The Court is a good mirror, an excellent mirror, of which historians for some reason have little availed themselves, of the struggles of dominant forces outside the Court.

FELIX FRANKFURTER

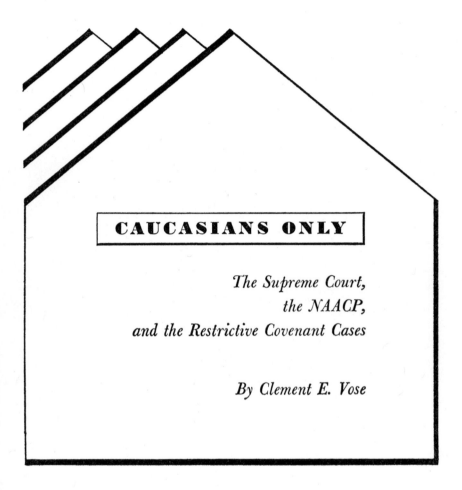

CAUCASIANS ONLY

The Supreme Court,
the NAACP,
and the Restrictive Covenant Cases

By Clement E. Vose

UNIVERSITY OF CALIFORNIA PRESS

Berkeley and Los Angeles 1959

University of California Press
Berkeley and Los Angeles, California
Cambridge University Press, London, England

© 1959 by The Regents of the University of California

Library of Congress Catalog Card Number: 59-8758
Printed in the United States of America
Designed by Adrian Wilson

PUBLISHED WITH THE ASSISTANCE OF A GRANT FROM THE
FORD FOUNDATION

TO DOTTY

"At no time shall said premises or any part thereof or any building erected thereon be sold, occupied, let or leased or given to any one of any race other than the Caucasian, except that this covenant shall not prevent occupancy by domestic servants of a different race domiciled with an owner or tenant." [1] This deed restriction is typical of thousands which are still part of property records in the United States despite the fact that none can now be honored by either a federal or a state court. In 1948, in four cases where neighbors sought to enjoin sale to and occupancy by non-Caucasians, the Supreme Court ruled that such covenants are not enforceable, and in 1953 the Supreme Court emphasized this ruling by holding that money damages could not be collected from a seller who violated a covenant. These decisions allow Negroes to rent or purchase property without the hindrance of such restrictive covenants. In effect, the Court withdrew governmental sanction for the established pattern of racial segregation in Northern cities. This book attempts to describe the sociological and political events leading to these decisions in the *Restrictive Covenant Cases* [2] and to appraise the practical result of the Supreme Court's rulings.

A number of contrasts follow the fact that the *Restrictive Covenant Cases* of 1948 and 1953 ended judicial support for private housing discrimination in Northern cities while the celebrated *School Segregation Cases* of 1954 and 1955 [3] insisted that state and local governments in the South may not require racial separation in public education. On the constitutional question, the ruling in the first cases was that judicial enforcement of racial restrictions in deeds was not a private matter but actually amounted to "state action" which was forbidden by the Fourteenth Amendment.

This reversed the generally accepted significance of the contro-
versial case of *Corrigan v. Buckley* [4] which since 1926 had given
the courts of the District of Columbia and nineteen states strong
justification for the enforcement of racial covenants. A different
line of constitutional history preceded the more recent school
cases. In the decisions there, the Supreme Court rejected flatly
the rule of *Plessy v. Ferguson*,[5] adopted in 1896, that "separate
but equal" facilities satisfy the demands of the equal-protection
clause.

The different origins of these two groups of cases tell a great
deal about residential segregation in the North and school segregation in the South. Because of the federal problem, a case came
up on both occasions from the District of Columbia. In addition,
the *Restrictive Covenant Cases* arose under urban circumstances
in St. Louis, Detroit, and Los Angeles. Various neighborhood property owners initiated actions to enforce restrictions against Negroes. These owners were well organized at the local level but
quite incapable of making a dent on national public opinion.
Attorneys for the Caucasians were not known outside of their
own cities and their defeat went practically unnoticed in the
United States Congress. On the other hand, the most important
of the *School Segregation Cases*, apart from the District of Columbia case, originated in the rural counties of Clarendon (South
Carolina) and Prince Edward (Virginia). Two additional cases
came to the Supreme Court from Claymont (Delaware) and
Topeka (Kansas). Government attorneys in these places prepared
the briefs and John W. Davis, an experienced and eminent advocate from New York, appeared before the Supreme Court in oral
argument for racial separation in Southern schools. In contrast to
the earlier covenant cases it was symbolic of general public interest
and agitation that the attorneys general of Arkansas, Florida,
North Carolina, Oklahoma, and Texas filed briefs *amici curiae* before the Supreme Court issued its 1955 decree in the school cases
while the officials of other Southern states loudly protested that
they would have nothing whatever to do with such displeasing,
and hence unconstitutional, proceedings. Although we are often
told that race relations in the North is also a problem, it is one
which, for the moment at least, is regarded quietly in national politics. Meanwhile the controversy following the *School Segregation*

Cases rages in party conventions, election campaigns, in Congress, and newspapers and magazines over the nation.

In the perspective of time, the significance of the *Restrictive Covenant Cases* may lie in what went into them rather than in what came out. There the National Association for the Advancement of Colored People made a full-fledged trial run in pressing for the expansion of Negro rights. This perfected the techniques the NAACP developed in twenty-five cases during the period from 1909, when the organization was formed, to 1947, when the Supreme Court agreed to hear the first four covenant cases. No earlier litigation was comparable in scope to the Association's task of working to eliminate the judicial enforcement of racial restrictions in housing. To overcome the legal precedent that stood against them, the NAACP relied on the constitutional theory of "state action" with the latest social and economic facts about discrimination in housing to win the day. A study of these efforts of the National Association for the Advancement of Colored People, made though it is with the knowledge of its role in later events, will inform us of the legal support for racial intolerance in the North and the basic methods employed to exterminate it. The fact that racial segregation in the residential areas of America's largest cities has not been altered to any substantial degree suggests the limited potency of court victories in some cases. Nevertheless the *Restrictive Covenant Cases* brought some material advantage to Negroes and meant even more as a symbol of power and a portent of the future.

I chose to study these cases for a number of reasons beyond their importance in the recent developments in race-relations law. My chief aim was to learn something of the role of interest groups in the judicial process, and perusal of the United States Reports showed that a record number of separate *amici curiae* briefs by organizations had been filed in these cases. This seemed enough to justify a fuller study. Another purpose was to investigate the interplay of historical forces in recent constitutional development. The rise and fall of court enforcement of racial covenants took place entirely in a period of four decades, a time of satisfactory length to consider economic, social, political, and intellectual developments and their impact on the law. Public policy on restrictive covenants had developed almost wholly

within the judicial branch of government, and this limitation not
only seemed likely to keep the study within manageable limits
but also might balance a tendency in writings about the Supreme
Court to overemphasize its power to review legislation.

Despite the reasons that led to my selection of the *Restrictive
Covenant Cases* as a focus I have no doubt that the study of any
number of other Supreme Court cases in diverse fields, and at
different times, would reveal similar patterns of organizational
activity. Even here the protective associations and real-estate
boards were for many years successful in persuading state courts
to enforce racial restrictions through injunction proceedings. It is
the nature of the judicial process and the power that courts have
in the American system of government which make organized
groups care about adjudication. I hope in studying other court
cases to refine an approach to the problem and to develop gen-
eralizations on the theme.

I wish to acknowledge the assistance I have received in preparing this volume. Many persons who worked for or against the
enforcement of racial covenants have provided information by
correspondence or by permitting access to legal and organization
files. These include Gerald L. Seegers, Emil Koob, Herman Willer
and Mrs. Margaret Bush Wilson of St. Louis; James Crooks and
Dean George M. Johnson of Washington; Loren Miller of Los
Angeles; Willis M. Graves of Detroit; and Charles Abrams, Joseph
B. Robison, and Mrs. Constance Baker Motley of New York. I am
also indebted to Robert L. Carter and Phineas Indritz who read
and made suggestions on the manuscript. This book began as a
doctoral dissertation at the University of Wisconsin, and I am
indebted to David Fellman for advice and encouragement. Finally, a grant from the Faculty Research Fund Committee of
Bowdoin College is acknowledged.

Permissions to quote correspondence and other unpublished
materials were granted by Charles Abrams, Roger Baldwin,
Robert L. Carter, James A. Crooks, Morris L. Ernst, Lewis Gan-
nett, Phineas Indritz, Newman Levy, Loren Miller, Joseph B.
Robison and Gerald L. Seegers. Permissions to quote copyrighted
materials were granted by Charles Wallace Collins and Little,
Brown and Company; the American Jewish Committee and the
Jewish Publication Society of America; and Charles M. Storey and

the Houghton Mifflin Company. Permissions to quote from my own articles were granted by William W. Falsgraf, editor in chief of the *Western Reserve Law Review;* David Fellman, editor of the *Midwest Journal of Political Science,* and Harold A. Basilius, director of the Wayne State University Press. The epigraph to this book was taken from Philip Elman, ed., *Of Law and Men: Papers and Addresses of Felix Frankfurter, 1939–1956* (New York: Harcourt, Brace, 1956).

A number of persons generously provided photographs of themselves. I also wish to thank the following for assistance in obtaining other illustrations: Mrs. Louis T. Wright for the photograph of Charles Houston; Mrs. Louis Wirth for the photograph of her husband; Dr. Davis McEntire for the maps prepared by the Commission on Race and Housing; P. L. Prattis, editor of *The Pittsburgh Courier,* for the reproduction of a front page of his newspaper and the photograph of George L. Vaughn; and Miss Barbara L. Clark of Harris & Ewing for a number of photographs.

Clement E. Vose

Brunswick, Maine

CONTENTS

ILLUSTRATIONS

(following page 44)

Louis Marshall (1856–1929)
City of St. Louis, 1940
City of St. Louis, 1950
Louis Wirth (1897–1952)
Robert C. Weaver
Dudley O. McGovney (1882–1945)
George L. Vaughn
Francis Dent and Willis M. Graves
116 Bryant Street, Washington, D.C.
Gerald L. Seegers
Henry Gilligan (1892–1950)
James Crooks
Charles Houston (1895–1949)
Thurgood Marshall
Loren Miller
Judge Henry Edgerton
Philip B. Perlman
Herman Willer
Phineas Indritz
Supreme Court of the United States, 1947–1948
The Pittsburgh Courier, May 8, 1948

I

LEGAL PRECEDENTS:

CAUCASIAN BULWARK

The Accommodation of Law to Segregation

Courts might regret that white hostility toward Negroes had led to segregation in American cities, but they commonly remarked that nothing could be done about it. You can't outlaw prejudice, they said. Nor could the discriminations which resulted from this attitude be eliminated by law. A justice of the Supreme Court of Michigan once put it, "The law is powerless to eradicate racial instincts or to abolish distinctions which some citizens do draw on account of racial differences." [1] This view had been widely held. [2] An indication of its predominance lay in the fact that racial residential segregation had become the established urban pattern. [3]

The enforcement of private agreements prohibiting the sale of property to colored persons, on the other hand, presented a sharp contrast to these confessions of the law's weakness. Positive legal sanctions had supported these embodiments of prejudice against Negroes. The assumption of the courts had been that whites "who own a home . . . have a right to protect it against . . . elements distasteful to them," and that white persons desiring segregation "should have confidence in the power and willingness of the courts to protect their investment in happiness and security." [4]

Neutrality had been claimed by the courts despite this ambivalence toward enforcing and preventing segregation. The law had been said to be impartial. When enforcing restrictions against Negroes, courts had stressed that "under similar circumstances the remedy granted here is equally available to all litigants, regardless of race, or color." [5] "Negroes have the same right in this respect as do those of other races." [6] It happened that these promises had never been exacted. The exception that proved the rule was a restrictive agreement against the use or occupancy by "persons of any race other than the Negro race" of certain property in the southwest section of Washington, D.C.[7] However there was no evidence that this restriction had been made by Negroes or enforced.

Only "Caucasians" had called upon America's judicial institutions to enforce racial residential segregation. This term is used advisedly to designate white persons whose preference for their own race caused them to restrict the purchase and occupancy of property to "none other than Caucasians." This narrow definition is convenient but not scientific since many white persons opposed racial segregation and some fought to end the judicial enforcement of restrictive covenants.[8]

Since feudal times the main tendency of Anglo-Saxon law had been toward the free and unrestrained sale and use of property. The practice was first given recognition by the statute of Westminster III, enacted in 1290, known as *Quia Emptores Terrarum,* reading, in part, "That from henceforth it shall be lawful to every freeman to sell at his own pleasure his lands and tenements, or part of them." [9] In the United States, property's free disposal, or unencumbered alienation, has become a marked characteristic of the system of land economics and property law.[10] This principle has been considered essential to the welfare of society because of "the necessity of maintaining a society controlled primarily by its living members," "facilitating the utilization of wealth," and "keeping property responsive to the current exigencies of its current beneficial owners." [11] Under the weight of these factors, therefore, freedom of alienation has become the established policy of the law.

While regulations or restrictions on the uses to which property may be put were considered to be out of place, exceptions were permitted when the objective aimed at by their imposition was of significant social importance.[12] Neither the constitutional limitation of due process of law nor the common law rule against restraints on the power of alienation were absolute. Restrictions on the disposal of land might sometimes be more compatible with the general welfare than complete freedom. A notable example of the police power of the state being used to control private property, over due-process objections, was found in the field of municipal zoning. The United States Supreme Court, in the leading case of *Euclid v. Ambler Realty Co.*,[13] had held valid an ordinance dividing a village into six districts with different residential, business, and industrial uses assigned to each. The Court held this to be a reasonable exercise of the police power despite the fact that the plaintiff company would lose financially because property it held would bring less when sold for residences (as would be necessary under the zoning requirements) than would be gained if sold for industrial development. Unless clearly arbitrary or unreasonable, the legislative judgment in zoning classification was allowed to prevail.[14]

This view was not followed in the legislative efforts to zone cities for the promotion of race separation. In *Buchanan v. Warley*,[15] decided by the Supreme Court in 1917, a Louisville, Kentucky, ordinance establishing exclusive residential zones for blacks and whites was invalidated on the ground that it unreasonably interfered with the rights of property owners freely to dispose of their property and therefore took their property without due process of law. "Dominion over property springing from ownership," the Court granted, "is not absolute and unqualified. The disposition of property may be controlled in the exercise of the police power in the interest of the public health, conveniences, or welfare." Nevertheless, restraint on the freedom of alienation based alone on the color of the occupant was not considered to be a legitimate exercise of the state's police power. It was looked upon instead as a "direct violation of the fundamental law enacted in the Fourteenth Amendment of the Constitution preventing state interference with property rights by due process of law." This and other decisions [16] have made clear that a citizen was protected by the Fourteenth Amendment from state or city legislation which limited his right to acquire, use, or dispose of property, solely because of race or color.

Thus in the *Buchanan* case the constitutional limitations against state action denying property rights were strictly applied. But although the Court recognized the existence of "a serious and difficult problem arising from a feeling of race hostility" which might well be solved by segregation, this factor was not important to its decision. To the Court, nonsegregation of the races was a lesser evil. To dispose of city lots by legislatively planned segregation of the races was an even worse interference with individual freedom because it upset long established Anglo-Saxon legal principles protecting the free alienation of property.[17]

When attempted by legislation, racial residential segregation was invalidated yet judicial power was later used to achieve this very same end. The free-alienation doctrine of the common law was adjusted to allow court enforcement of privately drafted agreements which excluded Negroes from specified property. This accommodation justifying a restraint "that the power of alienation can be freely exercised in favor of all persons except those who are members of some racial or social group" was summed up by the eminent American Law Institute.[18]

In its *Restatement of Property*, in 1944, the American Law Institute stated that all that was necessary to make an exception to the general rule regarding the free disposal of property was that "social conditions render desirable the exclusion of the racial or social group in question." [19] The restraint is reasonable and valid, it stated, even though the excluded group is "not small and includes so many probable conveyees that there is an appreciable interference with the power of alienation." Two benefits, "the avoidance of unpleasant racial and social relations and the stabilization of the value of the land" were said to overbalance "the evils which normally result from the curtailment of the power of alienation." Local circumstances or public opinion governed "the desirability of the exclusion of certain racial or social groups." Although "Bundists, Communists or Mohammedans," were cited as examples of such classifications, the only group affected in cases upon which the *Restatement* was based had been Negroes.

In this area of property law, developed solely through judicial action and without a controlling decision from the United States Supreme Court, the restatement of the American Law Institute was of great significance. Since its organization in 1923, the Institute had attempted to unify, in a series of restatements, diverse and often irreconcilable rules of the common law in orderly fashion. In fact, the project was undertaken out of concern that the common-law system's lack of clarity and certainty might force its abandonment.[20] The *Restatement of Property*, completed in 1944, was largely the work of nine leading authorities on property, who contributed time aside from their work in the classroom, on the bench, or at the bar, over a fifteen-year period.[21] The authority of the Committee on Property is emphasized by the prestige and influence of the American Law Institute as a whole. Founded by Elihu Root and guided for many years by George Wharton Pepper, it has always been composed of the top brass of the American legal profession. Its core is self-perpetuating. It also has official members which include the justices of the United States Supreme Court, the chief judges of the other federal courts and state supreme courts, executive board members of the American Bar Association, and deans of the leading law schools.[22]

The practices from which the exceptions to free alienation of land described in the *Restatement* stem were developed mainly after segregation by ordinance was held unconstitutional. When the ends sought could not be attained by legislation, they were gained by private agreements enforced under the common law. Caucasians who favored the separation of the races in residential areas could rely upon equity courts to support them. From World War I to 1948 privately adopted racial covenants provided an effective means of restricting Negroes from entering white sections in American cities. Quietly and unobtrusively, except for those against whom the covenants were directed, a legal means was developed to continue racial segregation despite constitutional and common-law doctrines of a contrary import.

Nature of Racial Restrictive Covenants

Like many summaries, the *Restatement* on the validity of racial restrictions on property concealed diversified and contradictory practices as to time, place, and doctrine. Most appellate court decisions on this subject had been made after 1920. Cases had arisen mainly in the border states between the North and South and usually had an urban setting. Their variety was shown in the first three decisions in which the application of racial covenants had been construed. Compared with later decisions, the earliest case was unique in two ways; the prohibition invoked was directed against Chinese, and the court refused enforcement. The decision of the United States Circuit Court for the Southern District of California, rendered in 1892, in *Gandolfo v. Hartman*,[23] held that the restriction discriminated against Chinese and thus denied them the equal protection of the laws. Under the Constitution, such unequal treatment could not be meted out by a state legislature or municipality. Therefore, the court reasoned that "any result inhibited by the Constitution can no more be accomplished by contract of individual citizens than by legislation, and the courts should no more enforce the one than the other." [24] The contrary rule of the *Civil Rights Cases* [25] of 1883 to the effect that private action was not controlled by the Fourteenth Amendment was not considered applicable.

In the next case, and for quite a different reason, the restrictive covenant against the sale of property to Negroes was not enforced. The case was heard in the Virginia Supreme Court in 1908.[26] There an amusement-park company, though organized and controlled completely by Negroes, was not affected by the covenant because the court ruled that since a corporation is not a person it has no "color" or race. More in tune with later developments was the third case [27] in which the Supreme Court of Louisiana, having the only civil-law jurisdiction in the United States, upheld as valid over all objections a covenant prohibiting the sale of certain property to Negroes for twenty-five years.

Racial restrictions varied in language, but their constant objective had been to make localities "more attractive to white people." [28] The clearest phraseology devised to express this purpose was found in a restriction which excluded "any person other than of the Caucasian race." [29] Such persons have been referred to as of "Negro descent," [30] "of African, Chinese, or Japanese descent," [31] and of the "Negro or African race." [32] The prosaic terms "Negroes" and "colored" have been most common but the quaint description, "Ethiopian Race" [33] has sometimes appeared. In the latter case the term had to be defined as being used in its popular sense to include Negroes. Only rarely has there been occasion for defining racial terms, and when done little light was added. For instance an Illinois court explained that the term "negro" included "every person having one-eighth part or more of negro blood, and every person who is what is commonly known as a colored person." [34]

No doubt, disputes over definitions did not arise more often because, in general, the identification of Negroes was not difficult, and attitudes toward them were crystallized. This was certainly true in the South, for the Alabama Supreme Court held that in the absence of a written restraint, an implied covenant existed against leasing an apartment to Negroes where they would have a common toilet with whites who lived in the next apartment, as this was "a well-known general custom vitally affecting the peaceful and quiet enjoyment of the premises." [35] Whether such a rule might have been made in the North was a moot question. [36] In 1928 the Michigan Supreme Court held that in a certain district where a consistent practice of exclusion of Negroes had been followed, a somewhat indefinite covenant providing that property should not be transferred to any person "whose ownership or occupancy would be injurious to the locality" was properly applied to Negroes. [37] In a more recent Michigan case, however, it was ruled that no racial restrictive agreement could be implied from the fact that there were building restrictions which sought to maintain property values and a high-class residential character in the neighborhood. [38] Verbal assurances and years of exclusion made no difference in that case, for the recorded restrictions lacked specific words excluding Negroes. In general, then, to have a binding covenant, the parties must have made clear their desire to exclude Negroes, although their use of racial terms did not need to be scientifically explicit.

Although the generic name of restrictive covenant covered all devices which aimed at limiting the sale or renting of property, two distinct types of devices were used to keep property out of the hands of Negroes. Restrictions might be placed in title deeds or signed as a separate agreement quite apart from the actual property titles. Deed covenants were made commonly by land companies or persons having a continuing interest in real estate they sold. At the turn of the century in Washington, D.C., the great land-development firm of Middough and Shannon [39] included this restriction in all deeds: "Subject to the covenant that said lots shall never be rented, leased, sold, transferred or conveyed unto any negro or colored person." [40] A similar provision made by a real-estate man in Denver, Colorado, was validated by the state supreme court which considered it good business and hence reasonable. [41] "A person who owns a tract of land and divides it into smaller tracts for the purpose of selling one or

more," said the court, "may prefer to have as neighbors persons
of the white, or Caucasian, race, and may believe that prospective
purchasers of the several tracts would entertain a similar preference, and would pay a higher price if the ownership were restricted to persons of that race. Surely it is not unreasonable to
permit such a person to insert in his deeds a provision restricting
not only occupancy but also ownership of the tracts conveyed by
him." Other cities where racial covenants were made as part of
real-estate developments include Los Angeles,[42] Shreveport,
(Louisiana),[43] and Winston-Salem (North Carolina).[44] It was the
more common practice, therefore, for real-estate interests to
subject property to covenants, but it was not unknown for individuals not in the real-estate business to restrict property to
Caucasians.

One person or real-estate firm could insert covenants into title
deeds, but a number of property-owners' signatures were necessary in the second type of device when it covered large areas.
Racial restrictive agreements were made when property owners
"agree with each other and mutually bind themselves, their
respective heirs, successors and assigns, the agreement of each
being made in consideration of the agreement to each other, to
keep and observe" [45] particular restrictions against the sale or
rent of their property to Negroes. The adoption of such restrictions ordinarily involved group efforts by neighboring property
owners organized as a protective association or by a real-estate
board.

Property-owners' associations had not originated solely to prevent the settlement of Negroes in an area, but many became pre-
occupied with this task in their broader quest of maintaining
property values and bringing about community improvement.
Because each of these organizations represented a small section of
a city they were usually decentralized and numerous. In 1944,
Chicago had seventy-eight organizations and Detroit fifty.[46] Only
in the District of Columbia, with sixty-eight so-called citizens
associations,[47] was there constant coöperation among them. Because the people of Washington are denied any direct part in
the government of the District, the Federation of Citizens' Associations developed as "the only organized opportunity they
have of stating their views on local matters." [48] The present asso-

ciations, which have been traced to 1887, regularly assisted the district commissioners on legislation after 1925.[49] In other cities protective associations also gave attention to the routine problems of city government, such as repairing streets, building sidewalks, providing school facilities and police and fire protection.[50] Yet most of these groups were touched by a Negro problem and have reacted by making restrictive agreements.

As Negroes moved into Northern cities from the rural South, the race problem ceased being merely sectional and became a matter of national concern. If anything, the difficulties were greater in the North than in the South. Above the Mason-Dixon line there were no established customs or mores restricting race relations. The great Negro migrations of the World War I and periods following raised new questions in the North. The answers, however, were old ones. Southern attitudes toward the Negro were easily adopted in the North, and their effect, untempered by tradition, thoroughly insulated the races from each other as huge colored districts of New York, Chicago, St. Louis, and Detroit developed. There the separation of the races "was even more complete than in the South." [51]

After the city segregation ordinance was invalidated in 1917,[52] the restrictive agreement became an important means of keeping Negroes in separate residential sections in urban areas. A study in 1944 by the Department of Race Relations of the American Missionary Association, an organization actively opposed to all such limitations on Negroes, indicates the pervasiveness of these restrictions.[53] In St. Louis it was found that 559 block areas, or 5½ square miles of land space and housing, were withdrawn from the use of Negroes through the operation of restrictive covenants and agreements. More than 11 square miles were covered in Chicago.[54] Even these broad restrictions do not alone explain the racial separation which exists in American cities. Gunnar Myrdal stressed that two other factors besides segregation enforced by whites account for residential concentration of Negroes. "Poverty preventing individuals from paying for anything more than the cheapest housing accommodation," he believed, and "ethnic attachment" were of great importance in producing segregation.[55] However, white real-estate interests and property-owners' associations apparently did not consider these influences as sufficient protection. Otherwise they would not have expended so much energy to the task of adopting restrictive agreements.

The size of the restricted areas in Northern cities was a tribute to the tenacity of the protective associations and to the few persons in each one who spent their energy on the project of adopting restrictive agreements. The difficulty encountered is well shown by the experience in 1923 of a group of residents on a single street in St. Louis who, wishing to preserve the area for the Caucasian race, formed a "property-owners association." With the help of a lawyer they drafted a restrictive agreement to prevent Negroes from buying or renting any houses there. Yet their plan failed when the efforts of paid solicitors gained only a small number of signatures.[56] In this situation, where a neighborhood scheme of restriction was contemplated, every property-owner's signature was essential "as anything short of that intention would have tended to defeat the very purpose of the restriction." [57] The agreement could have taken this difficulty into account ahead of time. Those who did sign could have indicated their own intention to be bound regardless of whether others might have refused to sign. Or they might have agreed to have been bound "upon the contingency that a certain number, but less than the whole, of the property owners should sign." [58] This was a possible solution and might have worked well in practice. But since it appeared "that no subscribing property owner intended to be bound unless all other property owners were bound," the court held that because it lacked final or complete assent, "the agreement never attained validity for the purpose of imposing a restriction upon any of the property within the district." [59] One court ruled that "the number of the parties to such an agreement is not the test of its validity." [60] Others seemed agreed that a percentage of owners could restrict their own property although they could not bind the nonsigning remainder.[61]

With certain exceptions both forms of restrictions went into effect when recorded in the customary sanctuary—the Office of the County Clerk or Register of Deeds. Even when officially registered, an agreement might not go into effect until the anticipated number of signatures were obtained. This arrangement was known as a "condition precedent." Under this plan the signers would not be bound "unless enough agreements were secured to render the proposed restriction reasonably effective." [62] Where unanimity was planned and not achieved, an agreement was not given effect because of the unfairness of restraining a property owner from transferring "his lot to any but a member of the Caucasian race, while adjoining him would be a lot that could be conveyed without any limitation whatsoever." [63] Even after the restriction was adopted and was on record it might become a dead letter under the terms of an "escape clause." This allowed any signer in the restricted area to treat the agreement as a nullity if a Negro entered the neighborhood and lived there for a period of four months.[64] Or it might be terminated by agreement of a specified percentage of the owners.[65]

When all signatures were authentic and in order and a covenant, using the term in its general or popular sense, was officially recorded, constructive notice of its existence for the indicated period was satisfied. Covenants commonly ran for twenty-five years,[66] but there was much variation between fifteen [67] and fifty.[68] Sometimes no duration was set.[69] Perpetual covenants have been upheld as just and reasonable as long as the conditions that existed when the restriction was adopted remained substantially unchanged.[70] Such perpetual covenants were not unusual.[71] The longest this side of eternity would have kept Negroes from entering or using certain property for ninety-nine years,[72] one of which designated the date for the convenience of interested persons as "March 16, 2025." [73] Agreements occasionally provided that the restrictions be inserted in all deeds and other transfers of the property to be made in the future,[74] but failure to do this did not affect the operation of a restrictive agreement, since it rested on contract and was valid standing alone.[75] Under this rule a person was considered to have notice by the mere fact that a restrictive agreement existed and was on file in the proper depository of the local government. The restriction did not need to appear in the deed title. Actual notice was not essential, although in a restriction being vague, notice requirements were satisfied by a correct explanation of its meaning to the affected party by a disinterested person.[76]

Most people are reluctant to break the law. The mere existence

of officially registered restrictive covenants, therefore, carried
an influence which had wide respect. With knowledge that the
deed contained racial limitations, few white persons were willing
to sell property to Negroes. The Negroes with enough temerity
to purchase were fewer still. Those who had done so usually received warnings that legal action would be taken against them.
Over a twenty-year period, one lawyer representing citizens' associations in Washington, D. C., sent to Negroes who bought covenanted property countless letters which included warnings like
the following: [77]

> As persons of the negro race or having negro blood you are
> prohibited from occupying the premises now occupied by you.
> This information was given to the Pasqual Real Estate Company,
> which sold you the property, and doubtless you were so in-
> formed both by Mr. Pasqualitchio and by the Title Company
> which searched the title.
>
> This letter will be presented to you personally. I trust you
> will discuss the matter with the gentleman or gentlemen who
> call on you [referring to representatives of the white property
> owners' association involved], looking to an amicable removal
> from the property. If you do not agree to move promptly I am
> instructed to bring an Injunction proceeding in the District
> Court to require you to move and prohibiting the occupancy
> by anyone of the negro race or having negro blood. I regret ex-
> ceedingly that you have failed to comply with the deed covenant,
> which has been upheld by the Court of Appeals as a good
> covenant. I assure you that it is the determination of white
> property holders under the same covenant as yours to enforce
> it. I am most hopeful you will save yourselves the necessity of
> court action and the expense incident thereto.

What remedies were available to enforce racial restrictions? An
indirect approach would be to sue for damages in order to punish
violators. But the direct and more practicable way, since damages
are difficult to measure in this regard,[78] was to get an injunction
to keep the Negroes out. Covenants sometimes provided that
"any owner shall have the right to sue for and obtain an injunction prohibitive or mandatory to prevent the breach of or
to enforce the observance of the restrictions." [79] Customarily
equity granted whatever remedies were needed to maintain the
covenant. If the property had been purchased, forfeiture was

ordered.[80] The white seller was restrained from transferring any real estate within the district to non-Caucasians, and the Negroes were ordered not to purchase property there.[81] In the most sweeping remedy granted, where a racial restriction had been violated, the deeds in question were canceled, court costs and attorney's fees were awarded to the plaintiff, and a lien was made on the lots involved, which finally were ordered sold to satisfy the costs.[82]

The parties to racial-restriction cases had different interests, and litigation took a variety of forms. Since each of the signatories to a restrictive agreement "granted to all of the others an easement in his or her property" a violation by one owner gave any other a cause of action.[83] Much the same theory applied to deed covenants which provided that in the event of violation the property "shall revert to grantor or sellers." [84] Under this provision the former owner might sue to enforce the contract against the white seller or the Negro purchaser, and on occasion both of them.[85] Litigation often arose without an overt violation of a restriction. Original parties to a restrictive agreement might later wish to sell property to Negroes. To do this they applied for injunctions decreeing the restrictions "to be clouds upon the titles of the owners thereof, impeding the free uses and enjoyment of their properties, and that the same in their entirety be cancelled, removed, and held for naught." [86] This plea was looked upon unsympathetically by the courts which believed that racial restrictive covenants were "valid and solemn contracts and should not be lightly set aside." [87] "Those who purchase property subject to restrictive covenants," were lectured that they "must assume the burdens as well as the benefits, for equity does not grant relief against a bad bargain voluntarily made and unbreached." [88]

Constitutional Considerations

When lawyers first began seeking court enforcement of racial restrictive covenants in 1920 they stood on firm constitutional ground. The remark that "our Constitution is color blind," made by Justice Harlan in a dissenting opinion twenty-five years earlier,[89] was still a minority view. The United States Supreme Court of that day had retracted little of its previously developed doctrines regarding the limited application of the Civil War amendments. The Thirteenth, Fourteenth, and Fifteenth amendments had been designed to protect Negroes particularly against state governments in the enjoyment of full citizenship and civil rights.[90] Originally many white persons were concerned that Negroes would rise too fast in the world as a result of this constitutional solicitude, but these fears were groundless. An observer noted in 1935 that "for fifty years or more, the relationship of the freedman to the fourteenth amendment has been practically lost to view." [91] Key Supreme Court victories by whites in cases involving Negroes before 1920, although unrelated to housing segregation, established strong constitutional defenses against attacks on restrictive covenants and their enforcement. The subject matter of these cases varied, but in the main the fashioning of constitutional meaning by the Court gave considerable aid and comfort to the larger Caucasian interest.

During the Reconstruction period after the Civil War the white Southern leaders lost control of the Negro. Military occupation of the South placed political power in the hands of the central government. A flurry of constitutional amendments and federal statutes adopted during that period made racial equality in civil and political rights the law of the land. During the years 1865–1870 the Thirteenth, Fourteenth, and Fifteenth amendments, abolishing slavery, protecting civil rights from state interference, and ordering that the Negro be not denied the right to vote because of his race or color, were adopted. To give greater force to these constitutional principles, Congress adopted the Civil Rights Act of 1866,[92] the Civil Rights Enforcement Act of 1870,[93] and the Civil Rights Act of 1875.[94] The provisions of the first law, which were reënacted in the 1870 statute, declared all persons born in the United States to be citizens and, among other things, extended to Negroes the same right "to inherit, purchase, lease, sell, hold, and convey real and personal property, . . . as is enjoyed by white citizens." [95] This was the only statute describing Negro property rights. On other matters the most radical feature of any legislation was contained in the Civil Rights Act of 1875. This ordered that "all persons within the jurisdiction of the United States shall be entitled to the full and equal enjoyment of accommodations, advantages, facilities, and privileges of inns, public conveyances on land or water, theatres, and other places of public amusement." [96] All in all, these laws gave the colored population of the South a position of potential equality, yet the Southern whites maintained actual superiority.

For in fact, it was possible to keep the Negro from gaining the equality that was his on paper. In 1877 the federal army was withdrawn from the South. In 1883 the Supreme Court rendered one of the most important of all its decisions in the *Civil Rights Cases,*[97] invalidating the key sections of the Civil Rights Act of 1875. It ruled that race discrimination by private persons could not be penalized by Congress. The Fourteenth Amendment, said the Court, does not prohibit the "wrongful acts of individuals, unsupported by state authority in the shape of laws, customs, or judicial or executive proceedings." [98] The rule established by this decision was that the Fourteenth Amendment could not be applied to prevent the misconduct of individuals when their action was not supported by the authority of the state. Historically, it has been said that the essence of the decision is to be found in the reality it accomplished—the return of the solution of the race problem to the South.[99]

Additional Supreme Court action favored the white position as opposed to that of the Negro. The privileges-and-immunities clause of the Fourteenth Amendment was defined so narrowly in the *Slaughterhouse Cases* [100] as to render it impotent. Although it was used many times to protect corporations, the original purpose of the due-process clause to protect Negroes was largely neglected.[101] Finally, the provision that a state deny no person "the equal protection of the laws" had its growth stunted by the ruling in *Plessy v. Ferguson,*[102] decided in 1896, that segregation was compatible with equality.

Therefore, to the question, "What positive gain has the operation of the Fourteenth Amendment been to the Negro race?" a Southern white intellectual answered in 1912, "We can point to nothing." [103] The commentator, Charles Wallace Collins, later the political theorist of the Dixiecrats,[104] added that this was right and proper. "It is the perversion of a noble idealism," he said, "that the lowest and most benighted element of the African race should in these enlightened days be the ones to rise up and claim the sacred heritage of Anglo-Saxon liberties." [105] The embodiment of these liberties in the Fourteenth Amendment was looked upon as a "fortune of circumstance" unrelated to the just deserts of the colored people. Collins believed that because "the African had no share" in gaining them, these constitutional rights are to him nothing more than "a strange and far-off language." "Unlike the charters of other people, it was written there not by his efforts nor dictated at his command." [106] The position taken by Collins, which is at once a commentary on the legal status of the Negro in 1912 and a rationale of the racial situation from a Caucasian viewpoint, follows: [107]

> The adoption of the Fourteenth Amendment could not make Anglo-Saxons out of Africans. It was unjust to the negro to force him to play a role for which by the forces of nature he was un-fitted. He deserves neither ridicule nor blame for the comedy and the tragedy of the Reconstruction. It is one of the funda-mental precepts of political science today that only those people in a community can participate equally in its civic, social, and political life who are conscious of a common origin, share a common idealism, and look forward to a common destiny. Where the community is composed of two divergent races rendering such a community of life impossible, the weaker and less favored race must inevitably and in the nature of things take the place assigned to it by the stronger and dominant race. The Republican Party, which controlled all branches of the government after the War, might have made the negroes wards of the nation . . . They, especially at that time, needed the protecting arm of the Federal Government thrown around them. Under this system of sympathetic tutelage the African might have been led to develop whatever latent powers that may be inherent in his race. Today he can truly raise the cry that many of the doors of opportunity are closed to him.
>
> As it now stands, the negro must look to his State for pro-tection. He must take his chances along with the other citizens. If in the unequal struggle he fails to gain for himself the full fruits of citizenship, there is no recourse left to him. The strong-est point in his favor is that he is human and his long sojourn in the midst of a naturally kind-hearted people has brought about certain tacit understandings and adjustments, the written Constitution to the contrary notwithstanding.

The superior legal status of white to colored persons was rarely challenged during this period. The Supreme Court did hold unconstitutional in 1915 an Oklahoma "grandfather clause" under which citizens whose grandfathers had voted before the adoption of the Fifteenth Amendment could register to vote without having to pass literacy tests. The Court found that Negroes were quite clearly discriminated against by the functioning of this rule.[108] In 1917, the Supreme Court held that a racial residential zoning ordinance was unconstitutional.[109] These were exceptions during an era when the chances of Negroes winning advances through the judicial process seemed small. Even the development of constitutional theories which might strengthen the Negro position were atrophied. In the early restrictive-covenant cases the constitutional argument against enforcement had been poorly worked out. The narrow scope which had been given to the Fourteenth Amendment and the various civil-rights acts was seldom understood; for appeals were constantly made to the Constitution in the most general terms. When the appropriate constitutional provisions were appealed to, it was not clearly argued whether the mere adoption of restrictions was under attack or whether court enforcement of them as state action was claimed to be invalid. Such lack of precision benefited those desiring continued segregation.

The landmark in constitutional interpretation of racial restrictive covenants was *Corrigan v. Buckley*,[110] which arose in the federal courts of the District of Columbia and, although dismissed for want of jurisdiction, was the only such case considered by the United States Supreme Court up to 1945. Thirty neighbors, including Corrigan and Buckley, executed an agreement in 1921 which restricted the sale or occupancy of their property to Negroes for twenty-one years. Later, Corrigan violated this by selling his restricted property to a Negro named Curtis. Still wishing to keep Negroes out of the neighborhood by means of the agreement, Buckley applied to the Supreme Court of the District for an injunction to restrain the sale. Corrigan and Curtis replied by filing a motion to dismiss which, in turn, was dismissed by the trial court.

On appeal, Judge Van Orsdel, for a three-judge panel of the Court of Appeals, defined the sole issue of the case as the power of the landowners to make and record such a restrictive agreement. The question did not involve the validity of a statute,

municipal ordinance, or other public law. There was no discrimination within the civil-rights clauses of the Constitution, because
if the Negroes owned the property they too could impose restrictions as to its disposal. Individuals might refuse to sell or
lease property if they wished, and the right of Negroes to possess
property did not allow them to compel its sale. Turning to the
specific contention that the equal-protection clause of the Fourteenth Amendment forbade racial restrictive covenants, Judge
Van Orsdel asserted that it was settled Supreme Court doctrine
that the clause inhibited only the power of the state. It did not,
he said, apply "to action by individuals in respect to their property." It naturally followed that the civil-rights statutes enacted
under its provisions "can afford no more protection than the
Constitution itself. If . . . there is no infringement of defendant's
rights under the Constitution, there can be none under the
Statutes." [111] The decree of the lower court granting the injunction
was affirmed.

Although the Supreme Court dismissed the appeal in *Corrigan
v. Buckley,* thereby allowing the injunction to stand, it did so
with an opinion. The reasons for declining jurisdiction were given
by Justice Sanford. He found the questions raised "so insubstantial
as to be plainly without color of merit and frivolous." Of the
constitutional objections Justice Sanford found none to be relevant
or applicable. The Fifth Amendment, he said, "is a limitation
only on the powers of the general government and is not directed
against the action of individuals." The Thirteenth Amendment,
aside from its prohibition of slavery, does not protect Negroes'
individual rights. Although the Fourteenth Amendment refers
only to state action and the District of Columbia is under exclusive federal jurisdiction, Justice Sanford without remarking
on this distinction stated flatly that the prohibitions of the Fourteenth Amendment "have reference to state action exclusively,
and not to any action of private individuals." In summary, he
asserted, "It is obvious that none of these Amendments prohibited
private individuals from entering into contracts respecting the
control and disposition of their own property." [112]

Justice Sanford relied on the rule of the *Civil Rights Cases* of
1883 [113] in looking upon the restrictive covenant and its enforcement in the *Corrigan* case as a matter of private action not af-

fected by the Fourteenth Amendment. By this same reasoning the
Civil Rights Act [114] providing that all persons and citizens shall
have equal rights with white citizens to make contracts and acquire property was held inapplicable. The statutes, said Justice
Sanford, "like the constitutional amendment under whose sanction they were enacted, do not in any manner prohibit or invalidate contracts entered into by private individuals in respect
to the control and disposition of their own property." [115]

After the *Corrigan v. Buckley* decision, the highest courts of
Kentucky,[116] Maryland,[117] Oklahoma,[118] Wisconsin,[119] and the
intermediate courts of Missouri [120] and New York [121] disposed of
the constitutional issue on grounds that the Supreme Court had
settled the matter once and for all.

Almost universally the restrictive covenants were looked upon
as involving only private action, and where the claim had been
made that judicial enforcement of covenants was state action, it
had been brushed aside.[122] In 1919 a California court looked at
the question in this fashion: "The fourteenth amendment, it is
true, applies to the judicial as well as the legislative department
of the state government. But the judiciary does not violate this
provision of the federal constitution merely because it sanctions
discriminations that are the outgrowths of contracts made by individuals." [123] A fuller exposition of this view was made in a decision by the same court in 1944, where it was said that "the right
of citizens to contract with each other with relation to their own
property . . . should not be confused with the power to legislate which is possessed by municipal and state governments." [124]
Under this view, then, the enforcement of a racial restrictive
covenant by a court was not "within constitutional principles,
action by the state through its judicial department." The rights
of the parties are derived from their contract so that "if the contract is valid it cannot be nullified under any theory that courts
are without the power to enforce it." [125]

Restraints on Alienation

The position of the *Restatement of Property*, that restraints on
the free disposal of property to Negroes were valid and enforceable,[126] rested on the rules of the courts of six states.[127] The

Restatement's view that race relations were benefited by the segregation imposed by restrictive covenants was not articulated in any of the cases. However, its other justification for covenants, that they supported property values, echoed a number of court decisions. One court ruled that when conveying a piece of land every property owner had full power to impose restrictions on its sale to Negroes in order subsequently to maintain the value of the part he retained.[128] It was assumed, in another jurisdiction, that "an absolute restriction on the power of alienation . . . is void" but this was differentiated from the imposition of "a condition or restraint upon the power of alienation in certain cases to certain persons or for a certain time, or for certain purposes." [129] Much emphasis was placed on the difference between total and perpetual inalienability and restrictions which were partial and temporary. A covenant was looked upon as "partial" when it applied only to Negroes. Twenty-five years have been considered to be "temporary." [130] Under this approach property owners who enacted racial restrictive covenants received legal support. They had the "right to use, enjoy and dispose of property" [131] and this included the power to prevent future owners from doing the same. Wishing to give certainty to the common law the American Law Institute adopted this rule as a correct statement in 1944. Within a year the *Restatement* position in support of racial restrictions was followed by a New Jersey court, which enforced a covenant against Negroes on its authority.[132]

But there were exceptions to the rule of the *Restatement*, in spite of the fact that they were not given attention in it. Beginning with the premise that "the right of alienation is an inherent and inseparable quality" of property ownership,[133] courts of four states refused to enforce restraints on the sale of property to Negroes.[134] It was crisply argued by a California court that to transfer the ownership of land and "at the same time restrain the free alienation of it is to say that a party can grant and not grant, in the same breath." [135] California courts based their holdings against the enforcement of a racial restrictive covenant on a literal reading of a section of the state's Civil Code providing that "Conditions restraining alienation, when repugnant to the interest created, are void." [136] Other courts had come to the same conclusion on the basis of the general property-law doctrine against restraints on alienation. This was applied to restrictions which were limited in time as well as to those which were perpetual on the assumption that "a restraint which would suspend all power of alienation for a single day, is inconsistent with the estate granted, unreasonable and void.[137] Not only was the aspect of time under attack. Exception was also taken to the reasoning which justified covenants when they apply to Negroes alone, and hence were only a partial limitation on the free disposal of property. One court speculated that if ownership "may be made to depend upon his not selling or leasing to persons of African, Chinese, or Japanese descent, it may be made to depend upon his not selling or leasing to persons of Caucasian descent, or to any but albinos from the heart a Africa or blond Eskimos.[138]

Even more biting language was used in an opinion by the West Virginia Supreme Court which would not enforce a fifty-year covenant against the sale of property to Negroes.[139] This was termed a "restriction on alienation to an entire race of people" and therefore "wholly incompatible with complete ownership." The court said:

> If large numbers of possible buyers are cut off by the hand of the grantor, then, to that extent, the grantee ceases to be in control of his own property. A fee simple title to real estate no longer would impart complete dominion in the owner if because of a restriction imposed by his grantor the market afforded by a whole race of the human family is closed. A distinction that would treat with more seriousness an absolute restriction for however short a period (the same being generally held invalid), than a restriction against alienation to a large race of people for half a century seems fanciful rather than real.

In this same case the Supreme Court of West Virginia, having allowed the Negroes to purchase restricted property, refused to permit them to live on it by enforcing a racial covenant against occupancy. The court held that a limitation on the sale of land to colored persons was wrong but "reasonable restrictions on use violate no principle lying at the base of untrammeled alienability of property." No court had held a racial restrictive covenant on Negro use or occupancy to be unenforceable. Those which had invalidated restraints on sale while enforcing those on occupancy hardly sensed the dilemma of the situation.[140] When the Mary-

land Supreme Court was confronted with this situation in 1938
it said, "The rules against restraints on alienation were only intended to make conveyancing free and unrestrained, and had
nothing to do with use and occupancy.[141] The court went on to
elaborate, "It may be an anomalous situation when a colored
man may own property which he cannot occupy," but so long as
the Negro's procedural rights were guarded, justice prevailed for
"if he buys on notice of such a restriction the consequences are
the same to him as to any other buyer with notice."

Considerations of Public Policy

Anglo-American courts have long recognized that the interests
of contracting parties were not necessarily identical with those
of the public. The rule developed that contracts whose objects
were opposed to public policy were unenforceable.[142] In regard
to racial restrictive covenants, however, freedom of contract was
equated with sound public policy. The power to bind one's own
property by contract was looked upon as an exceedingly important right "which the people of all races may exercise
freely." [143] Indeed, the almost universal enforcement of racial
restrictive covenants was said to be "the most satisfactory proof
of the public policy of the nation with respect to this phase of the
right to contract." [144]

Whether the covenants were enforced because people possessed the freedom to make covenants or because their object
constituted sound public policy mattered very little since either
line of reasoning led to racial residential restrictions. The frank-
ness of the latter rationale was displayed in 1915 by the Louisiana
Supreme Court: [145]

> . . . it would be unfortunate . . . if the public policy of the
> general government or of the state were so narrow, as to render
> impracticable a scheme such as the one in question in this case
> [a racial restrictive covenant], whereby an owner has sought to
> dispose of his property advantageously to himself and bene-
> ficially to the city wherein it lies.

The same viewpoint was expressed in the North when the Supreme Court of Michigan, in 1922, could find no interests of the

state that would be harmed by the enforcement of a racial restrictive covenant.[146]

The fact that equitable remedies were sought by persons wishing to have restrictive covenants enforced might have made their
task more difficult since equity traditionally stood for a liberal
and humane interpretation of law. Equity was synonymous with
"natural justice." [147] Furthermore, since the issuance of an injunction was not a matter of right, "it is the general rule that the
granting or withholding of equitable relief involves the exercise
of judicial discretion." [148] Yet these principles were not enough
to induce the courts to take a broader view of public policy concerning race covenants. The discretionary role of equity was rejected.[149]

> The responsibility of striking down the validity of racial re-
> strictions with respect to the use and occupancy of real prop-
> erty is one which no court or judge should assume on the strength
> of individual theories as to what constitutes the "present" public
> policy on the subject or of personal belief that the consequences
> would be for the general good.

If judges did not exercise their age-old function of keeping law
in tune with the better tendencies of the times, how was this to
be accomplished? In answer it was agreed by a California court
that: [150]

> The desirability of a more understanding and harmonious rela-
> tionship among the many races of our nation is something no one
> will deny, but it will come only with time and experience and it
> is a matter in which public thought and conscience cannot be
> directed or controlled by the courts through the uprooting of
> firmly established precedent.

The court reluctantly admitted that "public policy changes and
develops with the times." But there was insistence that "these
changes must have their sources in the citizenry." [151]

In New York a racial restrictive covenant was enforced because no public policy to the contrary had been expressed by
the state's legislature.[152] In New Jersey a number of antidiscrimi-
nation statutes had been enacted and these were claimed to indicate a general policy toward the full establishment of Negro
rights which should be carried forward by the courts. Since none

of these laws applied to discrimination in housing, however, a lower state court refused, in 1945, to declare racial restrictive covenants illegal on the basis of public policy.[153] Although recognizing that "the elimination of all discriminatory practice against all races and all peoples is a goal which someday may yet be attained in a democracy like ours," it stressed that "until the legislature, the supreme lawmaking power acts in the matter, it is not within the power or competence of the courts to do so." [154]

In the silence of the legislature and the citizenry social and economic facts might of themselves have spoken with a voice which courts would recognize. Actually sociological arguments were rarely urged in the restrictive-covenant cases under discussion. When employed they were unsuccessful. In 1938, a Missouri court was confronted with this situation: The defendants "urge that enforcement of the covenant will work a hardship on 50,000 negroes in Kansas City because they are said to be in difficulty in finding homes." [155] No consideration of public policy was seen to arise from this state of affairs. The court went on to say that it could not "agree that the property of any person may be confiscated for private purposes simply because some one regardless of race or color, fancies a particular house and covets it and no other." [156]

A tendency away from the general practice remains to be noted. One court's refusal to enforce a covenant was based partly on the intervention of a broad principle of public policy "to the extent that modern progress is doomed to necessitate a sacrifice of many former claimed individual rights." [157] The enforcement of racial restrictions in housing conflicted with sound public policy, said Judge Traynor of the California Supreme Court in a concurring opinion rendered in 1944.[158] He believed that there was a public interest in the fact that residential districts for Negroes in Los Angeles were crowded. And "that congestion is a consequence of residential segregation of the colored population," which was accomplished, asserted Judge Traynor, "not by ordinances, which would be unconstitutional, but by agreements between private persons which the courts have recognized as valid." [159] Citing considerable sociological evidence he concluded that these covenants "must yield to the public interest in the sound development of the whole community." [160]

The "Changed Conditions" Doctrine

While courts had been refusing to rule that public policy prohibited their enforcement, at the same time conditions had been changing within the many cities where covenants worked to maintain racial segregation. Old sections had grown older; new white residential developments had risen in the suburbs. More Negroes had arrived from the South, more had been born, and, all seeking places to live, had begun to overflow into formerly all-white districts. To the Caucasians who remained downtown these changes brought grave concern. To them, the physical closeness of the colored sections was ominous in itself, but of equal seriousness was the question it raised about the legality of racial restrictive covenants.

Racial restrictive covenants had as their purpose the maintenance of white neighborhoods and, in theory, gave mutual benefit to all properties covered. If Negroes moved into the area, the purpose failed to a degree. When an attempt was then made to enforce the covenant, the issue became one of how seriously the presence of Negroes challenged the segregated pattern of the restricted district. It was customary for courts sitting in equity to refuse to enforce an agreement

> when the neighborhood in question has so changed in its character and environment and in the uses to which the property therein may be put that the purpose of the covenant cannot be carried out, or that its enforcement would substantially lessen the value of the property, or, in short, that injunctive relief would not give a benefit but rather impose a hardship.[161]

Application of this rule led to the development of precedents which permitted breaches of racial covenants. Thus where Negroes were free to purchase and occupy homes in a restricted district and did so in such large numbers that the party seeking enforcement of the covenant was already living under the very conditions it was designed to prevent, no remedy was granted.[162] And in a case in Los Angeles changed conditions were declared to make enforcement of a covenant inequitable since the restricted area was so thickly populated by colored persons that it was known as the "Negro District." [163]

Since the entry of Negroes came about by degrees, the question of whether conditions were sufficiently changed had to be settled. When Negro occupancy in an area had progressed enough to bring about higher prices in the Negro housing market than in the white, that in itself was called "the beginning of an unmistakable trend." [164] In this case the court believed that enforcement of the covenant would depreciate property values in the block, and at the same time fail to accomplish the purpose for which the covenant was designed. Therefore the injunction was not issued and the properties were left "with a value commensurate to the conditions as they now exist." [165]

A somewhat different situation arose where there was a noncontiguous area covered by restrictions, for then the primary issue was not one of changed conditions but whether the neighborhood could be protected from Negro infiltration in the first place. The latter issue was settled by a California court which refused to grant a decree prohibiting a lot owner from renting his property to a non-Caucasian while owners of adjacent lots were at liberty to rent to whom they pleased.[166] This problem was elaborated by the Supreme Court of California, in 1944, in *Fairchild v. Raines.*[167] Enforcement was sought for an agreement in existence since 1927, where the restricted lots did not form a contiguous area. The agreement itself had never been violated, but Negroes had moved into the nonrestricted lots in large numbers. Because of this change within the neighborhood, the court ruled that the original purpose of the covenant could no longer be realized and thus made enforcement inequitable. Therefore if the battle had already been lost and the Negroes were living within the neighborhood, Caucasians could not persuade the courts to enforce a dead restriction.

When the changed conditions had been outside of the area, however near, restrictions had been upheld. There was only one exception to this latter rule. This was the case of *Clark v. Vaughan,*[168] decided by the Kansas Supreme Court in 1931. A restricted tract included one lot which was separated from the rest by a main thoroughfare. Negroes had occupied property behind and up to this lot before the covenant was adopted, and afterward they moved into all remaining lots on that side of the thoroughfare. Unable to dispose of his property to whites at a reasonable price, this lot owner arranged to sell to a Negro. Caucasians across the way then brought suit, but the court refused to grant an injunction because it would be inequitable and burdensome. This holding was criticized for failing to recognize that the restriction was imposed because the expansion of the neighboring Negro community was contemplated; therefore the actual expansion was hardly a changed conditions, but was the occurrence which the agreement was originally designed to prevent.[169] And a strong dissenting opinion emphasized that the Caucasians making the agreement knew that it could not and would not prevent colored people from acquiring property around the area covered, and that these outside changes should have no bearing on the validity of the agreement.[170] Another criticism of the rule was that to make an exception of borderline property encouraged successive successions pushing the boundary until the whole restriction would be eliminated.[171] As it turned out this case was an isolated one, for doctrine developed that changed conditions outside of a restricted area did not make enforcement of a racial agreement inequitable.

The insistence of courts that agreements must be enforced regardless of changed conditions outside of a particular covenanted district established important precedents for the Caucasians. Perhaps the most influential decision was that of the Court of Appeals of the District of Columbia in *Grady v. Garland,* decided in 1937.[172] There Judge Stephens dissented from the ruling of two colleagues because he considered barring of property from occupancy by Negroes when a nearby area had already been settled by them to be "unsuited to a growing community." [173] But the majority insisted and held that the object of the restriction was not to prevent "the invasion of the property surrounding it." If such a point of view were to be established in the law, said the court, "all that would be necessary to defeat such a covenant would be the settlement of a few colored families in the immediate vicinity of the restricted area." [174] To bring outside changes into play proof had to be made of radical changes, and of the fact that enforcement of the covenant would work an undue hardship on the defendant while giving no substantial benefit to the plaintiff.[175] Such results were never convincingly shown to any court, however, save in the case of *Clark v. Vaughan,* discussed above.

The courts' opinions in these cases taken at face value gave the sanctity of contracts a higher place than the rule of inequitability on account of changed conditions. The courts assumed just as they did regarding public policy that racial restrictive covenants were "vaild and solemn contracts and should not be lightly set aside."[176] Under such a contract parties "must assume the burdens as well as the benefits, for equity does not grant relief against a bad bargain voluntarily made and unbreached."[177] Even a decline in property values unless of a substantial nature would not negate a covenant because "there are some rights more valuable than money."[178]

Caucasian Position in 1945

The main claim made by the Caucasians upon the judicial system from 1915 to 1945, was for the enforcement of racial restrictive covenants. The courts made good this claim. The federal courts in Washington, D.C., consistently enforced racial restrictive covenants and the United States Supreme Court was generally assumed to have given tacit approval to the practice by dismissing for want of jurisdiction the case of *Corrigan v. Buckley* in 1926.[179] All state courts which faced the issue gave their sanction to racial restrictions, if the restrictions were properly drawn, signed, and recorded and if conditions remained the same.

The cases were scattered. The Caucasians had no program, and like many interest groups they were dormant at times, active at others. But in the totality of their separate and disconnected efforts, they gained for themselves a bulwark of legal doctrine. The covenants could not be touched by the Fourteenth Amendment because the restrictions were placed in contracts by private action, and citizens are protected only against discriminating state action. The traditional practice of freedom of alienation was made less important than freedom to contract to protect the value of one's own property. Also the principle of freedom of alienation was applied only to the sale of property; it was not applied to interfere with restrictions put upon its use or occupancy.

No considerations of public policy were discovered by the courts which were contrary to the enforcement of covenants. Changed conditions militated against the equitable enforcement of racial restrictions. But here the test of radical changes was developed and conditions were not often found sufficiently transformed to make the covenant unenforceable.

This history of racial restrictive covenants shows that court interpretation from 1915 to 1945 almost always favored the Caucasians. If *stare decisis* meant anything their future legal position was extremely secure. But the "threat" of Negroes moving into white areas was ever present as it had been for some years. In St. Louis at the February, 1940, meeting of the Marcus Avenue Improvement Association a speaker warned: "There are no blocks in St. Louis today that are safe. In less than six months it can change from white to Negro." [180] But he had a remedy: "You can be safe by signing a covenant and having responsible owners in the block sign it." He could give the assurance, finally, that "Under the law you can restrict any particular neighborhood that you want to, so as to absolutely prevent a colored person from occupying, using, or owning any property of that particular territory."

II

THE DEVELOPMENT OF
NEGRO STRENGTH

Organizing the NAACP

At the turn of the century the Negroes' low legal status was rationalized for them by Booker T. Washington, the former slave who had put into practice at Tuskegee Institute his ideal of vocational education for his race.[1] He stressed the middle-class virtues of reliance on practical learning, thrift, and obedience to duty as the best means for advancement, and he frowned on political action. When the Negro made himself useful to society, Washington believed, rewards would follow naturally. At the Cotton States Exposition in Atlanta in 1896, Washington declared that "the opportunity to earn a dollar in a factory just now is worth infinitely more than the opportunity to spend a dollar in an opera house." [2] Thus he accepted the estate in law which had been granted his race and begged other Negroes to do the same, warning that "the agitation of questions of social equality is the extremest folly." [3] Washington himself gained considerable political power,[4] a circumstance no doubt explained by the popularity of his words with white leaders, and found it to be of some utility. Yet he steadfastly opposed employing political methods to improve the lot of the mass of Negroes. In 1905, Washington declared: [5]

> I believe it is the duty of the Negro—as the greater part of the race is already doing—to deport himself modestly in regard to political claims, depending upon the slow but sure influences that proceed from the possession of property, intelligence, and high character for the full recognition of his political rights.

A reaction against the teachings of Washington and the first steps taken toward the later approach of the NAACP came in 1905 when W.E.B. DuBois, a Harvard graduate, organized a meeting of young Negroes at Niagara Falls to take determined action to secure their civil rights.[6] The following year the Niagara Movement, made up of fewer than one hundred Negro intellectuals, met at Harpers Ferry and pledged: [7]

> We will not be satisfied to take one jot or tittle less than our full manhood rights. We claim for ourselves every single right that belongs to a free-born American, political, civil and social; and until we get these rights we will never cease to protest and assail the ears of America.

Mary White Ovington, a social worker closely associated with Negro problems for fifty years, has said of that meeting: " 'Duties not rights' was then the watchword of the Booker Washington group, but at Harpers Ferry they were not afraid to speak of Negro rights."[8] The abolition of all distinctions based on race or color was demanded by the members of the Niagara Movement, but apart from its zeal the organization had little strength. Other Negroes who subscribed to the views of Washington criticized the movement as not representing members of the race living in the South. It was claimed, in an open reference to DuBois, that the race problem could not be solved by a "hot air artist." To the contrary, it was asserted, "one humble school teacher, or upright minister, or humble toiler in the wash tub or behind the plow, if frugal and persistent, is worth more to the race than a whole cart load of these perpetual wind jammers."[9] Indeed, the Niagara Movement existed for less than five years, but it was the leading attempt after the Civil War to organize a Negro protest.

The occurrence of a race riot in August, 1908, in Springfield, Illinois provoked a group of white leaders to lasting interest in the problems faced by Negroes.

The call for the first meeting of the National Association for the Advancement of Colored People was written by Oswald Garrison Villard, grandson of the great abolitionist leader, William Lloyd Garrison. This was issued on the centenary of Lincoln's birth in 1909 and was signed by fifty-three people including William

English Walling, John Dewey, Jane Addams, William Dean Howells, Lincoln Steffens, Rev. John Haynes Holmes, and Rabbi Stephen S. Wise.[10] Conferences were held in New York City in May of 1909 and again in 1910.

DuBois came from Atlanta to direct publicity and research and edit *The Crisis,* the official NAACP organ, published monthly since 1909. His belligerent spirit brought an intensity of purpose to the Association, but he did not dominate policy-making in regard to methods and objectives. For if the NAACP may be said to have had its origins in the Niagara Movement, that phase of ultraradicalism was the first of three stages through which, according to Arthur M. Schlesinger, Sr., every reform movement develops.[11] Then moderate leaders take hold. These are the men in every movement who win practical victories and bring their organization to the third stage in which the goals sought are at the point of gaining the sanction of social respectability.

The moderate leadership was exemplified by Moorfield Storey, a conservative Boston lawyer, who was president of the Association from 1910 until his death in 1929. Storey graduated from Harvard as the Civil War ended and served as secretary to Senator Charles Sumner during the critical days of President Johnson's impeachment. Then in Boston he built a prosperous law practice and in 1895 served as president of the American Bar Association. Soon after the NAACP was formed, Storey indicated his view of its function in these words: [12]

> The object of the National Association is to create an organization which will endeavor to smooth the path of the Negro race upward, and create a public opinion which will frown upon discrimination against their property rights, which will endeavor to see that they get in the courts the same justice that is given to their white neighbors, and that they are not discriminated against as they are now all over the country. We want to make race prejudice if we can as unfashionable as it is now fashionable. We want to arouse the better feelings of the white people, and broaden the sympathy which should be felt for the race to which we owe so much, and it seems to me that this is a field for our labor.

Joel Elias Spingarn succeeded to the presidency of the NAACP in 1929. Professor of comparative literature at Columbia from

1899 to 1911, Spingarn was a prominent literary critic and poet throughout his life. In 1914 he established the Spingarn medal to honor annually the outstanding Negro American. J.E. Spingarn died in 1939. His brother, Arthur B., who had long been interested in Negro betterment, became president of the NAACP in 1940. He graduated from Columbia Law School in 1901 and soon became a prominent attorney in the field of literary rights. As a young man, Arthur B. Spingarn became interested in the settlement house movement but transferred his main concern from immigrant to Negro problems soon after the formation of the NAACP. Thus there have been only three NAACP presidents, Storey and the two Spingarns, and all reflected the original interest of white civic leaders in Negro betterment.

Over the years the leadership of the National Association for the Advancement of Colored People had shifted from white to Negro. By 1949 the national office of the Association had a paid staff of seventy-two, only four of whom were white. The active leadership of the Association, in the position of secretary, has always been occupied by Negroes. The first secretary, James Weldon Johnson, was best known for his literary skill and poetic ability but his knowledge of Negro life and problems was profound.[13] In 1931 Walter White became secretary of the NAACP, a position he held until his death in 1955. His *A Man Called White* is a remarkable account not only of his own choice in being Negro but also of the NAACP story. A third Negro, Roy Wilkins, who had been a staff member for twenty-five years became secretary in 1955.

The strong leadership of the Association at the national level was strengthened by its growth in membership throughout the country. Local chapters were established in all major cities and many smaller ones—South as well as North. By the end of 1919, its tenth year, the NAACP had 310 branches with 91,203 members.[14] Nearly half of this membership was in the South.[15] When World War II ended in 1945, the size of the Association had grown to 300,000 members and 1,600 branches and youth councils.[16]

Colored leaders of NAACP have always urged members "to follow the course that leads to our becoming an integral part of the nation, with the same rights and guarantees that are accorded to other citizens, and on the same terms." [17] The pattern of action has been as broad as the goal: "petition and protest, legal redress, lobbying, legislative activity, education, and persuasion. And, implicit and explicit in all activities has been the theme of equality." [18]

Lobbying Congress

NAACP entry into national politics was signaled by its successful, though possibly misguided, campaign against Senate confirmation of the appointment of Judge John J. Parker to the Supreme Court.[19] At that time the Association had already won a number of cases in the United States Supreme Court and was alert to the personality factors in its operations. The NAACP believed, "in view of the many 5-to-4 decisions" rendered in previous years that "the character, social background and general education of each justice played an important part" in their outcome.[20]

President Hoover nominated Parker, a judge of the United States Circuit Court of Appeals for the Fourth Circuit and former leader in North Carolina Republican politics, on April 10, 1930. Before the Senate considered the nomination, the NAACP discovered what it considered to be an anti-Negro bias in his background. This was construed from a speech made before the North Carolina Republican Convention in 1920 in accepting the bid to be the party's candidate for Governor.[21] Parker expressed approval of a state constitutional amendment containing a "grandfather clause," the principle of which had been outlawed by the Supreme Court of the United States after the NAACP had carried its objections to it there in 1915.[22] In addition, Parker had said: [23]

> The Negro as a class does not desire to enter politics. The Republican Party of North Carolina does not desire him to do so. We recognize the fact that he has not yet reached that stage in his development when he can share the burdens and responsibilities of Government. This being true, and every intelligent man in North Carolina knows that it is true, the attempt of certain petty Democratic politicians to inject the race issue into every campaign is most reprehensible. I say it deliberately, there is no more dangerous or contemptible enemy of the State than

men who for personal or political advantage will attempt to kindle the flame of racial prejudice or hatred. . . . The participation of the Negro in politics is a source of evil and danger to both races and is not desired by the wise men in either race or by the Republican party of North Carolina.

When a subcommittee of the Senate Judiciary Committee held hearings on the nomination, Walter White presented this evidence and entered strong objections to Judge Parker on behalf of the NAACP. William Green, president of the American Federation of Labor, also urged that the Senate reject the appointment because of antilabor sentiments expressed in decisions affirming the validity of "yellow-dog" contracts.[24] The whole committee later reported out against confirmation of Parker by a vote of 10 to 6.[25]

In defense of Judge Parker, it was explained to the full Senate that in the labor matter he had been guilty of nothing beyond following the decisions of the Supreme Court of the United States. This was said to have been proper for a lower federal court. As to claims of race prejudice, Senator Overman of North Carolina pointed out that the speech in question, the authenticity of which neither he nor Parker denied or confirmed, was a political address and therefore should not be taken seriously, least of all by senators.[26]

Judge Parker pledged his support of the Constitution and all of its amendments in a letter to Overman [27] and in a telegram to Senator Kean of New Jersey.[28] He declared that "I do not believe in depriving any man, white or black, of his rights under the Constitution or the laws of our country, and have never advocated doing so." [29] Ironically Judge Parker had had only one chance to apply this general declaration, and had favored the protection of Negro rights in that single case. This was the case of *City of Richmond v. Deans* [30] questioning the validity of a segregation ordinance. In a *per curiam* decision the three-man court on which Judge Parker served ruled, under the doctrine of *Buchanan v. Warley*,[31] that a municipal residential segregation ordinance was a violation of the Fourteenth Amendment. The NAACP gained an affirmance in the Supreme Court when the decision was later carried there.[32] In debate over confirmation it was suggested to the Senate that in the light of Judge Parker's position in this case the white citizens of Richmond had more to fear from his appointment to the Supreme Court than did the Negroes.[33]

Oblivious to claims of Judge Parker's neutrality and judicial temper, the NAACP followed its criticism in committee with a letter and telegraph campaign to all senators. It was made clear that votes on confirmation would be taken as an acid test of sympathy to the Negro cause.[34] The biennial elections of 1930 were near at hand. With the A.F. of L. making a similar campaign against Judge Parker the Senate refused to confirm by the narrow margin of 41 to 39.[35]

Appraisal of the factors in Judge Parker's defeat is difficult. Resentment against the Hoover administration over the economic depression was rising, and this no doubt played a part. To look at the question in narrower terms, the objections of the A.F. of L. certainly counted for something but the efforts of the NAACP were at least of equal importance.[36] Herbert Hoover has recently attributed the defeat of his nominee to the organized efforts of labor and the Negro, recollecting that these groups cowed many senators who feared for their own reëlection.[37] The former president laments that this included many Republicans like Senator Arthur Vandenberg "who had often spoken of the sacredness of the bench from group pressures." [38] In sum, although the Negroes may have misplaced their fears in opposing Judge Parker—his later circuit-court decisions have been commended by Walter White himself [39]—the NAACP demonstrated that it was an able practitioner of the politics of pressure.

Despite large expenditures [40] the NAACP gained little in lobbying Congress. The institution was insulated against Negro claims. The size and character of the Southern delegation, the committee system, seniority, and cloture in the Senate doomed Negro efforts. In the 1920's Negroes failed to secure legislation making lynching a federal crime.[41] Over and over again bills to prohibit the poll-tax failed. During World War II, many Negroes became convinced of the uselessness of pressure-group activities in Congress with the defeat of proposals to create a permanent Fair Employment Practices Commission.[42]

The National Association for the Advancement of Colored People has not limited its lobbying to issues of primary interest to Negroes. For one thing, it has generally supported measures favoring workers and low-income groups. Specifically, the Association has advocated rent and price controls, public housing, federal aid to education, and stronger social-security laws.[43] On another front, the NAACP took a stand against the Mundt-Nixon Bill, later enacted as the McCarran Internal Security Act,[44] out of concern that under its sweeping provisions "any progressive organization striving for social, political or economic betterment" could be declared "subversive" by government officials who merely opposed its aims.[45] The Association also criticized the president's loyalty program.[46] It was instrumental in getting a Bureau of Immigration form abolished, so that all citizens could travel as Americans rather than some being designated as of African, Chinese, or other origin. While the general legislative work of the NAACP may be assumed to have directly benefited Negroes, the secondary value of building alliances with labor and liberal interest groups was also gained. Trade-union support for Negro objectives could be expected to grow after NAACP denunciations of the Taft-Hartley Act. Organizations specialize, but the American Civil Liberties Union, the American Jewish Congress, and the NAACP assume that the problems of civil rights are indivisible.[47]

Influence in National Affairs

After World War I, as numbers of Negroes increased in the North, their economic betterment and higher educational attainments served as spring boards for further advancement in all fields. Although the proportion of Negroes to the total number of inhabitants in the United States has decreased each decade since the first census, the settlement of Negroes in the large urban centers of the North helped enhance their importance. (See table.) Today the Negro population constitutes less than 10 per cent of the total as contrasted with 15 per cent in 1860. Yet the fact that there are now more than a million colored people in the New York metropolitan area has a political significance all its own.

The growth of the colored population in the North and their interest in influencing national policy made political realists out of many Negro leaders. Bloc voting for the Republican party until 1930 followed by the almost total switch to Roosevelt brought few concrete gains. After 1940 Negroes began to see a strategic advantage in the location of their population in Northern cities. This view was refined in an important study of the Negro vote by Henry Lee Moon, later publicity director of the NAACP.[48] In presidential elections Moon saw the Negro's influence deriving "not from its numerical strength" but from its strategic diffusion in the "marginal states whose electoral votes are generally considered vital to the winning candidate."[49] Thus even in 1944, Moon could show that "there were twenty-eight states in which a shift of 5 per cent or less of the popular vote would have reversed the electoral vote cast by these states. In twelve of these,

INCREASE OF POPULATION IN SELECTED STANDARD METROPOLITAN AREAS BY COLOR: 1940–1950 *

Standard metropolitan area	Total population			Nonwhite population		
	1940	1950	Per cent increase	1940	1950	Per cent increase
New York	11,660,839	12,911,994	10	668,854	1,045,512	56
Chicago	4,825,527	5,495,364	14	334,865	605,238	81
Philadelphia	3,199,637	3,671,048	15	336,843	484,644	44
Los Angeles	2,916,403	4,367,911	50	128,039	276,305	116
Detroit	2,377,329	3,016,197	27	172,778	361,925	110
Saint Louis	1,432,088	1,681,281	17	151,448	216,455	43
Cleveland	1,267,270	1,465,511	15	87,646	153,153	43
Washington	967,985	1,464,089	51	230,827	342,159	48

* Based on Bureau of the Census, Advance Population Reports, *Population of Standard Metropolitan Areas and Cities of 50,000 or More, By Color: 1950 and 1940*, Series PC-14, No. 1 (December 16, 1951).

with a total of 228 electoral college votes, the potential Negro vote exceeds the number required to shift the states from one column to the other."[50]

Despite some exaggerated claims, there can be no doubt of Negro influence in bringing about some favorable presidential policies. During Wilson's administration the NAACP opposed segregating civil servants in federal offices.[51] From World War I Negroes worked against segregation in the armed forces and eventually saw the practice ended by President Truman.[52] President Roosevelt by executive order established a temporary FEPC.[53] These actions indicate that when Negroes worked through national leaders they could often be successful.

Another attempt to make gains outside of government has been the NAACP ambition to gain for Negroes fair and equal treatment in all phases of life. Very early in its history the Association opposed the showing of the movie "The Birth of a Nation" because it vilified the Negro race.[54] It has since objected to the appearance of Negroes in motion pictures as comic or menial figures.[55] The barriers placed on Negroes by many types of private institutions—hospitals, colleges and restaurants, for example—have been attacked. Opportunities have been sought for Negroes, often highly skilled members of the race, to become members of bar and medical associations or participate in major league baseball. Gradual improvement has characterized most of these efforts; sometimes dramatic effect was gained. After the great Negro contralto, Miss Marian Anderson, was denied the opportunity to sing at Constitution Hall in Washington by the Daughters of the American Revolution, arrangements were made by Secretary of the Interior Harold L. Ickes for her to sing at the Lincoln Memorial, and on Easter Sunday, 1939, she sang outdoors to an audience of 50,000.[56]

The large numbers of Negroes located in urban production centers of the North have improved their economic position. Negroes have obtained jobs in heavy industry and shared in the wage increases gained by all laboring men in recent years. Even those who remained in traditional employments as menial servants also improved their economic lot. A. Philip Randolph's Brotherhood of Sleeping Car Porters increased the pay of pullman porters enormously through trade-union efforts. Opportunities in business and the professions opened too, for by 1946 in Northern cities about 85,000 Negro families were earning $5,000 or more annually.

Finally, in education Negroes made great strides. In 1940, more than half of the Negro population had completed more than five years of schooling, an important improvement relatively speaking. In that same year, 550,000 Negroes had graduated from high school while 80,000 had earned college degrees. Thus the mass of Negroes was better off and the pool of potential leaders was expanded.

NAACP Legal Defense

Beginning in 1915 the NAACP was active in nearly every Supreme Court case concerning the constitutional rights of

Negroes. It had the good fortune to obtain outstanding counsel in the very first cases and thereby began a confident tradition based squarely on careful preparation and dignified presentation. Moorfield Storey was already an exprienced advocate when he successfully represented the Association in the "grandfather clause" case in 1915.[57] Three years later Storey also prepared a brief and argued the cause in the Supreme Court against the constitutionality of a Louisville racial zoning ordinance.[58] In 1923, the Association gained its third victory when the Court overturned the death sentences of twelve Negroes convicted in an Arkansas court dominated by a mob.[59] The result of the Arkansas mob-rule case prompted Louis Marshall to volunteer his legal services without cost to the NAACP.[60]

Louis Marshall was a New York Republican with a conservative economic philosophy and a great humanitarian interest in working against racial and religious discrimination.[61] As president of the American Jewish Committee from its founding in 1906 he worked to create a climate of opinion that would bring about full equality in all walks of life. Thus it was characteristic of Marshall that in addition to Jews he defended Catholics, Indians, Japanese-Americans, and Negroes.[62] It has been said that Marshall "appeared in more cases in the United States Supreme Court than any one else, excepting the representatives of the government." [63] As we shall see, he and Storey worked together but failed in *Corrigan v. Buckley*, the restrictive covenant case.[64] Louis Marshall made a great contribution to Negro advancement by his brief in the first of the white-primary cases.[65] Here as in other early NAACP cases, Arthur B. Spingarn and Fred C. Knollenberg also played leading roles.

When Moorfield Storey and Louis Marshall died in 1929, the NAACP had already won a series of impressive constitutional gains and was organized to carry on its efforts in the courts. Arthur B. Spingarn had organized a national legal committee to advise the Association. Its first members included Clarence Darrow, Felix Frankfurter, Frank Murphy, Arthur Garfield Hays, and Morris L. Ernst. These men and their successors on the National Legal Committee contributed important help but volunteers could not give to the cause of Negro rights the broad continuity that was needed to present a large procession of cases to the Supreme

Court. Important school-segregation cases were lost when they came to the Court completely outside of NAACP control. The issues were not properly presented and "the cases were all argued and decided as if they were abstract legal problems, unrelated to real facts of life." [66] A Supreme Court justice remarked during this period that Negro rights were suffering because their cases were not always well prepared.[67]

In the early 1930's a foundation grant allowed the NAACP to make a broad survey of its legal problems. This financial support came from the American Fund for Public Service,[68] a foundation established in 1922 by a young millionaire named Charles Garland. The fund was certainly in great sympathy with Negroes, for its members in addition to James Weldon Johnson, then general secretary of the NAACP, were Roger N. Baldwin, Robert W. Dunn, Morris L. Ernst, Lewis S. Gannett, Benjamin Gitlow, Clinton S. Golden, Freda Kirchway, Charles Michelson, Scott Nearing, and Norman Thomas. Johnson went on leave from his NAACP position to become president of the fund and Ernst, also an NAACP attorney, became its secretary.

In 1929, three members of the board of the American Fund for Public Service—Ernst, Gannett, and Johnson—constituted as a Committee on Negro Work recommended that substantial financial help be given to protect the civil rights of Negroes. The spirit of the committee report is conveyed by the following passages: [69]

> The largest group of unorganized workers in America, the most significant and at present most ineffective bloc of the producing class are in the twelve million of colored people. . . . We believe that the largest single contribution which this fund could make to the release of the creative energies of the producing class in America would be to finance a large-scale, widespread, dramatic campaign to give the Southern Negro his constitutional rights, his political and civil equality, and therewith a self-consciousness and self-respect which would inevitably tend to effect a revolution in the economic life of the country. . . .
>
> Specifically, we recommend a dramatic, large-scale campaign to give the Negroes equal rights in the public schools, in the voting booths, on the railroads, and on juries in every state where they are at present denied them, and the right to own and oc-

cupy real property. These rights are the necessary basis of any real economic independence; their significance to later campaigns for unionization is obvious. . . .

. . . the campaign which we propose is a continuing battle because each time the Negro establishes a legal right, an effort is made to circumvent it by another restrictive law. . . .

We wish to emphasize that unless this campaign is conducted on a generous scale, it will lose most of its effectiveness. And we add that while the statement embarrasses one member of this committee, it seems to us all obvious that the only organization which could carry the brunt of such a campaign is the N.A.A.C.P.

Roger Baldwin questioned whether a legal campaign was what Negroes most needed. Upon receiving the recommendation of the Committee on Negro Work, Baldwin wrote this letter to a friend: [70]

Would you take the time to look over the enclosed report which is made by a committee of this Fund. It amazes me. My own view is that such a legalistic approach will fail of its object because the forces that keep the Negro under subjection will find some way of accomplishing their purposes, law or no law.

My personal view is that the whole problem should be approached from the economic standpoint and primarily that of the union of white and black workers against their common exploiters. This is a confidential document, but I would appreciate your view before October 30th when the Fund meets.

If you think of any Negroes outside of the Advancement Association who want to take a look at it, please suggest them.

Despite some difference of opinion among the directors, the sum of $100,000 was allocated to the NAACP for a coördinated legal program.

Money from the American Fund for Public Service was not immediately transferred to the NAACP, as a detailed program had to be designed and then acted upon. About $8,000 was paid beginning in May, 1931, to finance a preliminary survey.[71] And in June, 1933, $10,000 was transferred to the NAACP in connection with court cases for Negro rights.[72] Unfortunately for the NAACP, general economic depression in the 'thirties reduced the securities of the Fund for Public Service so that actual contributions to the legal campaign for Negroes were only $20,700. Even this sum, however, was of great value in stimulating the NAACP leadership to address itself to the broad problem of Negro advancement before the law.

The program planned by the NAACP constituted a full-scale attack on racial segregation in education, transportation, and housing. The Fund for Public Service and the NAACP agreed to entrust supervision of the program to the Committee on Negro Work. Members of the committee at this time were Roger Baldwin, Morris L. Ernst, Lewis Gannett, James Weldon Johnson, James Marshall, Arthur B. Spingarn, and Walter White. This committee in 1930 agreed to have Nathan Margold of New York, an experienced lawyer, direct the legal program. Walter White has said that Margold performed "a brilliant job of research," [73] and helped the committee map out an attack "on the basic causes of discrimination." Some cases, especially against the Texas white primary election system, were initiated through the efforts of Margold.[74] In 1933 Margold left the NAACP to become solicitor of the Department of Interior.

Margold was succeeded by one of the most capable Negro lawyers. In July, 1933, Walter White wrote: [75]

> The ideal person, in our opinion, is Mr. Charles H. Houston, Vice Dean of the Howard University Law School, a Harvard graduate, and Felix Frankfurter says he is one of the most brilliant and able students at Harvard within his memory. Mr. Houston is the attorney who did such brilliant work in the Crawford extradition case. His very deep interest would enable us not only to secure a man who would have all the intellectual and legal background necessary but one who will have a definite personal interest which would cause him to do the job better and less expensively than might otherwise be the case.

It was not until July 1, 1935, that Houston became special counsel for the Association. At that time he stressed that the legal campaign against inequality was "a carefully planned one to secure decisions, rulings and public opinion on the broad principle instead of being devoted to merely miscellaneous cases." [76] Houston left the NAACP in 1938 to return to private practice and to Howard Law School in Washington. His continued efforts to enlarge Negro civil rights were recognized, following his death in 1949, by the award of the Spingarn Medal. Dean Erwin Griswold of Harvard Law School, in making the award, said: "It is doubtful that there has been a single important case involving civil rights during the past fifteen years in which Charles Houston has not participated either directly or by consultation and advice." [77]

William H. Hastie, Houston's cousin, and himself a distinguished graduate of the Harvard Law School was closely associated with the legal work of the NAACP during the 1930's. Hastie's main contribution was made through directing the work of an enlarged national legal committee. In 1944 President Roosevelt appointed Hastie to be Governor of the Virgin Islands and in 1949 President Truman appointed him a judge of the Court of Appeals for the Third Circuit, located in Philadelphia. He was the first Negro to hold these two positions.

A third Negro played a more important role within the NAACP. Born in Baltimore in 1908, Thurgood Marshall graduated from Lincoln University and, in 1930, entered Howard Law School. Marshall studied there at the time that Houston, Hastie, and others were converting Howard into a laboratory for the enlargement of the legal rights of Negroes. After graduation Marshall practiced law in Baltimore but in 1935 was invited to join Houston at the NAACP in New York. Beginning in 1938 Thurgood Marshall as special counsel for the NAACP held what was "probably the most demanding legal post in the country." [78]

In 1939 the NAACP Legal Defense and Educational Fund was incorporated to provide a full-time staff to work on civil-rights litigation. There was another reason for separate organization. The Internal Revenue Code permits taxpayers aiding a corporation or fund when organized and operated for "educational purposes" to deduct contributions from gross income. In order to qualify for this tax advantage the code insists that "no substantial part of the activities" of an organization may be devoted to "carrying on propaganda, or otherwise attempting to influence legislation." The NAACP Legal Defense Fund, along with thousands of other organizations, has been held to be this type of organization by the Internal Revenue Service. [79]

The staff of the NAACP Legal Defense Fund is motivated primarily in establishing racial equality before the law on a broad

Louis Marshall (1856–1929)
Volunteer NAACP counsel in *Corrigan v. Buckley*

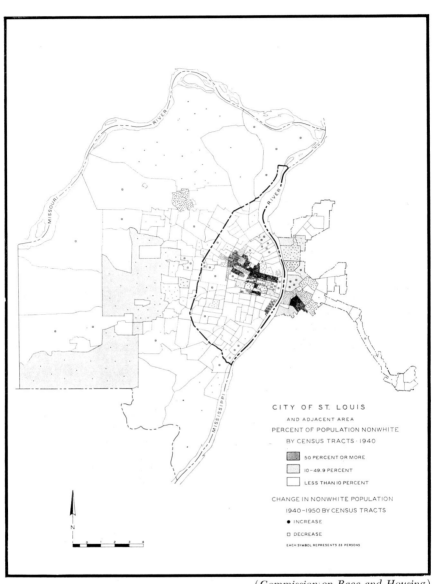

CITY OF ST. LOUIS
AND ADJACENT AREA
PERCENT OF POPULATION NONWHITE
BY CENSUS TRACTS · 1940

50 PERCENT OR MORE

10 – 49.9 PERCENT

LESS THAN 10 PERCENT

CHANGE IN NONWHITE POPULATION
1940–1950 BY CENSUS TRACTS
● INCREASE
□ DECREASE
EACH SYMBOL REPRESENTS 25 PERSONS

(Commission on Race and Housing)

CITY OF ST. LOUIS, 1940
Restrictive covenants reinforced racial residential
segregation in American cities

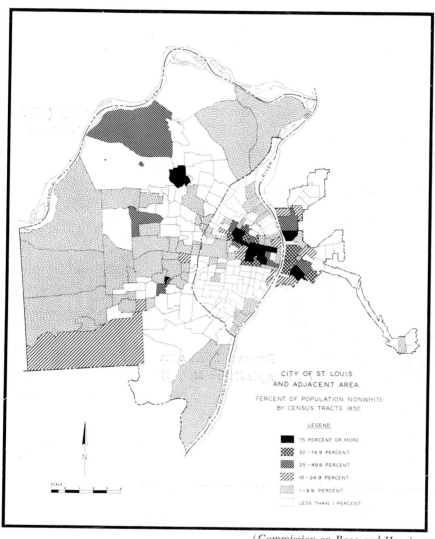

CITY OF ST. LOUIS
AND ADJACENT AREA

PERCENT OF POPULATION NONWHITE
BY CENSUS TRACTS 1950

LEGEND

■ 75 PERCENT OR MORE
▨ 50 - 74.9 PERCENT
▧ 25 - 49.9 PERCENT
▨ 10 - 24.9 PERCENT
▨ 1 - 9.9 PERCENT
□ LESS THAN I PERCENT

(Commission on Race and Housing)

CITY OF ST. LOUIS, 1950
The 1948 Supreme Court decisions freed the housing market
but did not end segregation

LOUIS WIRTH (1897–1952)
(*Photograph: Fabian Bachrach*)

ROBERT C. WEAVER
(*Photograph: Holmes Morgan*)

DUDLEY O. McGov[
(1882–1945)

GEORGE L. VAUGHN (1882–1950)
(*Photograph: Pittsburgh Courier*)

FRANCIS DENT AND WILLIS M. GRAVES
(*Photograph: Jimmie Johnson*)

(Photograph: Harris & Ewing)

116 BRYANT STREET, N.W., WASHINGTON, D.C.

GERALD SEEGERS
(*Photograph: Edwyn Portrait*)

HENRY GILLIGAN (1892–1950)
(*Photograph: Harris & Ewing*)

JAMES A. CROOKS
(*Photograph: Harris & Ewing*)

CHARLES HOUSTON (1895–1949)

THURGOOD MARSHALL
(*Photograph: Moss Photo Service*)

LOREN MILLER
(*Photograph: Bob Douglas*)

(Photograph: Harris & Ewing)

JUDGE HENRY EDGERTON

(Photograph: Harris & Ewing)

PHILIP B. PERLMAN

(Photograph: Rembrandt Studios)

HERMAN WILLER

(Photograph: Harris & Ewing)

PHINEAS INDRITZ

SUPREME COURT OF THE UNITED STATES, 1947–1948

Back row (*left to right*): Wiley B. Rutledge, Frank Murphy, Robert L. Jackson, Harold H. Burton. Front row: Felix Frankfurter, Hugo L. Black, Fred M. Vinson, Stanley Reed, William O. Douglas

NATIONAL EDITION of

Pittsburgh Courier
THE BEST WEEKLY
AMERICA'S

LIVE FEATURES · NEWS Leader in Advertising, Circulation and News CLEAN AND PROGRESSIVE

12¢ PER COPY

PITTSBURGH, PA., SATURDAY, MAY 8, 1948   PRICE TWELVE CENTS

VOL. XXXIX—No. 19

In Michigan, Missouri and D.C. We Can

'LIVE ANYWHERE!' HIGH COURT RULES

'Live Anywhere!' High Court Rules

(Continued from Page 1)

Court's opinion: Justices Frankfurter, Burton, Black, Murphy and Douglas.

The far-reaching decision means that a mortal blow has been struck at racial restrictions in homes, artificially created ghettoes, public utilities and public services, restaurants, neighborhood theatres and countless other jim-crow manifestations made possible because of the heretofore enforced segregation in home ownership.

The decision of the Court was that individual property owners could voluntarily enter into covenants, but that Court enforcement of such covenants contravened the Fourteenth Amendment. The Supreme Court further ruled that court action constituted State action, and will not henceforth be permitted in these covenant cases.

Yet to be considered by the Supreme Court is a case from Ohio.

In giving the Court ruling Chief Justice Vinson said:

"Upon full consideration, we have concluded that in these cases the State has acted to deny petitioners the equal protection of the laws guaranteed by the Fourteenth Amendment . . . the judgment of the Supreme Court of Missouri and the judgment of the Supreme Court of Michigan must be reversed."

Their decision in the cases in Washington, D. C., was patterned after the Michigan and Missouri reversals.

The ruling of the Supreme Court —which may upset the pattern of residential life in almost every State in the Union—supported a 1917 ruling by the U. S. Supreme Court in which it voided racial restrictive covenant ordinances enacted by the city of Louisville, Ky., and other municipalities.

Action Dooms Vicious Custom

By LEM GRAVES JR.
(Washington Correspondent)

WASHINGTON — A[ny]
American citizen can li[ve]
anywhere in the U. S. . . . [if]
he has the money to buy [or]
build a home. This was t[he]
ruling of the United Sta[tes]
Supreme Court Monday wh[en]
it outlawed restrictive cov[en]
ants in cases arising in [De]
troit, St. Louis a.id Washi[ng]
ton, D. C. The vote v[as]
unanimous in every case!

Reversed were rulings of [the]
Supreme Court of Michigan,
holding the legality of coven[ant]
restricting Orsel McGhee and [his]
family from living in a so-c[alled]
"white" residential area in De[troit]
and a similar ruling by the Mis[-]
souri Supreme Court against [Mr.]
Shelley and his family in St. [Louis.]
All were barred because they [were]
Negroes.

Adding totality to the final[ity of]
its decisions the Nation's h[igh]
tribunal also reversed the [U.S.]
Circuit Court of Appeals f[or the]
District of Columbia in two [cases]
in Washington, D. C. inv[olving]
James M. Hurd and famil[y and]
Robert H. Rowe and famil[y.]

Taken behind closed doo[rs sev]
eral months ago, the S[upreme]
Court justices had studie[d the]
dynamite-laden issue secret[ly . . .]
when the decision was ann[ounced]
three of the justices did n[ot vote.]
They were Justices Reed, [Jackson]
and Rutledge, who had [barred]
themselves from hearing t[he cases]
when it was argued, becau[se they]
was in some manner inve[sted in]
circumstances which had [a bear-]
ing on the cases.

Voting unanimously we[re eight]
Justice Vinson, who deliv[ered]

(Continued on Page 5, Co[l.]

The *Pittsburgh Courier*, a Negro newspaper, announces the
Supreme Court's decision in the 1948 cases

basis. The NAACP Legal Defense Fund is not a legal-aid society. Its limited resources prevent it from participating in all cases involving the rights of Negroes. To have the vital issues raised at the proper point so that the Supreme Court has a case with a record in good order, the NAACP attorneys commonly work on litigation from the beginning. A staff attorney has said: [80]

> Generally, we prefer to handle a case with local counsel from its inception through all of its appellate stages. Thus the staff is involved in the preparation of the complaint, the trial of the case, the preparation of briefs for use in the appellate courts and the Supreme Court and argument at the appellate levels and in the Supreme Court of the United States. [Actually] we do handle a significant number of cases which reach us after trial and sometimes we enter a case at the Supreme Court level.

The National Legal Committee has continued to be an important part of the NAACP. By 1947, when Charles Houston was chairman, the committee had thirty-seven members.[81] Since then its chairman has been Lloyd K. Garrison and its size has increased to forty-one.[82] The functions of the National Legal Committee are not clearly defined, but the committee can be said to be valuable in two ways. The members represent the NAACP in their localities and are frequently found to be in charge of race-relations litigation at the trial level. They are responsible persons and understand the general goals and methods of the organizations. All of the members form an advisory nucleus to the staff. Many conferences have been held through the years which deal with specific problems of strategy and tactics. Every evidence suggests that the National Legal Committee has provided real guidance and that the staff follows the counsel of the committee in many instances.

The Negro Bar

It is evident that an interest group which works primarily through the courts is highly dependent on lawyers. And it is essential when the issues are national in character but local in origin that able lawyers be on the job regularly in widely scattered places. Also, the delicacies of coördination demand that these lawyers be similarly motivated, compatible, and in basic agreement on objectives and procedures. These criteria have marked the Negro interest's activity in litigation. The great success of Thurgood Marshall as full-time special counsel of the NAACP, rests in part on the competence and camaraderie of Negro attorneys across the country who, for years, knew each other in law school, in business, and in fraternal and professional associations. To say this is not to discount the vital contributions made by white attorneys and professors, but merely to stress the leading roles played by Negro lawyers who felt themselves responsible for improving the legal status of all Negroes. Many have made substantial contributions of time to support the NAACP. The associational patterns of Negro lawyers were perhaps more casual and informal than can be shown here. Yet some attention to the unity of the Negro bar is necessary if the methods of the National Association for the Advancement of Colored People are to be understood.

The single most important training place for Negro attorneys has been the law school of Howard University, in the District of Columbia.[83] Organized in 1868 with almost complete financial support by the national government, the Howard Law School in recent years has had an annual student enrollment of 100 and a faculty of twelve. In the summer of 1956, the school occupied a new well-equipped building on the campus. Faculty interest in civil-rights problems has been shared by students and alumni. The school's publicity emphasizes that Howard has "the oldest and most fully developed civil rights course in any American law school." This course, begun early in the 1940's by Charles Houston and James Nabrit, has always centered on current problems in race-relations law. Professors and students have worked on litigation in process and their findings and recommendations have been relied upon in the presentation of briefs and arguments by the NAACP. Graduates of Howard Law School practice in many sections of the country. Asked to list those who have distinguished themselves in civil-rights activities, Dean George M. Johnson named twenty-two graduates and then added twenty-eight who have handled significant civil-rights cases in connection with their general practice.[84] Nevertheless, the part played by Howard Law School in the training of attorneys interested in civil-rights cases should be seen in perspective. A number of distinguished

Negro lawyers have graduated from other institutions, for example, Charles Houston and William Hastie from Harvard. Besides, many white lawyers, as students, faculty members, and practicing attorneys have been interested in and supporters of efforts to improve the general legal status of Negroes.

A study of Negro lawyers made in 1951 showed that there were 2,000 Negroes engaged in active legal practice.[85] One-third of these were concentrated in three cities, with 350 Negro lawyers in Chicago, and 200 each in Washington and New York. In 1951, the count stood at 11 in Alabama, 19 in Florida and 71 in Virginia but the number of Negro lawyers in Southern states has been increasing rapidly in recent years. The closeness of these attorneys in cities across the country to the problems of racial conflict and their part in channeling this conflict into the courts is significant. They are on the scene; it is part of their everyday life.

Not only are Negro attorneys participating in the affairs of their own community, but they also have professional contact with each other across the country. Excluded from the American Bar Association a small group of Negro attorneys in 1925 formed their own organization, the National Bar Association.[86] The purposes of the association include

> . . . working for a more equitable representation of all racial groups in the judiciary of our Cities, States and Nation, promoting legislation that will improve the economic condition of all the citizens of the United States, aiding all citizens, regardless of race or creed, in their effort to secure a free and untrammeled use of the franchise guaranteed by the Constitution of the United States . . . protecting the civil and political rights of the citizens and residents of the several States of the United States, and working for the integration of the American Bar.[87]

In the annual summer meetings of the association mainly problems of civil rights are discussed, especially for the legal profession itself. For a time the association published the *National Bar Journal.* Many of its most active members are graduates of the Howard Law School and have also served on the National Legal Committee of the NAACP. The interlocking nature of these organizations has been an important factor in the consciousness of Negro lawyers with respect to the legal barriers to equal treatment.

Communist and NAACP Legal Methods Contrasted

The organization that has most antagonized the association [88] has been the Communist party,[89] which sought to take over important NAACP cases. In the early 1930's the Communists fought strenuously for control of the Scottsboro cases, in Alabama, involving nine Negroes charged with rape. The rule that defendants in a criminal case have a federally protected right to the assistance of counsel in a state court was established after a brilliant effort by the great criminal lawyer Samuel Leibowitz.[90] This case was controlled by the NAACP until the legal principles were established, April 1, 1935. Thereafter Communists moved in and exploited the Scottsboro boys for Communist purposes.[91] The Communists won no further gains for the Negro, but publicized isolated cases of unfair treatment of Negroes for propaganda value in their attempts to discredit the American system of justice. In their appeals to the Supreme Court, the Communists' methods endangered the efforts of the NAACP to win advances for Negroes. For example, in 1951, in connection with the case of Willie McGee, a Negro who had been convicted of rape in Mississippi and was later electrocuted, the Supreme Court was picketed and deluged with telegrams largely from Communists and Communist sympathizers as part of efforts to gain McGee's freedom.[92] Justice Black, in giving a press conference, a rare occasion for a Supreme Court justice, severely criticized these tactics, saying that "the courts of the United States are not the kinds of instruments of justice that can be influenced by such pressures." [93] Referring to a five-inch stack of telegrams, Justice Black added, "I am not compelled to read these and have not and will not. It is a very bad practice."

These practices in cases involving Negroes and others attracted wide attention and were condemned by lawyers throughout the country. Numerous bills to restrict the picketing of courts were introduced in Congress.[94] Some restraint was expected of those who approached a court of justice. The picket line, the telegraph campaign, or other crude devices of publicity and influence would not do. A federal circuit court judge in Chicago, former Congressman F. Ryan Duffy, sent a communication to a congressional committee which was studying the problem in 1940 and expressed the typical sentiments of a wide segment of the bench and bar who were opposed.[95] "Assuming under our form of representative government pressure groups must be tolerated in our legislative and executive branches," he wrote, "I feel that there is no good reason why our courts should be subjected to such pressures." Congress became convinced that picketing of courts is a menace to justice and outlawed the practice in the Internal Security Act of 1950.[96]

In marked contrast to the tactics used by the Communists, the NAACP has adhered to established traditions of the American bar in sponsoring cases in the Supreme Court. Its success is not merely a tribute to its own work but to the American judicial system as well for its sensitivity to the Negroes' legal claims. The pressure exerted by the NAACP was unrelenting, but it was done with courtesy, dignity, and authority. Its briefs have often been models of legal craftsmanship. As we have seen, the Association's Legal Defense Fund has not functioned as a legal-aid society for Negroes. Rather it enters cases only when they involve racial discrimination, touch a fundamental right of citizenship, and establish a significant legal precedent. With care in the selection of issues, with the tact and maturity acquired by experience, and with the development of strong supporting organizations, the NAACP legal staff has become one of the ablest in the nation.

III

NAACP Opposition to Segregation in Housing: 1915 to 1940

Throughout its history the National Association for the Advancement of Colored People has fought against forced residential segregation. In 1915, for example, the Association declared: [1]

> The real crux of the matter lies in the fact that colored people, increasing in thrift and wealth, have been trying in the last decade to move out of the slums and unhealthy places of the cities into more desirable residential districts. They have been met by the plea that they are undesirable neighbors and that they depress real estate values. Hatred, riot, and even bloodshed have been the result of the controversy and finally the endeavor to prescribe the bounds of habitation by law.

Violence had to be opposed from the earliest years of the Association's life in order to protect the right of Negroes to live in any section of a city. Race riots have not developed solely from housing crises, but housing has been a leading source of them. In addition to ordinances, therefore, the NAACP discovered at a very early date "that the Negro may be segregated by intimidation and lawlessness." [2] The Association investigated instances of mob action associated with the race problem in housing in Kansas City,[3] Baltimore,[4] Philadelphia,[5] Cleveland,[6] Minneapolis,[7] Washington, D.C.,[8] Dallas,[9] and suburban New York.[10]

Legal action was often initiated after a housing riot. The most celebrated case in which the Association participated grew out of an incident in Detroit in 1925.[11] When a Negro surgeon, Dr. Ossian Sweet, moved into a newly purchased home in a white neighborhood, a mob gathered outside. Names were called and threats were made. Shots were fired at the Sweet home and shots were fired from the house into the mob. As a result one white man was killed. Ten relatives and friends of Dr. Sweet were in the house at the time and all were indicted on a charge of first-degree murder. The Detroit branch and the national office of the Association assumed responsibility for the defense. Clarence Darrow, the great criminal lawyer, was retained as chief counsel.[12] Frank Murphy was the presiding judge. After the jury disagreed in the first trial, a brother of Dr. Sweet was tried separately and acquitted. This was called the outstanding legal victory of the year.[13] The total cost of both trials was $37,849, three-fourths of which was paid by the national office of the NAACP.[14]

It had been hoped at first that the NAACP could help to eliminate discrimination in housing by merely pointing out its evils. Faced with the problem in its very first year the Association reported that it had encouraged among its members "the practice of writing letters to the press and magazines, in regard to any and all matters where the rights of the colored people were at issue, notably in the Baltimore segregation agitation." [15] The discovery was soon made, however, that a city ordinance could not be stopped by a letter to the editor. City councils in Baltimore, Richmond, Winston-Salem, Louisville, Birmingham, and a number of smaller communities had enacted segregation ordinances by 1915.[16] Dallas followed in 1916, and in St. Louis the first popular referendum on segregation ordinances showed that the public favored the device by a margin of two to one.[17] The NAACP was then faced with the fact that residential segregation was "sweeping the country." [18]

The NAACP carried to the courts its claims against the validity of segregation ordinances. The local branches of the Association successfully eliminated ordinances in Winston-Salem, Baltimore, Indianapolis, Norfolk, and Dallas through judicial action.[19] In the United States Supreme Court the NAACP won victories in 1917, 1926, and 1929. In the first case, *Buchanan v. Warley*,[20] a Louisville ordinance was invalidated, but its effect was limited, for within two years a number of new ordinances had appeared in various parts of the country.[21] The cost to the NAACP of *Buchanan v. Warley* was only $1,342, because Moorfield Storey rendered his services without charge.[22] However, after Louisiana courts had upheld a New Orleans ordinance,[23] over the objections of local NAACP representatives,[24] the national office of the Association appealed to the Supreme Court. Here they were successful, and the ordinance was held to be unconstitutional on the authority of the *Buchanan* rule.[25] In this case the cost to the NAACP was $8,182.[26] The Supreme Court adhered to its position once more in *City of Richmond v. Deans*.[27] The distinguishing feature of the Richmond zoning ordinance lay in its disguise of the principle of racial segregation by basing the separation on the legal prohibition of intermarriage and not on race or color. The Circuit Court of Appeals for the Fourth Circuit held that this restriction fell within the rule of *Buchanan v. Warley* because "the legal prohibition of intermarriage is itself based on race." [28] The cost of more than $2,000 of the case was borne by Negroes in Richmond.[29] When the case was appealed unsuccessfully to the Supreme Court by the City of Richmond, "the NAACP supervised the case, contributing the services of its legal committee." [30] Finally, then, the persistence of the Association was rewarded; since 1929, racial segregation by ordinance has been a rarity of no consequence.[31]

These Negro victories caused white supporters of residential segregation to rely upon the judicial enforcement of racial covenants. We have seen that these restrictions were widely enforced by the courts after 1918. In 1922 the breach of a covenant in the District of Columbia brought the NAACP into its first major effort to persuade the courts to hold such a restriction unenforceable.[32] In *Corrigan v. Buckley*, the attorney of record was James A. Cobb, a Howard Law School graduate in 1899, and thereafter a practicing attorney in Washington.[33] Having unsuccessfully contested enforcement of the restriction in the *Corrigan* case in two courts in the district, Cobb turned for help to the national office of the NAACP. Louis Marshall and Moorfield Storey agreed to prepare the appeal to the United States Supreme Court. Although the appeal was dismissed, it is instructive to observe the efforts made by Louis Marshall in that case as they place over-all NAACP strategy in perspective.

Planning the line of argument in *Corrigan v. Buckley*, Louis Marshall faced problems common to lawyers appealing from a record they had no hand in shaping. In September, 1924, Marshall wrote of "not being able to sleep last night" and so read the record of the case.[34] "The case is an exceedingly important one," he declared, "but there are technical difficulties which bother me." And a year later, after completing the first draft for a brief, Marshall blamed "its many imperfections" on the fact that he had "been obliged to steer a very cautious course between many rocks and shoals with which the channel of discussion is filled."[35]

With trepidation Marshall and Storey did contend in their brief in *Corrigan v. Buckley* that "the decrees of the courts below constitute a violation of the Fifth and Fourteenth Amendments to the Constitution, in that they deprive the appellants of their liberty and property without due process of law."[36] While preparing the brief, Marshall declared that "nothing can be gained by attempting to attack the conclusions of the Supreme Court in the *Civil Rights Cases*."[37] Indeed, at one point, Marshall expressed "fear that under the precedents the Court would not hold that the record presents any question that comes within the purview of the constitutional provisions on which reliance is placed."[38] At first, Marshall himself seemed to question the possibility of developing a theory of governmental action in restrictive-covenant cases for he explained that "in the present case no governmental body has acted, but merely individuals acting as such."[39] Yet Marshall developed a line of argument that presaged later efforts to have the judicial enforcement of racial covenants declared to be an unconstitutional expression of state action.[40]

> The court has been asked to restrain Corrigan from selling and Mrs. Curtis from buying property as to which a restriction has been created forbidding its use or ownership by colored people. If a judgment to that effect were rendered, the court would prevent Mrs. Curtis from buying this land because of her color. If it rendered such a decree, the court would be carrying out a policy which discriminates against colored persons and would thereby bring about segregation. The legislature may not segregate; the governing body of a city or village may not do so. Can a court, acting as a branch of the Government, by its mandate bring about segregation without running foul of the decision in *Buchanan v. Warley*, 245 U.S. 45? I think not.

"I believe that our principal hope must lie in securing a determination that a restrictive covenant of the character involved in this case is void because contrary to public policy." [41] Marshall knew that this was also a gamble. "Whether the record as made will enable the Supreme Court to decide that question under the technical rules affecting its jurisdiction," he said, "presents a problem of more than ordinary seriousness." [42] Speaking of *Buchanan v. Warley* once again, Marshall asked Storey if he was not correct in arguing public policy. [43]

> Public policy is largely based upon the constitutional and statutory definitions as to what the policy of a state is. When, therefore, the Constitution and laws enacted in accordance with it, and the decisions rendered interpretative thereof, indicate, as in this case, that segregation on account of color is not permissible, how can it be contended that a contract intended to do what the Supreme Court has decided that the State itself cannot do, is other than contrary to public policy?

Marshall added, "I have notes as to a large number of decisions which would support an argument on these lines," and these were cited in the actual brief. Finally, he believed that his position in the question of public policy was strengthened by the fact that this covenant was a restriction against alienation which "since the days of that statute *quia emptores* the courts have inclined against sustaining." [44]

Moorfield Storey, then over eighty years of age, and Louis Marshall, already seventy, participated in the argument for the NAACP in the Supreme Court. *Corrigan v. Buckley* was argued January 8, 1926, and on May 24 the Court handed down its decision that it lacked jurisdiction. Thus ended the first chapter in the long effort of the National Association for the Advancement of Colored People to have the judicial enforcement of racial restrictive covenants invalidated.

In 1930 the NAACP received encouragement for its goal from the American Fund for Public Service whose Committee on Negro Work recommended that the fund give priority to a campaign to end the enforcement of racial covenants. [45]

> The important problem in this issue is that of *segregation* by property owners' covenant. The N.A.A.C.P. has carried three cases to the United States Supreme Court. . . . In each of these the Supreme Court avoided decision, declaring itself without jurisdiction. . . . [46]

The issue is much broader than that of simply preventing discrimination against Negroes, for already such restrictive covenants have been used against Jews and Catholics.

Your committee proposes that funds should be provided to prepare a case in which the United States Supreme Court cannot avoid a definitive decision. Such a suit and the cost of subsequent test cases will, in our opinion, require the expenditure of not less than $10,000.

In spite of great interest the Committee on Negro Work was unable to develop any clear plan of attack on the current problem. On one occasion they recommended that "cases in this field should be started to test out various types of restrictions, and in various localities. Ten such actions would cost $4,000 each." [47] Later, in 1931, Walter White mentioned a more ingenious solution to the problem of getting the constitutional issue regarding racial deed restrictions before the Supreme Court.[48]

The attack on segregation by property-holders' covenants can best be made, in the opinion of the NAACP's attorneys, by preparing a case involving an attache or employee of a foreign embassy or consulate, in which original jurisdiction can be assumed by the United States Supreme Court. For such a case there would be no fee, as the case would be handled by Mr. Margold or the NAACP Legal Committee. Costs of arranging for course of action; court costs and costs of printing pleadings and brief . . . $500.00.

In practice the NAACP had no success in the 1930's although during that time efforts were made in "many cases involving restrictive covenants handled by NAACP attorneys in California, Michigan, Illinois, Missouri, Maryland, Virginia, New York, Ohio and the District of Columbia." [49]

A slight break came in 1940 when the Chicago branch of the Association carried the case of *Hansberry v. Lee* [50] to the Supreme Court of the United States. The attorneys for the Negroes in the litigation were Earl B. Dickerson, Truman K. Gibson, Jr., Francis Stradford, Loring B. Moore, and Irving C. Mollison. The case was decided in their favor on the ground that a prior state court decision upholding the covenant in question [51] could not bind persons who were not parties to it. By its own terms the covenant called for signatures of 95 per cent of the property owners, but this goal had not been achieved. The fact that the covenant had been improperly enforced in a previous case did not bind the court to repeat the error, for the doctrine of *res judicata* did not apply to this situation. The case had no significance in the development of legal doctrine which might be used to challenge the court enforcement of restrictive covenants generally. However, it had the immediate benefit of opening for purchase and rental to Negroes an entire area of twenty-seven city blocks in Chicago. But except for this the NAACP did very little toward ending the enforcement of racial restrictive covenants until after 1944.

Postwar Housing

In 1945 the Negroes' perennial shortage of good housing was worsened by the end-of-the-war scarcity. There had been a great influx of workers to the nation's industrial centers, yet there had been little increase in building. Negroes rarely received an opportunity to move into the more desirable dwellings. Therefore the enforcement of restrictive covenants, always irritating and clearly harmful to the Negroes' long-term hopes for improvement, frustrated immediate and pressing needs. In the past, perhaps, restrictive covenants had been looked upon as merely one of the many limitations on Negro action, and could be endured with the rest. As World War II was concluded, however, the enforcement of restrictions on an already circumscribed stock of residential housing provoked Negroes to fight back.

At the bottom of the postwar crusade against covenants were the bread-and-butter needs of Negroes. Throughout the nation, especially in the bigger Northern cities, large numbers were ready and willing to move to new homes. When the opportunity was presented, they purchased or rented property in restricted districts. Negro leaders encouraged this action. Some covenants remained idle, never enforced. In many instances, however, white property owners reached for their legal weapons. The Negro press urged its readers to stand firm. The National Association for the Advancement of Colored People gave assurances to individual Negroes that legal support would be provided.[52]

Soon at least a hundred injunctions to evict Negroes and dissolve their titles were sought by Caucasians. This estimate of the amount of litigation was made in 1946: [53]

During the past four years more than twenty covenant suits, probably affecting a hundred Negro families, have been entered in Los Angeles alone. Chicago had about sixteen such suits pending at the end of 1945, which affected about fifty Negro families. A dozen or more have been instituted in Washington, D.C., several in St. Louis and Detroit, and others in scattered cities in the North.

Much publicity resulted as suits were brought in Los Angeles against the well-known Negro actresses, Hattie McDaniel and Ethel Waters.

The enforcement of a restriction against an employee of the federal government in Washington, D.C., attracted considerable attention toward the end of World War II.[54] The employee, Miss Clara I. Mays, was defended by a group of Washington Negro lawyers including James A. Cobb, William H. Hastie, George E. C. Hayes, and Leon Ransom. Although the judgment of the district court enjoining the defendant from occupancy was affirmed by the Court of Appeals for the District of Columbia and certiorari was denied by the Supreme Court of the United States, hopeful signs appeared in the process. There were dissents by Justices Murphy and Rutledge from the refusal of the Supreme Court to hear the case, and on two occasions Judge Henry Edgerton wrote strongly worded dissenting opinions when the court of appeals acted to support enforcement. Judge Edgerton's dissent from the decision of the Court of Appeals provided a vivid picture of the difficulties Negroes faced in obtaining adequate housing in Washington at that time. Citing a large number of examples, Edgerton asserted that the shortage of housing for Negroes was so acute that enforcement of the restrictions was contrary to public policy. The decision in *Mays v. Burgess* discouraged the Negro attorneys, and yet Edgerton's dissent based on social and economic facts gave them heart.

The 1945 Chicago Conference

Since the enforcement of restrictive covenants was an important factor in limiting the supply of housing for Negroes at the end of World War II, the legal problem assumed priority on the NAACP agenda. The lawyers interested in seeing the enforcement of covenants ended began to restudy the entire question.

Therefore, since 1945 marks the beginning of a more intense period of development of opposition to racial restrictions the story will be told in greater detail.

A conference on restrictive covenants called by the NAACP in Chicago on July 9 and 10, 1945 was attended by thirty-three persons.[55] William H. Hastie, then governor of the Virgin Islands, was the presiding officer at the meetings. Thurgood Marshall, special counsel, explained that the purpose of the conference was to develop cases in order to question successfully in the Supreme Court the constitutionality of enforcement.

A number of lawyers attending the conference were actively engaged in restrictive-covenant cases. Willis Graves and Francis Dent reported on a case then being decided in Detroit. Charles Houston was working on two cases in Washington. Loren Miller in Los Angeles and George Vaughn in St. Louis were also trying to prevent the enforcement of covenants. With these and other lawyers were race-relations experts eager to share experiences and plan for the future.

From long hours of discussion emerged a clear-cut blueprint for attacking racial restrictive covenants. Every conceivable opportunity of attack was suggested, and the advantages of aggressiveness in and out of the court room were pointed out. There were comments on the trials, on which cases to select for appeal, what issues to raise, how to win in the Supreme Court, and how to exploit public opinion to advantage. A resume of the ideas presented before what the minutes call "Meeting of N.A.A.C.P. Lawyers and Consultants on Methods of Attacking Restrictive Covenants" show the individual lawyers' understanding of the problems faced. At the same time the development of legal and political strategy by an organization was clearly delineated.

What did the Negro leaders believe to be the origin and real nature of restrictive covenants? "There are property owners' associations," explained Spottswood W. Robinson, III, of Richmond, Virginia, "always composed partly of agitators, whose purpose and function it is to stir the neighborhood into the execution of segregation agreements." This fact creates in them an inherent weakness. "The agreements, in form a representation of the desire of all signers, are always the product of a few, which stands because of the aggressiveness of the few." Robinson expressed the belief that such agreements lacked stability, and with persistence by Negroes, could be broken. At another point in the discussion, Loren Miller, speaking of his experience in Los Angeles, said it was a good thing that a new suit was brought every time a Negro moved in. "The expenses of constant litigation are militating against those who desire to enforce the agreement." Miller believed there were more cases in Los Angeles than in any other city, with twenty different suits in progress.

But if the enforcement of restrictions reduced the Caucasian bank roll, it was no less expensive for Negroes. A St. Louis lawyer, David Grant, described the process of opening a covenanted area to Negroes as slow and costly. First, he explained, "some intrepid, energetic real estate operator" will purchase three or four houses in a white neighborhood. His sole motive is to make money. Having used straw parties in buying the property, he will then get "a Negro buyer and move him in there and sit back and wait and see what happens." If there is no objection he buys up more property because he knows it can be sold to Negroes at a profit. Sometimes the covenants are enforced; sometimes the brokers get into trouble with the Real Estate Commission and lose their licenses. "To what extent," asked Grant, "should Negroes go to the aid of these real estate brokers?"

"You should go completely to their aid," urged Charles Houston: "The pattern is the same in Washington."

Grant questioned this with a view to public opinion. "There is a lot of community disapproval on profiteering."

"I don't see how we can expect to break the agreements," said Loring Moore, an experienced attorney from Chicago, "if we don't have these law breakers."

This view and that of Houston's were supported by Thurgood Marshall. "This is not an ordinary service," the practical-minded special counsel advised. "You can't expect to break into a neighborhood at the regular rates."

An associated problem, the possibility that individual Negroes might become pawns in the larger struggle to end covenants, was talked over frankly. For one thing, in the movement into a traditionally white area, Charles Houston warned that leaders in all cities "must not let one Negro be stuck out there all alone. Negroes do not break covenants. They are broken by whites selling to

Negroes when the property becomes less desirable for white occupancy." Once a covenant is enforced against a Negro, a lawyer is faced with alternatives of trying to win the case on any ground as swiftly as possible, or managing the defense with an eye toward testing a broader point in an appellate court. If the latter approach were to be pursued, it would be appropriate for the Association to safeguard the individual by purchasing the property. Irving Mollison of Chicago said, "otherwise a lawyer might not be justified in giving up for a client other definitions which would win the case in order to test the point."

Perhaps a fair measure of success of any conference is whether it produces more questions than it answers. But there were answers too. Strong statements were made about techniques of attacking racial restrictive covenants. Undoubtedly the most respected lawyer present was Charles Houston, who expounded at length his philosophy of questioning the assumptions of the Caucasians as a method of education. In the District of Columbia, Houston explained, "we use the Court as a forum for the purpose of educating the public on the question of restrictive covenants because, after all, the covenants reflect a community pattern." The philosophy of segregation, he said, should be questioned as frequently as possible.

The legalistic methods of the Caucasians must be understood, continued Houston. He generalized that, "in the enforcement, the technique of those upholding covenants is to narrow issues as much as possible." Lawyers for the white property owners have clear sailing if they merely prove that the restriction exists, is properly recorded, and has been violated by a Negro. The plaintiffs "make a prima facie case by setting up the legal instrument and showing its violation." Against this, Houston had some advice for the defense lawyers.

> The person fighting it should broaden the issues just as much as possible on every single base, taking nothing for granted. We must make it just as difficult as possible for the plaintiffs. One technique is to start out denying that the plaintiffs are white. There has been a past tendency to draw clear cut lines by admitting that the plaintiffs are white and the defendants are Negroes. The first thing I recommend is to deny that the plaintiffs are white and the defendants are Negroes.

Here Houston evaluated this approach as an educational method.

> Every time you drag these plaintiffs in and deny that they are white, you begin to make them think about it. That is the beginning of education on the subject. In denying that your defendants are Negroes, you go to the question of the standards of race. There are many people who cannot give any reason why they are white. They don't have any standard about Negroes either.

Reminiscing, Houston told how successful this approach could be.

> I just tried a case involving about 20 whites. All were in court. After the first day I had them up a tree. The next day one woman said, "We were discussing that last night." The more you shake them, the better off you are. If they make a definition [of race] —you can't do it on color or hair—make them admit it will not hold.

The logic of racial definitions should then be applied to exploit the change of neighborhood doctrine, continued Houston. This claim had won cases in Washington when all others had failed. It will be recalled that under this rule a court will not order enforcement if the property has already been surrounded by Negroes sufficiently to make meaningless the covenant's purpose, to maintain the status quo of a white neighborhood. When this point is in issue, some percentage of Negroes in the white area must be accepted as the point where the section is no longer called "white." In reaching this point Houston would have the defense turn the whites' own definition of race to logical scrutiny.

> Establish the degree of penetration which makes the objects of the covenant unattainable. Play whites on their own prejudices —what degree of penetration changes a neighborhood from white to colored? One drop makes you colored, but one family in a block doesn't make the block colored.

Comments on local court politics were added to these strategic suggestions. A prominent Missouri Democrat and Negro lawyer George Vaughn, said that in St. Louis many of the decisions had " a political angle." For many years this had been an advantage to him in attacking restrictive covenants. "Because the Negro vote played such an important part in the election of judges, they were unwilling to offend it unnecessarily." But, Vaughn lamented, "the method of selecting judges now has been changed." A consultant to the conference, Dr. Robert C. Weaver of the American Council on Race Relations, speaking with Chicago in mind, claimed that "often political candidates can be defeated on the basis of their signature of racial covenants." The consensus was that political circumstances in all cities made the task of winning cases in trial courts next to impossible. Loren Miller, deeply involved in twenty Los Angeles restrictive-covenant cases, told the participants of the conference that the appellate courts in California were little better than the city superior court. "Our District Court of Appeals decisions are increasingly reactionary, and I believe hopeless." Complications make it worse, Miller declared when "the State Supreme Court evades the issue by sending all cases on appeal to the District Court of Appeals." This intermediate court had recently added insult to injury by refusing to permit the NAACP to file a brief *amicus curiae*.

A successful test in the Supreme Court of the United States was what everyone was hoping for. Working for this entailed a number of considerations. There are many unforseeable factors in the passage of a case through the judicial process to the Supreme Court, but one—the decision on what case to carry up —was in the hands of these lawyers. But there was disagreement among them. Loring Moore believed that the test case should come from a big city in the North like Los Angeles, Detroit, or his own Chicago. The public policy of Northern states was officially against segregation, while that of the South supported segregation. Believing that "the Supreme Court decision may turn on whether it will sustain a state policy," Moore reasoned that they should "get a case where public policy is favorable." It should come from a section where there has been "some tradition of freedom." He had worked to break a restrictive covenant in Kentucky, but declared: "I would not think of that case being appealed to the U.S. Supreme Court."

Echoing this argument, Irving Mollison raised special objections to appealing cases from Washington, D.C. He recalled that in the recently decided *Mays* case the Circuit Court there had "referred to the rules of law upholding restrictive covenants in the District as almost rules of real property law." The court did not wish to unsettle affairs in the capital where large amounts of real estate had been acquired in faith and reliance on the old rule. This led Mollison to the conviction that cases for an ultimate test should be selected from outside the District of Columbia. Here he added a seldom revealed thought on the full nature of the problem.

> As a practical matter, considering some of the things about judges, is it desirable that we have applications for certiorari so immediately close to the homes and the real estate investments of the judges of the Supreme Court? I don't believe they can properly separate themselves from their expensive homes and the terrain. We should select cases with greater care and take only a very excellent case up. But future applications should come from a state which on the face of it, by its law and constitution, has at least some outward expression against racial discrimination.

Leaders of the NAACP like William Hastie and Thurgood Marshall disagreed with this viewpoint. Hastie emphasized that restrictive covenants must be broken everywhere in the nation. But he said, "The Supreme Court will not forget that a decision from Illinois will affect Georgia and Mississippi." Thurgood Marshall also cautioned against "putting too much stress on the public policy angle alone." Eighty per cent of the Negro people live in states where public policy is against them respecting segregation. The loss of a case on this basis in a Northern state like Illinois "immediately becomes a precedent for enforcement in every other state."

Nonlawyers present were greatly interested in applying Houston's idea of using the courts as educational forums for molding national opinion. Homer Jack, a Unitarian minister from Evanston, Illinois, representing two organizations, the Chicago Council Against Discrimination and the American Civil Liberties Union, argued for a publicity campaign.

> . . . in the line of public relations it would be awfully important to ballyhoo a case similar to the Scottsboro Case and get the rank and file of NAACP and other organizations to highlight and understand the process of carrying it out and even though it is lost and there is a terrible let down, it would be terrifically educational and you should get public opinion on it. Even if it is an artificial case, it would be important to spend a good deal

of money to build a case and try to decide it on constitutional issues.

At the conclusion of this two-day conference in 1945 Thurgood Marshall announced that the national office of the NAACP would devote special attention to the problem of restrictive covenants. He promised a campaign of publicity against "the evils of segregation and racial restrictive covenants." Marshall would recommend that the Association maintain a full-time staff member on housing. Most important of all, he said, would be keeping in touch. Frequent conferences like the present one were important, he declared.

Some of the details of this conference, representing conflicting and repetitious comments on technicalities, must go unrecorded. There is, of course, no record of the informal discussion outside the meeting room. The very fact that this conference met presumed its value. Here was an opportunity for lawyers facing practically identical problems to exchange views. As we shall see, Graves and Dent in Detroit, Vaughn in St. Louis, and Houston in Washington, were already conducting defenses in cases destined to be carried to the United States Supreme Court. And the other leaders, drawn together by a common purpose, would return home with a fuller comprehension of the complicated problem with which they were dealing.

The Sociology of Law

Before Negroes could effectively register their claims against the validity of racial restrictive covenants they had to await the development of favorable social and economic theories. They could know, however, that once new data were available and widely known, they could serve as persuasive factors in reshaping the judicial mind. The growing political power of Negroes and their increasing effectiveness in pressure politics had to be supported by facts and theories. The interpretation of the Negroes' position in American society by sociologists after 1920 placed the race problem in an environmental setting and proved to be potent assistance in the struggle toward a higher status for colored people.

It was in 1908 that the sociological brief, created by Louis

Brandeis and the women of the National Consumers' League, had its first test. Acknowledging its influence the Supreme Court sustained the Oregon ten-hour law for women.[56] Statistics on the relationship of long hours of work to the health of women had convinced the Court of the reasonableness of the legislation. This was a departure from traditional legal method. The significance of this sociological brief lies in the fact that it "did not rely exclusively or even largely on legal reasoning and precedent, nor on such sketchy extra-legal materials as the court, or its own initiative, might have cared to take judicial notice of; but brought to the support of their arguments convincing arrays of historic, sociologic, economic, statistical and other similar data." [57] The approach to law taken by sociological jurisprudence was not immediately accepted on a wide scale. In fact the position of Brandeis himself as a dissenter on the Supreme Court after 1915 indicates the slow progress made by the new approach. But rapid gains were made after 1937 until, finally, the sociological method became "all but the official doctrine of the Court." [58] If judges were to be guided in this way [59] they could be expected to take into consideration the sociology of the race problem in deciding Negro cases.

At the time restrictive covenants were first applied in the United States, dominant social theory favored the segregation of the races.[60] It was commonly thought that the white race, whether termed "Nordic," "Caucasian," "Teutonic," or "Aryan," was superior and that it should protect itself from the "corrupting" influence of darker people. Social Darwinism, the interpretation of society in terms of the survival of the fittest, was in vogue.[61] The notion that Caucasians were in a position of power because of biological superiority was held not only by Southern intellectuals like Charles Wallace Collins, but was widely believed in the North, as well. The literature of sociology was dominated by the view that Negroes were inferior to the white race in every way.[62] This position of scholars both reflected and reinforced popular beliefs.[63] Thus a study of public attitudes toward Negroes in 1923 showed that the mental capacity of Negroes was ranked far below that of whites.[64] This was related to the notion that Negroes were predisposed to a life of crime, immorality, and emotional instability. The existence of this image in the popular mind was closely associated with justifications of segregation. The most important defense of the white race was established through state miscegenation laws which made it a crime for white and colored persons to marry. Residential segregation was the next most important means of maintaining racial purity. Thus the restrictive covenant can be viewed as a method of enforcing a social theory.

Explanation of Negro behavior and living habits in terms opposed to these racial theories developed slowly and spread gradually. The emphasis on biological inferiority was questioned by scholars long before it actually lost its grip on the popular imagination. In the field of Negro housing a beginning was made in 1912 with the *American Journal of Sociology* publishing a monograph on conditions in Chicago.[65] The article showed statistically that the Negro lived in dilapidated buildings, and suffered from crowding, and lack of ventilation and toilet facilities. As a result the occupants were in ill health. For all this the Negroes paid disproportionately high rentals compared to the housing white people could command. No broad social conclusions were drawn from this study. Its importance lies in the fact that it laid the ground work for new ideas based upon its objective presentation of economic and sociological data.

In 1922 came the report of the Chicago Commission on Race Relations. The commission had been established by Governor Frank O. Lowden following the riots of 1919 to study the broad question of the relations between the two races in Illinois and particularly in the metropolitan area of Chicago. The thirteen members of the commission were prominent representatives of the white and Negro communities. Its staff was likewise of mixed complexion. The associate executive secretary, Charles S. Johnson, provides an example of the talent enlisted. A Negro just then establishing himself as a leading sociologist, he later became president of Fisk University. The published findings of the commission, *The Negro in Chicago,* covered the whole gamut of racial problems in a large city and devoted considerable attention to housing.[66] Along with general information on the intricate evils of low-grade housing for Negroes, and histories of individual family difficulties, is the assertion that these conditions resulted from segregation enforced by organized prejudice. Real-estate dealers and property owners formed protective associations which pledged themselves to do everything possible to prevent the renting and selling of homes to Negroes in white areas. "In carrying out their program, they resorted to vilification, ridicule, and disparagement of Negroes, accusing them of destroying property values and robbing white people of their homes." [67] Along these same lines it was found that where Negro occupancy depreciated residential property values in Chicago it was due to "the social prejudice of white people against Negroes." [68] To white members of the public the commission addressed the recommendation that better Negro housing without segregation be developed. [69]

> Our inquiry has shown that insufficiency in amount and quality of housing is an all-important factor in Chicago's race problem; there must be more and better housing to accommodate the great increase in Negro population which was at the rate of 148 per cent from 1910 to 1920. This situation will be made worse by methods tending toward forcible segregation or exclusion of Negroes, such as the circulation of threatening statements and propaganda by organizations or persons to prevent Negroes from living in certain areas, and the lawless and perilous bombing of houses occupied by Negroes or by whites suspected of encouraging Negro residence in the district.
>
> We therefore recommend that all white citizens energetically discourage these futile, pernicious, and lawless practices, and either coöperate in or start movements to solve the housing problems by constructive and not destructive methods.

In the time since the report of the Chicago Commission on Race Relations the Negro has been viewed less as a Negro and more as an individual caught in a web of environmental misfortunes. In academic jargon, "the trend has been away from physical concepts and biological processes, through cultural analysis, and into a sociological and social-psychological study of social interrelations." [70] The 'twenties were the greatest years of urban sociological study, and Robert E. Park at the University of Chicago was the man responsible for most of the leading contributions. [71] Park had been an associate of Booker T. Washington and was particularly interested in the problem of the Negro. Among his students were E. Franklin Frazier, Charles S. Johnson, themselves Negroes, and Louis Wirth. The work of these and other scholars confirmed the findings of the Chicago Commission on Race Relations and placed the main weight of the sociology profession on the side of a sympathetic environmental explanation of the urban Negro's position.

There were two main themes in the shift toward scientific methodology in writing on the sociology of Negro housing.[72] One was the conclusion drawn from evidence that low standards in space, sanitation, and comfort cause unfortunate results: it was found that crime, juvenile delinquency and disease stem from these conditions. The second theme was that segregation was directly responsible for the poor housing. Too many people were forced to live in a space built to accommodate smaller numbers. Colored people had to pay higher rents than white people paid for comparable quarters. And since the segregated areas were overcrowded with inferior dwellings, there was no opportunity for those Negroes who had money to rent, buy, or build superior housing, to live at a standard equal to their income. All of this was related to restrictive covenants and other methods of enforcing segregation. These studies helped the Negro cause for, although the popular feelings of prejudice were not eliminated by their publication, it remained true that scholarly opinion was at last opposed to the racial restrictive covenant. These materials were not overlooked when the preparations for testing the enforcibility of covenants in the courts were being made.

New Legal Theory

In March, 1945, the *California Law Review* featured an article with the assertive title, "Racial Residential Segregation by State Court Enforcement of Restrictive Agreements, Covenants or Conditions in Deeds is Unconstitutional." [73] This conclusion was reached by the author, Professor Dudley O. McGovney of the California Law School, through two steps in reasoning. First, he argued that state-court enforcement of restrictive covenants is state action under the Fourteenth Amendment and, second, that this is forbidden because it denies Negroes the equal protection of the laws.

Legal theory was needed to blast the constitutional log jam built up behind the holding in *Corrigan v. Buckley*,[74] that the

Constitution did not prohibit "private individuals from entering into contracts respecting the control and disposition of their own property." Of course, Louis Marshall had argued against the constitutionality of court enforcement of racial covenants in his preparation of the *Corrigan* case in 1926, and NAACP attorneys more recently had successfully urged a "state action" theory in the white primary cases. Yet McGovney took a fresh view and made an important contribution to legal theory on the question. In his *California Law Review* article, McGovney agreed that individuals can make such a contract but stressed that *enforcement* of the restriction brought the government into the picture. This amounted to state action under the Constitution. The situation did not parallel the problem of the *Civil Rights Cases* [75] which held that private action unaided and unsupported by the state government could not be limited by federal statutes enacted under the authority of the Fourteenth Amendment.

Professor McGovney carefully distinguished between the private action of making a restrictive covenant and the state action of enforcing one.

> The discriminatory agreements, conditions or covenants in deeds that exclude Negroes or other racial minorities from buying or occupying residential property so long as they remain purely private agreements are not unconstitutional. So long as they are voluntarily observed by the covenanters or the restricted grantees no action forbidden by the Constitution has occurred. But when the aid of the state is invoked to compel observance and the state acts to enforce observance, the state takes forbidden action. The deed to the colored buyer cannot be cancelled by purely private action. The Negro cannot be ousted from occupancy by purely private action. When a state court cancels the deed or ousts the occupant, the state through one of its organs is aiding, abetting, enforcing the discrimination.

The claim that the enforcement of restrictive covenants was a violation of the equal-protection clause was based on a broad view of the line of cases beginning with *Buchanan v. Warley*,[76] which had disapproved of the enforcement of racial segregation by city ordinance or state legislation. The result in segregation was reached through either method, the legislative or the judicial.

If a statute or ordinance enforcing segregation was unconstitutional, enforcement by a court was also unconstitutional.

Professor McGovney's article in the *California Law Review* appeared toward the end of a teaching career of four decades during which he had published widely in the fields of contracts, administrative law, and constitutional law. Upon his death two years later, attention was called to the large volume of McGovney's publications which elaborated his belief that there was no rational justification for racial discrimination in any law. "Thus in one forceful article after another he has considered the problems of aliens and minority races, and has done perhaps more than any other man in the country to quicken in lawyers an awareness and a conscience about these problems." [77]

A number of law-review articles at that time and later criticized the enforcement of restrictive covenants, but none performed a comparable feat to McGovney's, which gave to the Negro cause a solid constitutional theory with which to attack the older notions of the law. Negro lawyers were active in attacking restrictive covenants, particularly through the organ of their own legal body, the National Bar Association. [78] Earlier articles had been dispassionate in discussing court enforcement of racial covenants, [79] but by 1945 there was open and sharp criticism of this practice.

Typical of the new view was the belief that "the litigation of constitutional issues and issues of land policy in a sociological vacuum has resulted in socially undesirable doctrines." [80] And it was suggested that the Negro defense in future litigation should include "relevant sociological data in the record and briefs."

> No court should be called upon to determine the validity of an anti-Negro restrictive covenant on the tacit assumption that only the parties litigant and the parcel of land as to which they assert rights will be affected by the decision. Instead, the relationship of the particular restriction to the entire community should clearly appear.

Unless the courts reversed themselves, terrible conditions would continue.

> Judicial failure to abandon a rule so costly in its social consequences to the community at large will ultimately require legisla-

tive correction, unless abominable housing conditions for Negroes, and the pernicious effects of such conditions on the general community, are to be accepted as a permanent condition of American life.

Charles Evans Hughes once said, "in confronting any serious problems, a wide-awake and careful judge will at once look to see if the subject has been discussed, or the authorities collated and analysed, in a good law periodical." [81] The Supreme Court of the United States has often followed the law reviews. In 1943, the Court reversed its 1940 position on the Jehovah's Witness flag-salute problem.[82] The first decision was the subject of sharp legal criticism which was marshaled by Professor Zechariah Chafee, Jr., of the Harvard Law School and brought to the Supreme Court's attention through an *amicus curiae* brief filed for the Committee on the Bill of Rights of the American Bar Association in the second case. Justice Jackson referred to these law-review articles in his opinion.[83] Earlier, in 1938, when the Supreme Court changed its position on the question of taxing the income of a federal judge, Justice Frankfurter took into account the fact that the first decision "met wide and steadily growing disfavor from legal scholarship and professional opinion." [84] The legal criticisms after 1945 of the judicial enforcement of racial restrictive covenants thus had an importance beyond the edification of the bar.

The Publicity Drive

Indicative of the growing importance of restrictive covenants and the gathering storm against them toward the end of World War II is a flyer printed in the spring of 1945 by the Chicago branch of the National Association for the Advancement of Colored People.

The flyer urged those to whom it was addressed to:

JOIN NAACP $50,000 CAMPAIGN TO BREAK RACE RESTRICTIVE
COVENANTS . . . NAACP IS LEADING THE FIGHT

It suggested what might be done by the Negroes themselves toward accomplishing the goals of the publicity drive.

What You Can Do

1. Hold living-room meetings.
2. Raise money.
3. Secure the help of your church.
4. Get petitions signed.

Your dollars will
* save lives and property.
* help to combat crime.
* educate the masses away from violence.
*** protect everybody's right to living space.

Lets buy freedom from

S L U M S !

This material was arranged around an editorial from the Chicago *Sun* entitled "The Fight Against Covenants." [85] It said that in Springfield at the state legislature a bill to invalidate racial restrictive covenants had been proposed and was to be the subject of a forthcoming hearing.

> The legislation ought to pass. Restrictive covenants based on racial discrimination are "unethical, undemocratic and uneconomic," as the Chicago Council Against Racial and Religious Discrimination has said. They are, in the words of the City Club, immoral and productive of racial tensions. The Metropolitan Housing Council, the Y.M.C.A. and many other organizations have called for their abolition.
>
> In the present low state of the legislature prospects for the legislation are not bright. The general Assembly finds it much easier to serve the lobbies of special interests than the general welfare. But whatever the outcome, the fight will not have been in vain. Someday restrictive covenants are going to be knocked out of American law & custom, because they are repugnant to American ideals.

And on the NAACP broadside the concluding paragraph of the editorial from the *Sun* was underlined:

> If the legislative fight is lost, *the campaign of the National Association for the Advancement of Colored People to obtain a definitive test of the covenants in the U.S. Supreme Court must be pressed with all possible vigor.*

A Conference for the Elimination of Restrictive Covenants was held in Chicago on May 10 and 11, 1946. It was called by the NAACP and the Chicago Council Against Racial and Religious Discrimination and sponsored by more than forty labor, civic, religious, housing, and veterans groups in Chicago.[86] Plans for legal procedures and briefs in restrictive-covenant cases were formulated there by lawyers who were working on these cases in all parts of the country.[87] Loren Miller and the Most Rev. Bernard Sheil, founder of numerous Catholic welfare organizations in Chicago, gave the major addresses at the conference.[88] The former speaker outlined the new legal arguments against the enforcement of restrictive covenants, while the latter condemned them as being immoral and anti-Christian. This meeting brought together the leading opponents of restrictive covenants and signified the new postwar interest in ending their effectiveness.

The value of this meeting or of loud efforts to drum up enthusiasm and support for the attack on restrictive covenants is debatable. It could play a vital role in raising money; it could stimulate interest in the broader problem of Negroes in American society—but whatever the positive usefulness of the publicity campaign, it surely reflects the approach of Negroes to the task of bringing about more favorable rules of law.

IV

COVENANTS IN THE CAPITAL

Introduction

By 1944 it was a routine part of Henry Gilligan's legal business to see that Negroes were kept from violating restrictive covenants. He had been stopping attempts to break covenants in Washington, D.C., for more than twenty years. His cases had sometimes gone beyond the trial level to the United States Court of Appeals for the District of Columbia Circuit. Gilligan was an old hand at this type of work, and had had unbroken success in pursuing it. There was nothing novel, therefore, in the fact that on June 30 of that year he should send off a letter to a man named James Hurd warning him that he had violated a restrictive covenant by buying a house at 116 Bryant Street, N.W., and moving into it.[1] Hurd and his wife had been advised that the covenant was in the land-developer's deed before they purchased. Because they were Negroes, Gilligan told the Hurds, they would have to move from their new home or "be forced out through injunction proceedings." Gilligan warned that he must be assured of Hurd's intention "to move amicably." Otherwise, he wrote, "I shall prepare and file for the property owners in that block of Bryant Street an injunction suit, and will make every effort to have the Court grant a preliminary injunction requiring you to move." Gilligan added that it was his "earnest hope that this suit may not be necessary." This wish was not based on any fear that the suit would not be successful, for Gilligan could boast that the "District Court has granted two injunctions within the past two weeks in cases brought by me."

Indeed, the federal courts having the District of Columbia as their sole and peculiar jurisdiction had enforced many restrictive covenants.[2] Enforcement had been refused only when "changed conditions" would prevent the objective of a covenant from being gained.[3] The most recent case prior to the Hurd trial, *Mays v. Burgess*,[4] added another precedent in line with the traditional rule. This decision by the District Court was to be upheld in January, 1945, in the Circuit Court, albeit with a pungent dissent by Judge Edgerton. Thus in Washington, as in other cities across the nation, the risk of litigation discouraged Negroes from purchasing property in white sections.

Most of these cases had been handled by the same attorney, Henry Gilligan, and they arose in the same area of the city, cut by North Capitol Street running north and south. As a residential district, it was hemmed in by permanent public establishments and so lacked room for expansion. A sprawling commercial development was advancing from the south just behind Negroes who had originally settled near the center of the city. On the southeast was Union Station with its appending railroad tracks and freight yards. Cemeteries lay to the east and northeast, and to the north were the city filtration plant and McMillan Park and Reservoir. Howard University bounded the North Capitol area on the west and northwest. White property owners in this area were therefore caught between these immovable barriers and the colored population pressing toward them from the south and southwest.

In the North Capitol area an Executive Committee of owners had been vigilantly opposing the advance of Negroes for some twenty years.[5] Its attorney was Henry Gilligan, and Henry K. Murphy was secretary-treasurer. After it had won the case of *Mays v. Burgess*,[6] involving property on First Street near McKinley High School, an *IMPORTANT STATEMENT TO OWNERS* was mimeographed and distributed telling of the need to adopt restrictions for the blocks not already covered by restrictive covenants or agreements.[7]

NOW IS THE TIME TO COMPLETE THE RE-EXECUTION AND RECORDING OF ALL RESTRICTIVE AGREEMENTS, AND YOU ARE URGED TO DO THIS IMMEDIATELY IN ORDER THAT THE WHOLE COMMUNITY OF A THOUSAND HOMES, SIX CHURCHES, HIGH SCHOOLS AND ELEMENTARY SCHOOLS MAY CONTINUE TO BE THE

STRONGEST PROTECTED WHITE SECTION IN THE DIS-
TRICT OF COLUMBIA. NO section of Washington is as safe
from invasion as is your section; LET'S KEEP IT SAFE! Make
sure the Restrictive Agreement in your block is being completed
NOW. DO IT AT ONCE.

Your contribution toward the expense of continuous litigation
is essential; please respond as liberally as possible immediately.

A later message from Murphy, who was now executive secretary,
was addressed *TO PROPERTY HOLDERS IN THE 2100 BLOCK
OF FIRST STREET, N.W.* It warned that the "unscrupulous
white or negro real estate men" who had reported that several
houses in the area had been sold to Negroes were wrong. The
house purchased by Clara Mays was to be bought back by the
Executive Committee of Owners in order to keep it in white
hands, and all other homes in the area would be protected. Therefore, the property owners were cautioned against selling out to
anyone.

If you own your own home, HOLD ON TO IT: remember
that the cost of a house elsewhere in the District is far above
the normal values, and NO COMMUNITY IN WASHINGTON
IS AS SAFE FROM NEGRO OWNERSHIP AS IS OURS OF
A   THOUSAND   HOMES,   SIX   CHURCHES,   AND   FINE
SCHOOLS. If you own as an investor, you have a FINE IN-
VESTMENT; DON'T BE STAMPEDED INTO LOSING THAT
GOOD INVESTMENT.

FROM   BOTH   THE   INDIVIDUAL   INTEREST   VIEW-
POINT AND THE COMMUNITY VIEWPOINT IT IS TO YOUR
ADVANTAGE TO SIT TIGHT, RETAIN YOUR PROPERTIES.

While publicity in the *Mays* case favored the general cause of
Negro opposition to restrictive covenants—the newspapers having played upon the human-interest angle of the government
worker, Clara Mays, and her family being put out on the street [8]
—the white property owners of the North Capitol area were
maintaining their area. The North Capitol Citizens' Association
retained Gilligan and his associate, James C. Crooks, largely on an
informal basis. The enforcement of racial restrictions became
confining work in Washington toward the end of the war as the
population of the city continued to grow despite efforts toward
decentralization of the national government's activities. An

example of formalizing the relationship of the association with its lawyer is shown by this petition form found in the lawyer's files,[9] opposing the sale of restricted property to Negroes.

> WHEREFORE, we hereby register our objections to such sale and we request the standing committee of the citizens association having matters of this kind in charge to authorize Henry Gilligan, Esq., to file suit for injunction to enjoin the consummation of such sale.
>
> FURTHERMORE, we all consent to the use of our names in the petition for such injunction, or as many as may be thought necessary . . .
>
> And FURTHERMORE, for our own benefit and for the benefit of all the property owners in the Block, we pledge ourselves to cooperate with attorney Gilligan in the prosecution of the suit.

With such unquestioning support from property owners, the long practice of Washington courts supporting the validity of restrictive covenants, and his own experience in the field, Gilligan could understandably speak with firmness to an offending Negro.

The network of interests supporting covenants and restrictive agreements in Washington was extensive. The Washington Real Estate Board had formalized its position as part of a code of ethics providing that no member sell property in a white part of the city to Negroes. Violating dealers lost memberships in the board.[10] Another factor assisting the maintenance of white areas was the practice of the Washington *Evening Star* in refusing to print advertisements offering restricted property for sale to colored people.[11] This was policed through the newspaper's coöperation with the real-estate board, whose Public Affairs Committee checked whether an address was in a covered area. This committee in turn consulted the citizen's association for the area in doubt.[12] Thus the sixty-nine citizens' associations in Washington exercised the final veto on what housing would be advertised and sold to Negroes. This aggregate of power—real-estate board, newspaper, citizens' associations, and the prevailing attitudes of numerous white persons—was highly effective in maintaining racial residential segregation in the city.

The one-hundred block of Bryant Street where Hurd purchased was unique, for it was nearly surrounded by Negro homes. These twenty dwellings, 114 to 152 Bryant Street, were row houses all located on the south side of the street facing McMillan Park across the way. The block had been developed by the huge real-estate firm of Middaugh & Shannon, Inc., between 1905 and 1910, and each house was sold subject to the following deed covenant, recorded among the land records of the District of Columbia.

> Subject also to the covenants that said lot shall never be rented, leased, sold, transferred or conveyed unto any Negro or colored person, under a penalty of Two thousand Dollars ($2000), which shall be a lien against said property.

To the demands Gilligan made for the Bryant Street owners, James Hurd's reply was a model of restraint and agreeableness.[13] "In connection with your threatened action to bring about removal of my wife and myself from [116 Bryant Street] for the sole reason that we are of Negro extraction," he wrote, "please be advised that we have no desire to litigate the matter and will be more than glad to move from the neighborhood in which we now find we are not wanted." Hurd had purchased the property, he said, because colored people lived in the vicinity and he assumed that it was legally permissible for Negroes to occupy property there. Consequently, Hurd said, that he and his wife "were greatly astonished when we received information that the people in this neighborhood desired that we be removed from the building which we purchased for our home." But since this was their attitude the Hurds were making an effort to find another house, after which they would dispose of their property "even if it means a financial loss." In fact, they already had a proposition to purchase another home, but could not do so until they raised another $600. And so Hurd promised Gilligan that if he would be "gracious enough to give us sufficient time within which to either find a rental or within which to purchase another home, we will make every effort to move from the premises as soon as is humanly possible." In remaining as occupants they were not attempting to establish residence for a period of time long enough to defeat a suit against them on that ground alone, technically called laches. Finally, Hurd asked for sympathy from Gilligan.

We earnestly hope that you will give us due consideration in the matter and treat us with a little human kindness by at least giving us sufficient time within which to comply with your mandate. The money that we invested in this house represents our lifetime savings and we would like to have the opportunity of selling the property after we vacate with as little loss as possible.

This plea may seem very touching to one removed from the immediate problem at hand, but to the white property owners there were higher values than inconvenience to a Negro or his financial difficulty. Gilligan could agree, in replying, to delay action for the white owners in order to permit the Hurds to find "a good home where there are no restrictions as to color." [14] He regretted the fact that they had purchased the house in the first place, for in such cases he had found that the colored buyer was usually the loser financially. "Unfortunately we have not reached that time when communities are satisfied when Negroes move into the white community," continued Gilligan. "The people of our community including the resident owners in your block, are determined to maintain their homes, and will seek Injunctions against any who sell to Negroes and any Negroes who buy where there are deed covenants or restrictive agreements." In conclusion, Gilligan restated his basic position.

I am informed that you are a most excellent family, and I am sorry you did not use better judgment in the purchase of your home. Our people intend to maintain their homes in the white community, and will bring injunction proceedings wherever necessary to do so.

Time proved that this was no idle threat, for action was taken in October, 1944, by the Bryant Street property owners to have the Hurds removed from their recently acquired home. The petition for an injunction by Gilligan was made on behalf of Mr. and Mrs. Frederic Hodge, Mr. and Mrs. Pasquale DeRita, Mr. and Mrs. Constantino Marchegiani, and Mr. and Mrs. Balduino Giancola. The petition asked that the Hurds be restrained from occupying the house and that the deed to it be canceled. The Ryans who had sold the house to the Hurds were also defendants in the action. The court was asked to grant an injunction restraining them from selling the house to any other Negro. The District

Court refused to issue a temporary injunction against the defendants, without prejudice, so that the Hurds were allowed to remain on their property until a full trial could be held.[15]

The wheels of justice moved slowly. Before the case could be brought to trial, three more houses in the one-hundred block of Bryant Street had been purchased and occupied by Negroes. They were houses that had been purchased by "straw parties," persons not actually interested in the homes, whose names are used to conceal the real buyers. Actual control was held by Raphael Urciolo, a lawyer and realtor, who had found it profitable to sell property in white neighborhoods to Negroes. Action was then taken against Urciolo and the Negroes, Robert and Isabelle Rowe, Herbert and Georgia Savage, and Miss Pauline Stewart and her family.

The Washington Real Estate Board had terminated Urciolo's membership because of his frequent sales of property in white sections of the city to Negroes.[16] Nevertheless he had succeeded very well in the real-estate trade without the board's approval.[17] In the cases at hand, Urciolo made a profit of from three to four thousand dollars on each of the houses sold, although the sale price was less than ten thousand dollars apiece. In the trial he agreed that he was interested in making as much money as possible in the houses he bought and sold. This question followed: [18]

> Q. Doesn't it make any difference to whom you sell?
> A. No, it makes no difference, except that I have an added reason, the reason being that since it is about five times as hard for colored people and foreigners to get houses, I always prefer, if I had a choice between selling to a colored man or a foreigner, and another—I would prefer to sell to the colored man because he has so much harder time getting a house than the other person.
> Q. So that no matter whether it is covenanted or not—
> A. I don't believe in covenants at all.

Urciolo was looked upon by Gilligan as solely responsible for the constant threat of the entry of Negroes into traditionally white neighborhoods—as though the 300,000 Washington colored population would stay put, were it not for this real-estate salesman. When rumors came to Gilligan about new Urciolo acquisitions on Bryant Street, he wrote to warn him that swift legal action would follow their sales to Negroes. Gilligan added a post-script: [19]

> In view of your full understanding of the terms of these deed covenants, I notify you also that in any action made necessary by you, it will be the aim of the complainants not only to enjoin but to enforce the penalty clause of the covenants.

When a similar circumstance arose later, Gilligan confided to Urciolo the key to better relations between them. "If, instead of constantly endeavoring to break the deed covenants and restrictive agreements in the community I represent," he wrote, "you would cooperate with us in helping to make and keep the community a fine white community, it would be a pleasure to work with you."

If Urciolo justified his profits in terms of lending a helping hand to Negroes in a housing shortage, Gilligan too could easily and sincerely justify his actions on the other side in defense of racial restrictive covenants. Gilligan not only believed that the enforcement of restrictions forwarded the interests of white owners, but was also the very best thing for Negroes. He articulated his philosophy on this score by protesting to the Washington Federation of Churches when its representatives joined in a local movement against restrictive covenants in 1946.[20]

> There is nothing unchristian in the desire of the people of my community to retain their homes among people of their own color, and there is no way that I know of to do this except through such covenants. The movements to destroy these covenants, legally and socially, are directed by people and organizations (generally speaking) that have no compunctions of any kind, and unscrupulous real estate agents—white and colored— are using unfortunate and frequently innocent colored people to amass fortunes for themselves and destruction of white communities. There is no minister or lay member of your organization that is more anxious for the welfare of our negro citizens than am I; the movement described is not in the real interest of negroes, and is certainly not conducive to the amicable settlement of their problems, nor is it in my considered judgment, Christian.

The Plaintiffs: Mrs. Hodge and Her Neighbors

At the trial which began before Judge F. Dickinson Letts on October 9, 1945, Lena M. Hodge agreed, when referred to as "the big chief" around the neighborhood, that she seemed "to have been looking after the place for more than twenty years." [21] She and her husband purchased their house at 136 Bryant Street in 1909 as the area was just being developed. One of the first things that the agent for Middaugh & Shannon showed the Hodges, she reported, was the "covenant that was in the deed to the house, which of course we liked." But they did not inquire whether restrictive covenants covered houses in the surrounding area, although they desired to live in a neighborhood where all the people were white. Through the passing years adjacent streets became occupied by Negroes. Adams Street immediately back of her own house became colored, and areas to the east and west of the one-hundred block of Bryant Street also changed. She could do nothing about that, for as she said, "I felt that I had enough to think about and fight for on my own street. I felt that somebody over there could take the reins over there and fight that out." So in her own block, made up of twenty houses, Mrs. Hodge was the leader who took over from Middaugh & Shannon the task of keeping the neighborhood white. She was asked the following questions at the trial:

> Q. . . . just how did you go about taking hold of this matter in connection with the whole community when the matter of the enforcement of the covenant in your block came up?
> A. You mean now, or earlier?
> Q. Any time.
> A. Well, I don't know, it is just one of those things. I got into it, I guess, and the different ones, as soon as they would hear or know of a colored person moving, they always called me and I just simply assumed the responsibility, I guess, because they wanted me to.
> Q. Did you get in touch with any of the people in the community, citizens associations, or executive committee of owners?
> A. I did earlier and later, too.
> Q. Did they cooperate with the people on your block?
> A. They certainly did.

Q. Are all the plaintiffs, knowing the costs, and others in the block, helping to take care of expenses of this suit?

A. Certainly.

At the time of the trial the neighbors had contributed $85, which had been turned over to the Executive Committee of Owners of the North Capitol Citizens Association to pay the retaining fee. Three families not in the case had contributed. However, the main burden of the case was on the shoulders of Mrs. Hodge and the other plaintiffs. The others had moved to Bryant Street more recently than the Hodges. Constantino and Mary Marchegiani had purchased their house in 1930 and were now renting it, having moved to Maryland themselves. Balduino and Margaret Giancola obtained their house in 1936, and Pasquale and Victoria DeRita acquired theirs in 1940. All had been emigrants from Italy, and the DeRitas were not yet citizens. None had seen Negroes before leaving Italy and claimed no difficulty in their limited relations with colored people since coming to the United States. But all of them supported the covenant and could agree with Mrs. Giancola, their most articulate representative, when she told Urciolo that "we feel bitter towards you for coming in and breaking up our block. We were very peaceful and harmonious there and we feel that you bought the property just to transact it over to colored people and we don't like it."

The plaintiffs' deep antipathy against Negroes was expressed by Mrs. Hodge. It was not a person's skin color but his race which she found intolerable. The defense attorney, Charles Houston brought out the feelings of Mrs. Hodge in cross examination.

Q. . . . Now, suppose, Mrs. Hodge, it was a very, very, light negro, say 99 percent so-called white blood. . . .

A. It would still be a negro, I think.

Q. And it would not make any difference?

A. No.

Q. If you got a person in the block who was supposed to be white and that person was undesirable, in the sense of untidy or something like that, you couldn't do anything about it?

A. No, certainly we couldn't.

Q. And you would prefer that untidy white person to a negro, no matter how educated or cultured?

A. As long as they are white, I would prefer them.

Q. No negro, no matter how, or whether he might be Senator or Congressman, it would not make any difference to you?

A. It wouldn't make any difference.

Q. Even if the white man just came from jail, you would prefer him?

A. Because he is white and I am white.

Her husband, Frederic Hodge, agreed with this expression of affinity for Caucasians. He said that the reason the movement of Negroes into sections near the Bryant Street neighborhood had not affected "the sociability of the neighborhood" was that the Negroes "stay by theirselves and white folks stay by theirselves."

These were the people to be protected by the enforcement of the restrictive covenant, and the following is the official complaint made by them to the United States District Court for the District of Columbia in the case of *Hodge v. Hurd.* The occupancy of houses on Bryant Street by Negroes, they said,

> . . . will be injurious, depreciative and absolutely ruinous of the real estate owned by plaintiffs, and will be harmful, detrimental and subversive of the peace of mind, comfort and property rights and interests of plaintiffs and of other property owners, and said neighborhood will become depreciative in value, and undesirable as a neighborhood wherein white people may live; that the continued occupancy and/or ownership by the defendants, Hurd, or any person or persons of the Negro race or blood, will constitute a continuing wrong and injury that is irreparable, and is incapable of ascertainment and compensation in damages, and the only adequate remedy is by way of injunction.

The Negroes' Defense

Charles Houston for the defense planned to dispute every possible assumption entertained by the white property owners. This strategy was dictated by Houston's conviction that the courtroom was an educational forum. Because he was smarting under the loss of *Mays v. Burgess* in the same court, Houston was determined to take every opportunity to raise doubts about the soundness of court enforcement of restrictive covenants. The plaintiffs drew the issues narrowly and assumed the outcome: The covenants existed; they were valid; Negroes had violated them; the court should enjoin the Negroes from ownership and occupancy. Houston broadened these issues and added new ones. As the trial opened he boldly denied that the plaintiffs were white, that it was a white neighborhood, and questioned whether the covenant was a valid instrument.

> We deny that all the defendants are colored. We say there has been a change of neighborhood. We say that the covenant is unenforceable, that an injunction should not issue because the object of the injunction could not be obtained, and that the purposes of the covenant can no longer be achieved.

In a separate tactic, Houston charged that the assigned judge, F. Dickinson Letts, had a personal prejudice and bias against the defendants and should be disqualified. The claim was based on the fact that Judge Letts lived in premises in northwest Washington covered by a racial restrictive covenant. Judge Letts declined to excuse himself, explaining that he was merely a "tenant by the month" of the house in question and did not know of the existence of the covenant.[22] The Court of Appeals for the District of Columbia Circuit in a *per curiam*, or unsigned, opinion, ruled that the refusal of Judge Letts to disqualify himself "was entirely proper." [23] The question to be determined, the court explained, was whether the defense had asserted facts "from which a sane and reasonable mind might fairly infer personal bias or prejudice on the part of a judge." It was held to be a "far-fetched conclusion" that the existence of a restrictive covenant "for which he is neither responsible or accountable" would "under any circumstances" create in Judge Letts' mind a personal prejudice against the defendants in this trial.

One of the basic defenses employed by Houston was that James Hurd was an American Indian. It seemed a dubious contention from the start, and Hurd's own testimony that he was a Mohawk Indian from the Smokey Mountains of North Carolina added little credence to it. But he explained away the implied admission of being a Negro made in his letter to Gilligan in which he had agreed to move. Hurd stated that Ryan, the person from whom he had purchased the house, had drafted the letter and that he signed it at work, when he was too busy to read it. The question of his automobile driver's license came up, for his own license showed that he had marked an "x" in the square for colored. But Hurd could point out that there was no space for Indian, so he had no recourse but to mark white or colored, neither of which were really applicable. Mrs. Hodge testified that Hurd had personally told her that he and his wife were Negroes. He had agreed to move originally, he said, because he was very nervous and high strung, and had always run away from trouble, but that the difficulty of finding another place militated against actually moving, in this instance. He had been constantly buffeted by questions about race. By now his resentment had become acute. As Hurd put it, "Everytime you turn around, somebody is asking your color. . . . You get tired of those things."

Frederic Hodge testified that Hurd "looked to me like a Negro, therefore I presumed he was a Negro." When called upon to define what was Negro about Hurd's features, he replied, "I would say the nose, for one thing." The nostrils were the distinguishing features, he said. Hodge admitted that Hurd had rather straight hair, which was not a Negroid characteristic. The other plaintiffs did not discuss Hurd's racial features, but did venture to define the meaning of race. Mrs. Hodge asserted that Negroes could be distinguished from whites. "There is always a look with regard to their eyes and nose that would give them away, as a rule." She has no specific test for telling colored people; "simply, you see they are colored, as a rule, you know." Mrs. Giancola never confused Assyrians, Turks, or Arabs with Negroes, because even though these people may be dark, "there is something about them that brings out the fact that they are of white blood." The plaintiffs agreed that they could be wrong, but all of them with Mrs. Hodge made clear that they had never been wrong yet.

The testimony on defining race by the experts called by the defense contrasts with that of the plaintiffs. The views of Monseigneur John M. Cooper, head of the Department of Anthropology at Catholic University, were those of a scholar dealing with a highly complex and difficult problem about which most knowledge was tentative. Dr. Cooper was asked this question:

Q. Could one make sure by any simple visible physical traits, such as fingernails, eyes, lips, nose, that a given light skinned individual thought to be partly negroid, is actually so?

A. None of these ordinary criteria are reliable. A highly frizzly hair is a very important criterion, but you get that occasionally even in caucasoids. One recent case has been reported in Norway of a family, typically blonde Nordics in which, however, there is a distinct kinky, grizzly hair. We do not know the cause of that. In most cases, highly kinky hair would be a very strong indication, but not absolutely infallible. These other criteria, such as the stripe in the fingernail, or coloring of the fingernail are not reliable.

He agreed that there were no reliable tests for making a distinction between the races, and that social concepts enter very largely into the problem.

A professor of bacteriology at the medical school of George Washington University, Dr. Leland W. Paar, was asked if there was any test by blood specimens by which it could be ascertained the race to which a group of heterogeneous people belonged. He answered that he did not know of any blood test or any other test that fell within the field of medicine. Thus the experts stressed the difficulty of telling the difference between members of various races. It was a personal or social matter which could not be corroborated by scientific means.

Another theme in the defense strategy was to probe into the feelings aroused in the plaintiffs by the presence of Negroes in their neighborhood. Houston kept asking them what it was about the Negro that made him undesirable. Mrs. Hodge, for example, admitted the fact that it was no special action on the part of a colored person that alarmed her. Thus if she were ignorant of one's race, there would be no objection. Houston then posed this query:

Q. . . . although she had not changed a bit in her conduct or anything, if later you heard she was a negro, you would object?

A. I certainly would.

Q. Although she would be the same one and you would object, and on appearance you can't tell whether she is white or colored?

A. I would object until I found out.
Q. It is the label of "negro"?
A. Not entirely, it is the color—yes, the label.
Q. It can't be the color, because you can't tell whether that lady is white or colored.
A. Yes.
Q. So it is the label?
A. Yes.

At this point Urciolo entered the colloquy.

Q. Mrs. Hodge, in other words, if I am labeled negro and I want to move into one of those houses you would ask that I be put out?
A. I would.

Pinpointing the actual objection to the proximity of Negroes proved difficult for the plaintiffs, who at times seemed almost to have turned into witnesses for the defense. Thus Mr. Hodge testified that he had had no trouble with the Negroes in the area, and that the occupancy of nearby covenanted houses by the Hurds, Savages, Rowes, and Stewarts, had not disturbed his peace of mind a bit. Since, in addition to being emotionally content over the new state of affairs, he had not moved out of his house, he was asked what disturbed him so far as the Hurd occupancy was concerned.

A. Well, Mr. Houston, I feel this way—as far as the colored coming in, I have nothing against them having their home, but it does, in a way, take away from the—well you might say the sociability of the white people in the neighborhood, that is, in our block. That is the only reason that I can give.

Even though it was shown that neighborhood peace had always been maintained, that the few children there of whatever race played together, and that on the whole all including the plaintiffs had customarily stayed to themselves, Hodge insisted that sociability within the block would be affected by the Negroes' presence. If a person was not known to be Negro, it would make no difference, Houston discovered through cross-examination. What then would be the result if this person was found to be a Negro, even though he stayed to himself? Hodge repeated that this would affect the sociability. How? He couldn't say, but it would "in a general way."

In addition to attacking the foundations of the plaintiffs' racial and social ideas, the defense attorneys also disputed the claim that the occupancy of the covenanted property by Negroes would be "injurious, depreciative, and absolutely ruinous of the real estate" in the neighborhood. Some of the plaintiffs did not understand the meaning of the clause. Mr. Marchegiani could only answer, when asked to explain how property would depreciate because of Negroes' presence, that it would depreciate "in every way." Mrs. DeRita came through cross-examination even more poorly.

As might be expected, Mrs. Hodge did the best job of explaining the reasons for the decline in property values. Although her statements were not based on evidence but on personal observation, it was her considered belief that if colored people entered an area, the value of all houses nearby would be depreciated. She thought that in most cases the homes of Negroes "are not kept up as well; the majority understand, I am saying,—as possibly my house is, and naturally if houses are not kept up, I would say the market value would go down, and of course, if that went down, mine naturally would have to go down, I would think." However, she agreed that some Negroes kept up their homes well. Even the Hurd house at 116 Bryant Street she agreed was "being kept up very nicely." Mrs. Hodge was then asked by Houston whether depreciation would follow when neat Negroes moved into a neighborhood:

> A. Well, if the property was sold to Negroes, I think the property would depreciate in value, as far as having them further occupied by white persons is concerned.

Hodge said that he did not believe that a white person would buy it after other property in the area had been sold to Negroes. "I wouldn't be able to dispose of my property to advantage unless I sold to a negro." She would not say, however, that the property could be sold to a Negro for what it was worth.

The defense presented the testimonies of Urciolo, a rent-control official,[24] and a Negro real-estate dealer[25] to support the claim that the value of real estate was higher as Negroes moved into an area. Urciolo's statement that Negroes pay from 30 to 40 per cent more both for rents and sales of property in the Washington area than do whites for comparable dwellings was corroborated by these disinterested authorities. This fact was closely related to the limited availability of housing for Negroes. Because of restrictions, both legal and tacit, the supply of housing for Negroes was small; but the continually increasing population of Negroes made the demand great. It was a simple case of supply and demand. The defense therefore appeared to have scored in its effort to show that property appreciated as the real estate changed from a white to a Negro market.

The scarcity of housing for Negroes had another result besides increasing the prices they were forced to pay; it was no easy task for Negroes to find a place to live at all, whether or not they had the money. All Negro defendants, it was shown, had moved to Bryant Street only after they had been forced to move out of their last abode.[26] They claimed to have looked far and wide for housing and taken the Bryant Street places only after the most exhaustive search. Although one witness, a social welfare board consultant, said that the housing shortage prevailed among whites as well,[27] most testimony supported the claim that it was more serious for Negroes. Upon this basis the defense attorneys argued that the difficulty for Negroes in the circumstances was so serious that under the doctrine of balancing equities the covenants should not be enforced.

One more defense was made for the Negroes who had purchased homes on Bryant Street. Houston said that conditions had changed considerably since the restrictive covenants had been placed in the deeds about 1906, and that the entry of Negroes was but the final chapter in the progression of a neighborhood. Thus he tried to establish that Negroes were now closer to the Hodges than the Hurd house. When he sought Mrs. Hodge's answer to the question of whether the injuction would be of any use unless the Negroes in the surrounding area were diminished, the opposing attorney Gilligan objected, and the court sustained the objection. Houston then stated his design:

> I want to put my objection in the record on the ground that a court of equity or a court exercising an equity jurisdiction will not do a vain thing and if the defense can establish, out of the plaintiff's own mouth, on cross-examination that it would be futile to issue the injunction, I say the question is a proper question and should be allowed, sir.

Although dogged by objections from the plaintiffs' attorney, which were sustained by the court, the defense was able to show that times had changed in the neighborhood since the Hodges occupied their home as a young married couple in 1909. At that time most people in the area were young. Now, in 1945, they were older, many had moved away; the children of the original owners had grown up and moved elsewhere. In recent years Italian and Assyrian immigrants had replaced the older people. Houston showed the point of his examining efforts by quoting from a study of the Federal Housing Administration entitled, *Growth and Structure of American Cities:*

> Forces constantly and steadily at work cause a deterioration of existing neighborhoods. A neighborhood composed of new houses in the latest model, all owned by young married couples with children, is at its apex. At this period of its vigorous youth, the neighborhood has a vitality to fight off the disease of blight. The owners will strenuously resist the encroachment of inharmonious forces because of their homes and their desire to maintain a favorable environment for their children. The houses being in the newest and most popular styles do not suffer from the competition of any superior houses in the same price range, and they are marketable at approximately their reproduction costs under normal conditions. Both the buildings and the people are always growing older. Physical depreciation of structure and the aging of families constantly are lessening the vital powers of the neighborhood. Children grow up and move away. Houses with increasing age are faced with higher repair bills. This steady process of deterioration has been signed by obsolescence. A new and more modern type of structure relegates these structures to the second rank. The older residents do not fight too strenuously to keep out inharmonious forces. A lower income class succeeds the original occupants. Owner-occupancy declines as the first owners sell or move away or lose their homes by foreclosure. There is often a sudden decline in value due to a sharp transition in the character of neighborhood or to a period of depreciation in the real estate cycle. These internal changes due to depreciation and obsolescence in time cause shifts in the location of neighborhoods. When in addition there is poured into the center of the urban organism a stream of immigrants or members of other racial groups, these forces all will cause dislocations in the existing neighborhood pattern. The effects of these changes vary according to the type of

neighborhood and can best be described by discussing each one in turn.

Support for this interpretation came from testimony given by Dr. E. Franklin Frazier, head of the Department of Sociology at Howard University. He believed that the area in question had changed over a period of years. For one thing the municipal plant of the water department, and the garbage-disposal unit in the area, made it vulnerable to changing of population. The large foreign element was also cited as an important indication that through a process of sociological succession the neighborhood changed hands. Gilligan was particularly quick to object to allowing this type of material into the record, and Judge Letts sustained him. Dr. Frazier was not allowed to answer the question, "Will you state what the effect of perpetual covenants are, on the natural growth of the city?" And when he was asked if the Negro population movement into the North Capitol area had "followed any well established, recognized, sociological principles," Gilligan's objection to the question of "sociological principles" was sustained. Frazier was stopped so often in testifying that he would answer a particular question, "That is, if I can say it."

The defense attorney, Charles Houston, had made a notable effort to show why the covenants were not enforceable; he had introduced expert testimony to corroborate the points in their legal defense. He had revealed the attitudes and feelings of the plaintiffs on race, had probed into the network of interests keeping Negroes segregated in Washington, had tried to prove that there were changed conditions in the neighborhood, and had presented the individual defendants' housing hardships against the broader problem of housing for Washington's 300,000 Negroes.

The Covenants Enforced

The findings of fact and conclusions of law determined by Judge Letts for the District Court favored the plaintiffs and led to his judgment that the restrictive covenants in question must be enforced.[28] It was therefore ordered that the various deeds to the Negro defendants be "declared null and void and of no effect." The titles were declared to be in the last previous owners of the properties. It was ordered, in addition, that these owners "and all persons in active concert or participation with them, and each of them be and they hereby are, permanently enjoined from renting, leasing, selling, transferring or conveying any of said lots unto any Negro or colored person." Finally, the Hurds, Rowes, Savages, and Miss Stewart were ordered "to remove themselves and all of their personal belongings, from the land and premises now occupied by them within 60 days from November 20, 1945."

Judge Letts based his decision on two main points. First, the covenants involved in the action were valid under decisions of the Court of Appeals for the District of Columbia and the Supreme Court of the United States. Second, Judge Letts ruled that there had been no trend of penetration by Negroes in the area to bring these actions within the exception to the rule upholding such covenants. Many more than sixty days were to pass, however, before the Negroes could be forced out of Bryant Street for Charles Houston appealed the injunctive order to the Court of Appeals of the District of Columbia Circuit, and action was slow in coming.

Before 1946 when the two *Hodge* cases came before it, the Court of Appeals for the District of Columbia had heard seven racial covenant cases. No other appellate court had passed so often on this subject. During this period of two decades a total of fifteen judges served on the Court of Appeals, twelve had sat on one or more of these cases, and ten assumed with Judge Josiah Van Orsdel that "these covenants constitute valid and solemn contracts and should not be lightly set aside." [29] Each case was decided by a panel of three judges named by the chief judge, as he is called, who is simply senior in service on the court. The two judges who questioned the validity of enforcement were never fated to serve together. They were Wiley B. Rutledge and Henry W. Edgerton.

Judge Rutledge's misgivings were expressed in a concurring opinion to a 1942 decision that "changed conditions" made an otherwise valid covenant unenforceable.[30] Chief Judge Lawrence Groner wrote the main opinion and Fred M. Vinson, a member of the Court of Appeals between 1938 and 1943, was also on the panel. Rutledge separated himself from Groner and Vinson in an opinion of only one sentence, as follows: "I concur in the result for the reason that if such a covenant as is involved in this case is valid in any circumstances, as to which I express no opinion, it is not valid and enforceable in the conditions shown on the present record and stated in the opinion of the court." This tentative expression of difference between Rutledge and the other judges is of special interest because he and Vinson were later fellow members of the United States Supreme Court.

Judge Edgerton's disagreement with his colleagues was stated explicitly in strong dissenting opinions in *Mays v. Burgess*,[31] which came twice to the Court of Appeals, once on appeal and later on rehearing. It will be remembered that this case was something of a *cause célèbre* in Washington during World War II, and Edgerton's forceful dissents stimulated interest in the whole problem of discrimination in housing. Chief Judge Groner wrote the opinions of the court in both phases of the case and was supported in the first stage by Justin Miller and in the second by Bennett Champ Clark.

When the consolidated cases of *Hurd v. Hodge* and *Urciolo v. Hodge* came before the Court of Appeals in November, 1946, the panel designated to sit was composed of Clark and Edgerton, two knowns, in the sense that they had previously decided a racial restrictive covenant case, and Wilbur K. Miller, an unknown. The decision was not announced until May 26, 1947, when enforcement of the restriction was upheld by a two to one vote. Judge Clark's opinion was supported by Miller while Edgerton again dissented.

Because the courts of the district had consistently upheld the validity of restrictive deed covenants and agreements over a period of twenty-five years, Judge Clark held that the settled law of the jurisdiction made such covenants valid and enforceable in equity by way of injunction. Under this influence he indicated that the Court of Appeals was "not prepared to reverse and annul all that we have said on this subject, and to destroy contracts and titles to valuable real estate made and taken on the basis of our decisions."

Judge Clark's remarks on the changed-condition doctrine were drawn in totality from the court's recent decision in *May v. Burgess*. There the answer to the question was negative regarding whether "the purpose of the restrictive condition has failed by reason of a change in the character of the neighborhood, so that its enforcement would impose a hardship rather than a benefit upon those who were parties to its terms." [32] Likewise, in this instance, time had passed, but the change in this neighborhood was considered to be insufficient to consider setting aside a rule of law which had been in force and followed for a period of twenty-five years.

Finally, the court reported having "thoroughly considered the contention that such a restriction constitutes an illegal restraint on alienation." And again, it was declared that for twenty-five years the courts in the District of Columbia had upheld restrictions against races regardless of their time period and whether they applied to sale or use. Precedent then, the old bulwark of the white property owners, was enlisted successfully in 1947 for the aid and comfort of Lena Hodge and her Caucasian neighbors. Not only did Judge Clark find, in conclusion, that "in other jurisdictions the majority of recent decisions are in accord with our holding," but could cite as well the ruling of the American Law Institute's *Restatement of Property* dealing with "perpetuities and other social restrictions." [33]

Judge Edgerton, Dissenting

Incorporated into the dissenting opinion of Circuit Judge Henry W. Edgerton were the main intellectual criticisms of segregation and racial restrictive covenants.[34] Disdaining the majority's emphasis on precedent in earlier covenant cases, he relied on other constitutional decisions and modern sociological and legal writings to show that the precedents in the racial-covenant litigation were erroneous. Judge Edgerton cited Professor McGovney's claim that court enforcement of restrictive covenants was unconstitutional.[35] He integrated information in articles by Robert C. Weaver, a Negro sociologist,[36] and in Myrdal's *An American Dilemma*[37] into his dissenting opinion. A speech by President Truman[38] and sections of the United Nations Charter[39] were referred to by Judge Edgerton to show that wise public policy left no room for racial restrictions in housing.

In a preliminary analysis, Judge Edgerton argued that the

majority erred in believing that the United States Supreme Court
had ruled on the questions of the validity of racial restrictive
covenants or their enforceability by injunction in *Corrigan v.
Buckley*.[40] The Supreme Court in that case had merely held that
neither the Civil Rights Act of 1866 [41] nor the Constitution prohibited private parties from agreeing to covenants. The Supreme
Court did not consider whether the Constitution or the Civil
Rights Act prohibited *enforcement by injunction* of such covenants. Nor were any other issues before the court in the present
case settled by the *Corrigan* decision. Aside from the point on
which the Supreme Court did rule, Judge Edgerton noted that the
Circuit Court's present decision rested only on its own past decisions, which he believed were erroneous and should be overruled.

Closely following his earlier dissent in *Mays v. Burgess*,[42] Judge
Edgerton argued that the lower court's enforcement of the Bryant
Street restrictive covenants should not be affirmed. He gave five
reasons, "each independent of the other four." Enforcement of
the covenants by injunction, he said, was (1) inequitable, (2)
contrary to the due-process clause of the Fifth Amendment, (3)
violative of the Civil Rights Act of 1866, (4) void as an unreasonable restraint on alienation and (5) contrary to public policy.

In the first place, Judge Edgerton believed that the principle
of "balancing equities" precludes the issuing of an injunction.
The extreme hardship which the injunctions would inflict upon
the Negroes because of the local housing shortage greatly out-
weighed any benefits which their white neighbors might derive.[43]

Secondly, in a skillful discussion of the police power and the
due-process limitation, he balanced them perfectly to show that
"Negroes have a constitutional right to buy and use, and whites
to sell to Negroes, whatever real property they can without direct
government interference based on race." [44] He said that, of course,
there is no doubt of a state's power to adopt whatever policy may
promote the public welfare, and even to enact zoning ordinances,
unless they "are clearly arbitrary and unreasonable, having no
substantial relation to the public health, safety, morals, or general
welfare." [45] In *Buchanan v. Warley*,[46] he recalled, the Supreme
Court held that enforcement of a city ordinance forbidding
Negroes to live in certain areas was an arbitrary and unreason-

able use of the police power because its only purpose was to bar people, solely because of their color, from these particular areas.

Turning to the constitutional question, Judge Edgerton asked if a court of the United States has power to cancel deeds "which willing sellers have made to willing buyers, and evict the buyers from the property, because the buyers are Negroes." [47] Restrictive covenants were not, he pointed out, self-executing. If all persons owning property burdened by such agreements refused to sell to Negroes, then only the action of private individuals would be involved, and the situation would be similar to the refusal of the innkeeper in the *Civil Rights Cases* [48] to serve Negroes.

> But in this case private means have failed to produce compliance with the covenant and a court has been asked to enforce it. If the colored applicants refuse to vacate the premises in obedience to the court's decree it will be enforced against them through the court's power to punish for contempt; they may be imprisoned or fined, and dispossessed by force if necessary. The action that begins with the decree and ends with its enforcement is obviously direct government action.[49]

Thus the injunction in this case was like the city ordinance in *Buchanan v. Warley;* [50] such enforcement by a court should have been banned because it likewise was government action.[51]

Thirdly, argued Judge Edgerton, the enforcement of racial restrictive covenants violated the federal Civil Rights Act,[52] for there was no civil right clearer or more vital than "the right to buy a home and live in it." [53] This declaration of a federal right by statute meant that courts should recognize it and protect it. Colored citizens had the same right to own and occupy property as is enjoyed by white citizens, and it was wrong to deny this by the enforcement of a restrictive agreement made more than forty years ago.

The next objection centered on freedom to alienate, a principle of property law which Judge Edgerton believed was subverted by restrictive covenants. Relying entirely on the assumptions and reasons of the American Law Institute's *Restatement of Property,* Judge Edgerton showed that freedom of alienation is essential to the welfare of society because of " 'the necessity of maintaining a society controlled primarily by its living members, in part upon the social desirability of facilitating the utilization of wealth, and in part upon the social desirability of keeping property responsive to the current exigencies of its current beneficial owners'." On the basis of the very factors which the institute lists as tending to make restraints on alienation reasonable and valid, that is, instances where the restraint is limited in time, to a small number of people, or for charitable or "worthwhile" purpose, Judge Edgerton felt that the covenants in *Hurd v. Hodge* were "clearly unreasonable and void considered merely as restraints on the freedom of owners to alienate their property." He thought it was quite inconsistent that the institute "qualifiedly" endorsed racial covenants.

Finally, Judge Edgerton asserted that racial restrictive covenants are contrary to public policy. The defense that covenants increase the value of restricted property and prevent racial conflict was answered by the point that due to the acute postwar housing shortage the price of homes was already "inflated above any level that can be thought socially desirable" and that in fact "enforced housing segregation increases rather than diminishes the possibility of racial conflict." "If the satisfaction which many of the whites in restricted areas may derive from excluding Negroes is to be given weight," reasoned Edgerton, "it must be weighted against the dissatisfaction which Negroes may feel at being excluded." He also contrasted the role of covenants in aggravating the serious shortage in Negro housing with some of President Truman's words on the need of Americans to live together in peace, with equal justice for all. He also cited the public policy expressed in the United Nations Charter to which the United States has subscribed. In summation, Judge Edgerton said:

> Suits like these, and the ghetto system they enforce, are among our conspicuous failures to live together in peace. In another suit, this court recently argued that "if the two races are to meet upon mutually satisfactory ground, it cannot be through legal coercion. . . ." This premise, instead of supporting the court's conclusion that racial restrictive covenants should be enforced by injunction, is one more argument against it. The question in these cases is not whether law should punish racial discrimination, or whether law should try to prevent racial discrimination, or whether

the law should interfere with it in any way. The question is whether law should affirmatively support and enforce racial discrimination. Appellants do not ask that appellees be forced to sell them houses. Appellees alone have come to court with a claim. They ask the court to take away appellants' homes by force because they are Negroes. There is no other issue in the case.

This dissenting opinion was immediately regarded by leading civil-rights lawyers as one of the best formulations of reasons against judicial enforcement of racial covenants. Judge Edgerton had improved upon his earlier dissent in *Mays v. Burgess.* The intrinsic merit of the reasoning was matched by Edgerton's reputation as one of the ablest and most influential judges on the federal appellate bench. Born in Kansas, he studied at Wisconsin, Cornell, and the University of Paris before completing a law degree at Harvard in 1914. Following several years of practice, Edgerton became a professor at Cornell Law School and in 1937 was appointed by President Roosevelt to the Court of Appeals. In a recent tribute to Edgerton's twenty years of service on that court Felix Frankfurter has said: "The range and depth of his academic experience and of his legal writings, and his awareness of the recalcitrances of practice and of government, singularly well prepared him for a judgeship." [54] On the bench he has been praised for creating "a body of judicial writing that will have an increasing impact upon the development of the law." [55] In 1952, a study showed that the Supreme Court commonly granted certiorari in cases where Edgerton dissented, and of the 23 dissents reviewed there were 17 reversals of the decisions against which he voted.[56] It was said that the influence of Judge Edgerton's work "rests in part upon the enlightened and progressive precedents his decisions have set; in part upon his creative use of the implements and materials with which a judge must work; and finally upon his courageous declaration of principles in the most honored traditions of our democracy." [57]

V

The Marcus Avenue Improvement Association

One of the streets that bound the densely populated Negro district of St. Louis, Missouri, from outlying white residential areas in the northwestern part of the city is Marcus Avenue. It was by no accident that this street, for more than thirty years before 1948, stood as a line of separation between the two races. The continuity of white solidarity in that section was the result of the planning and calculated hard work of white property owners. They were united in the Marcus Avenue Improvement Association,[1] which drew the color line along the most northerly blocks on Taylor, Cora, Marcus, and Euclid avenues, and along the western blocks on Easton, Cote Brilliante, Leduc, Hammett, Cupples, Northland, St. Louis, and Labadie avenues. When the Supreme Court of the United States ruled in 1948 that judicial enforcement of restrictive covenants was no longer valid, the phase of defending this white section from occupation by Negroes through legal action ended. But it did not end through any default on the part of the Marcus Avenue Improvement Association, which had spent $10,000 [2] in the case of *Shelley v. Kraemer*.[3] This major defeat marked the decline of the association and its activities for the perpetuation of a white neighborhood.

Racial restrictions had been placed in some deeds in the area as early as 1911, the year following the founding of the association. Between 1921 and 1928 the neighborhood had been checked thoroughly to see that covenants covered all property. But available records show that in 1937 the Marcus Avenue Improvement Association held its first meeting in five years. Significantly, the meeting was called, as the secretary's minutes show, "regarding the sale of property located at 4610 Labadie Ave., to negroes." [4] Fear that colored people might burst their existing bounds brought about renewed interest in building a strong association. Early in the following year more meetings were held and the purpose of the association was summarized: [5]

> . . . to start a plan of action in which property owners, business men and institutions would combine under the banner of THE MARCUS AVE. IMPROVEMENT ASS'N; to help in keeping up the good work of the Ass'n, in this district and to improve or eliminate any nuisances that might exist.

Those present at the meeting were reminded by one of the older members, Martin Seegers, that their labors of the past had succeeded, and he urged them to "go on from there with the same spirit to keep up the standard of this neighborhood indefinitely." [6] Although there was an "excellent turnout," it was moved that a letter be sent to every property owner, businessman, and institution for support. Finally, volunteers agreed to survey various blocks in the area as to property changes.

Since the organization was making a new beginning, at the next meeting in April, 1938, two of the older leaders explained the role of racial restrictive covenants in keeping their neighborhood white.[7]

> Mr. [Martin] Seegers then spoke about the very pertinent question of restrictions as regards their stability in the eyes of the law. Mr. Seegers and Mr. Vornbrock collaborated in explaining to the meeting that the constitution provides that all citizens irrespective of color and creed enjoy all liberties alike, and particularly in our case the owning of property located anywhere in St. Louis, New York, New Orleans etc. Now the white people living in these towns who feel that the negroes should not be denied their liberties but prefer to live separately can do this by banding together in a community and draw up an agreement as property owners not to sell to negroes, this agreement after being signed becomes part and parcel of the deed. By doing this the white people are not transgressing against our constitution and bill of rights, they are simply availing themselves of the liberties that are existent in our laws, and which have been proven in numerous cases in all courts that they are iron clad.

These remarks suggest very clearly that one important purpose of the Marcus Avenue Improvement Association was to keep the area it represented an exclusively white neighborhood, but to accomplish it by strictly legal methods.

The activities of the association were mostly limited to the maintenance of racial restrictive covenants and their enforcement in cases of violation. Parts of the area had been restricted at different times, and from 1937 to 1948 it was necessary to renew these restrictions. Court action was seldom necessary to prevent Negroes from becoming residents there, because property owners were discouraged from selling to Negroes. The association was also alert to warn its members against selling to a wildcat real-estate operator who might deliberately ignore the restrictions and resell the property to colored people. At one meeting assurances were made that "in the event an attempt was made to sell to colored, the Association would back up the property owners to the fullest extent of the law." [8]

Restrictive covenants were the primary means for achieving the group objective, and were supplemented with other activities by the association to maintain the racial purity of the environment. Great efforts were made to keep the Cote Brilliante primary school for white children only.[9] This meant working to arouse the interest of all citizens in the community to protest against possible School Board action which would change it to a school for Negroes only. Another example of association activity to keep Negroes outside the area was its opposition to the assignment of a Negro mail carrier to serve the section.[10]

The Marcus Avenue Improvement Association also displayed some general community interests. Its greatest success in this field came when it secured the coöperation of city, state, and federal governments in filling an old quarry in the vicinity,[11] which changed a treacherous and unusable pit into a playground. The association assisted in the campaign to build an addition to a small hospital in the neighborhood.[12] Further, the association asked for additional bus service, but the Public Service Commission did not order it.[13] During the war the association solicited funds to erect a memorial honor roll of the sons of the community in the armed services.[14]

The organization of the Marcus Avenue Improvement Association began and ended with a small group of leaders who generated the ideas, managed the meetings, determined the policies, and led in carrying them out. Most of them were older men. Martin Seegers, active from the beginning in 1910, was 81 years old in 1947. In 1942, he had retired from the presidency and was replaced by Emil Koob, 45-year-old bakery operator, who dominated the work of the association for the next half-dozen years. He was a man with deep convictions about the values inherent in a white neighborhood, and had already worked as secretary of the organization for several years.[15] He was eager to push the work ahead.[16]

> Mr. Koob, received the election of himself as President, and stated that he was not interested in a mere title, but wished to impress upon the other Directors present, that this work was not the responsibility of only the President, but every Director was expected to take upon himself, the activity that is necessary to keep the Organization an active and alert working body and everyone was to keep this district which we have undertaken to keep white, and if all felt this as deeply as he did, he would consider to fill this office.

Koob has recently stated that less than forty people formed the nucleus of the organization, and that fewer than this did the leg work necessary to maintain the district for white residents. The board of directors and the officers were elected by the total membership in open meeting, and these positions too were filled by men who were willing to work hard and who felt most strongly about the need for fulfilling the purposes of the organization.

The Marcus Avenue Improvement Association claimed to speak for more than 2,000 property owners in the area and a membership of more than this number. Efforts were often made to convince property owners of the value of restrictions and the good work performed by the association. This is illustrated by the concern revealed at a meeting in 1944: [17]

> Mr. Vornbrock asked for assistance in trying to establish the fact the district for 20 years is good for white people to live in. The one way to establish this fact is to secure new restriction agreements when the existing ones lapse, also to secure agreements where none exist. He cited the instance of Wagner Place, where

meetings were called to try to interest people, but without success.

Yet the work of the association was effectively continued by the leaders. Lamentations were regularly made; consider this statement made in 1941: [18]

> Mr. Floescher states briefly that there are over two thousand families in our district and yet there is only about fifteen men who really take an active interest in this group. He announced that the Association would be unable to carry on their work without assistance from more of the members.

There was no increase in membership or of participation by the rank and file. The association was successfully operated because its leaders were able, and they were interested in the objectives of the organization.

While the success of the Marcus Avenue Improvement Association depended on the work of its leaders, democratic forms were maintained. Quarterly meetings were held to which the officers and board of directors reported and answered questions raised by members. Where convenient, the membership was asked to ratify decisions about the work of the organization, and it did so without dissent. The lack of opposition indicates that all those who participated, even tacitly, approved of the purposes and means of operation of the association. At many meetings some person there for the first time voiced his whole-hearted approval of the group and promised full participation.

The association was financed from membership dues of $1 a year, but those collections could hardly keep the treasury up to the capacity needed to pay the expenses engendered by the cases carried to the court after 1945. This litigation was paid for by large contributions of from $50 to $500 dollars by other protective associations and businessmen, especially in the real-estate field. In 1938 the balance on hand was $444.50; in 1940 it was $413.63. But in 1943 it was $2,609 and stood at nearly $5,000 in January, 1948 [19] after legal actions had already drained off a large amount.

Soon after its rebirth in the late 'thirties, the Marcus Avenue Improvement Association was incorporated under the laws of Missouri. A proponent of this action made clear its wisdom to a meeting held in 1940: [20]

To start out with I want to say this, an Unincorporated organization, such as this, can neither sue, nor can it be sued, and whatever action may be taken, it is not the Organization that suffers from it, but the individual members. I am not saying that with a view of scaring anyone because it is very seldom that we hear of Officers or Members of an Improvement Association hurting anyone else's feelings or rights;

However, if Incorporated and anyone sues, then instead of suing the individuals, the Corporation will be sued and no individual.

Plainly this would be advantageous to the members of the association, who could then advocate or take action in the corporate name.

One feature of the internal organization of the Marcus Avenue Improvement Association remains to be described. Although they were paid for their services to the association, two lawyers actually became leaders in its activities, for they were the authorities on the crucial question of enforcing restrictive covenants. The legal strategy had to be worked out by a lawyer and accepted by the leaders and the membership. D. Calhoun Jones was the counsel for the association for a number of years, having been recommended by the St. Louis Real Estate Exchange. Later Gerald Seegers, a nephew of one of the first leaders, Martin Seegers, became the attorney. Both men attended meetings and advised the membership about all legal matters before them. The members were given this advice by one of their attorneys in 1941: [21]

Mr. D. Calhoun Jones addressed the chair stating that it was impossible to stress too much on what the Board of Directors and Officers have advised about getting behind the Association and helping in every way. He too stated that the few men now interested in the work could not possibly complete the job without assistance. He advised that when the restriction agreements are presented to the property owners, care should be exercised that the proper names of man and wife, or whoever owns the property, are given and that the property owners are to appear before a Notary Public and acknowledge that they executed the instrument. He advised all present that they should impress upon their neighbors the importance of these restriction agreements being in the proper form, etc., and that every property owner on every block should sign the restriction agreement without fail.

The interest of each of the lawyers in the objectives of the group kept fees at a minimum.

The methods of operation of the Marcus Avenue Improvement Association, so far as they can be reconstructed from available records, were the techniques common to most legitimate political organizations. First, the association established alliances with other groups for the mutual assistance. It coöperated with associations just beyond the border of its own jurisdiction and interest, lest the common enemy take advantage of the middle ground not subject to primary protection by either. These associations sometimes contributed money to the Marcus Avenue purse, and were called upon more and more as the legal entanglements sent costs up after 1945.

There was coöperation with other organizations within the Marcus Avenue area. Thus, when the problem over the Cote Brilliante School arose, the Marcus Avenue Association joined with various parents' organizations to put sustained pressure on the school board to keep the school in white hands. There was likewise coöperation with the businessmen's association of that community. Finally, members of the association were urged to join all the organizations they could, in order to keep posted on all activities and also to carry their own concern for protection of the area against Negroes into the councils of other groups whose *raison d'être* was something else.

Most important of the liaisons established by the Marcus Avenue Improvement Association was that with the St. Louis Real Estate Exchange, later Board; their interests crossed and complemented one another. It was a standing policy of the exchange that its members not sell property in predominantly white sections to Negroes. It supported the principle of residential segregation. The bylaws of the St. Louis Real Estate Exchange contain the following provision: [22]

> Committee on Protection of Property.—The Committee on Protection of Property shall consist of thirteen (13) members, and it shall be their duty to co-operate with local Improvement and Protective Associations to maintain certain restrictions and shall have authority to make investigations, to hold hearings, to file charges on violations of restrictions by Active Members of the

Exchange and to perform such other duties as may logically come
within the provisions of such committee.

The coöperation between the Real Estate Exchange and the
Marcus Avenue Improvement Association was very close. In fact
the association became an associate member of the exchange,
and paid dues of $50 to it.[23] The two organizations worked hand
in hand both to keep unaffiliated dealers in real estate out of the
area and to maintain the white domination there. The primary
goal of each was the secondary consideration for the other. The
association's essential interest was in blocking Negro entry, while
the Real Estate Exchange was interested in checking wildcat
realtors.

The policing of real-estate sales was a common method of gaining the objectives of the Marcus Avenue Improvement Association. But other informal methods were equally effective. For
example, leaders of the organization arranged personal conferences with the members of the school board in order to persuade
them not to turn over the Cote Brilliante School to Negroes.[24]
The following item taken from the secretary's minutes of a meeting of the association held in 1938 discloses the application of
pressure for a familiar purpose.[25]

> Action on a letter written to Mr. Gerling of the School Board
> asking his intersection with Miss Anna Evans school teacher at
> Beaumont High School to sign restrictions for 4652 and 4653
> Greer Av., was taken on the secretary's report that so far we had
> no reply. It was decided to call on Anna Evans again to see if
> she has had a change of heart rather than provoke her superiors.

The informal methods of operation were even applied to the
courts by the Marcus Avenue Improvement Association. During
the 1940's it initiated several actions against Negroes in the trial
courts of St. Louis. In each action it sought a quick decision because the law had always been on its side, and it was confident of
the outcome. Delay was exasperating, so on one occasion the
association sent this letter to a trial court judge.[26]

> We have been advised by our attorney, Mr. D. Calhoun Jones,
> that you are of the opinion that some members of this organiza-
> tion are complaining about the long period of time which has

elapsed between the trial of the case of Dolan v. Richardson and the yet unrendered decision therein, and that you should have rendered such a decision prior to this time.

Mr. Jones has told us that due to his illness, he was unable to file a reply brief until the first week in August, and because of that fact it would have been impossible for you to render a decision prior to that time. He also states that you were on your vacation at the time he filed that memorandum, and, therefore, no decision could have been rendered during the June Term of Court which did not expire until the 12th of September, and that because of the momentus nature of the issues it would be necessary for you to give the case exceptional consideration in order to do justice to all parties in arriving at a proper decision. We wish to assure you that this organization fully understands the conditions which made it impossible to render a decision up to this date, and that by no stretch of the imagination could it be said that you were in any way responsible for such delay.

However, as you can readily understand, our people would appreciate an early decision of this very important case, and we sincerely hope that before long you will be able to enter one.

Respectfully yours,

[*signed*] Emil Koob, President

Marcus Avenue Improvement Association, Inc.

(special delivery)

Not all the efforts of the association were behind the scenes. Its work on the quarry project was publicized in the city newspapers. And in return for the favors extended by Congressman Cochran in filling the quarry, the Improvement Association coöperated and gave its support to him in his bid for reëlection in 1942. Although the association claimed not to be in politics, it accepted one-hundred dollars from Cochran, added more to this amount and sent out a printed form letter to all members urging his reëlection.[27]

Since the security of the position of the Marcus Avenue Improvement Association depended on reciprocity with other organizations and people, it is not surprising that it would go on public record in return for a favor. Its deep involvement with the real-estate board necessitated that a stand be taken against public housing. In 1947, the executive secretary of the real-estate board of St. Louis appeared before a meeting of the association.[28]

> Mr. Lang addressed the group, complimenting everyone for their interest in this neighborhood group, stating that the M.A.I.A. has achieved great accomplishments to the interests of all property owners. Mr. Lang stated that he had a very important message to give all the residents of the City of St. Louis, regarding a bill before the House Legislature, being House Bill No. 91, proposing Public Housing Projects for St. Louis, and Kansas City. He suggested that members of the various Associations should be represented at the meeting in Jefferson City, Wednesday afternoon, February 19, in the Capital Building, Jefferson City, Mo., to oppose this bill. He stated that public housing is a step towards National socialism—that ownership and management of housing by the government discourages individual home owners, as these projects are tax exempt. He appealed to everyone in attendance to support the effort to defeat further public housing in St. Louis. He urged as many as possible to attend the meeting before the Legislative Committee. Mr. Koob suggested that perhaps a group could be appointed to attend this Jefferson City meeting. Mr. Seegers made a motion which was seconded and carried, that a Committee be appointed to go to Jefferson City on February 19— and the Real Estate Board Members will arrange transportation.

The main method employed by the association to maintain the neighborhood beyond Marcus Avenue as a sanctuary for Caucasians during those years was by suits brought in trial courts of St. Louis to gain court enforcement of restrictive agreements. Using the names of individuals, the association brought action and conducted these cases as an organization concerned with the larger goal of protecting its district against the entry of Negroes. It hired lawyers and, of course, followed the forms and methods of the judicial system in pursuing its goal. The details of the case of *Shelley v. Kraemer* tell the story.

Kraemer v. Shelley

J. D. Shelley and his wife bought and occupied a house located at 4600 Labadie Avenue in St. Louis on September 11, 1945. The Shelleys were Negroes. They had told Robert Bishop, a colored salesman for the Bowers Real Estate Company, two months earlier, that they wished to buy a house and he showed a number to them. Bishop, who was also the minister of their evangelical church, noticed that the two-apartment house at 4600 Labadie Avenue was for sale, and purchased it through another real-estate firm for $4,700. Bishop acquired the property in the name of Mrs. Geraldine Fitzgerald, as a straw party. This is what Bishop said as a witness under examination about this transaction: [29]

> A. . . . I secured the property through Mrs. Fitzgerald, a straw party, which I found that using a straw party, especially a white, my previous case using a straw party has been an advantage to me in financing.
>
> Q. Will you explain what you mean by that statement, if you please?
>
> A. Well, I bought 1238 north Obert, a 4-family flat, about a year ago through a straw party, and I was enabled to secure a much larger first deed of trust than I would have been able to do at the present home on Garfield.
>
> The Court: I understand what you mean: It's easier to finance?
>
> A. Yes, easier to finance through white. That's common knowledge.
>
> Q. You mean if property is owned by a white person it's easier to finance it?
>
> A. White can secure larger loans, better loans. I have a 5% loan.

Although securing better financing was given by Bishop as the reason for using a white straw party, another reason was more basic. Until the Fitzgerald purchase the property had been owned by a signatory to the restrictive agreement. Consequently before the property was deeded to a colored person it was put in the name of a white straw party so there would be no breach of contract. This meant that since the seller (Fitzgerald) was not a party to the original restriction, sale to the Shelleys was an arm's-length transaction between "a willing seller and a willing buyer."

With Mrs. Fitzgerald as the fictitious owner, Bishop then sold the house to the Shelleys for $5,700. This sizable profit was attacked as unethical by attorneys who later sought to have the Shelleys removed from their home because of their being Negroes.

> Q. Mr. Bishop, what was the sale price of the property when it was sold to the Shelleys?

A. Oh, I think 57.

Q. So there was a clear $1,000 profit in this deal?

A. No; there was cost of financing in there.

Q. Well, how much did that amount to, do you say?

A. That amounted to around in the neighborhood of $300.

Q. You mean to say you bought this property for 4700 and sold it to Shelleys for 5700?

A. Approximately that; I am telling you the price, you asked for it, your Honor.

Q. Are you aware you owe the Shelleys a thousand dollars?

Certainly the Shelleys themselves were not aware of the fact that Bishop had made this profit; nor were they conscious of the fact that they were moving into a hostile neighborhood, part of the bailiwick of the Marcus Avenue Improvement Association. But having moved in on the morning of September 11 they had a lawsuit on their hands that evening. At the trial of the suit, which was underway within two weeks, Mrs. Shelley was asked if the real-estate salesman, Bishop, had told her why they had been sued. Mrs. Shelley answered:

A. Seems like he told me, from the way the papers read, that the place was restricted; something like that, I don't know definite how he explained it. But he told me he let me know when I have to come down.

Q. Do you understand anything about this lawsuit now, why you have been sued and why you are here?

A. Well, I understand the white people didn't want me back.

The Court: You understand what?

A. That's what I understand. And I don't know why; I see other people on the street, that's why I bought it. If I hadn't a-seen them I never would.

In time the interest of the Shelleys in keeping this particular house became mere embroidery on the larger interest of the St. Louis Negro leaders who were opposed to the whole concept of residential segregation, and especially to restrictive covenants and their enforcement by the courts. Earlier in 1945, Scovel Richardson had written a note for the *National Bar Journal* entitled "Some of the Defenses Available in Restrictive Covenant Suits Against Colored American Citizens in St. Louis." [30] It was his central hope that the United States Supreme Court would soon declare restrictive covenants to be unconstitutional. But until that great day came, Richardson stated that [31]

> we cannot overemphasize the importance of being alert to those defenses which state courts have condescended to recognize, particularly change of neighborhood and defects in the execution of the instrument sued upon.

He then proceeded to point out some of the prevalent defects in restrictive covenants in St. Louis. First, agreements are intended to be acknowledged by every owner in a block, but in fact the full number of signatures is seldom obtained. Such agreements are not valid without all the intended signatures, even though the agreement may be recorded. Second, signers sometimes sign for themselves and others without proper acknowledgments. When not properly notarized, the signatures are not legally authentic. Thirdly, agreements are defective where no mention of them is made in the deeds, for a buyer "is not expected to look outside his chain of title for encumbrances upon property purchased by him, and an instrument lying outside the chain of title imparts no notice to him." Fourthly, Richardson, a leading colored attorney in St. Louis, attacked the real-estate exchange in the city for fostering these restrictive agreements. The express powers of the exchange, as it was then named, did not include any authority to become a party to a restrictive agreement. In participating in agreements it violated "both its certificate of incorporation and the 14th Amendment to the Constitution of the United States." Richardson's suggestions, general as they were, helped to forward the hopes of all Negroes in St. Louis to eliminate the operation of racial restrictive covenants. George Vaughn, St. Louis Negro attorney and Democratic politician, took up the defense of the Shelleys and at the trial used the tactics suggested by Richardson.

The Marcus Avenue Improvement Association, in attempting to have a court enforce the restrictive agreement covering the block on Labadie Avenue where the Shelleys had moved, brought action in the name of Fern and Louis Kraemer, who lived at 3542 Labadie Avenue. Any nearby resident could have been the plaintiff but Mrs. Kraemer was chosen because her parents had signed the original restriction. Of course, she was willing to be the plaintiff and testified at the trial to prove her inheritance of the property from a signatory. Later, as the case grew in interest and importance, Mrs. Kraemer became nervous and upset by the publicity.[32] However, her part in the case was limited to this brief appearance at the trial.

The restriction, which the complaint filed on behalf of the Kraemers, asked the Circuit Court for the City of St. Louis to apply against the Shelleys, read as follows: [33]

> This contract of restrictions made and entered into by the undersigned, the owners of the property fronting on Labadie Avenue in blocks 3710-B and 3711-B between Cora Avenue on the West and Taylor Avenue on the East, Witnesseth: That for and in consideration of one dollar and other valuable considerations paid by the undersigned persons hereby contract and agree with the other and for the benefit of all to place, and do place and make upon the Real Estate fronting on Labadie Avenue and running back to the alley on the North and South sides of Labadie Avenue between Taylor Avenue and Cora Avenue, a restriction, which is to run with the title of said property in favor of each and every one of the undersigned parties, and their assigns and legal representatives and successors as the owners of this property, which shall not be removed except by the consent of all of the property owners by some instrument or Deed, made and Executed and put of record, the said property is hereby restricted to the use and occupancy for the term of Fifty (50) years from this date, so that it shall be a condition all the time and whether recited and referred to as not in subsequent conveyances and shall attach to the land as a condition precedent to the sale of the same, that hereafter no part of said property or any portion thereof shall be, for said term of Fifty-years, occupied by any person not of the Caucasian race, it being intended hereby to restrict the use of said property for said period of time against the occupancy as owners or tenants of any portion of said property for resident or other purpose by people of the Negro or Mongolian Race. It is further contracted and agreed that upon a violation of this restriction either one or all of the parties to this agreement shall be permitted and authorized to bring suit or suits at law or in equity to enforce this restriction as to the use and occupancy of said property in any Court or Courts and to forfeit the title to any lot or portions of lot that may be used in violation of this Restriction for the benefit of each and every person that may

now or hereafter, after the recording of this restriction, become
the owner of any property on said street. To have and to hold
each to the other their said property, subject, however, always
and under all conditions to the terms of this restriction, each war-
ranting to the other the compliance in every respect of the above
restrictions. In testimony whereof, the parties hereto have signed
their name and seal this the 16th day of February, 1911.

The signers included the owners, in 1911, of the property, owned
in 1945 by the Kraemers and the Shelleys.

On the basis of this restrictive agreement the plaintiffs said to
the Circuit Court for St. Louis that the violation by the Shelleys,
who were Negroes, would inflict "irreparable injury and ir-
remediable damages to their property." They asked the court to
issue a temporary restraining order to keep the Shelleys from occupying the property, to have the defendant show why such an
order should not be made, and upon a final hearing to make the
injunction permanent and perpetual. This would mean that the
Shelleys would have to give up their title and return it to some
person "wholly of the Caucasian race."

The Circuit Court of St. Louis ordered the defendants to refrain from taking possession of their property until a hearing
could be held. The plaintiffs had to give a bond in the sum of
$500, with surety, in connection with this order. This temporary
restraining order was made on October 9, 1945.

The defendants' answer to the petition of the plaintiffs was
filed by George Vaughn and was a carefully designed piece of
legal work. It raised some searching questions about the particular
restriction and introduced into the record objections on public
policy and constitutional grounds. Vaughn claimed that the
Shelleys had no knowledge of the existence of the restrictive
agreement until after the sale was completed. They had relied
upon the fact that Negroes had owned and occupied homes in
the same block for more than fifteen years. Since the agreement
was made in 1911, this meant that the plaintiffs in this action had
failed to enforce the restriction in so many previous instances
that it had lost all force and effect. The blocks could not be
kept free of Negroes and preserved for dwelling places for Caucasians alone since Negroes were already present. In sum, the
enforcement of the restriction, said the defendants, would not

accomplish its purpose, would work a hardship on them and other Negroes, and limit the market so much that other owners in the block would be unable to dispose of their property at a fair price. Broader defects were also recounted by the defendants. Enforcement of the restriction against them would be a violation of the Fourteenth Amendment and the provision of the Civil Rights Act of 1866 which assured to all citizens the right to have, hold, control, and dispose of property. Rights under the Missouri Constitution would also be abridged. The agreement was termed an unreasonable restraint on the right of free alienation of property, as well.

The defendant's attorney bolstered his argument with sociological evidence, contending that the courts should not use their equity powers to aggravate terrible housing conditions under which Negroes were forced to live by the pattern of segregation imposed upon them. Vaughn pointed out that the Negro population had grown at a rapid rate until it stood at that time, 1945, at 117,000. Despite this increase the defendants noted that the portions in which Negroes could live in the city of St. Louis had been "narrowed, surrounded and circumscribed almost completely." A ghetto had been created and the responsibility for it lay with the courts for having enforced restrictive covenants and agreements such as the one then invoked against the defendants. The congested conditions that followed from the limitations on the housing supply had spun a web of disease, crime, and juvenile delinquency which was a serious problem for the whole community.

It was a fact agreed to by all parties at the trial held in October, 1945, that when the restriction was signed there were 39 owners of the 57 parcels of land which made up the district sought to be restricted. Only 30 of these owners had signed the agreement. Their holdings constituted 47 parcels of land. It was also agreed that five of the lots in the immediate vicinity of 4600 Labadie Avenue where the Shelleys had made their purchase had been occupied by Negroes for varying periods of time. The earliest time was 1882, but others had lived there for 25 or 30 years.

The plaintiffs' explanation of the state of this restrictive agreement was made in detail at the conclusion of the trial, with a request for findings of fact and conclusions of law. While a small percentage of property had been occupied by Negroes for some length of time, the plaintiffs stressed the fact that the colored people were old residents and that since 1923, "the character of the neighborhood (that is the two city blocks covered by the restriction agreement in evidence as well as the surrounding area for a radius of 3 blocks) has not changed."

The court was not convinced, for on November 19, Judge William K. Koerner found that "the plaintiffs are not entitled to a temporary injunction or to the relief prayed for in their petition." The main reason for this holding was that an insufficient number of owners had signed the agreement. Judge Koerner inferred from the words of the agreement that it was to be signed by the owners of *all* real estate within the designated district. Provisions of such an agreement should be strictly construed, said Judge Koerner, and it was his opinion that the parties intended it to be signed by all landowners within the district.

> Consideration should also be given to the purpose of the agreement. The signers certainly did not intend to be bound unless that purpose was accomplished. If the agreement had been signed by only 25% of the landowners it would clearly have been ineffective and not binding. . . . The wording of the agreement indicates that it was contemplated all of the landowners should sign; but if this is not so it was intended that at least enough should sign to make the restriction effective. In the Court's opinion that requirement has not been met.

It was also ruled that the defendants had not had adequate notice of the existence of the restriction, although the real-estate salesman, Bishop, did know of it. Since his interest was antagonistic to that of the Shelleys, he did not tell them this crucial fact.

While holding for the defendants in the case of *Kraemer v. Shelley*, Circuit Judge Koerner did not accept any of their broader claims. He followed the leading Missouri precedents in ruling that the restriction was not a violation of the constitutions of Missouri and the United States, the federal civil-rights statutes, and public policy.[34]

The Missouri Supreme Court Enforces the Agreement

From the judgment of the Circuit Court of St. Louis holding the restrictions invalid the plaintiffs appealed to the Missouri Supreme Court and won a reversal. The opinion of the court, written by Judge James N. Douglas, and handed down on December 9, 1948, interpreted the sense of the agreement much differently than had Judge Koerner at the trial level. The Supreme Court ruled that it was not the intention of the parties to the agreement that all property owners in the district sign the agreement.[35]

> The agreement by its terms intended to cover only the property of those owners who signed it. It is limited to "the undersigned," who are then described as "the owners of the property fronting on Labadie Avenue." . . . It would seem to us by the repeated use of the term "undersigned" and the reference to the "parties" to this agreement that the agreement was intended to cover only the parcels owned by those who became parties to it and to be effective as to them whether all signed or not. There is no mention in the agreement that its validity is conditioned on the joining of all or any particular number of the owners.

Judge Douglas found even stronger support for this view of the intent of the agreement by looking at the surrounding circumstances. As we have seen, five parcels in the district were owned by Negroes at the time the agreement was executed. The court stated emphatically that they could not have been expected to join in the agreement. The intent of the parties could not have been to prevent all Negro occupancy, since this much already existed. And although these five properties were occupied by colored people, the nearest predominantly Negro district was then some distance away. Consequently, "it must have been their intention to prevent greatly increased occupancy by negroes." This plan had succeeded, for no more Negroes have moved in since the agreement was made. The court concluded that the transfer to the Shelleys, defendants in this case, was the first attempt to violate the restriction.

As a general rule, the Missouri court said that any number of owners, however small, could make a technically valid restrictive agreement. The fact that some owners in a district did not join the agreement did not necessarily affect its validity. This was true because the general purpose of the agreement restricting an area against Negroes might still be accomplished without the acknowledged coöperation of every single owner. Thus in this agreement there was no practical result from the failure of some of the owners to sign the agreement, and the purpose of the restriction was realized.

Upon this basic construction of the terms of the agreement and its history, the court disposed of all other possible objections to its enforcement in this case. The plaintiffs were entitled to equitable relief for there had been no change in conditions. On the ground that the Supreme Court of the state had always enforced valid racial restrictions, the court could see no public policy grounds for refusing enforcement here. It was ruled that the defendants, the Shelleys, had notice by the mere fact that the agreement was recorded, since "every instrument in writing which affects real estate imparts notice by being recorded."

The Missouri Supreme Court likewise followed precedent in ruling that the enforcement of this racial restrictive agreement did not violate any constitutional rights of the Shelleys. The Supreme Court of the United States had decided this, it said, in the *Corrigan* case, and the Circuit Court of Appeals for the District of Columbia Circuit had just reiterated this rule in *Mays v. Burgess*.[36] Neither the Thirteenth or Fourteenth Amendments prohibited private persons from entering into contracts respecting the control and disposition of their own property. An answer was also made to the Shelleys' claim of state action: [37]

> Nor can it be claimed that the enforcement of such a restriction by court process amounts to action by the state itself in violation of the Fourteenth Amendment, which relates to a state action exclusively. To sustain such a claim would be to deny the parties to such an agreement one of the fundamental privileges of citizenship, access to the courts.

Finally, Judge Douglas addressed his attention to the overcrowded conditions under which Negroes in St. Louis live, since the trial judge had apparently been influenced somewhat by these facts. He felt this problem was not one for the courts to grapple with.[38]

Such living conditions bring deep concern to everyone, and present a grave and acute problem to the entire community. Their correction should strikingly challenge both governmental and private leadership. It is tragic that such conditions seem to have worsened although much has been written and said on the subject from coast to coast. . . . But their correction is beyond the authority of the courts generally, and in particular in a case involving the determination of contractual rights between parties to a law suit. If their correction is sought in the field of government, the appeal must be addressed to its branches other than the judicial.

The Real Estate Brokers Association

Negro leaders in St. Louis who were made complacent by the trial court holding for Shelley were rocked into action by the adverse Missouri Supreme Court decision. As a result the Real Estate Brokers Association of St. Louis was organized in the winter of 1946–1947. It was formed partly because Negroes were excluded from the St. Louis Real Estate Exchange and its parent, the National Association of Real Estate boards. The brokers' association complained of the "restrictions with reference to living quarters available to colored citizens," and declared that it was "one of the purposes of this organization to peaceably and lawfully endeavor to remedy this condition.[39] In March, 1947, the association was incorporated to consist of "any and all persons of good character, regardless of color, race or creed, who are engaged in the real estate business and who desire to become a member of the organization." Soon afterward the Negro brokers of St. Louis were affiliated with the National Association of Real Estate Brokers.

The immediate aim of the association was to publicize the *Shelley* case in order to obtain funds for an appeal to the United States Supreme Court. James T. Bush, president, and Robert A. Bishop, secretary, organized a large advisory committee led by St. Louis leaders like David Grant, president of the NAACP chapter there and Scovel Richardson, president of the National Bar Association. Soon afterward a public appeal was launched with this advertisement in a Negro newspaper, *The St. Louis Argus:*

THIS IS A CALL TO ACTION
THE MENACE--RESTRICTIVE COVENANTS!!
Present and future home ownership and residential expansion threatened

THE NEED FOR ADEQUATE AND DECENT HOUSING is the gravest problem facing all groups in every city in America. There are not enough places in which to live. Yet, in spite of this grave situation, which is a menace to good citizenship and health, there are a few, a very few Americans, who persist in using un-American methods to deny 13,-000,000 citizens of our country the right to decent housing.

ONE OF THE METHODS USED IS THE ADOPTION OF RESTRICTIVE COVENANTS, neighborhood agreements among property owners which provide that their property shall not be sold to, or occupied by, persons not of the Caucasian race. The real object, of course, is to prevent Negroes from buying or renting property in the neighborhood covered by the agreement. After careful survey, we find that these agreements would never be entered into except for the activity of a few individuals in these neighborhoods who are steeped in racial prejudice or have selfish motives behind their activities. These individuals make a house to house canvass, spread vicious propaganda and picture a calamity that will occur if Negroes move into the block. They have even threatened violence to those who hesitated to sign the agreements.

RECENTLY, THE SUPREME COURT OF MISSOURI, in the case of KRAEMER vs. SHELLEY, ruled that restriction agreements based on race were valid, reversing the decision of our local Circuit Court to the contrary. If this ruling is allowed to stand it means the Shelleys will lose their home and with it their life savings. More serious than the Shelley's loss is the fact that FURTHER EXPANSION OF NEGRO NEIGHBORHOODS IS AT AN END!

THE REAL ESTATE BROKERS ASSOCIATION OF ST. LOUIS REGARDS THE COURT'S DECISION AS A CHALLENGE NOT ONLY TO THE NEGRO BUT TO ALL PEOPLE WHO BELIEVE IN TRUE CHRISTIAN AND DEMOCRATIC IDEALS. WE, THEREFORE, ACCEPT THE CHALLENGE AND ARE APPEALING THE CASE TO THE UNITED STATES SUPREME COURT. WE HAVE 100 CITIZENS SUPPORTING OUR MOVEMENT AND WE WELCOME SUPPORT AND SUGGESTIONS FROM ANYONE WHO BELIEVES WE ARE JUSTIFIED IN THE ACTION THAT WE HAVE UNDERTAKEN.

REAL ESTATE BROKERS ASSOCIATION OF ST. LOUIS

■ ■ ■ ■ ■ ■ ■ ■ ■ ■ ■ ■ ■ ■ ■ ■ ■ ■ ┑ ■ ■ ■ ■ ✦ ■ ■ ■ ■ ╲ ■ ■ ■ ■ ■ ■ ■ ■ ■ ▪

Real Estate Brokers Assn., 3912 Finney Ave: I believe the validity of restrictive covenants based on race should be settled for all times and am enclosing $———to be used to help pay the costs of an appeal to the United States Supreme Court.

Name_____

Address_____

Similar appeals were mimeographed as flyers and distributed in the Negro community. George L. Vaughn spoke on legal aspects of the case at meetings in October, 1947, at Pleasant Green Baptist Church "under direction of the local branch of the NAACP in cooperation with the Real Estate Brokers Association and other interested organizations" and in December at Central Baptist Church under sponsorship of the Inter-denominational Ministerial Alliance to support the "Citizens Committee—Shelley Restrictive Covenant Case Fund." The proceeds from all these efforts apparently reached no more than $1,500 which meant that leaders of the effort, especially Vaughn, bore special burdens.

The Real Estate Brokers Association, with its rather narrow economic interest in the outcome, was supporting its only court case but Vaughn was more experienced. Yet his scope was basically local and he seems to have stood apart from the main stream of leading Negro lawyers in the country. A native of Kentucky and boastful of being the son of a slave, Vaughn attended Lane College in Jackson, Tennessee, and obtained a law degree at Walden University in Nashville. He then set up practice in St. Louis where he became first president of the Mound City Bar Association and served many years as chairman of the executive committee of the local NAACP. He was also a lay leader in the local Afro-Methodist-Episcopal Church, the Masons, and the Elks. His active interest in the Democratic Party was rewarded for he was a delegate to the Democratic National Convention in 1948, a Justice of the Peace in St. Louis and, for a time, Assistant Attorney-General of Missouri. In April, 1957, eight years after his death, the City of St. Louis named a 1350-unit public-housing project The George L. Vaughn Apartments and School in his memory.

VI

The Education of Willis M. Graves

For Caucasians in Michigan the restrictive-covenant case of
Parmallee v. Morris [1] was an important precedent, but for Willis
M. Graves it was a needle pricking his skin. Graves was a Negro
attorney and real-estate broker. As a lawyer, he was a leader in
the Detroit chapter of the NAACP and a member of the National
Legal Committee. He also worked to organize the National Association of Real Estate Brokers, later serving as its president and
counsel. [2] His business brought many Negroes to his office, and if
he prospered from the fees of the middle class and the well-to-do,
he suffered in more ways than one from his contact with the poor.
Racial restrictive covenants applied to all Negroes, and these
peculiar institutions of twentieth-century America provoked a
special interest in Graves.

Born in Raleigh, North Carolina, just before the turn of the
century, Willis M. Graves had been fortunate in the educational
opportunities afforded him. In Raleigh at Shaw University, a
Negro college started in 1865 by the Baptist Church, he earned a
bachelor's degree in liberal arts. Graves then moved on to law
school at Howard University, and, in 1919, received his LL.B.

Upon graduation from Howard, Graves moved to Detroit,
Michigan, where he planned to hang out his shingle. While pre-
paring for the state bar examination at the Detroit College of
Law, he was aroused by the decision of the Supreme Court of
Michigan in the *Parmalee* case. A covenant restricting a lot from

being "occupied by a colored person" had been enforced by a Pontiac trial court. This action was supported by the state supreme court against all constitutional and public-policy objections. *Parmalee v. Morris* became the leading case on restrictive covenants in Michigan. Graves was instinctively critical of the decision, and his growing professional interest in law magnified his interest in the legal arguments of the case.

In his own mind Graves found everything wrong with the judicial enforcement of racial restrictions in housing. As a part of the ever-increasing Negro population of Detroit he was personally aware of the refusal of many white persons to sell or rent homes to members of his race. When on occasion a white person agreed to sell or rent to a Negro, a covenant drawn up years before was invoked to prevent the transaction. The prohibition was backed up by a court of law, a public governmental organ. The consequences of this were disturbing. The legal rationale for the enforcement of restrictions against Negroes was equally distasteful to Graves. A court of justice had no business supporting private discrimination, he thought. It was contrary to sound public policy for a democratic government. Moreover, it seemed to a young Negro attorney to go against the plain words of the Fourteenth Amendment. The constitutional limitation that no state shall deny any person the equal protection of the laws meant that no state court could enforce a restrictive covenant.

In the 1920's, Negro attorneys in Detroit formed the Harlan Law Club, a professional and social association named after Mr. Justice John Marshall Harlan. The club's members thereby honored the spirit of the Justice who had written hopefully, in dissent in *Plessy v. Ferguson* in 1896, that "the Constitution is color blind." [3] Later the Harlan Law Club evolved into a state organization known as the Wolverine Bar Association. In Michigan, as elsewhere during this period, many Negro attorneys became members of the National Bar Association which had been organized in 1925. Meanwhile, white attorneys found their own voluntary associations inadequate to police the profession and in 1937 persuaded the Michigan Legislature to create an "integrated bar" to which all lawyers must belong. Supervised by the state judiciary, Negro attorneys were then obliged to be members of the Michigan Bar Association. This was an important step, but while Negroes had a generally inferior legal status, their attorneys in Michigan kept their own associations alive.

Working together to wipe out legal impediments against Negroes, the Wolverine Bar Association sponsored many social activities, topped by an annual banquet. Willis M. Graves, president of the organization in 1937 and 1938, took what he regarded as rather brash action at the 1941 dinner. Before a distinguished audience, including the entire Supreme Court of Michigan, Graves in the major address of the evening denunciated the legal enforcement of racial restrictions in housing. His argument centered on the fallacy of *Parmalee v. Morris!* At that time, in 1941, there were no restrictive-covenant cases pending in the state. But events that would soon bring cases to the fore had already begun to develop under the pressures of war production increases in Detroit, the hub of the "arsenal of democracy."

Housing and Race Riots

In 1940 as the industrial plant of the nation was being geared for military production, the Negro population of Detroit stood at 150,000. There were jobs in Detroit. Its population went soaring. But during the succeeding decade the proportion of increase for the Negro population was by far the greater. By 1950 the number of Negroes had doubled over the 1940 figure. The additional number of Negroes had noticeable social consequences.[4]

As in all industrial areas there was a shortage of housing in Detroit. The federal government was indirectly responsible, for its orders had speeded up the work of the factories. Hence, upon the influx of population, the government took action to provide the necessary housing during the early part of World War II. As part of the defense housing program the United States Housing Authority constructed a low-cost housing project in Detroit to be set aside for Negroes. Named after a famous free Negro of Civil War Days, the Sojourner Truth Homes were to be opened in February, 1942.

White pickets blocked the entrances of the Sojourner Truth Housing Project on February 28, 1942, when Negroes attempted to move in.[5] A riot developed as fights between white persons and Negroes broke out. One hundred and fifty policemen were enlisted to quell the violence. The disturbance continued intermittently for three days during which more than one hundred arrests were made. Negroes picked up the slogan "WE WANT HOMES NOT RIOTS," but the emergency was not treated energetically enough. The following year new and more fearful outbreaks between the races took place in Detroit. The riots of June, 1943, produced seventeen deaths, of which all but three were Negroes. A study by two Wayne University sociologists asserted that overcrowding in dwellings was once again one of the most serious causes of these riots.[6] The riots in Detroit came to an end, but restrictive covenants continued to keep the Negroes from entering white sections of the city. Supporting segregation in housing were numerous property owners' associations in the Detroit metropolitan area. For example, it appears clear that leaders of the Seven-Mile–Fenelon Improvement Association of Detroit helped precipitate one of the Sojourner Truth riots of 1942.[7] Undoubtedly there was greater extremism in Detroit politics than in any other city in the nation during the early 'forties. Given the size of the Negro population, its growing proportion to the whole in a northern city and the lack of housing available, a crisis may be viewed as inevitable. The improvement associations of Detroit made clear that they would not budge from a policy of full segregation in housing.

Trial: Sipes v. McGhee

By 1945 the organized property owners of Detroit had asked the courts to enforce twelve restrictive covenants. Among these was one suit brought by the Northwest Civic Association. Under its auspices the owners of property on Seebaldt Avenue, between Firwood and Beechwood avenues, drew up in 1934 and 1935 the following agreement: [8]

> We, the undersigned . . . do hereby agree that the following restriction be imposed on our property above described to remain in force until January 1st, 1960, to run with the land, and to be binding on our heirs, executors and assigns:
> This property shall not be used or occupied by any person or persons except those of the Caucasian race.
> It is further agreed that this restriction shall not be effective

unless at least eighty percent of the property fronting on both sides of the street in the block where the above property is located is subject to this or a similar restriction.

This was a reciprocal negative easement which gave each of the owners protection against a non-Caucasian occupying any other lot in the defined area.

After ten uneventful years, the restriction was invoked on January 30, 1945 by twenty-one owners of property covered by it in an action against Orsel and Minnie S. McGhee and their family, to oust them from the home purchased at 4626 Seebaldt Avenue. The white owners sought a temporary injunction from the Circuit Court for Wayne County to keep the McGhees from remaining on the property until a trial could be held. This was denied. At the trial which followed in May, 1945, Benjamin Sipes, who lived next door to the house occupied by the McGhees, testified that they were colored people.

> I have seen Mr. McGhee, and he appears to have colored features. They are darker than mine. I haven't got near enough to the man to recognize his eyes. I have seen Mrs. McGhee, and she appears to be the mullat-o [sic] type. Any white man to me is a Caucasian, and I haven't heard of any colored people who are Caucasians.

Upon this basis Sipes had called a meeting of taxpayers in the neighborhood together and gained their approval in making joint efforts to have the McGhees removed from the area. He composed a letter, and a group of the white home owners went with him to McGhee's house and read it to him. Sipes's testimony on the contents of the letter follows:

> I says, "We are a group of taxpayers in the neighborhood, who are representing the [Northwest] Civic Association. We are a group and we are asking you to kindly vacate the property. . . . We also wish to inform you that unless you vacate this—unless you move out, the Civic Association will take you to court."

When the McGhees failed to move, Sipes and the other Caucasians filed for an injunction in the Wayne County Circuit Court. They complained that the restriction had been imposed on the McGhee property by John and Meda Furgeson, through whom the McGhees claimed title, and was recorded on September 7,

1935, at the Wayne County Register of Deeds Office. They asserted that the McGhees were not of the Caucasian race and had moved into their house in direct violation of the restriction. They said further:

> The restricted character of Seebaldt Avenue, and particularly of the block where defendants' property is located, as an exclusively white residential neighborhood, has been uniformly observed since the property was subdivided and the continued violation of said restriction will cause irreparable injury to these plaintiffs and all other owners in the vicinity by greatly reducing the desirability and value of their properties.

The plaintiffs asked, therefore, that a temporary injunction be issued by the Wayne County Court restraining the McGhees, defendants in this action, from using or occupying their property or permitting its use or occupancy by any person except those of the Caucasian race. Upon hearing the cause it was asked that the injunction be made permanent.

The McGhees called upon the Detroit branch of the National Association for the Advancement of Colored People for help. Their defense was taken up by Willis Graves, who now had an opportunity to apply to a concrete case his long-felt feelings against restrictive covenants. Joined with him was Francis Dent, likewise a member of the NAACP National Legal Committee. Dent had a wide acquaintance among Negro lawyers and had been a schoolmate of Charles Houston at Amherst in addition to attending the Detroit College of Law.

Lawyers for the defense admit as little truth to the complaint as possible. Graves and Dent denied a number of contentions in their answer, but chief among these was their refusal to admit the claims regarding the race of their clients. They asserted that the McGhees lacked "sufficient knowledge of their ancestry to say to which race they belong." Nor did their answer to the bill of complaint concede the validity of the restrictive covenant in question.

If technicalities could win their case, Graves and Dent were armed with many detailed objections. One of the restrictive agreements was not properly notarized, they claimed, because it was signed in Indiana and no certificate of the notary's appointment and authority was included. Another agreement was signed by the officers of a corporation on its behalf and that too was without authority. Then again, an executor of an estate filed one of the agreements without authority from the probate court. For the rest of the names appearing on the other agreements, it was claimed that more than the mark of the notary public should appear to make the signature authentic and binding. The notary "should name the people who appeared before him in the certificate and the dates that they appeared before him in the certificate. The certificate itself must bear a date and there is no date in the certificate." Supporting these arguments were a mass of technical comments on the legal process of notarization.

If broader constitutional claims would work for their benefit, Graves and Dent were prepared to push them. It was unnecessary to treat the constitutional question exhaustively, but it was imperative to plead that question properly in the court of original jurisdiction. Otherwise a review could not be had later in the United States Supreme Court. Graves and Dent said first that enforcement of the restrictive agreement against the McGhees would violate the due-process clause of the Michigan Constitution.[9] This contention was expanded when the trial began in late May, 1945. Graves reiterated an old belief that "the restriction against occupancy based upon race or color of the occupant is void under the 14th Amendment to the Federal Constitution." Furthermore, it was argued that "the issuance of an injunction by this court, as prayed for, would prevent defendants from occupying their property, because of their race or color, and would therefore contravene the 14th Amendment to the Constitution." Finally, it was said that "the restrictive covenant, relied upon by the plaintiffs, would prevent occupancy of the property because of the race or color of the occupant, and is therefore void as against public policy."

The trial between Sipes, sponsored by the Northwest Civic Association, and McGhee, defended by Graves and Dent of the NAACP, took place in the Circuit Court of Wayne County before Judge Guy A. Miller on May 29, 1945. The plaintiffs entered documentary evidence to show that the restrictive agreements were indeed properly acknowledged and recorded. The opinion of Sipes was relied upon to support the truth of the view that the McGhees were colored persons.

The only other witness for the plaintiffs was a real-estate man in the district, Charles R. Robert, who commented on the depreciatory effects of Negroes moving into the area.

> I have seen the result of influx of colored people moving into a white neighborhood. There is a depression of values to start with, general run down of the neighborhood within a short time afterwards.

This was the general rule although he had known of an exception to it in this area of Detroit. However, the reaction against the McGhees was disturbance and grave economic concern.

> As a result of this particular family moving in the people in the section are rather panic-stricken and they are willing to sell— the only thing that is keeping them from throwing their stuff on the market and giving it away is the fact that they think they can get one or two colored people in there out of there. My own sales have been affected by this family. Since the fact got around there and it seems to have gotten around the northwest section that colored people are on Seebaldt, which is one of our nicest streets, and nine out of ten calls on the telephone—that, of course, is the section I operate in—they ask which side of Grand Avenue it is on, and the south side is where the colored people are. Six or seven weeks ago I sold a house at 5673 Seebaldt and got a deposit one day and got the owner's acceptance to the purchaser, he found out there was a colored family in the district and he called me and stopped the deal, and on the request of the Securities Commission, we returned the deposit. I am familiar with Seebaldt Avenue.

He said that the property occupied by the McGhees at 4626 Seebaldt Avenue was worth $5,200, while if there were no colored family in it the property would be worth $7,000.

This issue of depreciation was not joined by the defendants, whose only witnesses discussed the question of race. Dr. Norman D. Humphrey, an assistant professor of sociology and anthropology at Wayne University, was the main expert. He testified that there are three major races in mankind: Mongoloid, Caucasian, and Negroid.[10] But there was no single or simple criterion for determining membership in a particular race. Determining this was a highly complex scientific problem which only an expert could solve. He did not think that the average person could look at an individual and tell what racial classification he should be put in, because the average person "is unfamiliar with the anthropological scientific determination of racial stocks." Skin color was said to be a very poor index of race.

Letting these scientific definitions stand, the plaintiffs questioned Dr. Humphrey about racial terms used in popular parlance, in order to bring out that the words of the restrictive agreement were sufficiently meaningful to apply to the McGhees. The tenor of the plaintiffs' cross-examination efforts showed that popular beliefs, like the ones expressed by Sipes about the color of the McGhees, were as clear as the carefully elaborated language of science.

> Q. Doctor, the approach that you have testified to here, has been the purely scientific and academic approach, has it not?
> A. It has been the scientific and academic approach, yes, sir.
> Q. In other words, you are not testifying to the popular concepts of these things, you are testifying solely as to the academic concepts?
> A. Yes, sir.
> Q. In just ordinary language that the man in the street uses, what does the Negroid consist of? What is the common word for that?
> A. The average person in the street calls it "nigger" and spells it with two "g's."
> Q. What is the Mongoloid? What is the term for that?
> A. Again, the man in the street uses variable language—he may use Mongolian.
> Q. And the Caucasoid, what is the common word for that?
> A. Well, the commonly used term is the white race, so to speak, but actually there is a variance here between the man in the street's usage of the term and the anthropologists', just as there is a difference between the chemist—
> Q. I understand, but I am talking about common ordinary meaning of the man in the street—the Negroids are known as the black race?
> A. That is right, but I am not competent to talk about the lan-

guage of the man on the street because it is an ambiguous language.

Q. I grant you that, but generally speaking, the Negroid is the black race?

A. It is commonly felt that the Negroids are black.

Q. Isn't it a fact that they are commonly called black?

A. Commonly—to me they would be more brown than black.

Q. Or black or brown; but the Mongolians or Mongoloids are talked of by the ordinary people as a yellow race?

A. In some references, yes, and in some references, no.

Q. They are talked about commonly in ordinary language as the "Yellow Race," isn't that so?

A. Yes, sir.

Q. And the Caucasoid is what is commonly considered to be the white race?

A. Yes, sir.

Dr. Melvin Tumin, an instructor of sociology and anthropology at Wayne University, testified that he had no "substantial disagreement" with his colleague's words. There was no follow-up on the question of the McGhees' race by their lawyers, but the plaintiffs entered as evidence copies of their marriage license showing that they described themselves as Negroes. This ended the trial.

Three months later, on August 23, 1945, Judge Miller, for the Circuit Court of Wayne County, granted the injunction requiring the McGhees to leave their home. This meant, of course, that the claims of the plaintiffs were accepted while the contentions of the defendants were turned down. The acknowledgments to the restrictive agreement were accepted as valid because the defendants had offered no positive proof that they were not authentic. Judge Miller ruled that the covenants were founded on mutual considerations, for each signer had agreed with all the others thereby binding the property under the restriction for twenty-five years. In terms they ran with the land and bound heirs, executors, and assigns. Because the agreements were recorded, each lot owner had notice. "Each purchaser," he said, "who takes subject to such negative restrictive easements agrees with all others subject to them that he will observe them."

The broader question of the validity of racial restrictive covenants and their enforcement by courts was answered on the basis of precedents. Judge Miller held that the restriction did not violate either the federal or the state constitutions, for his court was bound on the point by two state cases, *Parmalee v. Morris* [11] and *Schulte v. Starks* [12] and the United States Supreme Court's decision in *Corrigan v. Buckley*.[13] The Michigan Supreme Court had ruled that a restriction preventing sale of property to any class of persons entitled to hold interests in land is an invalid limitation on alienation.[14] But Judge Miller held that this rule did not apply to the McGhee case because the limitation there was merely on use or occupancy. The judge disregarded the anomaly that the McGhees owned a house they could not occupy.

The restriction was iron-clad, and the precedents supported its general validity. Was there a violation of it? Judge Miller found that the McGhees were "not of the Caucasian race" but were "of the colored or Negro race." Furthermore they had purchased their property with full knowledge of the restriction and were using and occupying it as their residence. Therefore a violation existed. The decree of the Circuit Court of Wayne County reads:

> It is Ordered, Adjudged, and Decreed that defendants Orsel McGhee and Minnie S. McGhee, within 90 days from the date hereof move from said property, and that thereafter said defendants be and they are hereby restrained and enjoined from using and occupying said premises, and
>
> It is Further Ordered, Adjudged and Decreed that after the expiration of 90 days from the date hereof that said defendants and all persons claiming through or under them be and they are hereby restrained and enjoined from violating the above restriction and from permitting or suffering said premises to be used or occupied by any person or persons excepting those of the Caucasian race.

First, the attorneys for the Negroes—taking exception to the court's holding on the McGhees' race—moved the Wayne County Court to set aside its decree. Filed two months after the original decision, the motion for a rehearing listed the same arguments on which the defendants had fought their case at the original trial. However, it stressed that "there is no valid proof of record that the defendants are not of the Caucasian Race." Circuit Judge Miller handed down an opinion denying this motion for rehearing on November 13, 1945. He said that as the evidence stood, a *prima facie* case showing that the McGhees were of the Negro race had been made. They had described themselves as Negroes in their marriage license, which constituted an admission by them. Furthermore, he said that they did not deny being of the Negro race, and they were in court during the trial but did not take the stand.

The case was then taken to the Supreme Court of the State of Michigan. That court ordered a stay of the injunction on December 5, 1945, and continued this in full force indefinitely on January 28, 1946, when it granted the defendants leave to appeal from the decree of the Circuit Court for Wayne County. The McGhees would stay in their house for at least a year until the state supreme court decided the case on its merits.

The McGhees as Appellants

The brief filed with the Supreme Court of Michigan by Willis Graves and Francis Dent was based on two claims.[15] One questioned the findings of fact and conclusions of law of the trial court, and remained close to the narrow issues of the particular case in which they were engaged. The other claim made for the appellants was the broader one that the restriction concerned was void because it was contrary to the state and federal constitutions and to sound public policy. Considering the lawyers' association with the Detroit chapter of the NAACP, the brief was notable for its omission of sociological material. It did rely on McGovney's article [16] to support its constitutional point. Thus the Negroes' brief was legalistic, designed apparently to defeat the white property owners on their own ground.

The questions of fact which the appellants raised in the state supreme court had been canvassed in the trial. Again it was claimed that the owners of 80 per cent of the lots on Seebaldt Avenue did not validly execute the restrictive agreement so as to constitute notice to third parties.[17] They went beyond this somewhat in claiming that even if 80 per cent had properly signed and acknowledged the restriction, it could not have been effective for the entire block, because the remaining 20 per cent had failed to sign. Support for this theory came from the District of Columbia case of *Hundley v. Gorewitz*,[18] where it had been said that if some of the property in an area remained unrestricted, contrary to an agreed plan, the agreement could not possibly achieve its purpose of segregation since Negroes were free to occupy the unprotected 20 per cent.[19]

The contention that the McGhees had not been proved to be non-Caucasian was made once more before the Michigan Supreme Court.[20] The burden of proof, it was declared, was upon the plaintiffs to establish the racial identity of the McGhees. The testimony of Sipes that McGhee "appears to have colored features" while his wife "appears to be the mulatto type" was indefinite and insufficient. It was claimed that the marriage licenses entered as exhibits were not connected with the plaintiffs. The appellants' brief denied that either of the McGhees ever appeared in the courtroom and so the assumption of the Wayne County Court that the McGhees had conceded that they were Negroes was erroneous.

The appellants amplified their position on race by avowing that the restriction against all persons "except those of the Caucasian race" was void for uncertainty. "The term itself is a general expression," it was said, "but for the purpose of construction it must be definite to a degree certain and all proofs submitted must be equally certain." [21] Reliance was placed on *Re Drummond Wren*,[22] a decision of the Supreme Court of the Province of Ontario. There the phrase "Land not to be sold to Jews or persons of objectionable nationality" was declared to be uncertain. It was said of this terminology that "no court could conceivably find legal meaning in such vagueness." The case had been won by the Canadian Jewish Congress,[23] and this fact together with the references in the decision to the ideals of the Charter of the United Nations so soon after its adoption earned the case much publicity. Negroes, Jews, and other racial and religious minorities found it tonic to their interests and so widely advertised it. If in the *Wren* case "Jews or persons of objectionable nationality" was ruled to be too vague for judicial application, the appellants reasoned that essentially the same difficulty was raised in identifying "persons except those of the Caucasian race." [24]

Two new points springing from the facts of the case were also made in the appellants' brief. One was that the general plan of developing the subdivision had been abandoned because a large number of Negroes had resided in the area for a number of years. The parenthetical words of Sipes and the real-estate dealer in their testimony that some Negroes lived near the section covered by the restrictions in question were the only support for this claim. Little more substantiation was provided in the brief for another of the appellants' contentions: that plaintiffs did not establish either in law or fact, the proper application in this case of the doctrine of reciprocal easement. The restrictive agreements in the McGhee case lacked the appropriate elements of a reciprocal negative easement, the brief asserted, for the agreements had not started with a common owner. Therefore the brief argued that a different rule applied to this case, a rule holding that restrictions on the use of land should be construed strictly against those claiming to enforce them, and that all doubts should be resolved in favor of the free use of the property.

In laboring these technicalities, counsel for the McGhees certainly took attention away from the broader points which despite their basic importance had then to be considered as after-thought material. This strategic dilemma illustrates a common problem of lawyers, who must balance the importance of raising every possible issue against the value of emphasizing a few well chosen ones.

When the brief finally turned to the constitutional issue it rephrased the distinction made by Professor McGovney between the adoption of a covenant and its enforcement. The appellants' argument was as follows:

> The discriminatory agreements, conditions or covenants in deeds that exclude Negroes or other racial minorities from buying or occupying residential property so long as they remain purely private agreements, are not unconstitutional. So long as they are voluntarily observed by the covenanters or the restricted grantees, no action forbidden by the Constitution has occurred. But when the aid of the State is invoked to compel observance, the State takes forbidden action. The Negro cannot be ousted from occupancy by purely private action. When a State Court cancels the deed or ousts the occupant, the State through one of its organs is aiding, abetting, enforcing the discrimination.

On this reasoning it was contended that a decree of a court of equity upholding a residential restriction was a violation of the Fourteenth Amendment of the Constitution and the Michigan Constitution.

Lastly, it was claimed that the restrictive agreement was void as being against public policy. This was true, the appellants related, because "the public policy of Michigan, as set forth by Constitution, statutes and court decision, is clearly opposed to all forms of discrimination or segregation on account of race or color." After reciting the language of an assorted group of public pronouncements on the subject the appellants concluded that "the plain and simple truth is that race restrictive covenants run directly counter to the spirit and genius of Michigan's laws and traditions." Additional support for this point was furnished by the Ontario decision which had ruled that the racial or religious restrictive covenants were invalid because the principle involved was offensive to public policy.[25] A 1943 decision of the Superior Court of Orange County, California, was also cited to support this claim.[26] The conclusion in the *Wren* case was reinforced "by the wide official acceptance of international policies and declarations frowning on the type of discrimination which the covenant would seem to perpetuate." [27] The decision of the Canadian court was printed in full as an appendix to the appellants' brief.[28]

The NAACP and Other Amici Curiae

The base of the attack upon the enforcement of the restrictive agreement against the McGhees had been set by the pleadings and testimony before the trial court. Only the questions raised there could be considered on appeal, and these questions were covered thoroughly in the appellant's brief. Several Negro, liberal, or labor organizations in six *amici curiae* briefs elaborated upon these themes in their own way. In addition to *McGhee v. Sipes*, two other covenant cases,[29] were then before the Michigan Supreme Court. This fact no doubt encouraged the *amici curiae* to make rather broad arguments in condemnation of the judicial enforcement of racial restrictions.

The brief *amicus curiae* of the National Association for the Advancement of Colored People,[30] signed by Thurgood Marshall,

Robert L. Carter, and Marian Wynn Perry of the national office in New York, Spottswood Robinson III of Richmond, Virginia, and Edward M. Turner of Detroit, outlined the interest of the organization in the outcome of these cases. In asking the court for leave to file a brief as *amicus curiae* the Association declared:

> The National Association for the Advancement of Colored People is a membership organization which for thirty-five years has dedicated itself to and worked for the achievement of functioning democracy and equal justice under the Constitution and laws of the United States.
>
> From time to time some justiciable issue is presented to this Court, upon the decision of which depends the course for a long time of evolving institutions in some vital area of our national life. Such an issue is before the Court now. In the above entitled appeals, this Court is asked to decide whether enforcement by state courts of a restrictive covenant against use or occupancy of land by Negroes violates the prohibitions of the Fourteenth Amendment to the Constitution and is against the public policy of the United States and the State of Michigan.
>
> It is to present written argument on this issue, fundamental to the good order, welfare and safety of the community, that this motion is filed.

The first of two points made by the NAACP was that judicial enforcement of the covenant in question violated the Constitution of the United States. The right to take and hold property was guaranteed by the Fourteenth Amendment and the Civil Rights Acts of 1866. In the city segregation ordinance cases the Supreme Court had upheld these rights and had denied that the power of the state could support such discrimination, the brief said. Now these property rights were being taken away from Negroes by the action of the trial court in enforcing restrictions by injunction, the NAACP brief continued. This constituted state action in violation of the Fourteenth Amendment.

The National Association for the Advancement of Colored People's second claim was that restrictions upon the use of land by Negroes was against the public policy of the state and the nation. The words of the two constitutions, various statutes, and court decisions as well as the ideals of the United Nations, were cited.

Support for this point on public policy was carefully culled from sociological evidence. Its general position, based on the *Report* of the Committee on Negro Housing of President Hoover's Conference on Home Building, was that:

> Residential segregation, which is sought to be maintained by court enforcement of the race restrictive covenant before this Court, "has kept the Negro occupied [sic] sections of cities throughout the country fatally unwholesome places, a menace to the health, morals and general decency of cities, plague spots for race exploitation, friction and riots!"

Local studies for Detroit were emphasized. They showed that colored people had less living space than white people, and that this was due in large part to legally imposed restrictions. With the Negro population growth continuing at a high rate, this situation, said the NAACP, would steadily worsen unless the courts removed their sanction of racial residential restrictive covenants.

> The dangers to society which are inherent in the restriction of members of minority groups to overcrowded slum areas are so great and are so well recognized that a court of equity, charged with maintaining the public interest, should not, through the exercise of the power given to it by the people, intensify so dangerous a situation.

In concluding its argument on public policy, the NAACP drew attention to the role of protective associations and real-estate groups in maintaining residential segregation. Restrictive covenants were not "the spontaneous product of the community." Rather they resulted "from the pressures and calculated action of those who seek to exploit for their own gain residential segregation and its consequences." The NAACP brief cited a featured article in the *Detroit Free Press* estimating that 150 protective associations were functioning in Detroit. Thus the brief attempted to portray the covenants as the result of an unholy conspiracy among selfishly motivated groups rather than the work of individuals who had strong feelings in the matter.

Another Negro organization, the National Bar Association, stressed the legal objections to the enforcement of racial restrictive covenants in its brief *amicus curiae*.[31] The brief was prepared for the organization by four Chicago attorneys, Earl B. Dickerson, Loring B. Moore, Richard E. Westbrooks, and George N. Leighton. Six years earlier Dickerson and Moore had a lead in carrying *Hansberry v. Lee* to the Supreme Court, and they hoped to take up another test case from Chicago. Their brief showed that they were abreast of new developments for it very effectively presented the "state action" theory along the lines which McGovney had recently set.

In sharp contrast to the thirty pages of tightly argued legal reasoning presented by the National Bar Association was the *amicus curiae* brief of the International United Automobile Workers, C.I.O. which devoted barely three pages out of sixteen to traditionally accepted methods of argument.[32] The rest of the U.A.W.-C.I.O. brief related its own interest and experience in race relations. As a labor organization with a claimed membership of 800,000, the U.A.W.-C.I.O. had sought not only to raise the economic position of its members, but also to unite all employees under its jurisdiction into one organization "regardless of religion, race, creed, color, political affiliation or nationality." The union had an even larger goal in mind; as stated in its brief the U.A.W. "seeks actively to break down and eliminate among its members and among the public generally, prejudice, ill-will and discrimination against persons in all minority groups." In its work the U.A.W.-C.I.O. had learned that few people are prejudiced, but that many are influenced by those who have a professional interest in creating racial strife. Government opposition to discrimination has been effective. The sanctity of authority, said the brief, goes far in erasing discrimination against Negroes. The union mentioned the success the government had in the enforcement of fair-employment practices during World War II. It applied the same reasoning to the race problem in housing.

> So also the attempt to secure adequate housing for Negroes would be tremendously enhanced by the official recognition by this Court that restrictions upon use or occupancy on the basis of color are contrary to public policy and are unenforceable in equity. We are convinced that the refusal of this Court to enforce by injunction restrictive covenants against use or occupancy by Negroes

would have a tremendously salutary effect on the citizenry of our state. The people would abide by the Court's decision, irrespective of such prejudices as they may have.

It was on this theory that the U.A.W.-C.I.O. urged the Michigan Supreme Court to reverse the lower court's decision in *Sipes v. McGhee*.

The three remaining *amici curiae* briefs which supported the position of the appellants were filed by Michigan groups. Two of these were by organizations of lawyers, the Wolverine Bar Association [33] and the Detroit Chapter of the National Lawyers Guild.[34] The former added little to the argument, devoting separate sections of its brief to public policy, the "state action" theory, and the United Nations Charter. Although most organizations filing *amici curiae* briefs describe themselves, the Wolverine Bar Association did not explain either its membership, history, or purpose. The brief of the Lawyers Guild was equally lacking in information about itself, but the latter group was well-known as a national union of lawyers which had supported liberal causes for many years.

The Lawyers Guild took a fresh approach to the enforcement of restrictive covenants by asking the Michigan Supreme Court to reëxamine the law on the subject laid down twenty-four years earlier in *Parmalee v. Morris*. Its reasons, which were elaborated at length, were hinged to the developments in gains of civil and political rights for Negroes, social theory, and legal criticism. Times have changed since 1922, it was argued. In the 'twenties it had been thought that restrictive covenants were necessary to keep the race problem from erupting. The Lawyers Guild brief claimed that this notion had been shown erroneous.

> Not only have the events of the past 24 years disproved this, but recent investigations have demonstrated that law itself helps to mould the mores and prejudices of the people. A decision holding such restrictive covenants to be constitutional fortifies and increases existing prejudices by permitting such prejudices to be exercised under the encouragement of legal approval. On the other hand, a decision holding the law unconstitutional would give legal sanction and support to people who do not believe in segregation and discrimination.

Another marked feature of the brief *amicus curiae* entered by the Detroit chapter of the National Lawyers Guild was the suggestion that the court look upon the widespread and organized increase in the use of restrictive covenants as a public problem rather than a private one. It lashed out at the groups which it believed had perpetuated the covenants among an unwilling population, and argued that action by these associations creating a segregated pattern in American cities was quasi-public and not isolated individual action. It summed up the evils of such action as follows:

> During recent years, real estate interests and property associations have sprung up at an amazing rate in the larger cities for the avowed purpose of "protecting" the interests of the white residents. These associations and organized groups have increasingly adopted the restrictive covenant as an effective and legal technique for accomplishing their objective. The result has been that Negroes are effectively barred from any normal or natural residential expansion, and are relegated to slum areas. The resentment on the part of Negroes toward such injustice and the concomitant fears engendered by these associations in the white neighborhoods, have been major factors in making it possible for race riots to occur.

An analogy was then drawn between the organized action of these associations and the discrimination against Negroes by a trade union or a political party, both being groups which the Supreme Court of the United States had found to be sufficiently public in nature to fall under the ban of the prohibitions against discrimination in the Fourteenth and Fifteenth amendments.[35] In conclusion the Lawyers Guild expressed its theory in the following words:

> For the courts to permit private organizations to practice a form of racial discrimination which is contrary to public policy and which would be prohibited if committed directly by the state, is an evasion of constitutional guarantees. It is the substance and not the form to which this Court should look in determining whether to issue an injunction or not. A court of equity should not close its eyes to the fact that associations which seek to establish a pattern of race segregation in America through the device of the restrictive covenant are attempting to circumvent the Constitution.

The *amicus* brief entered by the American Jewish Congress, Detroit section, was straight-forward in designating its brief as "dealing with the broad social, ethical and constitutional issues, rather than any narrow legal principles." [36] However, the brief did not restrict itself to the broader issues because of any weakness in the legal position. It was "rather because courts, lawyers and litigants have tended to forget the basic principles, while losing themselves in a maze of legalisms and technicalities."

The first point made by the Jewish Congress was the unequivocal claim that racial restrictive covenants were contrary to "every moral and ethical principle." Public denunciation of restrictive covenants by civic leaders and officials in a variety of groups in the Detroit area were skillfully massed to support this general statement. Catholic and Protestant church groups, the mayor's interracial committee, and housing authorities were quoted to show the large disapproval of covenants that existed in Detroit.

The second point in the brief, the familiar one that racial restrictions in housing "create overcrowding, poverty, disease, delinquency, crime, tensions and other social evils," was supported by more documentary evidence than was supplied in any of the other briefs filed in this case. Urging that the court not be "blind, deaf, dumb or heartless" the Jewish Congress asked that as this was a suit in equity, the facts should not be looked at "in a narrow manner, but in a large way, so that the essential truth may be known and acted upon." Statistics were given which showed that Negroes were in fact segregated in Detroit, and that they occupied a large proportion of the substandard housing in the city. In this colored area, deaths from all causes were more numerous, more people were on relief, more crimes were committed and juvenile delinquency was many times greater than in other parts of Detroit. The brief of the American Jewish Congress, Detroit chapter, asked: eliminate covenants so that fuller freedom will be opened for colored persons.

> His white neighbor, even an immigrant, may readily look forward to moving to better areas, more wholesome areas for himself and his children. The Negro, being marked indelibly by his skin, must stay where permitted to live, subject to crime, delinquency, disease and ill-health. *One answer is to permit him access to modest sanitary surroundings by the removal of restrictive racial housing covenants.*

Briefs for Appellees

Having gained an injunction from the Wayne County Circuit Court to have the McGhees ordered from their home, Sipes and his neighbors had nothing more to ask of the Michigan Supreme Court than that the decree be affirmed. The appellees' brief therefore was short and constituted little more than an answer to the appellants' contentions.[37] In the end it concluded that the action of the lower court enforcing the restrictive agreements was valid since "every court of last resort in the United States, to which this question has ever been submitted, has upheld the validity of racial restrictions against occupancy." The appellees mocked the claim of the Negroes that the action enforcing the covenants was contrary to the constitutions and public policy of both Michigan and the United States. For, they said, if this be true, "it is passing strange that the only decisions they can find to support their contentions, are one by the Supreme Court of Ontario, Canada, and one by the Superior Court of Orange County, California."

In the brief for the appellees we come for the first time to the Caucasians' answer to the increasingly emphasized claim that the judicial enforcement of a racial restrictive covenant is state action under the Fourteenth Amendment, and is consequently invalid. The appellees first phrased the argument "that the court, as an arm of the State, has no power to do that which the State itself may not do by virtue of its sovereignty." With the comment that "superficially this may sound reasonable, but a little thought will demonstrate its fallacy," the appellees launched into their analysis. They pointed out that the Negroes had admitted the validity of the restriction as a purely private agreement, but had balked at the enforcement of it by a court.

> Our whole economic and moral structure rests on the sanctity and enforceability of valid contracts. To say that a contract is valid between the parties, but cannot be enforced by the court because of a constitutional provision, which applies only to State action, is sophistry of the lowest order.
>
> The fundamental difference between State action through the legislature and State action through the civil courts is that, in the former the citizen is compelled to do or refrain from doing with-

out his personal consent, whereas in the latter case he is required to do or refrain from doing only that which he has personally and voluntarily undertaken.

Here a contract had been signed by all property owners in the neighborhood. It provided that none would allow a Negro to live in any place in the specified area. Since this was a valid contract the appellees argued that it could be enforced, even though it was granted that the state could not pass a law restricting a neighborhood in this way.

After the deluge of opposing briefs arrived, the appellees expanded their discussion of the "state action" theory in an answering brief.[38] They observed that all *amici curiae* briefs had argued that enforcement of a racial restriction by a court was state action prohibited by the Fourteenth Amendment. But they noted that "Professor McGovney's is the most elaborate presentation of that thesis" and proceeded to answer him. Reciting the Fourteenth Amendment, they found its language to be "clear and unambiguous" and stated that it was beyond their powers of perception to see how it could be "interpreted or construed to prohibit a court from enforcing a contract which a party has voluntarily assumed and the validity of which is not questioned."

> This Amendment does not say that "no State shall make or enforce any contract * * *," yet that is the result reached by the Professor. We believe that the underlying error which pervades the whole argument is that the Professor overlooks or ignores the fundamental difference between enforcing a law and enforcing a contract. He starts with the premise, "The test should be * * * whether a state statute embodying the same rule would be violative of the Equal Protective Clause." This is obviously false. The obligations imposed on parties by their own contracts would, if imposed upon them by statute, be clearly unconstitutional in the vast majority of cases. No court would enforce a statute requiring A to sell his house to B, yet the courts without question enforce A's contract to sell his house to B.
>
> When the court enforces a law, whether it be legislative law, judge-made law or common law, the effect is to control the actions of the individual without regard to his personal consent. But when a court enforces a contract, the indispensable prerequisite is the individual's voluntary agreement, either expressed or implied, to do that which the court decrees he shall do.

But the appellees felt they had more than logic on their side; they pointed to the fact that no court of the last resort in the United States had ever held that the enforcement of a valid contract was state action prohibited by the Constitution.

The appellees asserted that the Supreme Court's action in *Corrigan v. Buckley,* had been the subject of some "deliberate misrepresentation." Attorneys for Negroes had long claimed that the constitutionality of state court enforcement of restrictive covenants had not been settled because the *Corrigan* case had arisen in the District of Columbia which was solely under federal jurisdiction. The appellees noted that the United States Supreme Court had itself based its decision not only on the Fifth Amendment but also on the Thirteenth and Fourteenth. Therefore the brief claimed that "the Corrigan case is a clear-cut, unequivocal decision that racial restrictions do not violate the United States Constitution, notwithstanding the claims of all opposing briefs to the contrary." It suggested that the Michigan court should merely read the *Corrigan* case rather than read "reams of arguments." But the counsel for the appellees could not resist one last swipe at their main opponent in this matter:

> We only wish to observe that anyone who can garble and misread an opinion as clear as that in the Corrigan case, as Professor McGovney does, can hardly be trusted either as to his judgment or his intellectual integrity.

The appellees also derided the opposing briefs' reliance on social and economic data, and said such material was quite beside the point in the case under consideration.

> The briefs *amicus curiae* are addressed principally to the sociological problems of the negro and are based on alleged facts, consisting of statistics, mostly prepared by protagonists of the intermixture of the races.
>
> These sociological problems were not raised in the court below, the reasons and grounds of appeal make no mention of them and the alleged facts (statistics) were not offered in evidence. In short, these matters are not properly before this court.

New precedents had appeared since the filing of its first brief. *Mays v. Burgess,*[39] in particular, was added, and the court was referred to the recent *American Law Report's* annotation [40] for the still growing list of precedents which favored the position of the white property owners in these cases.

Taking final issue with the briefs *amici curiae* supporting the claims of the McGhees and other non-Caucasians, the appellees in their answering brief agreed that human rights were equally important with property rights, but insisted that "white people have rights as well as negroes." And among these rights, continued the counsel for the appellees, is the one "to live and rear their families in white neighborhoods, and the right not to be driven from their homes." These rights could only be protected through the operation of racial restrictive covenants because otherwise Negroes might move into a white area. As soon as an entering wedge was made, little could be done to stop the area from going black.

> Regardless of theory and claims made for intermixture of the races, all past experience proves that when negroes begin to move into a neighborhood the whites are driven out. If the principle of restriction is broken down the practical result will be that negroes can take over any section of the city into which they choose to move.

Since the white people were there first it seemed to the appellees that their established rights should take precedence over the rights of Negroes who came later and purchased property with "full knowledge of the situation and a deliberate intent to violate the contractual obligations they assume when they accept deeds subject to the restrictions."

Briefs for The Property-Owners' Associations

The Supreme Court of Michigan received only one brief *amicus curiae* aiding the appellees in the case of *Sipes v. McGhee*, but that single document represented the interests of twenty-six organizations.[41] All were property owners' associations from the section of Detroit surrounding the neighborhood of the principal case. The brief filed by these groups described the area as embracing a population of 800,000 inhabitants, "made attractive to the home owner because of a plan or pattern of development in which building restrictions, so-called, controlling use and occupancy, have been the constant guide." The court was urged to prevent a violation in this case and all other cases, for it should realize that if violation of racial restrictions were permitted, dire results would follow.

> Soon the general character of the entire area will change and those who have acquired their homes in reliance upon use and occupancy restrictions will be forced to seek other locations and will suffer irreparable, economic loss. The long range character of the home establishment controlled by use and occupancy restrictions will have ended. We feel certain that the court will not lightly consider the rights of so vast a number of residents who have attempted through constant vigilance to protect their homes.

The economic basis of the interest of these property-owners' associations, indicated by their concern over property values, appeared to be no more important than their wish to maintain homogeneous and socially stable neighborhoods. The home, they said, is the foundation stone of American society. In harmony with this universal truth was the home-owner's consideration of environment for his family. Numerous families in Detroit had counted upon racial restrictive covenants to assure the maintenance of congenial and harmonious communities.

> Certainly, the average family unit acquiring a residential property in an area so restricted gives great consideration to the long range character of home ownership in order that the home may have stability at least as to time, and children of the home may grow up and mature in a neighborhood or surrounding similar to that existing at the time the residential property was acquired.

The Michigan Supreme Court should again acknowledge the importance of segregated housing, pleaded the property-owners' associations, by enforcing the restrictive agreement in this case.

The great freedom of choosing one's own surroundings and maintaining them, said the *amicus curiae* brief of the twenty-six groups, had been embedded in the law of the land as the right of contract. This was called "the greatest right which a free member of a free society possesses." Property has long been subject to planning and control by private contract and these contracts were very properly valid in law.

The property-owners' associations reminded the court that the right of free contracts had created a free country for Negroes as well as white people. Restrictive covenants represented this right of contract; they did not discriminate against Negroes. If freedom of contract, the linchpin holding society together, was taken away, everyone would be the loser.

> This free right to contract has been exercised by an overwhelming majority of the owners of homes in a subdivision area entirely white, which the negro now seeks to destroy. If the argument of the negro is to be considered, then it would appear that in order to exist as a free member of a free society, he must destroy the freedom of contract of other members of the same free society. This obviously cannot be the case, and consequently, those of the Caucasian race who have exercised their free right to contract work no discrimination upon the Negro.

Pointing out that the opinion in *Parmalee v. Morris* [42] had settled the questions of the enforcement of racial restrictions on use and occupancy in Michigan, and was the correct expression of the law on the subject, the property-owners' brief quoted it in full lest the Supreme Court overlook the decision.[43] This *amicus curiae* brief also answered the claim that the enforcement of racial restrictive covenants by a court of equity constituted state action in violation of the Fourteenth Amendment. It quoted at length from the discussion of that amendment in a well-known summary of precedents, *Ruling Case Law*.[44] The argument there was the familiar one that the Fourteenth Amendment was intended to secure the civil rights of Negroes against the acts of the states. It was not designed as a protection against the acts of persons. Consequently, the argument continued, racial restrictive covenants were valid as the voluntary contractual acts of individuals.

The Michigan Supreme Court Enforces a Covenant

The eight judges then constituting Michigan's Supreme Court unanimously affirmed the judgment of the Wayne County Court.[45] The court first accepted the facts as found by the Wayne County Court and insisted upon by the appellees. The testimony of Sipes was found to be sufficient to sustain the finding that the McGhees

were not of the Caucasian race. The Supreme Court ruled that
the signatures to the agreement were authentic, asserting that under state policy courts will uphold acknowledgments "wherever
possible" and will not let them be defeated by "technical or un-
substantial objections." The trial court's holding that the terms
of the covenant were not uncertain was also affirmed with the
remark that it was "difficult to see how language could be more
certain than that employed." This indicated that the popular
meaning of racial descriptions was acceptable to the Supreme
Court of Michigan.

Justice George E. Bushnell, who wrote the opinion for the
court, credited the several *amici curiae* briefs as containing "valuable material with respect to the related social and economic
problems." He was impressed with the rapidity with which the
Negro population of Detroit had increased until it amounted to
12 per cent of the total in 1944. But he was not sure that this
should affect the court's position in this case.

> The arguments based on the factual statement pertaining to
> questions of public health, safety and delinquency are strong and
> convincing. However, we must confine our decision to the matters
> within the record submitted to us and questions raised in the
> briefs of the parties to the cause.

Much the same view was taken toward the declarations of the
Atlantic Charter and the United Nations which the Negroes and
their friends said had made the device of restrictive covenants
against minority groups a matter of public concern rather than
private contracts. Justice Bushnell stated for the court:

> We do not understand it to be a principle of law that a treaty
> between sovereign nations is applicable to the contractual rights
> between citizens of the United States when a determination of
> these rights is sought in State courts. So far as the instant case
> is concerned, these pronouncements are merely indicative of a
> desirable social trend and an objective devoutly to be desired by
> all well-thinking peoples.

But these high ideals, though desirable, were not to be taken
seriously in practice. "These arguments are predicated upon a
plea for justice," explained Justice Bushnell, "rather than the

application of the settled principles of established law." Thus the Michigan Court found its first obligation was to support traditional ways.

This commitment of the Supreme Court of Michigan to the support of legal precedent was displayed in its consideration of all other arguments made against the enforcement of racial restrictions. The prohibitions of the Fourteenth Amendment were not applicable against these private contracts. To accept the reasoning that the enforcement of the restrictive agreement in this case would deprive the defendants of constitutional rights, said Justice Bushnell, "would also at the same time deny 'the equal protection of the laws' to the plaintiffs and prevent the enforcement of their private contracts." It was held, therefore, that the action of a state court in enforcing these private contractual rights was not within the prohibitions of the Fourteenth Amendment.

> To hold otherwise would be to nullify many statutory enactments and overrule countless adjudicated cases. The unsettling effect of such a determination by this Court, without prior legislative action or a specific Federal mandate, would be, in our judgment, improper.

The main precedent applicable to this case, held the Court, was *Parmalee v. Morris,* where a similar restriction against the use or occupancy of property by colored people was enforced. Restrictions against the sale of property had been held invalid because of the applicability of the principle of free alienation. But here there was no question of ownership. It was merely a matter of use or occupancy, to which the ban against limitations on free alienation did not apply. Justice Bushnell considered the restriction enforceable and continued that "rules of property, which have existed during most of the life of the State, should not be brushed aside in the absence of strong and cogent reasons." The decree entered by the trial court was affirmed.

VII

Cases to Choose From

The continuing failure of Negroes to convert a major appellate court to their viewpoint in a racial covenant case made it urgent for them to reach the Supreme Court of the United States. While this was their underlying hope, caution was necessary lest the opportunity of obtaining not only a hearing, but also a favorable decision would be lost. On January 26, 1947, this problem was met at a conference of Negro leaders at Howard University in Washington.[1] Because the Supreme Court had refused certiorari in *Mays v. Burgess* [2] only two years earlier, William Hastie, who was still governor of the Virgin Islands, agreed with Thurgood Marshall that if another failure was to be avoided, "the next record on which we apply for certiorari would have to contain something substantially stronger." [3] All eighteen persons present subscribed to the sensible plan of seeking the best possible case in which to apply for certiorari.[4]

Loring Moore, who had been on the *amicus* brief of the National Bar Association in the *McGhee* case before the Michigan Court, told the conference the basic components of a case he was working on in Chicago.[5] From this he presented an analysis of the ideal record to build for presentation to the United States Supreme Court.[6]

1) Testimony of an economist on the effects of covenants upon availability of housing;
2) Testimony of a sociologist as to the effect of overcrowded

            slum conditions and black ghettos upon both the victims of
discrimination and their fellow citizens;

3) Introduction of a map of racial occupancy in the community;
4) Superimposed upon [this map] . . . a map of the restrictive
covenants indicating the extensiveness of the restrictions;
5) Thereafter, further testimony by a sociologist as to the effect
of the type of restriction proved by the two maps upon housing
conditions;
6) Evidence as to the fact that thirty (30) or more other restrictive covenant cases are pending in the community to show
that the effect of enforcement would be extensive private
zoning in the areas.

Actually, Moore's ideal was a mustering of the standard approaches used by intelligent lawyers in all parts of the country.
Charles Houston had amply illuminated the total effects of racial
restrictions in the Washington cases. And sociological factors had
by no means been neglected by George Vaughn in St. Louis, or
Graves and Dent in Detroit. When their cases reached the appellate court, the social and economic implications of residential
restrictions on Negroes had been stressed even more. The pattern
found in these cases was the same elsewhere.

A case in the Court of Appeals for Franklin County, Ohio,[7]
raised the novel question of whether a church corporation in
Columbus, whose congregation was largely composed of Negroes,
could be enjoined from allowing its Negro pastor to live in a
house on the restricted property which it owned. The deed
covenant provided that the property not be sold to or used by
non-Caucasians. Ownership of the property by the church was
allowed on the theory that as a corporation it was separate and
distinct from its shareholders and therefore was without racial
identity. At the same time, the court granted an injunction to
prevent the colored minister or any other Negro from occupying
the premises. The case, decided October 30, 1946, stimulated a
great deal of interest. The Eastwood Civic Association of Columbus, "and others," filed an *amicus curiae* brief urging enforcement
of the restriction. Briefs supporting the Negro position were
entered by the American Civil Liberties Union, with Arthur Garfield Hays and Osmond K. Fraenkel among the attorneys; an

individual, Edward B. Paxton; and the Columbus Council for Democracy. That the Franklin County Court of Appeals felt and resented the pressure represented by the briefs filed on behalf of the church and its Negro clergyman cannot be doubted from this passage in its opinion.

> We well recognize that vociferous minorities of our citizens, instigated by politicians not statesmen, clamor for judicial denial of public rights under the guise of public welfare which is to say public policy. However, the courts ought to be and are ever mindful of that basic thought which underlies representative democracy: "Give all power to the many and they will oppress the few, give all power to the few and they oppress the many, so that each should retain within themselves the power for their own self-preservation." That reservoir of protection is to be found in our guaranty of constitutional rights, for example, the right to private contract, and in the hesitancy of the courts to be swayed by that which is seemingly popular for a moment but which finds little or no sound reason or precedent, either in law or equity.

The appeal to the Supreme Court of Ohio was dismissed on March 5, 1947, but preparations were made to carry the case to the United States Supreme Court.

Rapid population growth in Los Angeles caused Caucasians to enforce racial segregation by restrictive covenants as they were commonly doing elsewhere. Loren Miller conducted the legal defense of Negroes in numerous cases.[8] Although not blessed with success, the tendencies as far as the Negroes were concerned pointed in the right direction. In the last restrictive-covenant decision of the California Supreme Court, *Fairchild v. Raines*[9] decided in 1944, the Negroes had found one voice of sympathy in Justice Roger Traynor, who wrote a sharp dissenting opinion. Another heartening development for Negroes came in September, 1946, when the attorney general of California filed a brief as *amicus curiae* in eight companion cases then pending before the state supreme court.[10] Robert W. Kenny, sometime president of the National Lawyers Guild, was the state's attorney general at this time. His "special advisor" on this brief was Professor D. O. McGovney, whose law-review article of the previous year had given impetus to the movement to end court enforcement of racial covenants. In a foreword to the brief, the attorney general made a sharp-edged rationale of the position he was taking for the state.[11]

> Although these actions are entitled as though they were between private litigants this is not really the fact. Whole sections of the population are to be affected by the outcome of this litigation. Some persons of one race seek to fence in all persons of another race and by agreement among themselves have attempted to fix the bounds of the habitations of that other race.
>
> But this is not all. Some of the parties to the agreement, either because of avarice or change of heart, have failed and refused to live up to their agreement. The other parties to the agreement now call into play all of the machinery of the State for the purpose of giving effect to this agreement.
>
> The State as a whole is interested in this matter. The aid of the Courts, nisi prius and appellate, has been sought; its clerks, sheriffs and constables have been called to issue and serve writs which issue in the name of the People of the State of California; ultimately (if the hopes of plaintiffs and appellants are realized) even the jails of the State may be called upon to play a part in these actions.
>
> Under such circumstances we do not feel that the legal arm of the State should remain inactive.
>
> When the State is called upon to take State action in its own name against a large segment of its law-abiding citizens the law officers of the State should be heard.

Further evidence of the nation-wide agitation against legal enforcement of restrictive covenants came in New York in the case of *Kemp v. Rubin*,[12] decided on February 11, 1947, by the Supreme Court of Queens County. The participation of interest groups in the litigation was greeted enthusiastically by Judge Livingston who prefaced consideration of the issues in his opinion with this generous remark: [13]

> The court wishes to express its deep gratitude to counsel for plaintiffs, defendants, and the various organizations which have intervened in this action as *amicus curiae*, for their able and enlightening arguments and for their scholarly briefs.

The record in *Kemp v. Rubin* identified the real plaintiffs as the Addisleigh Park Improvement Association. Lawyers for the

Negro defendants were Andrew D. Weinberger and Vertner W. Tandy, Jr. Will Maslow filed an *amicus curiae* brief for the American Jewish Congress and the American Civil Liberties Union; and Marian Wynn Perry, an employee of the NAACP at that time, for the City Wide Citizens Committee on Harlem. *Amici curiae* briefs were also submitted for the New York State and Greater New York Industrial Union Council, C.I.O., the Social Action Committee of New York City Congregational Church Association, and the Methodist Federation for Social Service. Although Judge Livingston asserted his personal agreement with Justice Murphy that "distinctions based on color and ancestry are utterly inconsistent with our traditions and ideals," [14] he ruled that "regardless of what its sentiments may be, this court is constrained to follow precedent and govern itself in accordance with what it considers to be the prevailing law." [15] The covenant was enforced.

To the Negro leadership the accumulating defeats in Washington, St. Louis, Detroit, Columbus, Los Angeles, New York, and other cities [16] might well have made their cause seem hopeless. The Caucasian fortifications were greatly strengthened by the addition of these fresh precedents from the postwar years. On the other hand, hindsight shows that nothing new had been added to the law that already favored the enforcement of restrictive covenants, while the increased litigation created greater opportunity for the Negroes to press the Supreme Court of the United States into reviewing the problem.

Certiorari: The Crucial Writ

Under the Judiciary Act of 1925 [17] the Supreme Court was given almost complete discretionary control of its appellate business, through grant or denial of the writ of certiorari. The statute settled the modern principle that the Supreme Court's function was, "not to see justice done in every case, but to decide the more important policy issues presented within the frame of a 'case' or 'controversy,' concerning the federal balance, the relations of the branches of the federal government, or the fundamental rights of the individual in relation to government." [18]

Lawyers have not always understood the meaning of the

Supreme Court rule that "a review on writ of certiorari is not a matter of right but of sound judicial discretion and will be granted only where there are special and important reasons therefor.[19] Elaborating upon these reasons, Chief Justice Fred M. Vinson in 1949 told the American Bar Association that "to remain effective, the Supreme Court must continue to decide only those cases which present questions whose resolution will have immediate importance far beyond the particular facts and parties involved."[20] His view was that the Court could best fulfill its unique appellate function by considering representative cases. "What the Court is interested in is the actual, practical effect of the disputed decision—its consequences for other litigants and in other situations." Thus practitioners have been advised that petitions for certiorari "must disclose not only the technical basis of the Supreme Court's jurisdiction to review, *but why the party claims that power should be exercised in this case.*"[21]

The Supreme Court had been petitioned repeatedly to review decisions upholding the judicial enforcement of racial restrictive covenants. After *Corrigan v. Buckley,*[22] the court refused to grant a writ of certiorari in 1929 in two cases from the District of Columbia.[23] In 1937 a petition to grant the writ in a District case was again rejected.[24] From the states, certiorari was granted in *Hansberry v. Lee,*[25] but the Supreme Court declined to rule on the constitutional and public-policy issues and restricted itself to the question of fraud in the acknowledgments to the covenant.

In 1945, an order denying the Negroes' petition for a writ of certiorari in *Mays v. Burgess* revealed disagreement within the Supreme Court, for it told that "Mr. Justice Murphy and Mr. Justice Rutledge are of the opinion that certiorari should be granted."[26] This indication that two justices favored review of the decision of the Court of Appeals had a special significance because of the development of the so-called "rule of four," under which the Supreme Court takes cases under consideration when four Justices favor granting certiorari.[27] Thus the dissents from the denial of certiorari in *Mays v. Burgess* signified that only two more votes would be needed in any later petition for the review of a restrictive-covenant decision.

This was a hopeful consideration at the conference meeting at

Howard University in February, 1947, and yet it was felt important "not to build up a record of many applications for certiorari denied." [28] The conference was uncertain which cases would be best to carry to the Supreme Court.

Willis Graves and Francis Dent urged that their case in Detroit would be a suitable test. But the conference felt that additional cases should be allowed to develop before applying for certiorari in any single one. However, all agreed that once other cases in Michigan and elsewhere were decided the group would "meet once more and discuss any other decisions which have come down in the meantime to determine what action we will take." [29]

Before another meeting of NAACP lawyers was held, George Vaughn took unilateral action by filing a petition for certiorari with the Supreme Court of the United States in *Shelley v. Kraemer,* on April 21, 1947. This provoked NAACP leaders in New York into taking quick action, and on May 10 a petition was also filed for *McGhee v. Sipes.* This was a critical period of waiting. On May 26, the Court of Appeals for the District of Columbia announced its adverse decision in *Hurd v. Hodge* and *Urciolo v. Hodge* so that Judge Edgerton's dissent may have been known to the Supreme Court, which was considering the petition in the state cases. In any event, on the last Monday of the term, June 23, 1947, the Supreme Court granted petitions for writs of certiorari to the Supreme Courts of Missouri [30] and Michigan.[31]

The Supreme Court was in recess during the summer until its new term opened on the first Monday of October. This allowed ample time for the filing of petitions for certiorari in the *Hodge* cases. The petitions in the two District of Columbia cases were filed with the Supreme Court on August 22. It was assumed that the writs of certiorari would be granted, and so immediately the attorneys began preparing the briefs on the merits. This assumption was correct; the Supreme Court granted certiorari in both cases on October 20.[32]

Earlier denials of certiorari in cases from the District of Columbia may have concealed a willingness of some justices to review a racial restrictive covenant case. This could have been true if they believed that the best basis of decision would be the equal-protection clause of the Fourteenth Amendment as this would require a state case. This limitation did not cover federal action because the Bill of Rights, which did apply, lacked an equal-protection requirement.

The deliberateness by which the Supreme Court agreed to review the judicial enforcement of racial covenants is seen in its choice to hear two state and two federal cases. During the summer (June 26) a petition for certiorari was received in the Columbus, Ohio case,[33] and early in the autumn (November 6) petitions came to the Court to review two Los Angeles cases.[34] Those cases raised peripheral issues of church-state relations and the rights of aliens, and one may speculate that, since these were irrelevant to the constitutional questions raised by judicial enforcement of racial covenants, the Court did not wish to hear them. In any event, the Supreme Court took no action on these petitions preferring instead to consider the question by limiting itself to four cases. Therefore the District of Columbia cases were set down for argument immediately following the Missouri and Michigan cases. This conscious planning by the Supreme Court may be assumed from this statement by Chief Justice Vinson: [35]

> Those of you whose petitions for certiorari are granted by the Supreme Court will know . . . that you are, in a sense, prosecuting or defending class actions; that you represent not only your clients, but tremendously important principles, upon which are based the plans, hopes and aspirations of a great many people throughout the country.

Managing the Test Cases

Consolidation of the four restrictive-covenant cases by the Supreme Court did not produce perfect coördination in brief-writing and oral argument by the attorneys in the different cases. A coöperative spirit was established, but in each city—Detroit, Washington, and St. Louis—the lawyers managing the cases planned their work differently. The national office of NAACP, it will be remembered, had entered the Michigan case as *amicus curiae* at the state supreme-court level. Now the Detroit lawyers, Willis Graves and Francis Dent, were willing to allow NAACP to take full responsibility to prepare the brief in the United States Supreme Court. The names of Graves and Dent appeared on the briefs, but Loren Miller of Los Angeles and Thurgood Marshall and the NAACP legal staff in New York did the preparation.[36] Of the four cases, only *McGhee v. Sipes* was an NAACP case in the strict sense.

The burden of work in the Washington cases had been carried by Charles Houston at the trial and first appellate levels. Raphael Urciolo had provided some legal and financial assistance but did not wish to carry the responsibility of preparing briefs for the Supreme Court. Spottswood Robinson, III, the Negro attorney from Richmond, Virginia, did some work on the brief. But Houston's chief help came from Phineas Indritz, a white attorney in Washington whose interest had been aroused by reading the dissenting opinions of Judge Edgerton. Indritz believed strongly that a "full sociological presentation" should be made in the Supreme Court.[37]

> Houston and I feel that the brief should be accompanied by a separate appendix reprinting all the major articles, or excerpts, dealing with the effects of these covenants. Although the Justices might have the library to send them the articles and books to which we make reference, there would be greater likelihood of their reading the references if we place such a compilation before them.

In order to prepare a brief of this character, a group of lawyers, sociologists, and economists were organized to coöperate with Houston and Indritz. When a draft of the brief was prepared it was mimeographed through the courtesy of Robert C. Weaver in the office of the American Council on Race Relations in Chicago and then circulated to about fifty lawyers. Comments on the returns were invaluable to Houston and Indritz in preparing the final brief.

Preparations of *Shelley v. Kraemer* for the Supreme Court were also largely separate from the NAACP in New York. The St. Louis Real Estate Brokers Association had borne the main expense of prosecuting the case. This local sponsorship was insufficient and there arose some difficulty with the NAACP in New York over financial assistance. There also were some differences over legal strategy. George Vaughn was an able and successful municipal-court lawyer but his experience in appellate practice was limited. Vaughn was not versed in the newer style of sociological argument. On the constitutional question, quite differently than

the attorneys in the other cases, Vaughn believed that the slavery
provisions of the Thirteenth Amendment gave the Negroes a
defense equal in merit to the equal-protection clause of the Fourteenth Amendment. This view was not shared by any of the
attorneys in the other cases. However, Thurgood Marshall was
in communication with Vaughn so that the resources of the
NAACP were made available. In preparing the final brief Vaughn
received the help of Herman Willer, a white attorney in St. Louis,
and Willer later joined Vaughn in oral argument before the
Supreme Court.

Amassing the Facts

If the Negroes were to win the restrictive-covenant cases they
had carried to the Supreme Court in the 1947 term they would
have to rely heavily on nonjudicial material. The precedents
seemed to favor the Caucasians overwhelmingly. To offset this
advantage the Negroes would try to persuade the court that
judicial enforcement of covenants was state action which violated
the Fourteenth Amendment, as Professor McGovney had suggested.[38] They would also point to the social results of the practice of enforcement. But reasoning by itself is not enough, nor
are raw statistics considered to be sufficient for presentation in
legal briefs. Citations of articles and books where the facts and
ideas had been published would surely make a better appeal to
the learned justices. At least this was the theory of the lawyers
working on these cases. In order to meet this and other problems,
Thurgood Marshall sent out a call for another NAACP conference for the fall of 1947: [39]

> In order that we may present every issue as clearly as pos-
> sible, and cover all conceivable arguments which might be pre-
> sented to the court, we are calling a conference of lawyers who
> have worked on these cases with us and lawyers for various organ-
> izations interested in the problem. . . . We particularly urge
> that attorneys come to this meeting after having given consider-
> able thought to the manner in which they believe that the issues
> should be presented to the Supreme Court. Prior to the date of
> the meeting, we will also send to you an outline of the material
> in the record in the two cases and any other written material

which we have which will be helpful in preparing for discussion on these cases.

Forty-four persons attended the all-day conference in New York on September 6.[40]

The first round of discussion at the conference centered on the twin problem of preparing sociological material and getting it published so that it could be used in briefs to be presented to the Supreme Court. Phineas Indritz suggested that the maps should be "published by a reputable magazine."[41] Charles Houston urged that "evidence and data which is not already in the record should be published and put in some acceptable form." Marian Wynn Perry of the New York office of the NAACP commented: "Among the organizations here represented there must be a great many publications. We should get our joint public relations committees together and tell them that we want it published in the best kind of space available in the October issues." Harold Kahen believed that "the sociologists should gather the material and get it published in some journals and then supply it to a group of lawyers."

The NAACP had already published some material. It had sponsored a pamphlet, *Race Bias in Housing* by Charles Abrams, together with the American Council on Race Relations and the American Civil Liberties Union.[42] Abrams had also attacked covenants in the monthly magazine, *Commentary*,[43] published by the American Jewish Committee. These blasts served the purpose of bringing the evils of racial restrictive covenants to the attention of the public. The object of future publication would be to gain new sources which might be cited in the briefs to be filed with the Supreme Court.

However, the publications on the housing problem did not by any means all stem from NAACP efforts. A large number of independently written short articles came out at this time.[44] Full-length articles were published in *The Annals, Yale Law Journal, University of Chicago Law Review, National Bar Journal, Architectural Forum, National Lawyers Guild Review, Journal of Land and Public Utility Economics,* and *Survey Graphic.*[45]

So much independent work had been done in assembling sociological material that the leaders of the movement to end restrictive covenants hoped to coördinate work by appointing a committee to handle the problem. Dr. Louis Wirth of the University of Chicago, who was not present at the meeting, was made chairman. Others agreeing to serve on the committee were Loring Moore, Robert Ming, Harold Kahen, Byron Miller, and Dr. Robert Weaver, all of Chicago; Ruth Weyand of Washington; James T. Bush of St. Louis; and Annette Peyser of New York.

A bulky memorandum on the social and economic significance of racial covenants was prepared in a matter of weeks by a team of sociologists under the direction of Professor Louis Wirth and Dr. Robert C. Weaver, who were then president and director of community services of the American Council on Race Relations in Chicago. The Council functioned between 1944 and 1950 as a national clearing house whose purposes included "the stimulation of research bearing upon basic factors underlying the problems of racial and cultural relations, the perfection of sound policies and techniques, experimentation with methods for evaluating the practical results of programs and procedures, together with persistent efforts to call these findings to the attention of the policy-makers and technicians in the field." Weaver had combined research with administration ever since gaining a doctorate in sociology at Harvard in 1934 for he had served for a decade in labor and housing agencies in Washington and acted as executive director of the Mayor's Committee on Race Relations in Chicago. He had published a book on Negro labor, and numerous articles on Negro housing which he brought together as a book published in 1948 under the title *The Negro Ghetto*.[46] In the preface of that book, Weaver has explained how the nonlegal material was put together for the briefs in the covenant cases.

> After the manuscript had been completed, the American Council on Race Relations undertook to prepare a memorandum on the economic and social aspects of race restrictive covenants for use of lawyers engaged in litigation on such covenants then before the Supreme Court. The author of this book was assigned principal responsibility for the project, and he drew heavily upon the manuscript he had completed. At the same time, preparation of the memorandum revealed additional materials, principally those in graduate theses in the Department of Sociology of the University of Chicago and in a forthcoming study of the Chicago Census Advisory Committee. Dr. Louis Wirth made these materials available

and, in editing and supervising the preparation of the memorandum, offered valuable criticisms. This study, no less than the memorandum, benefited from Dr. Wirth's suggestions.

The memorandum of several hundred pages which resulted from this work was mimeographed and circulated to the lawyers who were preparing the briefs. Some brief-writers used parts of the material whole, some refined it through revision and adaptation and others ignored it. This was the first time that such a substantial amount of factual data was presented to the Supreme Court in civil rights cases.

NAACP's "Friends of the Court"

With plans made to prepare sociological data for use in the briefs, the NAACP conference of September 6, 1947, turned to the question of *amici curiae* briefs.[47] Charles Houston took a poll of the organizational representatives in attendance and found that fourteen planned to file briefs as friends of the court. These were: the American Jewish Congress, American Jewish Committee, Protestant Council of New York City, Japanese American Citizens' League, National Bar Association, Anti-Defamation League, American Civil Liberties Union, Negro Elks, Congress of Industrial Organizations (CIO), Anti-Nazi League, Board of Home Missions of the Congregational Church, National Lawyers Guild, American Indian Association, and the American Indian Council.

Leaders of the NAACP were no doubt gratified to have so much support offered in carrying the fight to the Supreme Court, but they had the practical problem of winning the cases and feared that a show of force without careful planning might be disastrous. Governor Hastie made this warning:

> The question of who shall file *amici* briefs needs some coordination. We will get a large group of *amici* briefs saying the same thing and some of them will be good and others will be poor which will not do very much for the cases. Suggested there should be an *amici* brief committee.

Phineas Indritz was quick to agree.

> We should strive not to flood the court with too many briefs. Suggested that a limited number be filed and that other interested

organizations should merely indicate that they concur in everything that has been said by the organizations filing these briefs.
Should ask the five lawyers, Graves and Dent, Vaughn, Ransom
and Houston to decide how we are going to present these *amici*
briefs.

A representative of the nonsectarian Anti-Nazi League to Champion Human Rights, Irving Brand, put the dilemma in a nutshell
when he remarked that "too many friends are sometimes just as
bad as too many enemies." The motion was seconded by Harold
Kahen who urged that a committee be established to take up
"the task of convincing some of the organizations that what they
have has already been said and that they should merely sign the
brief as concurring." He also suggested that the organizations
that did file briefs should outline the theme they were going to
follow.

Although the minutes of the New York meeting show that
consensus was reached on limiting the number of briefs and coördinating their content, little was done afterward to insure this.
The following rule governed the filing of *amici curiae* briefs in
the Supreme Court: [48]

> A brief of an *amicus curiae* may be filed when accompanied by
> written consent of all parties to a case, except that consent need
> not be had when the brief is presented by the United States or
> an officer or agency thereof sponsored by the Solicitor General,
> or by a state or a political subdivision.

None of the lawyers managing the cases for the Negroes thought
of using their power of refusal to limit the number of *amici curiae*
briefs filed to support their position. Consent was freely given to
all who wished to prepare briefs. Likewise the lawyers for the
white property owners gave their permission to all organizations
against them.[49]

The NAACP did not wish to alienate any of the groups so
eager to provide assistance but some gentle hints were made to
gain limited coördination. Thus when Thurgood Marshall granted
consent to file a brief *amicus curiae* to William Strong of the
American Indian Citizens League of California he included these
suggestions: [50]

I believe that it would be very helpful if you would check with Mr. Loren Miller, of your city [Los Angeles], who will join in arguing this case before the Supreme Court, so that you will be familiar with the points raised and the general discussion which has occurred among the attorneys for various organizations interested in filing briefs amicus. We are particularly anxious, in securing the cooperation of attorneys for organizations who are interested in filing briefs amicus, to eliminate as much as possible the repetition of arguments which are fully presented in other briefs. This does not mean, of course, that we do not want briefs filed but rather that we are hoping that each brief can present a new angle of the case.

So far as is known the NAACP took no other measures to see that the *amici curiae* briefs favoring them were worked up together. Thurgood Marshall and his staff were fully occupied with the preparation of the main brief in the *McGhee* case. Eventually a total of nineteen briefs were filed by friends of the court which argued for the Negro position but except for the fact that those interested could draw from the same published sources and could correspond among themselves for information and ideas these briefs were not coördinated.

As an isolated example of the manner in which one *amicus curiae* brief developed, the experience of the Independent, Benevolent, Protective Order of Elks of the World is instructive. This large Negro fraternal organization's full-time counsel, Perry Howard, a Republican National Committee man from Mississippi, has explained how this came about.[51] George Vaughn came to him and suggested that the Elks file a brief *amicus curiae*. Howard then discussed the matter with the executive board of the Elks and gained consent to file a brief which he and Vaughn had prepared.

Some broad problems of what should be said in a brief and who should say it are illuminated by the New York housing consultant, Charles Abrams, in connection with the *amicus curiae* briefs filed in the covenant cases by two organizations. The American Civil Liberties Union had entered numerous Supreme Court cases and therefore had the experience and know-how to write its own brief, but it sought Abrams's advice and asked him to sign it.[52] In the meantime, Newman Levy of the American

Jewish Committee sought Abrams's comments on the brief Levy was writing for that organization. In November, 1947, Abrams responded with a letter setting forth his ideas on the proper function of the *amicus curiae* brief.[53]

> It is an excellent "main brief" written with your fine straight style. But I question the adequacy of its emphasis as a brief *amici*.
>
> I have always viewed the function of the *amici* to take up and emphasize those points which are novel or which, if stressed in the main brief, might dilute or weaken the main forceful arguments.
>
> I never thought there was much cumulative force in the repetition of logic by eighteen briefs. Unlike good poetry, repeated it has a tendency to bore. But a weak legal argument, with a moral quality, forcefully presented by an "outsider" will not detract from the force of the main argument. If it creates a healthy doubt or insinuates even a slight justification for itself on moral grounds, it may bend the judge toward adopting the law advocated in the main brief.
>
> Novel arguments in a brief *amici* may serve another purpose. Sometimes the court is not ready to adopt the arguments of the main brief. In our case for example it may entail upsetting *Corrigan v. Buckley*. Or it might be loath to annul a contract between private parties or impinge upon the states' rights doctrine.
>
> The *amici* should be providing the arguments that will salvage the judges' consciences or square with their prepossessions should they lean toward holding for us.
>
> The TVA decision [Ashwander v. Tennessee Valley Authority [54]] is a case in point. Upholding TVA as an exercise of the War Power is about as reasonable an analogy as the Laws of Mohammed are to our law of Domestic Relations. But the Court did not then wish to expand the welfare power so drew upon the war power, which surprised everybody.

In conclusion, Abrams suggested that sociological arguments were useful for furnishing the moral background for a judicial holding.

> Play up what entailment of all land would mean socially. Use the relevant references by Gunnar Myrdal; give the British background for exclusion of non-conformists and their migration to America where the freehold and the fee simply became one of our earliest and greatest traditions. Show how Jefferson and the States immediately after Independence adopted laws excluding

primogeniture and entail. Quote from these constitutions and the debates that prompted their enactment. What if covenants in Washington, D.C. become as common as in Chicago and Los Angeles? Will that not bar Negroes, Jews or other Americans from holding office? May people band together to bar a race from food and clothing? These are a few of the important irrelevancies that occur to me.

Why desert all these rich and adventurous passages to jam the safe waters that should be reserved for the main advocates?

There can be little quarrel with these sentiments as an expression of the ideal *amicus curiae* brief, but the various organizations had their own interests, and these did not necessarily coincide with Abrams's ideal. Newman Levy explained this problem in an answer to Abrams.[55]

I enjoyed your letter and I wish that time permitted me to adopt your suggestions. As you know the briefs have to be filed before Dec. 1st so I have to send mine to the printer next week.

I thoroughly agree with everything that you say about the function of an *amicus* brief. So far as the court is concerned I am inclined to think that it is pretty much like an endorsement on a note. Its purpose is to tell the court that we agree with the appellant and we hope that it will decide in his favor. . . .

When this brief was first contemplated I discussed it with my legal committee, and they agreed that I should confine myself exclusively to the constitutional question. That was why I omitted the sociological stuff, the United Nations Charter and the rest of it. You see, if the Supreme Court should happen to mention in its decision that restrictive covenants are illegal upon the authority of Buchanan v. Warley, we all will be able to say to our members, "Isn't that exactly what we told the Court?"

Even though the brief was not changed, Abrams consented to having his name appear on the brief.

Later, Marian Wynn Perry, assistant special counsel of the NAACP Legal Defense and Education Fund, who was put in charge of coördinating the various briefs, wrote to Abrams to thank him for a copy of the letter he had written to Levy. "I wish I'd had the courage to write that kind of letter to all the *amici*," she said.[56]

The United States as Amicus Curiae

Organizational efforts were also made to gain the United States Department of Justice as an ally in the Supreme Court. This aim was accomplished only after President Harry S. Truman, his Committee on Civil Rights, and officials in the Department of Justice were won over by the claims of interested groups. No doubt the Truman Administration was disposed favorably toward action, but prodding seemed essential.

During President Truman's first year in office he was often told of ugly instances of racial discrimination and later recalled "the repeated anti-minority incidents immediately after the war in which homes were invaded, property was destroyed, and a number of innocent lives were taken." [57] On September 19, 1946, members of the National Emergency Committee Against Mob Violence, formed at the call of the NAACP, visited the White House.[58] The group included Walter White, its chief spokesman, along with James Carey, C.I.O.; Leslie Perry, Washington bureau of the NAACP; Frederick E. Reissig, Federal Council of Churches; Boris Shishkin, A.F. of L.; and Dr. Channing Tobias. Representing forty-seven national organizations the National Emergency Committee urged the president to call Congress into special session to protect minority groups against violence. The president was asked to initiate a study of the state of race relations in the country.

By an executive order on December 5, 1946, President Truman created a committee known as the President's Committee on Civil Rights.[59] The fifteen members of the Committee designated in the executive order were as follows: Charles E. Wilson, chairman; Mrs. Sadie T. Alexander, James B. Carey, John S. Dickey, Morris L. Ernst, Rabbi Roland B. Gittelsohn, Dr. Frank P. Graham, the Most Reverend Francis J. Haas, Charles Luckman, Francis P. Matthews, Franklin D. Roosevelt, Jr., the Right Reverend Henry Knox Sherrill, Boris Shishkin, Mrs. M. E. Tilly, and Channing Tobias. The committee was authorized "on behalf of the President" to determine how governmental action might safeguard the civil rights of the people. The executive order also specified that the committee report its studies to the president in writing which would terminate the committee's life. This was indeed the President's Committee on Civil Rights as it had no connection whatever with Congress, and its report eventually laid the basis of President Truman's civil-rights program which was bitterly opposed in Congress.

The President's Committee on Civil Rights met first at the White House on January 15, 1947. President Truman told the fifteen members of the committee that he wanted the Bill of Rights implemented in fact.[60] The committee then determined that it could be most helpful by focusing on the bad side of the national record—"on what might be called the civil rights frontier." [61] To do this in a single year the committee engaged the services of a fourteen-member professional staff led by Professor Robert K. Carr, an authority on governmental protection of civil rights, as executive secretary.

The work of the Committee on Civil Rights promptly won the attention of numerous groups. Between January and September, 1947, the committee held a series of public hearings where more than twenty spokesmen for interested groups made statements and were questioned. The committee reported that it had correspondence with nearly 250 private organizations and individuals. Some twenty-five agencies of the federal government also provided assistance.[62] In May, Will Maslow, director of the Commission on Law and Social Action of the American Jewish Congress proposed that the President's Committee make a number of recommendations for government action against restrictive covenants.[63] This was but one of many communications received by the committee on this subject.

In its report, entitled *To Secure These Rights,* three of the committee's forty recommendations dealt with racial covenants.[64] One favored "the enactment by the states of laws outlawing restrictive covenants" and another asked for legislation by Congress to the same end in the District of Columbia. A third recommended that court attack upon restrictive covenants be renewed "with intervention by the Department of Justice." Although the committee was divided on some other matters, it was unanimous on these recommendations.

The report of the President's Committee on Civil Rights, issued on October 29, 1947, was followed the next day by a decision of the Department of Justice to file an *amicus curiae* brief in the

Restrictive Covenant Cases. Solicitor General Philip B. Perlman
has explained that this "decision was reached during informal conferences which I had with Attorney General Tom C. Clark at
the time and was announced by him during the course of press
conference." [65] Perlman added that "there were a number of letters filed with the Attorney General and also with me by different
religious, racial, welfare and civil rights organizations, urging the
Government to enter the litigation."

The NAACP also announced that the attorney general was "re-
quested by many organizations to file a brief on behalf of the
United States government." [66] Walter White spoke for the Association when he wrote to Attorney General Clark that "the Department of Justice owes . . . minorities a deep responsibility to
help the court to understand the issues involved." [67] Irving Miller,
chairman of the executive committee of the American Jewish
Congress, wrote Clark that the Department has a responsibility
to act because of its duty to enforce civil-rights statutes.[68] Miller
stressed the provision of the United States Code that all citizens
"shall have the same right, in every state and territory, as is enjoyed by white citizens thereof to inherit, purchase, lease, sell,
hold and convey real and personal property." [69]

Unquestionably, the Department had authority to commit the
United States to a position even though the *Restrictive Covenant
Cases* were between private parties. In his letter to Clark, Miller
noted that the Department had filed a brief *amicus curiae* in 1944
in a civil suit in which a Negro fireman challenged the validity
of a contract entered into between a railroad and a labor union.[70]
Although not mentioned in the correspondence the United States
Code grants discretion to act in this way by providing that "the
Attorney General may, whenever he deems it for the interest of
the United States, either in person conduct and argue any case
in any court of the United States in which the United States is
interested, or may direct the Solicitor General or any officer of
the Department of Justice to do so." [71] Reinforcing this is a section in the Supreme Court Rules to the effect that consent of the
parties is unnecessary when a brief *amicus curiae* "is presented
by the United States or an officer or agency thereof and sponsored by the Solicitor General." [72]

In his reply to Irving Miller, Attorney General Clark promised to tell him "of any decision that may be made," but did not convey how a decision might be reached.[73] In the body of the letter Clark said: "I have asked the Assistant Attorney General who has jurisdiction of the Civil Rights section to make a study of the cases, and to make a recommendation as to whether, all things considered, it would be appropriate and desirable to take the action you suggest." But to this was added a postscript, in Clark's own hand: "The Solicitor General makes such decisions and I shall refer to him after receiving the recommendation of the assistant."

It is tempting to overweigh the influence of the organizational efforts to bring the Department of Justice into the *Restrictive Covenant Cases*. But there were other factors bending in the same direction. Among these was the political orientation of the Truman administration and the Department of Justice. President Truman was moving toward an open break with Southern Democrats as he kept reiterating the theme of federal responsibility to protect minority rights. When Irving Miller wrote to Tom Clark, he had cited the President's latest statement on the subject: [74]

> The extension of civil rights today means not protection of the people *against* the Government, but protection of the people *by* the Government.
>
> We must make the Federal Government a friendly, vigilant defender of the rights and equalities of all Americans. And again I mean all Americans.

President Truman had spoken these words on June 29, 1947, at the 38th Annual Conference of the NAACP before the Lincoln Memorial in Washington.[75] He told the NAACP of his confidence that the product of his Committee on Civil Rights "will be a sensible and vigorous program for action by all of us." And he added, "we must strive to advance civil rights wherever it lies within our power."

The president meant business. An editorial in *The Crisis* praised his address to the NAACP conference as "the most comprehensive and forthright statement on the rights of minorities in a democracy, and on the duty of the government to secure and safeguard them that has ever been made by a President of the United States." [76] By February, 1948, President Truman had formulated his civil-rights program, largely on the basis of the re-

port *To Secure These Rights.* His aggressive interest in this program became a key issue in his campaign for nomination and
reëlection as president.

Tom Clark worked closely with Truman to win a civil-rights
reputation for his administration and to obtain the president's
reëlection. Upon Clark's appointment as attorney general in 1945,
Truman told him how he wanted the Department of Justice run.[77]
"I emphasized to him," Truman has written, "the need to be vigi-
lant to maintain the rights of individuals under the provisions of
the Bill of Rights." Truman stressed this so much that "Tom Clark
thought I was 'hipped' on the subject—and I was." Clark himself
had no name in the civil-rights field. He had worked up the administrative ladder since coming to the Department from private
law practice in Texas in 1937. His appointment as attorney general was, according to the president, "strongly endorsed by the
whole Texas delegation." Later, Attorney General Clark's activities were geared closely to the spirit and needs of the Truman
administration. In 1947 alone Clark addressed at least eight major
Jefferson and Jackson Day dinners to praise the Democratic administration and to recommend the reëlection of Harry S. Truman.[78]

The solicitor general has long had the unique function of representing the interest of the federal government in the Supreme
Court. This was back-breaking work as the government, in 1947,
was a party in 57 per cent of the cases argued orally on the merits,
and in 41 per cent of all appellate cases.[79] Philip B. Perlman was
new to the job. He had been nominated by President Truman in
February, 1947, but opposition by Senator Homer Ferguson, who
believed Perlman to be the Democratic party boss of the State of
Maryland, held up confirmation until late July.[80] Perlman had
been in private law practice for twenty years but had earlier
worked in the Maryland State law department and served as city
solicitor of Baltimore for three years. Like Attorney General
Clark, he had strong Democratic loyalties and had regularly attended national party conventions. Also like Clark, Solicitor General Perlman was without any public record as a supporter of
civil rights.

The staff of the Justice Department and other administrative
agencies was also part of the constellation of interests moving

toward government participation in the covenant cases. The place of the staff is dimly seen for there is no documentation of its role. Yet consultants at the NAACP planning session in September, 1947, believed that it was "important to get government in on it." [81] And to bring this about, Phineas Indritz advised "that it would be a good idea for the directors of the various organizations represented to visit the heads of the various departments. There should be a well-coördinated group action to get behind these agencies." Indritz was sure that the Bureau of Indian Affairs, Department of the Interior, would file a memorandum on the Indian aspects of restrictive covenants. Later events showed that the Justice Department received promptings from other agencies as well.

Announcement of the report of the President's Committee on Civil Rights was the occasion for the decision of Clark and Perlman to enter the covenant cases as *amicus curiae*. In calling for intervention of the Department, the report said that the restrictive covenant "is providing our democratic society with one of its most challenging problems." The report also disclosed: [82]

> The effectiveness of restrictive covenants depends in the last analysis on court orders enforcing the private agreement. The power of the state is thus utilized to bolster discriminating practices. The Committee believes that every effort must be made to prevent this abuse. We would hold this belief under any circumstances; under present conditions, when severe housing shortages are already causing hardship for many people of the country, we are especially emphatic in recommending measures to alleviate the situation.

On October 30, the day following the publication of *To Secure These Rights*, Irving Miller expressed again to the attorney general the interest of the American Jewish Congress.[83] Miller wrote that "the Department of Justice should take prompt and firm action to implement and give effect to the committee's recommendations. We urge again that the Department bring its massive influence to bear in the fight to outlaw restrictive covenants by filing a brief *amicus curiae* in the pending cases."

The decision of the Department had already been made. On the same day, Solicitor General Perlman wrote to Miller: "The Attorney General has asked me to inform you that he has decided to file a brief *amicus curiae* in the *Restrictive Covenant Cases* now pending in the Supreme Court." [84]

The White Neighbors Prepare

Unlike the Negroes, the protective associations in St. Louis, Detroit, and Washington did little to coördinate their presentations to the Supreme Court. The untimely death of the Detroit attorney, Charles Chockley, in the autumn of 1947, forced the leaders in that city to turn to Gilligan and Crooks in Washington to write their brief in the *McGhee* case. But this was a matter of expediency rather than of coöperation. Gerald Seegers, representing the Marcus Avenue Improvement Association of St. Louis, became acquainted with the lawyers in Washington and exchanged greetings with them, but they worked independently. Eventually, organizations in other cities entered the cases as friends of the court but no effort was made by the protective associations on the front line to secure a general alliance.

The absence of coördinated planning of briefs and arguments for the white property owners is best explained by the local nature of their organizations. Improvement associations have sprung from a neighborhood. Functionally their work has been bound to a geographical area within a city, and as the records of the St. Louis group indicate, their primary purpose has been to police relatively small districts against infiltration by non-Caucasians. Therefore, their work has been confined with very little communication outside a restricted area. Within a city a number of associations have worked together, and there has been effective coöperation between them and the local real-estate interests. Similar groups have existed in most large cities of the country but all operated independently of each other. Each organization had been largely successful in its own area for state courts had consistently enforced their restrictive agreements. Under attack by a national organization in the Supreme Court of the United States, these local white property owners' associations faced a contest new and different.

Before the Supreme Court, the property owners' associations were opposing national organizations, and they understood this full well. In St. Louis, the leaders of the Marcus Avenue Im-

provement Association sought financial and moral support from
all sections of the city by organizing the Council for Community
Preservation. Detroit citizens were solicited for support, too. In
the fall of 1947 this appeal was made to maintain the defense of
the Caucasian position in *McGhee v. Sipes:* [85]

> This case, which involves restrictions prohibiting negroes from
> occupying property in our neighborhood, has been successfully
> fought by the Northwest Civic Association through the Wayne
> County Circuit Court and the Michigan Supreme Court and the
> cost has been a heavy drain on our treasury.
>
> [Money is needed] so we can properly finance this battle with
> the National Association for the Advancement of Colored People
> which draws upon the whole United States and is our opponent
> in this case.
>
> If we lose this case, the negroes will be able to move in next
> door to you. . . .
>
> So let's all pull together for the protection of our homes, and
> if everybody does his bit no one will be hurt and we will give
> them the fight of their lives.

This was a characteristically local appeal. No attempt was made
by Caucasians to broaden the campaign to defend the validity of
the enforcement of restrictive covenants into a nation-wide
movement.

Another handicap in the Supreme Court contest with the well-
organized Negroes was the lack of argumentative support in the
law reviews. By any standards they had little help in legal periodicals but in contrast with the volume of writing which assisted the
Negro cause, the position of white property owners was particularly weak. Although some case comments were neutral, most
notes and all articles favored the end of court enforcement of
racial restrictive covenants. Only one lengthy discussion questioned the efficacy of the Negro position.

Recognizing that Negroes faced an admittedly difficult housing
problem in all large cities, the editor-in-chief of the *Michigan
Law Review,* John A. Huston, nevertheless took issue with the
opponents of race restrictive covenants.[86] "The striking fact about
the attack on court enforcement of race restrictive covenants,"
he declared in April, 1947, "is the unlikelihood that a statute outlawing such covenants could be obtained in any jurisdiction in

the country. This stamps the current agitation as a conscious plea for judicial legislation." The main feature of Huston's comment was that it took issue with the state-action theory employed by the Negroes, while at the same time granting the assumptions the theory demanded. Taking as a text the general point of view on state action expressed by Professor Robert L. Hale of Columbia University,[87] lately associated with the NAACP in its battle against covenants, Huston made this statement: [88]

> In a final sense, state action permeates society, for the existence of anything and the action of any individual or group is permitted, commanded or forbidden by the state: it can be fairly said that everything in the social organism takes character from its relation to the central collective purpose manifested by the government.

All private action which society permits, it sanctions. But what was true in theory, Huston observed, was not necessarily wise in practice.

> But a distinction is made in the common understanding between action by the state and the action of private persons and it is in terms of this distinction that the Fourteenth Amendment has been held to speak. Perhaps the only logical principle on which to found the distinction is to attribute that action to the state which embodies a purpose of the government or of one entrusted with its authority which is separable from the purposes of private individuals. It may be difficult in particular cases to say whether action by the state or a private person is primarily responsible for a result; but every concept blends into others at some point in the melange of the law, and what we must treat in practice as vitally different ideas owe their singularity at least to a distinction between border line cases.

Then came the "parade of horribles."

> If it should be held that court enforcement of racial restrictive covenants is state action, the basis for this distinction would be obscured; and on the theory that the state is sanctioning final consequences whenever it protects a citizen in the exercise of any of his property or contract rights, the Fourteenth Amendment would emerge with unforseeable implications for our daily lives.

VIII

The Roosevelt Court

In the 1947 term of the Supreme Court seven of the justices sitting
had been appointed by President Franklin D. Roosevelt. In order
of appointment they were Hugo Black, 1937; Stanley Reed, 1938;
Felix Frankfurter and William O. Douglas, 1939; Frank Murphy,
1940; Robert H. Jackson, 1941; and Wiley B. Rutledge, 1943.
President Harry Truman had appointed Harold H. Burton in 1945
and, as Chief Justice, Fred M. Vinson in 1946. In ten years these
changes on the Supreme Court had been reflected in the decisions
of the court, for since 1937, thirty-two former decisions had been
overruled. These departures from precedent revealed tendencies
to permit new government regulations of the economy, to broaden
the rights of trade unions, to recognize the necessity of bureauc-
racy and to respond to the claims of Negroes for greater civil
rights.[1]

What were the predilections of the Roosevelt Court toward
competing claims in the controversy over judicial enforcement of
racial covenants? Most germane to this issue was the way in which
decisions by the Court had expanded the "state-action" theory in
civil-rights cases. In the first of these cases in 1944 the Court ruled
that a primary election conducted by the Democratic party in
Texas was state action.[2] Accordingly, the party's exclusion of
qualified Negro voters violated their right to suffrage under the
Fifteenth Amendment. In Texas, political parties had been en-
trusted with the supervision of primaries by the state legislature.
Subsequently the South Carolina legislature wiped all laws regu-
lating primary elections from its books, but lower federal courts

there broadened the meaning of state action to prohibit the Democratic party from discriminating against Negro voters.[3] By denying certiorari the Supreme Court did not review the case.

Enlargement of the concept of state action, so successful in ending the white primary, was paralleled in two other decisions. In a 1944 case [4] involving discrimination against Negroes by the Railroad Brotherhood of Locomotive Firemen and Enginemen the constitutional issue was avoided. However, Chief Justice Stone indicated that if the Railway Labor Act were construed to confer power on the union as the authorized bargaining agent, its practice of discrimination might be held to violate the Fifth Amendment. He observed that "the representative is clothed with power not unlike that of a legislature which is subject to constitutional limitations on its power to deny, restrict, destroy or discriminate against the rights of those for whom it legislates and which is also under an affirmative constitutional duty equally to protect those rights." [5] In a Jehovah's Witness case [6] a year later, the right to distribute literature on the sidewalk of a company town was upheld. The Court did so against the contention that First Amendment rights did not apply to privately owned sidewalks and over the fact that the State of Alabama had permitted the corporation to govern the community in this manner. Broadening the state-action doctrine to private property was too much for three members of the Court; and Chief Justice Stone was supported in his dissent by Justices Reed and Burton. Despite these dissenting views, the Court had put life into the state-action concept on which Negro chances in the restrictive covenant cases heavily depended.

The Court that made these decisions was, of course, composed of nine men with individual tendencies. It was of capital importance, therefore, when Justices Reed, Jackson, and Rutledge declined to participate in the *Restrictive Covenant Cases*. In withdrawing from these cases each of the three justices acted individually, on his own initiative and in silence. Justice Jackson had earlier had occasion to explain the Supreme Court practice on disqualification of judges.[7]

> No statute prescribes grounds upon which a Justice of this Court may be disqualified in any case. The Court itself has never undertaken by rule of Court or decision to formulate any uniform

practice on the subject. Because of this lack of authoritative standards it appears always to have been considered the responsibility
of each Justice to determine for himself the propriety of withdrawing in any particular circumstance.

Under this custom it is impossible to make an accurate inference
of the reasons why Reed, Jackson, and Rutledge disqualified themselves. Newspaper stories said their ownership of property subject to restrictive covenants explained their action.[8] Another report
told of "an alternative rumor floating around Washington that the
reason for the disqualification was that one or more Judges had
spoken before groups which had taken positions against restrictive
covenants." [9] The reasons for disqualification here are no less
mystifying when it is recalled that Justice Rutledge had earlier
sat on a racial covenant case when a member of the Court of
Appeals for the District of Columbia. He had also registered a
public vote against denial of certiorari in *Mays v. Burgess*. Moreover, while three Supreme Court justices disqualified themselves
in these cases, District Court Judge F. Dickenson Letts had earlier been permitted to preside over the hearing of the two *Hodge*
cases against the protest of counsel that his residence in restricted
property made for bias.

As for the six justices who did participate in the covenant cases,
the knowledge that all eventually sided with the Negroes makes
retrospective analysis of each personality easier. Yet, even before
the cases were decided, attorneys for the property owners doubted
their chances of winning.[10] They believed that the justices were
sufficiently disposed against their position to discount the mathe-
matical advantage of a six-man court.[11] Under the rule that an
evenly divided result affirms the lower court's decision, only three
justices were needed to produce the tie that would mean victory
for the Caucasians. It was estimated that Burton and Vinson would
be most amenable to the property-owners' arguments but persuading one from among Frankfurter, Black, Douglas, and Murphy
seemed doubtful.

The public career and judicial behavior of each member of the
Court who took part in the covenant cases reveals his possession
of some values in tune with the subsequent decision. The most
patent correlation is apparent in the personality of Justice Frank
Murphy.[12] Recognized by the NAACP as early as 1925 for fairness

in presiding over the Detroit race riot case,[13] Murphy later joined the Association and served on its national legal committee during the 'thirties. In party politics, as Democratic mayor of Detroit and governor of Michigan, his achievement rests on successful appeal to the Negro voters in his constituency. His three years in the Philippine Islands as governor general gave him new insight into the problems of race relations by acquainting him with Oriental criticism of American treatment of Negroes. These influences showed in Frank Murphy's brief tenure as attorney general of the United States. In the Justice Department he created the Civil Rights Section to prosecute violations of the nearly forgotten civil-rights statutes enacted more than fifty years earlier.[14] Murphy thereby showed his willingness to use the positive power of government to prevent interferences with the rights of Negro citizens.

From this career, Frank Murphy carried strong feelings against the color line to the Supreme Court. He stated his position clearly in a concurring opinion in the *Steele* case: [15]

> The Constitution voices its disapproval whenever economic discrimination is applied under authority of law against any race, creed or color. A sound democracy cannot allow such discrimination to go unchallenged.

Murphy's staunch support of Negro rights as a justice support the truth of the observation of Justice Jackson, as attorney general, that "the Supreme Court conference chamber is the forum where each fundamental cause has had its most determined and understanding championship." [16] Certainly the intensity of devotion to the cause of racial equality was very great in Justice Murphy. If others on the Court were uncertain, Murphy could be counted upon to exercise some persuasion on them.

In Justice Murphy's system of values, interest in forwarding civil rights was accompanied by a belief that the power of the Supreme Court should be employed for such a desirable end. Like his brothers Hugo Black and William Douglas he was a judicial activist for whom the test of a decision is its result. The voting behavior of these justices can frequently be explained by reference to their personal predilections. The opinion of a student of Justice Douglas' work on the Court is that his "approach to any kind of case is the most deliberately and consciously political of any Justice. That is to say, I believe that he makes the greatest effort to work out an opinion that squares with his policy preferences."[17] As a judicial activist, Justice Black is not far behind. A former clerk, John P. Frank, in a biography of Black has this to say:[18]

> He is a representative of that movement in American history which we have variously called the Grange, the Populists, the New Freedom, and the New Deal. He is one of the tiny handful of representatives of that movement ever to reach the Supreme Court of the United States. His significance as a Justice is that he knows what to do with the power thus given him.

The pre-judicial careers of Black and Douglas provided little hint that on the Supreme Court they would choose the Negro position as frequently as Murphy. As an expert in corporation finance on the faculty of Yale Law School and as first chairman of the Securities and Exchange Commission, Douglas had no occasion to deal with race problems. In contrast, Hugo Black, as a Democratic Senator from Alabama from 1927 to 1937, could not escape racial controversy. As a Southern Democrat he supported New Deal social and economic programs which tended to benefit Negroes as well as other depressed groups. At the same time, Black spoke against bills which would have made lynching a federal crime and participated in filibusters to prevent civil-rights measures from coming before the Senate for a vote. In spite of this, Black was claimed as a close friend by Walter White, secretary of the NAACP who supported his appointment to the Supreme Court and stood by him after Justice Black acknowledged one-time membership in the Ku Klux Klan.[19]

On the Court, Black after 1937 and Douglas after 1939, consistently supported the expansion of the state-action doctrine and of Negro rights. One clerk to Black said that if one concern or belief influences the justice's decisions more than others it is this: "A profound sense of the value of individual dignity and freedom, and a belief that this value can best be protected and promoted by a wide dispersion of power through many public and private institutions."[20] The NAACP attorney, Charles Houston, told about this incident after a concert by Marian Anderson:

"Negroes sought Mr. Justice Black's autograph more than that of any other person except Marian Anderson herself. People have an uncanny instinct for recognizing their friends." [21] That this reputation was deserved is indicated by remarks made by Black in a 1940 decision.[22]

> No higher duty, no more solemn responsibility rests upon this Court, than that of translating into living law and maintaining this constitutional shield deliberately planned and inscribed for the benefit of every human being subject to our Constitution— of whatever race, creed or persuasion.

Compared to the libertarian activists, Felix Frankfurter's personal social predilections have had a limited bearing on his work as a justice. It may be that his "reputation for radicalism" was unjustified.[23] But he had directed the preparation of the sociological brief to support protective labor legislation in Supreme Court cases; [24] he had worked to limit the use of the injunction in labor disputes; [25] and he had attacked the conviction of Sacco and Vanzetti.[26] From his position at Harvard Law School during the 'thirties, Professor Frankfurter had fed the best of his graduates to important positions in the New Deal. Interested in the progress of Negroes, teacher to William Hastie and Charles Houston, friend to Walter White, Frankfurter had served several years on the National Legal Committee of the NAACP.[27] These activities stamped Frankfurter as a great friend of civil rights. The disappointment at Frankfurter's performance as a justice felt by those who regarded him as a friend of civil rights has been owing to his notions about the function of the Supreme Court in the American system of government. Holding to a line of judicial self-restraint, Justice Frankfurter has rarely interfered with legislative action, not because he liked the policy of Congress but because he thought in a democracy Congress should set public policy. This delicate problem was not the issue in the covenant cases. There the Supreme Court was concerned with the use of the judicial power, not the legislative power, to enforce racial restrictions in housing. No doubt Frankfurter was personally opposed to the application of equity for this end; how he would behave as a self-conscious justice would be difficult to predict.[28]

When Harold H. Burton came to the Supreme Court he held

a strong respect for the importance of following precedent. Burton's respect for precedent grew from his experience in private practice and as law director of the City of Cleveland. He understood the great utility of certainty for the bar. Republican senator from Ohio for six years before his appointment, it was expected that his constitutional views would flatly disagree with the New Deal appointees. But it is relevant that Justice Burton was born into a Massachusetts family with abolitionist roots. He is a great admirer of Abraham Lincoln. His leadership in the Unitarian church taken with these other associations insure that he is sentimentally attached to the desirability of full racial equality. In the 'thirties his election as Republican mayor of Cleveland was due in part to the support he received from the large Negro population in the heart of that city. As a United States senator he favored ending the poll tax in the South. On the Court he dissented alone when the majority held a Virginia statute requiring segregation on buses could not apply, because of the commerce clause, to buses operating in interstate commerce between Virginia and the District of Columbia.[29] In his study of the Roosevelt Court, Herman Pritchett regarded Burton as "extremely negative toward personal liberty claims." [30]

One thing stands out about Fred Vinson's work as chief justice of the United States from 1946 to 1953—his consistent support of the Democratic administration.[31] A life-long Kentucky Democrat, Vinson served six terms in the House of Representatives. Then he gained five years of judicial experience on the United States Court of Appeals for the District of Columbia before resigning, toward the end of the war, in order to work in various top positions in the executive branch. Vinson had thus gained the outlook of the administration as he took his seat at the center of the Supreme Court. On a great variety of issues, from the regulation of business to the regulation of Communists, Chief Justice Vinson voted with the government. In 1947, when the United States enjoined John L. Lewis, Vinson infuriated his colleague Murphy by asking for help "to get the Administration out of this jam." [32] Throughout his tenure as chief justice, Vinson's associations with President Truman were exceedingly close. Vinson's position might then be determined in part by his view of the president's civil-rights program.

Main Briefs in the State Cases

The briefs submitted to the Supreme Court for the petitioners reflect the thoughts of many lawyers and sociologists and the great labor of counsel consumed in the preparation. These briefs were based on fresh research and were often strikingly different in form and content from the contentions made in the lower courts. Also there were differences among the briefs for the petitioners which arose because three groups of lawyers in St. Louis, New York, and Washington worked separately.

A sociological brief of ninety-two pages was prepared for the petitioners in *McGhee v. Sipes* by Marshall, Miller, Graves, and Dent as counsel.[33] In submitting that the judgment of the Supreme Court of Michigan should be reversed this brief advanced six arguments. First, restrictions of occupancy were said to have developed through a distortion of doctrines concerning restrictions on the use of property. Limitations of *how* property shall be used had been improperly applied to limitations of *who* shall occupy property. While restrictions on use affected all persons equally and in the same way, restrictive covenants in America had the new and unrelated purpose of preventing the ownership and occupancy of homes by unpopular minority groups. For this, the brief argued, there was no resulting social or legal justification. Second, the right to use and occupy real estate as a home was asserted to be a civil right guaranteed and protected by the Fourteenth Amendment and the Civil Rights Act. Third, the brief presented the well-known view that no state may deny a person his civil rights solely because of race. Fourth, it was urged that judicial enforcement of the racial restrictive covenant in the case constituted a denial by the State of Michigan of the petitioners' civil rights. No efforts were spared in spelling out the view that the decree of the state court was based solely on the race of the petitioners. Under state precedent eviction was required only if the petitioners were found to be of other than "the Caucasian race." If the petitioners had not been Negro and if the state courts had not acted, "they would be occupying their home peacefully without threat of eviction." These were among the logical points made to persuade the Supreme Court that judicial enforcement of racial covenants was invalid state action.

The sociological argument was the fifth point in the petitioners' brief in the Detroit case. Much data was included to show that judicial enforcement of covenants had created a uniform pattern of overcrowding and congestion in the housing of Negroes. Using the census standard that a dwelling is overcrowded "when there are fewer rooms than there are persons to live in them," the brief showed that 27 per cent of all housing occupied by Negroes in Detroit was overcrowded in 1944. Statistics were provided to indicate that this situation was paralleled by conditions in other cities. It was also shown that Negroes were paying high rentals for inferior housing. Because of restrictive covenants "only a small portion of the total housing supply is opened to the Negro," so that the opportunity of improving his living conditions are cut off. Slums have resulted, and, the McGhee brief argued, these conditions have in turn resulted in a serious rise in disease, crime, vice, racial tension, and mob violence. Factual evidence to support these contentions were drawn from more than sixty articles, books, and official reports on living conditions for Negroes in American cities.

In addition to this sociological claim, the petitioners' brief in *McGhee v. Sipes* insisted that there were no economic justifications for restrictive covenants against Negroes. A survey of Negro housing undertaken by the National Association of Real Estate Boards was cited to show that three-fourths of the realtors polled believed Negroes were good economic risks and whose occupancy did not depreciate property. Additional studies were listed to support the conclusion that "Negroes are able to pay for better housing in large numbers, but the wall of racial covenants that surrounds their areas of concentration and excludes them from most newly constructed suburban housing prevent their securing it."

Finally, the brief of petitioners in *McGhee v. Sipes* also argued that "judicial enforcement of this restrictive covenant violates the treaty entered into between the United States and members of the United Nations under which the agreement here sought to be enforced is void."

In conclusion, the brief for petitioners in *McGhee v. Sipes* said that their case was "not a matter of enforcing an isolated private agreement." Rather it was "a test as to whether we will have a

united nation or a country divided into areas and ghettos solely
on racial or religious lines." Thurgood Marshall and Loren Miller
were the major and Willis M. Graves and Francis Dent the minor
architects of this brief. Several other attorneys were listed as being
of counsel. They were William H. Hastie, Charles H. Houston,
George M. Johnson, William R. Ming, Jr., James Nabrit, Jr., Marian
Wynn Perry, Spottswood W. Robinson, III, Andrew Weinberger,
and Ruth Weyand.

For *Shelley v. Kraemer* the arguments of George Vaughn and
Herman Willer were different in form but not in kind.[34] Sociological points were made, but they were drawn almost wholly
from the trial record and they were subordinate to the legal and
constitutional claims. Main reliance was placed upon the standard argument that judicial enforcement as state action in enforcing covenants is contrary to public policy and to the Constitution.
This brief was more like the arguments made in the lower courts
and for that reason need not be reviewed.

The brief of seventeen pages submitted by Gilligan and Crooks
for the respondents in *McGhee v. Sipes* suggests that they were
surprised by the sociological and economic data used to support
the petitioners' brief in that case.[35] Thurgood Marshall had submitted his brief on November 17, and Gilligan and Crooks filed
theirs on December 1. This did not allow them time to answer the
carefully elaborated facts of the petitioners. Their brief was short
and repeated the position that had been expressed in the numerous
precedents under which judicial enforcement of racial restrictions
had been justified. This brief does reveal the reaction of these
lawyers to the sociological arguments of the NAACP, as follows: [36]

> It must be emphasized that such matters as health, housing, crime
> and the other problems that undoubtedly are acute among Negro
> citizens, must be addressed to the legislature of the state in the
> exercise of the police power. Neither this Court nor the courts
> of the State of Michigan can correct the conditions complained
> of. The thirty-six pages of petitioners' brief devoted to these soci-
> ological problems would indicate many varied individuals, organ-
> izations and even governmental agencies have devoted much time
> and effort to the problem. The Supreme Court of Michigan, not
> unmindful of these problems, although not a part of the record

in the case, nevertheless declared the indentures to be not against the public policy of that State, and that declaration is conclusive.

The respondents' brief in *Shelley v. Kraemer*, prepared by Gerald L. Seegers with the assistance of St. Louis attorneys, Walter H. Pollman and Ben F. York, was more thorough as its arguments filled eighty pages.[37] Yet the brief did not contain much that was new. The *Michigan Law Review* article by John Huston [38] was cited, but there was little else that was new on the subject and so the argument was a distillation of the three decades of decisions upholding judicial enforcement of covenants.

Main Briefs in the Federal Cases

The consolidated brief for the petitioners in *Hurd v. Hodge* and *Urciolo v. Hodge* was masterful in its blending of legal and sociological claims.[39] Its 149 pages had been prepared by Houston, Indritz, and Robinson and was filed with the Supreme Court on November 17. The addition of new counsel together with the demands of argument at the Supreme Court level may account for the fact that this brief was radically different from the argument made in the lower courts. Many points that had been labored before were now omitted. The changed-condition argument, and the contention that Hurd was not a Negro, for example, were discarded. The details of the record were passed up in order to incorporate substantial material derived from sociological and economic publications. Altogether there were more than 150 separate articles, reports, and books cited, and there were numerous charts and maps to accompany these arguments. The brief contained an expression of thanks to a number of sociologists for "technical assistance in assembling material and in the preparation of the brief." [40] Louis Wirth and Robert C. Weaver of the American Council on Race Relations; Charles H. Johnson and Herman Long of Fisk University; Joseph B. Lohman of the Julius Rosenwald Fund and Robert C. Wasson and Leon Zitver were mentioned. Certainly the brief indicated the work which had gone into it, for the whole argument was polished and developed to a pitch never before done.

This brief struck hard even in framing the question the Supreme Court was being asked to decide.[41]

> These cases involve this fundamental issue: Shall we in the United States have ghettoes for racial, religious and other minorities, or even exclude such minorities entirely from whole areas of our country, by a system of judicially enforced restrictions based on private prejudices and made effective through the use of governmental authority and power?

In answering this question, the brief called the Court's particular attention to four discussions of the problem. Thus Houston, Indritz, and Robinson acknowledged their own debt to these analyses: [42] (1) the dissent of Judge Edgerton in this case in the Court of Appeals; (2) the law-review article by D. O. McGovney; (3) an article in *Survey Graphic* by Loren Miller; (4) the law-review article by Harold Kahen.

The legal analysis was especially incisive and made the point that this was unconstitutional state action in a lucid way. Boldly but with strong logic, the brief urged that their contentions to invalidate judicial enforcement of racial covenants as improper state action were "not novel legal doctrines." On the contrary, "they have been applied by this Court in numerous prior cases in other contexts." The thesis argued was that "racial discrimination is forbidden by the Constitution if directly supported in any way by governmental power, whether by laws or through judicial or executive proceedings." It was this view which the brief said had been a basic assumption of the Court since the *Civil Rights Cases*.

The argument that judicial enforcement of racial covenants constituted government action was well made through the use of analogies. The Court was reminded that on three occasions it had held legislative racial zoning unconstitutional and that the *Hodge* cases involved "governmental action which achieves precisely the same end through the judiciary." The brief pointed out that "judicial action, not involving any statute has been held by this Court to be state action" in deciding numerous cases arising under the due-process clause of the Fourteenth Amendment. There were also recent examples of holdings that "constitutional rights are not to be denied through court action at the behest of private parties seeking to utilize government power to effect a result which the legislation itself could not constitutionally effect." The following parallel from the brief indicates the quality of reasoning on this point:

> In *A.F. of L. v. Swing*,[43] this Court expressly held that a court injunction against peaceful picketing, based on the state's common law policy, was as unconstitutional as was the statute against peaceful picketing in *Thornhill v. Alabama*.[44] The cases at bar (invoking a court injunction against sale or occupancy of land solely because of race) are no different from the *Buchanan, Harmon* and *City of Richmond* cases (holding that statutes providing for racial zoning were unconstitutional) than *A.F. of L. v. Swing* was different from *Thornhill v. Alabama*.

Since these were federal cases, the consolidated brief for the petitioners could not rest on the Fourteenth Amendment but rather claimed that the due-process clause of the Fifth Amendment had been violated. In supporting its argument on this and other points, the brief bristled with data drawn from the literature of sociology and economics. Certainly this portion of the brief was more extensive than the brief of the NAACP in the Michigan case.

A twenty-five page brief prepared by Gilligan and Crooks for the respondents was much like their brief in the Detroit case with adaptations for the federal problem.[45] Precedents from the District of Columbia were stressed and the early Supreme Court decision of *Corrigan v. Buckley* was repeatedly endorsed as having settled the issue. The law of the land on this question was firmly established and should not be tampered with. The brief was devoted also to answering the Negroes' contentions. It was said that the racial restrictions were private agreements; consequently enforcement of them by courts did not deny Negroes any constitutionally protected right. In fact the action of the courts in these instances supported the contract rights of individual white property owners. The public-policy issue was answered by citing legal precedents. It was added that the position of Congress was a more authoritative expression of public policy than the political speeches of President Truman and the declarations of other executive officials. Congress had refrained from enacting any legislation questioning the wisdom of segregation; rather, it had long supported racial separation in the District of Columbia. From all of this it was urged that the enforcement of racial covenants was in tune with public policy.

The opinion of Chief Judge Groner in the Court of Appeals decision in the *Mays* cases was drawn upon to support the argument that the injunctive relief granted by the District Court was not contrary to the federal Constitution or implementing legislation. Neither the Fourteenth Amendment, the Fifth Amendment, or the Civil Rights Acts prohibited judicial enforcement of these restrictive covenants. Speaking of the social results attributed by the petitioners' brief to restrictive covenants, the respondents' brief said,[46]

> Petitioners fail completely to recognize or deliberately ignore the fundamental rule of judicial construction that courts are not concerned with purely political issues. Alleviating over-crowding, crime, sub-standard health conditions and the like are the "legitimate exercise of the police power of Congress in the District of Columbia. Neither this Court nor the trial court can correct or remedy the conditions complained of."

This provoked a "reply brief" of twenty-five pages filed for the petitioners on January 13, 1948.[47] Houston, Indritz, and Robinson had thus worked on the petition for certiorari in July and August, then turned immediately to prepare a substantial main brief filed with the Supreme Court in November, and finally just before oral argument completed another document to support their contentions. This reply brief expressed its function well, for it not only dealt directly with the arguments advanced in the respondents' main brief but also replied to the views expressed in *amici curiae* briefs of various protective associations. It said that these briefs "demonstrate that the covenants are devices for community zoning." And this permitted the petitioners to stress again that the protective associations in this way achieved "by circumvention the very results of racial restrictive zoning which this Court has held to be unconstitutional." The brief spoke sharply of the respondents' claims by saying that they failed utterly "to show any basis other than the perpetuation of their racial prejudice, for the continued enforcement of racial restrictive covenants."

The United States as Amicus Curiae

On December 5, a brief *amicus curiae* for the United States was submitted to the Supreme Court by Tom C. Clark, attorney general, and Philip B. Perlman, solicitor general.[48] Although this brief presented a thorough argument on the constitutional questions supported by a wealth of documentation, its emphasis was on the responsibility of the federal government "for the protection of the fundamental civil rights guaranteed to the people by the Constitution and laws of the United States." Speaking of the fact that racial restrictive covenants were widespread and were to be blamed for the overcrowded housing conditions, the brief of the government argued that racial minorities cannot escape from the ugly residences to which they are confined by these restrictions. The Court was told that "this situation cannot be reconciled with the spirit of mutual tolerance and respect for the dignity and rights of the individual which give vitality to our democratic way of life."

Four prepared statements by different agencies in the government were included in this brief to indicate the fact that racial restrictive covenants enforced by the instrumentalities of government are a source of serious embarrassments. Each of these statements were in the form of letters to the Department of Justice during October or November of 1947. The letter of Raymond M. Foley, administrator of the Housing and Home Finance Agency asserted that racial restrictive covenants had affected every phase of public-housing administration since the beginning of the program in 1934.[49] These covenants have controlled the access of Negroes to sites and dwelling units and generally restricted minorities to sharply defined neighborhoods.

> The ultimate effect of covenanted land restrictions is to place the Federal agency, required as it is to clear and replace slum areas, in the position of appearing to place the stamp of government approval upon separate residential patterns and to render it most difficult for the agency to administer public funds in such manner as to assure equitable participation by minority racial groups.

The administrative problems faced by the Housing and Home Finance Agency then were spelled out in detail in Foley's long statement.

In a much shorter letter, Dr. Thomas Parran, surgeon general of the United States Public Health Service, expressed a more tentative criticism of racial restrictive covenants as harming the health of the nation.[50] He said that "the relationship between housing and health is extremely difficult technically to assess" but health authorities agreed that housing lacking basic sanitary facilities and other deficiencies was "a serious deterrent to improved national health." Dr. Parran reached this carefully stated conclusion: "To the extent that racial restrictive housing covenants would deny a citizen the opportunity to provide himself a sanitary and healthful environment, such covenants would, in my view, be prejudicial to the public health."

The Undersecretary of the Interior Oscar L. Chapman, presented information showing the implications of racial restrictive covenants for the 400,000 Indians in the United States.[51] "One of the main goals of the Indian Service," he said, "is to aid the Indians to participate equally and fully in the life of the Nation." On occasion Indians had not been able to accept federal employment in Washington because of these restrictions. Chapman also said that "the effort to eradicate old injuries to Indians and to aid in their participation in the national life is stultified by their being categorized as inferior by the exclusions caused by restrictive covenants." The undersecretary also said that 25 per cent of the people of Puerto Rico, 50 per cent of the people of Alaska, and nearly all of the people in Hawaii and the Virgin Islands would be classified as "non-Caucasians" and "thus would be within the scope of most restrictive covenants." It was admitted that none were being applied in the territories, but it was deemed important that "restrictive covenants are being applied against them in the United States and may well spread to the territories." Finally, a plea was made by the Interior Department that enforcement of "racial covenants be ended because their implications are entirely inconsistent with the future national and international welfare of the United States in its relations with the 'non-white' peoples."

In a fourth statement, Ernest A. Gross, Legal Advisor to the Secretary of State, advised the Department of Justice that "the United States has been embarrassed in the conduct of foreign relations by acts of discrimination taking place in this country."[52]

Nothing was said specifically about restrictive covenants as Gross's statement was drawn entirely from a letter sent a year earlier from the Department to the Fair Employment Practices Committee. Its view simply was to insist that acts of discrimination handicap American relations with other countries.

Finally, in stressing the nation's responsibilities, the experience of the Department of Justice was mentioned, and several paragraphs were quoted from the report of the President's Committee on Civil Rights, issued just a short time before, on October 29, 1947. This brief *amicus curiae* for the United States also dealt thoroughly with the constitutional issues, with public-policy considerations, and with restraints on alienation. However, the special responsibility of the government to help bring about equal opportunity in all departments of life pervaded the document.

Government participation in these cases sufficiently irritated Henry Gilligan and James Crooks to elicit a reply brief for the respondents.[53] One argument centered on the statements by different government agencies. They told the Court that these views were not a part of the record in the cases and should not be considered. But at a minimum the Justice Department was asked to produce the original correspondence leading to the use of these statements.[54] This reply brief also criticized the Justice Department for arguing for one side in private litigation between citizens.[55]

> Neither the records in the present cases, nor the decisions of this Court or any State Court, justify the pernicious statements in the Government's brief. . . . The government presumably serves all citizens, yet it charges these respondents and others with ignorance, bigotry and prejudice. It is understandable that private litigants may make statements of this kind in their effort earnestly to press their cases, but the government must not only be criticized, but condemned, for such practice.

Organizations as Amici Curiae

The eighteen briefs *amici curiae* on the Negro side fall into five fairly well-defined categories of interest in these cases. These were led by the racial, ethnic, or religious minorities which suffer directly when prejudice is translated into acts of discrimination. Thus a Negro fraternal organization—the Independent, Benevolent, Protective Order of Elks of the World—pointed out "some of the conditions from which its members and others of the millions who belong to the colored race are suffering." [56] The National Bar Association, composed mainly of Negroes, did the same.[57] The brief *amicus curiae* of the American Indian Citizens League of California reminded the Supreme Court: [58]

> The American Indians and their descendants, have not only suffered various indignities for years, but are now being denied, in many parts of the United States, as non-caucasians, a place to live upon the continent which was once entirely theirs, all as a result of land restrictions prohibiting occupancy of premises by Indians and their descendants.

The Japanese American Citizens League stated that "discrimination or unfair treatment against any minority redounds to the detriment of all minorities." [59] Its brief also told of the difficulties of its own members in finding housing. Referring to the forced evacuation by the army in World War II, the brief made its own explanation of the root of the trouble:

> Were the Japanese not forced, by reason of race restrictive covenants, to live in definite areas, they would presumably have lived normal lives throughout the area and consequently the "clanishness" which General DeWitt found so inimical to national safety would not have existed.

The interests of the Jews in these cases was much the same as those of the Indians and Japanese Americans. The Court was told that Jewish interests are threatened whenever any group of human beings is humiliated because of race, religion, or national origin. One brief was filed by the American Jewish Congress.[60] Another was a consolidated brief *amici curiae* in behalf of four organizations, the American Jewish Committee, B'nai B'rith (Anti-Defamation League), the Jewish War Veterans of the United States of America, and the Jewish Labor Committee.[61] Also in the category of minorities was the only brief filed for several individuals under the misleading title, "California Amici Curiae." [62] Sponsored by a Negro defendant in a Los Angeles covenant case then before the appellate courts there, this brief documented the widespread use and effectiveness of property restrictions on the West Coast.

The briefs of the two large national labor organizations stressed their direct interest in the outcome of these cases in a manner very similar to that of the minority groups. The American Federation of Labor told the Supreme Court that 750,000 of its members were Negroes and said that it desired "to help in every possible way to secure for its members—and for all Americans—the opportunity to live in decent homes." [63] It asserted that restrictive covenants had been responsible for the scarcity of housing for Negroes and the resulting high prices.

> All that the A.F. of L. has accomplished in raising the income of Negro workers in the past—all that may be done in the future— is rendered virtually worthless when members cannot use their increased means to leave the ghettos and move to more congenial surroundings.

The same was true for the members of the Congress of Industrial Organizations, whose brief was signed not only by its general counsel, Lee Pressman, but also by twenty-six attorneys representing member international unions.[64] "The effect of these covenants on our own members has not been confined to depriving them of adequate shelter at reasonable prices and endangering their livelihood," the C.I.O. brief said. "These covenants have forced our members into slum areas which breed vice, disease and delinquency."

A third batch of briefs came from religious organizations. In a brief without a legal citation, counsel of the Congregational Church sought to persuade the justices to abstain from evil by preaching them a sermon.[65]

> We repent of the sin of racial segregation as practiced both within and outside our churches, and respond to the mandate of the Christian Gospel to promote with uncompromising word and purpose, the integration in our Christian churches and our democratic society of all persons of whatever race, color, or ancestry on the basis of equality and mutual respect in an inclusive fellowship.

> Segregation is a sinful denial of fellowship between men and women who are equally chosen of God whatever their color or national ancestry may be. Because of the evil consequences of segregation—psychological, economic, sociological—this com-

monly practiced form of discrimination on the basis of race and creed denies the very basis of our democratic creed and undermines our moral influence in international affairs. We believe that race restrictive covenants are unconstitutional, immoral, and against the public interest and welfare. They increase and perpetuate hostility between groups and are a persistent threat to peace and progress in our society. It is our conviction that a great moral victory would be achieved by this Nation if the constitutional and democratic principles of America were to be upheld by a decision of the Supreme Court of the United States invalidating these unjust and discriminatory agreements so far as they are now enforceable by court action.

The brief of the Human Relations Commission of the Protestant Council of New York City was confined to routine legal arguments,[66] but the third religious *amicus curiae,* the American Unitarian Association, emphasized the incompatibility of racial restrictive covenants with the concept of the brotherhood of man.[67]

Other support for Negroes was furnished by a half dozen organizations primarily devoted to various liberal political ends. In their *amici curiae* briefs the American Civil Liberties Union [68] and the unaffiliated St. Louis Civil Liberties Committee [69] reiterated the theme of the main briefs. However, their briefs in defense of the Bill of Rights was an important overtone in their exposition. Another group, the American Association for the United Nations,[70] noted the impact of racial inequality in the United States on foreign affairs. The Supreme Court was told that legal enforcement of restrictive covenants prevented the country from living up to United Nations ideals. An *amicus* brief from the American Veterans Committee [71] pointed out that many Negroes were former soldiers and that these veterans were prevented by covenants from living in decent homes. Two other organizations, the Non-Sectarian Anti-Nazi League to Champion Human Rights [72] and the National Lawyers Guild [73] argued in separate briefs as friends of the court that such racial practices as these were contrary to the American democratic creed.

Only one thing further needs to be said about the briefs filed with the Supreme Court in support of the Negro position in these cases. It is the dual appearance of some persons on briefs filed by different organizations. Much of the interplay between groups is unknown. But from the briefs themselves it can be seen that Francis Dent, attorney for the petitioners in the Detroit case, signed the brief of the American Civil Liberties Union. Joseph Proskauer was a signer of the briefs of the American Association for the United Nations and the American Jewish Committee; William Strong for the Indians and American Jewish Congress; Luther Ely Smith, Victor B. Harris, John R. Stockman, and Eugene H. Buder on the American Civil Liberties Union as well as the St. Louis Civil Liberties Committee brief. Harry Merican was on the *amici curiae* briefs of both the A.F. of L. and the American Veterans Committee, and Phineas Indritz, counsel in the *Hodge* cases, was also counsel for the American Veterans Committee.

Amici curiae briefs were filed with the Supreme Court by property-owners' associations in three cities, Baltimore, Los Angeles, and Washington, D.C. These organizations closely resembled the Marcus Avenue Improvement Association of St. Louis. Thus, the Arlington Heights Property Owners Association of Los Angeles, speaking for itself and five other organizations [74] told the Supreme Court that they represented "several thousand Caucasian property owners . . . who are united in their desire to maintain their homes and raise their families in communities inhabited by persons of their own race." [75] The Mount Royal Protective Association, Inc. of Baltimore said its main function "has been to represent the interest of the property owners in such matters as zoning laws, the invasion of this residential district by commercial or otherwise undesirable enterprises and in general to support the efforts of the inhabitants to secure the amenities of life within the neighborhood." [76] Similarly, the Federation of Citizens Associations of the District of Columbia boasted that it was speaking for sixty-nine white-citizens associations "interested in the general improvement and civic betterment of the District." [77] Its *amicus curiae* brief went on to declare that its interest in the question at issue had arisen from a

> firm conviction that it is in the mutual interest of the two dominant races, that the rule of law, established by numerous decisions of the highest court of the District of Columbia over a quarter of a century, validating and enforcing restrictive covenants, be confirmed by this court.

The arguments made in these briefs were based on the theory that segregation was the most desirable solution to the race problem. The Washington property-owners' associations told the Court that a purely legal question had been raised which was unrelated to "sociological theories." It set forth a viewpoint of the value of segregation.

> There is no reason to believe that the national crisis in housing, which affects all races, will be solved, or that racial tolerance will be enhanced, by a decision which would permit non-Caucasians to invade a neighborhood which the other residents desire to maintain as a Caucasian community.

In Baltimore, the Mount Royal Protective Association claimed the colored and white areas are equivalent. Describing the Negro section the brief explained: [78]

> These are not in any sense of the word slum districts, and although there are slums in Baltimore, both white and negro, it would be utterly untrue to say that the practice of voluntary restrictive covenants in Baltimore has resulted in forcing the large negro population to congregate in districts of sub-standard housing and inadequate public services.

The brief made a full-fledged defense of the segregated solution to the race problem achieved in Baltimore.[79]

> The City of Baltimore is one of the few very large cities in this country containing a large proportion of negroes which has been singularly free from the race riots that have disfigured and disgraced many other communities. Any impartial observer conversant with the facts of city life would testify that this immunity is not unconnected with the fact that the races have been physically separated to a great extent and for the most part are not closely mingled in the same blocks. It should be remembered, of course, that in this city, as in other eastern cities, the bulk of the population resides in solid rows of houses, not in detached dwellings, so that neighbors are in much closer physical proximity to each other than in the newer cities of the West. That there was much crime and disorder during the war years when the working population, white and black, were very much congested is true, but the fact remains that outbreaks that could properly be called riots have not occurred.

A fourth *amicus curiae* brief favoring the enforcement of restrictive covenants was presented by the National Association of Real Estate Boards.[80] Its Code of Ethics provided that a "realtor should never be instrumental in introducing into a neighborhood a character of property or occupancy, members of any race or nationality, or any individuals whose presence will clearly be detrimental to property values in that neighborhood." In explaining its interest in the enforcement of racial restrictive covenants to the Supreme Court, the National Association of Real Estate Boards said:

> The application of constitutional law principles to real property law is of utmost interest to those whose business it is to buy and sell land. In the making of sales, entering into of contracts, evaluation of real property, and in the making of decisions as to the soundness of investments in real estate, those in the real estate business are vitally interested, not only in the existing constitutional law, but also in the predictability of future judicial determinations of the validity of the various types of legal devices used as the everyday tools of the real estate man.

Oral Argument

In the *Restrictive Covenant Cases* seven hours' time was set aside for oral argument on January 15 and 16, 1948. The Supreme Court granted the request of the Justice Department to hear the solicitor general for one hour as *amicus curiae,* and three hours were allotted to each side. For the appellants, George Vaughn and Herman Willer argued in the St. Louis case; Charles Houston and Phineas Indritz argued in the District of Columbia case, while Thurgood Marshall and Loren Miller argued in the Detroit case. For the appellees, Gerald L. Seegers was the advocate in the St. Louis case, and Henry Gilligan and James Crooks together represented the white property owners from Detroit and Washington.

NAACP attention to the preparation of oral argument, as at other stages of its cases, was truly remarkable. Of course, Association lawyers were experienced in Supreme Court practice, and Houston, Marshall, and Miller had often appeared personally since 1935. Before each appearance in the Court they have customarily tried out their lines at Howard Law School in major practice sessions. An enormous benefit to the Negro attorneys is indicated by this description of these "dry runs." [81]

> These are arduous, all-day rehearsals at the law school, where Marshall and his assistants try their arguments on a simulated Supreme Court made up of professors. Nine of them sit at a long table, and each one tries to act as much as possible like a specific Supreme Court justice, sticking the lawyers with tough questions that might crop up in the court itself. Law students form the audience and are encouraged to ask rough questions too.

On this occasion also Dean Johnson arranged a rehearsal, and it is said that a second-year student asked a question later raised by Justice Frankfurter. The NAACP lawyers had the answer worked out.[82]

No one outside the Supreme Court knew that justices Reed, Jackson, and Rutledge were disqualifying themselves from participating in the decision of these cases until time for oral argument on January 15. No announcement is made on such occasions; the chairs of the nonparticipants are simply unoccupied when the Court convenes for argument. This meant that in these cases the briefs had been written and oral argument planned without the knowledge that the decision would be made by six rather than nine justices. The argument was opened by Philip Perlman, solicitor general of the United States, who spoke for the government on behalf of the Negroes in all four cases.[83] He relied on the report of the President's Committee on Civil Rights in attacking the evils of restrictive covenants. Their enforcement, he told the Court, hampered the national government in doing its duty in the fields of public health, housing, home finance, and in the conduct of foreign affairs. And in addition to these practical evils, the solicitor general urged the justices to declare these restrictions to be contrary to public policy and unconstitutional. In its brief the government had suggested in a footnote that the decision in the *Civil Rights Cases*, holding that the Fourteenth Amendment applied only to state action, was still open to reëxamination. When Justice Frankfurter asked Perlman if the government meant to question this rule in these cases, he received the answer that it did not. Justice Murphy asked a single factual question: did the nineteen states which had enforced restrictive covenants have civil-rights laws comparable to the federal statute? Solicitor–General Perlman answered that they did not.

The Missouri case, *Shelley v. Kraemer,* was first argued. George L. Vaughn presented an argument for the Negroes which he later incorporated into a speech for civil rights which he gave before the Democratic National Convention in the summer of 1948. He did repeat the state-action theory and stressed the claim that the judicial enforcement of racial restrictions contravened the Civil Rights Act of 1866. But political argumentation was used too. Vaughn characterized racial restrictive covenants as "the Achilles heel" of American democracy and, as the son of a slave, stated that the Negro knocks at America's door and cries, "Let me come in and sit by the fire. I helped build the house." The justices never once interrupted him. Herman Willer followed Vaughn with a summation of the main legal points which the Negro petitioners wished the Court to take into consideration.

Gerald L. Seegers, who had come to Washington with Emil Koob, president of the Marcus Avenue Improvement Association and the Council for Community Preservation in St. Louis, told the Supreme Court that it should disregard the sociological and political claims of his adversaries. However, he acknowledged that the question was an important one and that the decision would affect the lives of millions of citizens, adding that they were white and not colored people. But even so, Seegers added, "this is a law suit, this is a court of law, and the problems before the Court are legal ones." Later he declared that "the problem of racial discrimination cannot be solved by judicial decrees and the current housing problem is no justification for a judicial amendment of the Constitution."

Turning to his basic legal arguments, Seegers criticized the Negroes' claim that the state court had no right to enforce the covenant in the St. Louis case. That argument, he maintained, is based on the notion that the people received their rights from the state. This was a wrong idea. The people of the State of Missouri, Seegers continued, hold all their rights, except those which they have given up to the state. He claimed that restrictive covenants are valid because the people of Missouri had not authorized the state to prohibit them. The right to like and dislike, to pick and choose, comes from human nature, from natural law. Racial restrictive covenants represent an exercise of these natural rights and as legal contracts must be enforced.

This line of reasoning brought a question from Justice Frankfurter, "Are there any contract clauses which your courts have struck down as contrary to public policy?"

"Yes."

"Where did they get that power?"

Seegers answered, "From the Constitution or from the pronouncements of the people."

"Then they have struck down clauses," asked Justice Frankfurter, making his point, "although a reading of the Constitution and a reading of the statutes show no affirmative sanction has been given?"

"The courts have just said they are not going to enforce it."

In a separate exchange with Justice Murphy, Seegers took the position that there was no essential difference between a price covenant, prohibiting the construction of a house costing less than $25,000, for example, and a racial restrictive covenant. Justice Murphy pointed out that a price contract would not involve race or color, but Seegers answered that it discriminates against poverty and, in principle, could not be distinguished. Although Seegers did not say what constitutional provision would make it so, he stated that if the covenant in the *Shelley* case should fail, then a price covenant would also fall.

Next on the agenda was the Michigan case, handled for the Negroes by NAACP attorneys Loren Miller of Los Angeles and Thurgood Marshall of New York. They reiterated the arguments that: the State of Michigan denied the Negro petitioners their civil right to occupy residential property; the decree of the state court was state action which was contrary to the Fourteenth Amendment. Thurgood Marshall referred to the sociological information in the briefs and urged the High Court to take into consideration the effects of racial segregation on housing problems, crime, disease, and Negro morale. Justice Frankfurter, himself a pioneer in the development of sociological jurisprudence, then asked: "What's the relevance of all this material? If you are right about the legal proposition, the sociological material merely shows how it works. If you're wrong, this material doesn't do you any good." Marshall had to agree that it was not necessary to rely upon it, but that it had legal significance and was essential in the District of Columbia cases where the state action theory was not applicable. There, he continued, the question of public policy was basic and the social and economic data should be an ingredient in any decision relating to the wisdom of enforcing restrictive covenants. Justice Frankfurter thereupon agreed that the sociological material might be of some legal significance, especially in the cases from the District of Columbia.

The NAACP was answered when Henry Gilligan and James Crooks took up the argument for the white landowners from Detroit. First, Gilligan said that there was nothing wrong or immoral in choosing one's associates. He then drew attention to other examples of selection which are socially acceptable. James Crooks tried to convince the Court that the white property owners who had signed the covenant were protecting a right, and if the right meant anything the courts should enforce it.

Justice Frankfurter then asked, "What do you conceive to be the significance of the state action which follows?"

"The decree of the court enforcing the private contract is not an act of the state enforcing discrimination," said Crooks in emphasizing his point, "but is a decree enforcing the rights of citizens."

"I agree," replied Justice Frankfurter, "but the citizens couldn't enforce it themselves. They need the full strength of the state's judicial power to enforce something which the state could not itself declare as state policy. Is that a fair statement of the case?"

"Yes, I think so," answered Crooks.

Moving on to the two cases from Washington, D.C., those who sought to break the racial restrictions, as petitioners, addressed the Court first. Charles Houston gave great attention to the record in these cases in order to make the point that there had been no racial conflict in the neighborhood involved, and no tension, and that the white property owners had not even had their peace of mind disturbed. He also referred to Mrs. Hodge's remark that she would rather live next door to a white criminal than a distinguished Negro. Houston also discussed the sociological material. To this, Justice Frankfurter responded, "I take it that this all goes to the inequities of the case?" Phineas Indritz, also appeared for the Negro position in the District of Columbia cases.

On their home ground, Gilligan and Crooks showed great confidence in answering Houston and Indritz in the *Hodge* cases. Gilligan stressed the long-time policy of the courts of the District toward racial restrictive covenants. And he added that in recent years the Supreme Court had denied certiorari in four restrictive covenant cases. This, he contended, had established "the right of citizens to live in homes in a neighborhood of their own selection unhampered by the dealings of greedy real estate speculators posing as friends of the Negroes."

James Crooks admonished the six justices not to substitute their judgment on policy for that of Congress. The problems of this case should have been solved by Congress, if any part of the government was to intervene. As it was, nothing had been said about restrictive covenants or housing segregation by the national legislative body. Crooks asked the Court, "Has Congress, with its exclusive jurisdiction over the District of Columbia, done one thing to indicate a public policy against segregation?" Finally, Crooks warned that the Court should not lose sight of the fact that as these were cases in the District of Columbia, the Fifth Amendment rather than the Fourteenth was involved. This meant that the issue of equal protection of the laws was not a part of the controversy.

In conclusion, Crooks cited the statement of Chief Judge Groner in the *Mays* case as a commendable guide to sound public policy in this matter.[84]

> That the broad social problem . . . is both serious and acute, no thoughtful person will deny. That its right solution in the general interest calls for the best in statesmanship and the highest patriotism is equally true. But it is just as true that up to the present *no law or public policy has been contrived or declared whereby to eradicate social or racial distinctions in the private lives of individuals.* And it should now be apparent that if ever the two races are to meet upon mutually satisfactory ground, *it cannot be through legal coercion or through the intimidation of factions, or the violence of partisans,* but must be the result of a mutual appreciation of each other's problems, and a voluntary consent of individuals. And it is to this end that the wisest and best of each race should set their course.

Charles Houston appeared briefly in rebuttal to tell the Court that "racism in the United States must stop." He referred to the housing problems of veterans and Japanese Americans to illustrate how the housing problem had become the focal point of a struggle between powerful economic groups and minorities. He asked the Supreme Court to rule that judicial enforcement of racial restrictive covenants was invalid. For as it was, Houston concluded, "the courts, by making racial unity impossible, are endangering national security."

The Court's Decision

On May 3, 1948, Gerald Seegers in St. Louis received a telegram sent at one o'clock in the afternoon from Washington containing the terse message: "ALL COVENANT CASES DECIDED ADVERSELY WAS IN COURT WHEN OPINIONS RENDERED LETTER WILL FOLLOW." [85] The sender was James A. Crooks. As this telegram between two of the leading attorneys for white property owners' groups indicated, the Supreme Court had ruled that judicial enforcement of racial restrictive covenants was invalid. The six justices who participated in the *Restrictive Covenant Cases* were unanimous in this conclusion. Since Chief Justice Vinson discussed the state and federal cases separately, we shall consider his two opinions in turn.

In narrowing the question to the simple and clearly defined question of the validity of court enforcement of privately drawn restrictive covenants whose purpose was to exclude Negroes from owning or occupying property, the chief justice remarked that "basic constitutional issues of obvious importance have been raised." [86] He proceeded then to summarize the history of *Shelley v. Kraemer* and *McGhee v. Sipes.* At the end of these preliminaries he made clear that the main proposition to be considered was the petitioners' claims that judicial enforcement of the restrictive covenants in these cases violated rights guaranteed to them by the equal-protection clause of the Fourteenth Amendment.

Chief Justice Vinson cleared the decks for a consideration of this question by explaining that it had never been before the Court. The *Corrigan* case, he said, raised the limited question of the validity of racial restrictive covenants. The separate issue of court enforcement was not raised in that case. In fact, he pointed out that because it was a federal case, *Corrigan v. Buckley* [87] could not present issues under the Fourteenth Amendment, for the limitations of that amendment apply only to states and not to the national government. Only one other case involving racial covenants had been considered by the Supreme Court. But in that case, *Hansberry v. Lee*,[88] the constitutional issues raised in the *Shelley* and *McGhee* cases were not reached by the Court.

Scrutinizing the terms of the restrictions involved in the principal cases, the chief justice, striving to spell out the issue in its simplest terms, stressed the fact that the covenants were directed toward a designated class "defined wholly in terms of race or color." [89] The restrictions prevent Negroes from owning or making use of certain properties for residential purposes. At this point Chief Justice Vinson added the pertinent comment "that among the civil rights intended to be protected from discriminatory state action by the Fourteenth Amendment are the rights to acquire, enjoy, own and dispose of property." This was established by the Civil Rights Act of 1866, "enacted before the Fourteenth Amendment but vindicated by it." The Supreme Court had protected this right by declaring invalid state statutes and city ordinances which limited Negroes from establishing homes wherever they desired.

It was an established principle, therefore, that restriction on the right of occupancy like that created by the covenants in the present cases could not have been validly imposed by state legislatures or city councils. But here the discrimination was first determined "by the terms of agreements among private individuals." This was private conduct, and under the rule of the *Civil Rights Cases,* the Fourteenth Amendment erects no shield against it no matter how discriminatory or wrongful.[90]

> We conclude, therefore, that the restrictive agreements standing alone cannot be regarded as a violation of any rights guaranteed to petitioners by the Fourteenth Amendment. So long as the purposes of those agreements are effectuated by voluntary adherence to their terms, it would appear that there has been no action by the State and the provisions of the Amendment have not been violated.

So before moving on, the chief justice underlined his devotion to precedent.

Chief Justice Vinson observed that while the formation of restrictive covenants was by private action, their purposes "were secured only by judicial enforcement by state courts." This raised two questions. Did the judicial enforcement of private agreements amount to state action? If so, did the action of the state courts in these cases deprive the Negroes of rights guaranteed by the Fourteenth Amendment?

To set the stage for a consideration of these questions Chief Justice Vinson reviewed a number of Supreme Court decisions, and found that it had long been established "that the action of state courts and of judicial officers in their official capacities is to be regarded as action of the State within the meaning of the Fourteenth Amendment." This had been spelled out in the early cases construing that amendment as well as many more recently decided. It was pointed out that the Court had reversed criminal convictions in state courts because those courts had failed to provide a fair hearing. In addition to these examples the chief justice noted that the action of state courts in enforcing a substantive common-law rule had been held to be state action of the sort prohibited by the Fourteenth Amendment. On the basis of this summary he reached the following conclusion: [91]

> The short of the matter is that from the time of the adoption of the Fourteenth Amendment until the present, it has been the consistent ruling of this Court that the action of the States to which the Amendment has reference, includes action of state courts and state judicial officials.

"Against this background of judicial construction," Chief Justice Vinson announced that the Court had "no doubt that there has been state action in these cases in the full and complete sense of the phrase." The properties involved had been willingly sold by the owners and the Negroes were willing purchasers.[92]

> It is clear that but for the active intervention of the state courts, supported by the full panoply of state power, the petitioners would have been free to occupy the properties in question without restraint.

These are not cases, as has been suggested, in which the States have merely abstained from action, leaving private individuals free to impose such discriminations as they see fit. Rather, these are cases in which the States have made available to such individuals the full coercive power of government to deny to petitioners, on the grounds of race, or color, the enjoyment of property rights in premises which petitioners are willing and able to acquire and which the grantors are willing to sell.

The facts that the judicial action was taken in connection with the state's common-law policy, or that the discriminatory pattern was first defined by a private agreement, did not alter the conclusion that enforcement was state action.

Coming at last to the second issue, whether this state action denied the Negro petitioners the equal protection of the laws insured by the Fourteenth Amendment, Chief Justice Vinson stated his affirmative answer succinctly. There had been discrimination. It was imposed by the state courts in these cases. As a denial of the rights of ownership or occupancy of property equally with other citizens this was state action which could not stand.

The remainder of the chief justice's opinion was in the nature of a mopping-up operation. The claim of the respondents that since the state courts stood ready to enforce restrictive covenants against white persons, enforcement against colored persons did not deny them the equal protection of the laws was answered bluntly. He replied that it was no answer to this discrimination against Negroes "to say that the courts may also be induced to deny white persons rights of ownership and occupancy on grounds of race or color." Chief Justice Vinson disposed of the whole matter with the aphorism, "Equal protection of the laws is not achieved through indiscriminate imposition of inequalities." Nor could he find merit in the notion that the refusal of the judiciary to enforce the restrictive covenants would deny white property owners access to the courts. "The Constitution confers upon no individual the right to demand action by the State which results in the denial of equal protection of the laws to other individuals."

Speaking again for a unanimous six-man court, Chief Justice Vinson reached the same result in the federal cases by a different line of reasoning.[93] The Civil Rights Act of 1866 provided the first ground for the Supreme Court's decision. This statute which guaranteed to all citizens the equal right to have and to hold property included the District of Columbia within the phrase "every State and Territory." Repeating the line of thought laid down in the state cases, Chief Justice Vinson stressed these principles: Congress had power to enact this legislation and to apply it to the District of Columbia. The statute did not invalidate private agreements, voluntarily enforced. It was directed only against governmental action. The scope and purpose of the statute was identical with the Fourteenth Amendment, for they were passed by the same Congress and were part of the same policy. The chief justice then applied these interpretations to the facts of the cases before him and found that the Negro petitioners were denied the right to own and occupy property by virtue of the action of the federal courts of the District of Columbia.[94]

> The Negro petitioners entered into contracts of sale with willing sellers for the purchase of properties upon which they desired to establish homes. Solely because of their race and color they are confronted with orders of court divesting their titles in the properties and ordering that the premises be vacated. White sellers, one of whom is a petitioner here, have been enjoined from selling the properties to any Negro or colored person. Under such circumstances, to suggest that the Negro petitioners have been accorded the same rights as white citizens to purchase, hold, and convey real property is to reject the plain meaning of language. We hold that the action of the District Court directed against the Negro purchasers and the white sellers denies rights intended by Congress to be protected by the Civil Rights Act and that, consequently, the action cannot stand.

Even in the absence of the statute, Chief Justice Vinson declared that judicial support of racial restrictions was contrary to the nation's public policy and should be corrected by the Supreme Court. Where this is true, federal courts have an obligation to refrain from using their power to enforce covenants. State court enforcement of racial restrictions violated the Fourteenth Amendment. This limitation did not touch federal action, and so the chief justice concluded: [95]

> It is not consistent with the public policy of the United States to permit federal courts in the Nation's capital to exercise general

equitable powers to compel action denied the state courts where such state action has been held to be violative of the guaranty of the equal protection of the laws. We cannot presume that the public policy of the United States manifests a lesser concern for the protection of such basic rights against discriminatory action of federal courts than against such action taken by the courts of the States.

In a short concurring opinion, Justice Frankfurter agreed that the judicial enforcement of racial restrictive covenants was unconstitutional, but not "for any narrow or technical reason." [96] Frankfurter thought that there had been a violation of "rights so basic to our society that, after the Civil War, their protection against invasion by the States was safeguarded by the Constitution." For the courts to enjoin citizens from using these rights he thought particularly ironic, because "equity is rooted in conscience" and involves "the exercise of a sound judicial discretion."

IX

ADJUSTMENTS UNDER
THE NEW RULE OF LAW

The Negro Victory

To the National Association for the Advancement of Colored People, the favorable decision of the Supreme Court in the 1948 *Restrictive Covenant Cases* was doubly sweet. A new rule that courts may not enjoin violations of racial covenants had been established without sacrificing the interests of the Negro families involved in the test cases. In Detroit, Orsel McGhee and his family were "mighty happy." McGhee said, "We've tried to be good neighbors. If some of them don't like us, we just can't help it." [1] The Shelley family of St. Louis, depicted by the press as "one of the spearheads of a great legal battle," [2] was jubilant. It was reported that another defendant, James Hurd in Washington, had expected to win and was pleased to be confirmed.[3] In addition, the Supreme Court's decision assured other Negroes on Bryant Street in Washington that they could remain in their new homes. One newcomer, a messenger at the Pentagon, was told the news and exclaimed, "Well, what do you know? That's a great thing. I knew it couldn't stay that way. This is America, brother." [4]

Since these cases were merely representative, the new rule which was produced from them was quickly applied to benefit other Negroes. A Negro in California had been imprisoned for refusing to vacate restricted property. On the authority of the *Shelley* rule, he was granted a writ of habeas corpus by the state supreme court and released from jail.[5] The other cases were less dramatic. The United States Supreme Court acted on its own rule in three cases on May 10, 1948. In the *Monroe Avenue Church* case, certiorari was granted and the judgment of the Ohio courts reversed without opinion.[6] The Supreme Court dealt similarly with two California cases in which a Korean and a Chinese might otherwise have been evicted from their newly acquired homes.[7] Within months, the *Shelley* rule was followed in several state supreme courts. In Illinois, *Tovey v. Levy*,[8] and in New York, *Kemp v. Rubin*,[9] were summarily dismissed. The California Supreme Court refused injunctive relief in nine racial restrictive covenant cases.[10] Additional actions against Negroes were eliminated from the dockets in New Jersey,[11] Maryland,[12] Michigan,[13] Missouri,[14] and Oklahoma.[15]

Litigation appeared to be ended, but the full implication of the 1948 decision would be difficult to calculate. A Negro newspaper, the *Pittsburgh Courier*, told its readers via headlines that the Supreme Court's message was, "Live Anywhere You Can Buy." [16] Yet, it was evident that few colored persons would be able to act upon this invitation. Loren Miller felt that it would be "folly to expect an overnight reversal of social attitudes implemented by court decisions and rooted in custom." [17] In an editorial, the *Washington Post* observed that the removal of a legal barrier to housing for Negroes did not end economic and social limitations. "No one need either hope or fear," it continued, "that the Supreme Court's action will change the situation quickly. The Ghetto wall is merely breached, not demolished." [18] Others, too, believed that Negroes had gained a limited victory. This opinion appeared in the *Notre Dame Lawyer:* [19]

> No great change in the race patterns of America's housing accommodations will come overnight. The Negro purchaser can now drive a sharper bargain and, as a result, prices in Negro neighborhoods will drop. However, the Negro who seeks entrance into the holy of holies, a "white neighborhood," still must face onerous difficulties.

Although it was understood that the millennium had not arrived, the covenant decisions were widely hailed. One writer said "a tremendous victory in the struggle to protect and preserve the civil liberties the Constitution intended to share" had been achieved.[20] "The decision of the Court represents a significant advance in the protection of human rights." [21] John Frank called the decision "the most important of the year in terms of legal theory." [22] There was a prediction that the new rule would "go far towards effectuating the goals which the Fourteenth Amendment was designed to achieve." [23] In the *New Republic,* the Court's action was regarded as "a reaffirmation of the basic principle that the law can't be used as a weapon to deprive Americans, regardless of their color, creed or social condition, of equality of opportunity." [24] The new rule was endorsed in a number of other newspapers,[25] periodicals,[26] and law reviews.[27]

Among commentators who approved of the newly established rule, there was disagreement as to its meaning in the context of the Negro's place in American public law. One critic could not reconcile the *Restrictive Covenant Cases* "with decisions of the Supreme Court sanctioning state segregation in schools, and public carriers." [28] Another believed that the anomaly would be ended to the advantage of Negroes.[29] A third writer specified that "in destroying the force and effect of racial restrictive covenants, the Court appears . . . to have seriously undermined the foundation of an extensive field of state segregation laws previously deemed unassailable." [30]

Whatever its implications, the 1948 decision ending enforcement of racial restrictions in housing was highly regarded by the Negro community. In an editorial titled "Let Freedom Ring," the *Chicago Defender* looked back to the bad old days: [31]

> These covenants have been responsible for more human misery, more crime, more disease and violence than any other factor in our society. They have been used to build the biggest ghettoes in history. They have been used to pit race against race and to intensify racial and religious prejudices in every quarter.

The editorial saluted Chief Justice Vinson and the Supreme Court for bringing "to a dramatic close one of the ugliest developments in American history."

In accounting for the victory, Negro and white opponents of covenants had themselves, as well as the Supreme Court, to congratulate. For the NAACP, Walter White calculated that $100,000 had been spent during thirty-one years of litigation.[32] The *Chicago Defender* had this to say about the organized work that had been accomplished.[33]

Tribute must be paid to the Negro press, the National Association for the Advancement of Colored People and to all the organizations and their leaders, white and colored, who have fought so valiantly to abolish restrictive agreements. Special honors must go to Thurgood Marshall and the legal department of the NAACP which he heads.

In this gallant fight, however, we found an ally in the Federal Government itself. It was Solicitor General Philip Perlman at the bidding of Attorney General Tom Clark and President Truman who opened the argument against restrictive covenants in the hearings before the Supreme Court.

The profound and eloquent appeal of the Federal government before the Court on behalf of full citizenship for all Americans marked a high point in this historic struggle. President Truman threw the whole weight of the Executive branch of the government behind the fight to emancipate us from these restrictions which have for so long despoiled our lives and impeded our progress.

In spite of the gains made, Negroes were reminded by Walter White that a complex of interest groups had fought against them.[34]

. . . the fantastically financed real estate boards, national, state and local, neighborhood associations, a goodly number of anti-Semitic and anti-Negro organizations, some of the press, and the vast resources of many banks, trust companies, holding corporations and insurance companies.

The veteran leader of the NAACP could not expect this powerful aggregation to fade away. The Negro victory was, therefore, a limited one which, White concluded, would have to be protected and defended.[35]

The fight is not over. Just as it took four Supreme Court decisions over a period of more than twenty years to wipe out finally disfranchisement by white primaries, so will the vast interests attempt to find some other means of maintaining residential segregation. But we have moved forward a long way through this decision and those who believe in democracy now are on the offensive and have put the enemies of decency on the defensive as they have never been before.

Caucasian Comment and Criticism

"Of course, I'm very much disappointed," said a former president of the District of Columbia Federation of Citizens Associations, "but I don't think anyone has the right to expect anything
else from the present Supreme Court." [36] However, he hoped that
residential segregation could be continued.

> I shall do everything in my power to urge the people not to
> sell property to anyone unless they are sure that the buyer is go-
> ing to occupy it himself; that they not sell to the whelps who
> traffic in the welfare of decent citizens.

As onetime leader of the sixty-nine neighborhood groups included
in the Federation in Washington, he felt sure that the decision
would not change the attitudes of the people. If feelings stood
still, he was certain that attorneys could accommodate them to
the law.

> I'm sure that there will be methods devised that will protect
> people who want to have neighbors who think along the same
> lines. I have no compunctions against deserving colored people
> trying to get ahead, but I think they would be happier living
> among their own people, just as we feel better among our own.

The most extreme criticism of the Supreme Court's action in
the covenant cases came from Southern politicians who had previously shown no interest in that particular problem. On the
floor of Congress, Representative John Rankin of Mississippi
shouted: [37]

> Mr. Speaker, there must have been a celebration in Moscow
> last night; for the Communists won their greatest victory in the
> Supreme Court of the United States on yesterday, when that once
> august body proceeded to destroy the value of property owned
> by tens of thousands of loyal Americans in every state in the
> Union by their anti-covenants decision.

Another Mississippi congressman, John Bell Williams, complained
to the House of Representatives that "white Christians seem to
have no rights which the present Supreme Court feels bound to
respect." [38]

In contrast to these voices of doom, many individual white

property owners adjusted to the implication of the *Shelley* rule by accepting Negroes as neighbors. "It's all over now," Mrs. Frederic Hodge lamented in Washington. "There's nothing to say. But we're staying right here." [39] The Hodges said they would retain their house on Bryant Street as a matter of principle, but did not indicate under what principle. Perhaps there was a limit to their interest in segregating themselves from colored people. Another plaintiff in the 1948 cases, Benjamin Sipes of Detroit, also stayed in his home after the Negroes secured their tenure next door.[40]

Criticisms of the new rule of law by legal writers sprang from the premises long held by white property owners. First was the view that the past should be conserved which meant in particular that the favorable precedents should not be abandoned.

> When placed against their proper background, the Supreme Court's rulings in the recent covenant cases unquestionably constitute bad law. The employment of such covenants for generations both in the states and the District of Columbia, the refusal of a single state legislature . . . to nullify them, the silence of Congress for years in the face of their widespread use, and the uniform sanctioning of them and their enforcement in equity by state and federal courts alike make any other conclusion unrealistic.[41]

It was observed that precedent had been ignored for the express purpose of protecting the civil rights of minorities. But in doing this, it was argued that the Court made a poor bargain for its new rule jeopardizing the rights of contract and property held by whites.[42] This situation, said James Crooks who had argued the Washington cases before the Supreme Court, left the lawyer as well as the individual high and dry.[43]

> In those cases involving contract and property rights in conflict with the Court's conception of civil rights, the decisions have resulted in confusion as to just what remains of prior well-established rules of contract and property. How and what to advise a client becomes ever more difficult.

From St. Louis, Gerald Seegers shared these sentiments, saying, in reference to his work in the *Shelley* case, that he "failed sufficiently to stress the fact that a court determination of contract rights is one of the rights of a free people." The deprivation of these rights, Seegers believed, would itself become "a violation of constitutional rights, both human and property." [44]

Secondly, attack was leveled against the Supreme Court's expansion of the state-action concept. The president of the Virginia State Bar Association devoted a full convention address to what he described as the "spurious" interpretation by the Court.[45] He pointed out that, as the concept stood, state action could be used to invade all remaining areas of private life. Another critic agreed: [46]

> It is submitted that if all state court judgments are "state action" within the meaning of the Fourteenth Amendment, it may be wondered whether a union shop agreement is enforceable lest it discriminate against non-union labor as a class, or whether any contract of hire is enforceable, lest it discriminate against those who were not hired. Similarly, one may wonder whether a dealer-producer marketing agreement, the lease of an apartment, or any executory contract, could be enforced without an examination by the Court to determine whether the parties had treated all persons with that scrupulous regard for fairness and equality which the Fifth and Fourteenth Amendments demand of those who enjoy the public trust as state and federal officers.

Thirdly, Chief Justice Vinson's distinction between the validity of a covenant standing alone and its invalidity when enforced by a court was scoffed at. "The effect of the decision," said one writer, "is to leave the landowner with a perfectly valid contract, for the breach of which he has no remedy—he has a right without a remedy." [47] James Crooks especially regretted this, for "the inseparability of validity and remedy has been destroyed; the Constitution has been invoked to deprive citizens of the use of their courts for the enforcement of valid contracts." [48]

Finally, the Supreme Court was charged with having enacted judicial legislation and thereby having gone beyond its proper function. One writer said: [49]

> There is a sizable school of thought in the country which embraces the notion that when the people or their representatives lag in their social thinking, the judiciary should bring them up to date. Some such idea apparently motivated the Supreme Court in deciding the restrictive covenant cases. But this doctrine is a

pernicious one for it allows the courts to become creators of
public policy, contrary to the principles and the traditions on
which our constitutional system is based.

This view, in the *South Carolina Law Quarterly,* was shared by
the President of the Virginia State Bar Association: [50]

> There is no reason to believe that the national crisis in housing,
> which affects all races, will be solved by eliminating judicial
> enforcement of restrictive covenants. The correction of the soci-
> ological problems relied upon by the appellants is the responsi-
> bility of the legislative and executive branches of the govern-
> ment. Neither will racial tolerance be enhanced by a decision
> which permits non-Caucasians to invade a neighborhood which
> the other residents desire to maintain as a Caucasian community.

The Debate Over Property Values

The end of equitable enforcement of racial covenants in 1948
changed few attitudes about the desirability of having Negro
neighbors. Some home owners confessed to racial prejudice, pure
and simple. A larger number claimed to abhor discrimination,
but defended residential segregation with economic arguments.

> "WHAT'S MY HOUSE GOING TO BE WORTH?" is the ques-
> tion almost everyone asks when he hears that colored people are
> moving into the house down the street. Someone almost always
> answers, "Property values always go down when Negroes get
> into the neighborhood." [51]

This concern was said to be widespread by those who sought to
improve their housing conditions and opportunities. Evidence of
how widely held is the view that values dropped when colored
persons arrived came directly from white property owners, too.
Fear that this would come about after the *Shelley* case, was revealed by the remarks of Emil Koob to the Marcus Avenue Improvement Association in St. Louis, in September, 1948. [52]

> We feel if we can curb this hysteria now—we know people
> are running for cover—they can't get the price for their property
> —real estate men are telling them "you can't sell to whites, you
> might as well start to unload to Negroes." We know this is true
> because the men who are out approaching the residents in this
> area are using these tactics.

Public opinion believing in the depreciative effect on values of homes with Negro neighbors extended to many professionals in the American Institute of Real Estate Appraisers. The Institute's publication, *The Appraisal Journal,* "a medium for the expression of individual opinion," presented both views on the relation between Negroes and values. But its parent body, the National Association of Real Estate Boards, had supported the continuation of restrictive covenants in its brief *amicus curiae* in the *Shelley* case.[53] In a regular feature of the journal, "The Appraisal Docket," the validity of court enforcement of covenants had been urged before the 1948 decision.[54] When the decision went contrary to its wish, the Supreme Court was promptly condemned.[55]

> We cannot resist the parenthetical remark that the present Supreme Court, while free from precise *stare decisis* of its own past making, has certainly disregarded its own past dictum in this type of case. Such a circumstance has not been unusual in the last ten years; indeed, prior determinations of the same court, made by judges presumedly as wise as those now gracing its august bench and written to serve as signposts to us poor benighted as we grope our way, have fallen like blighted leaves after the autumn frost of the last ten years. The unusual is now to be expected of our highest court; the professor of the law may well now include in his curriculum the subject of abandoned precedent.

The affiliation appraisers have with realtors has made them honor-bound not to introduce into a neighborhood, as owners or occupants, "members of any race or nationality, or any individual whose presence will clearly be detrimental to property values in the neighborhood." [56] In 1923, one professional appraiser, Stanley L. McMichael, wrote, in effect, that Negroes should coöperate in this ethical principle.[57]

> They must recognize the economic disturbance their presence in a white neighborhood causes and forego their desire to split off from the established districts where the rest of their race lives.

Twenty-five years of experience reinforced McMichael's belief in the economic desirability of racial segregation. In 1949 he passed on to the appraisal profession the following observations: [58]

> That the entry of non-Caucasians into districts where distinctly Caucasian residents live tends to depress real estate values is

agreed to by practically all real estate subdividers and students of
city life and growth. Infiltration at the outset may be slow, but
once the trend is established, values start to drop, until properties
can be purchased at discounts of from 50 to 75 per cent.

This race consciousness has been echoed in the writings of
another expert on the valuation of residential real estate, Arthur
A. May. "It is people who make value," May has written,[59] but
some people create more value than others. He has said that
what counts is "the homogeneity of the people who live within
the area, their sameness of income and their sameness of social
habits." [60] As a professional appraiser, May told a client, in judg-
ing the worth of a property, to be sure that his prospective neighbors

> were of about his same economic level, that culturally they were
> approximately his equal, and that they were of his same race and
> preferably his same religion in order to assure him that the in-
> terests and living habits of himself and his neighbors would be
> parallel.[61]

It has been made clear by May that the highest values are
attached to white sections. The presence of nonwhite groups or
even "people of foreign birth" and "of their children" scales down
the worth of property.[62]

After 1948 the traditional views on real-estate values were
challenged and contradicted. Men who wished to see the psycho-
logical barriers to a larger housing market for Negroes go the
way of legal barriers disputed the standard appraisal gospel. The
"statement that people should live in homogeneous neighborhoods with those of their race, religion, and economic status"
has been attacked by Charles Abrams of New York as a "social
judgment, not a real estate appraisal." [63] Abrams lectured the
appraiser to "realize the limits of his calling." Speaking of
McMichael and May, Abrams said that the appraiser should "as-
certain the value of a property at a given time or place" and
leave to others the work of the economist, sociologist, and social
psychologist.

Disagreeing flatly with the appraisers who placed high value
on homogeneity, Abrams gave four reasons why such communities
are socially and financially unstable. First, they lack diversity

and are dull and monotonous. Second, one-class communities are poor places to raise children because they see only their own kind, color, race, and culture. Third, these neighborhoods run contrary to the American tradition of the melting pot. An established system of homogeneous neighborhoods, says Abrams, "would constrict social mobility, stratify living patterns, lose us the precious democratic dividends of free contact, free movement, and fluidity of culture which are the nub of the Americanization process." Communities which would end these traditional advantages are un-American, he said. Finally, Abrams argued that it was unrealistic to expect a neighborhood to remain static with similar neighbors for a long period of time. Individuals would do well to permit mixed communities and learn to live with them. He thinks the home owner "would feel less disturbed if his neighborhood were a miscellany of creeds and cultures from the start. Stabilized heterogeneity is a better investment in the long run than unstabilized homogeneity."

Charles Abrams's preferences for mixed neighborhoods were supported by the contention that "there are among all minorities, good and bad folk, cultured and ignorant, socially abominable." Therefore the racial restrictions should be eliminated. He believed, moreover, that because of the great differences within particular racial and religious groups, no economic value could be ascertained solely on that basis. Substantiation for these views has recently come from an intensive study in San Francisco of the effects of nonwhite purchases on market prices of residences.[64] The conclusions, which appeared in *The Appraisal Journal*, in July, 1952, indicate that no deterioration in prices followed changes in the racial pattern.[65]

> In San Francisco during the period 1949–1951, areas which experienced nonwhite purchase and occupancy during or shortly before that period did not display the price behavior which the popular theory would predict. Instead, transactions took place at prices closely corresponding to those in comparable all-white areas, although a small fraction of sales differed by plus or minus amounts which may have reflected unusual circumstances: (1) a premium price extracted from a nonwhite buyer anxious to get into that particular locality, (2) a sacrifice price agreed to by a seller desirous of dumping a property in an area believed by him to be on the verge of rapid deterioration.

The idea that nonwhite groups do not lower property values and the new facts supporting this view have been utilized by organizations eager to see Negroes accepted in traditionally white neighborhoods. Typical of the line of reasoning advanced are the following excerpts from a pamphlet, *If Your Neighbors Are Negroes*.[66]

SO YOU WANT TO LOSE MONEY

Yes, if you want to lose money on your house it can be arranged. Here's how and why. When one or more Negro families move into a neighborhood the old property-loss scare usually crops up. Sometimes people talk themselves into the scare, but often the scare is deliberately trumped-up for money-making reasons—huge profits can be made by panicking the market, buying fast and then reselling. Not having the facts, white home-owners get panicky and are ready to sell at any prices, just to unload before the expected "drop in values."

So here's what happens: The white owner sells cheap. The middleman buys cheap. The Negro buyer pays more than the original price of the days before the scare. *Who wins?* Add it up yourself!

Right enough—every time there's a panic *white owners themselves* break down property sales values for a brief period—until the Negro buying begins and prices *boom* far upward.

The moral? Don't panic; sit tight; save your own vested interest in your home and neighborhood.

BUT WAIT—WHAT ABOUT COVENANTS?

Unfortunately, some people still make voluntary agreements to keep "non-Caucasians" out. But any person who wants to can break the agreement at any time and sell to anyone. The racial covenant is now worth slightly less than the paper it is printed on.

From any point of view such covenants were poor protection. They never kept out the really undesirable people—the murderers, law-breakers, wife-beaters, drunks and moral degenerates. Many neighborhoods "protected" by covenants remained all-white *but* filled up with small factories, criminal and near-criminal elements, and the worst kinds of rooming-houses—so that the home-owners' property values were seriously hit.

The educational campaign to make Negroes acceptable has not been a great success. Negroes are being excluded from the largest new suburbs in the country and most white residents acquiesce. Levittown, the prototype of the new suburb, is the largest community in the United States that has no Negro population. In a study of the mass-produced suburb, published in *Harper's Magazine*, Harry Henderson demonstrated that racial myths in housing live on.[67]

> Those who have the greatest conflict are those who call it "disgraceful" but cannot down their worries about "property values." They put the blame for the situation on the "Communists," meaning people who raise the issue and who, in point of fact, are often actually anti-Communist. If this is shown to the complainants, they then blame the builder who "started it," Negroes, and "society," in that order; and again they cite "property values" as a reason for not disturbing the "disgraceful" situation.

Real-Estate Boards and Segregation

Without legal support but with the compulsion to segregate remaining, white property owners in all parts of the country received the coöperation of real-estate boards in keeping Negroes from buying homes in residential areas traditionally reserved for whites. In the past, realtors ordinarily respected the force of restrictive covenants. The Supreme Court's decision in the 1948 cases did not change the minds of most real-estate salesmen. That decision made their position of greater importance for they could enforce segregation whereas the Court would not. Within a month the power of real-estate organizations was being felt. This is how Gerald Seegers described the system to an inquiring Virginian: [68]

> The method now being employed here in St. Louis . . . is to have the Real Estate Exchange zone the city and forbid any member of the exchange under pain of expulsion to sell property in the white zone to a Negro. If the real estate men refused to participate in the sale, the breaches will at least be minimized to those who deal with each other directly or through a . . . nonmember of the exchange who could be easily identified and boycotted more or less by all the people to whom the knowledge comes.

The Marcus Avenue Improvement Association of St. Louis became increasingly interested in close coöperation with the real-estate interests as a means of keeping colored persons from its section of the city. The association took some action of its own. Thus at a meeting in September, 1948, President Emil Koob announced that "block committees of no less than 3 or 4 people [were needed] to see that real estate in their block is not advertized to Negroes." The committees were urged to "find out who is advertizing and hound them by telephone calls." [69] However, the association received splendid coöperation from the St. Louis real-estate organizations.

A communication to an errant real-estate salesman from the Real Estate Board reveals its willingness to forward the purposes of the neighborhood property-owners group. The letter was written on September 25, 1948, addressed to H. F. Mahler, Inc., with headquarters in Maplewood, Missouri, a suburb of St. Louis. It was signed by the executive secretary of the board.[70]

> We are in receipt of a copy of a telegram sent to you by the Marcus Avenue Improvement Association, Inc. in connection with your apparent offer of sale to Negroes of property at 4807 Cupples Place, St. Louis.
>
> The information contained in the telegram regarding the restriction placed by the Members of the St. Louis Real Estate Board is the matter of where they may deal in property with Negroes is correct.
>
> While you are not an Active Member of the St. Louis Board, you are an Active Member of the County Board and therefore a "REALTOR." We would therefore request that you not be a party to a transaction involving property in the jurisdiction of the St. Louis Board which its members are restricted against in the interest of the welfare of the community and also in keeping with Article 34 of the Code of Ethics of the National Associations of Real Estate Boards, which all Member Boards are compelled to have their members observe.
>
> We realize that you may not have been familiar with the rules and regulations of our Board in the matter of where Members may deal in property with Negroes; therefore, this comminique is sent to you as one of information and not condemnation. We hope to have your full coöperation in this matter, the same as though you were an Active Member of this Board, because you are a "REALTOR."

Insurgent real-estate salesmen in all parts of the country were disciplined by local boards. In Atlanta, the Georgia Real Estate

Commission revoked the license of a broker who sold property in a white area to Negroes.[71] Reports from Madison, Wisconsin; [72] Portland, Oregon; [73] and Washington, D.C.[74] indicated that real-estate boards in those cities had ruled it "unethical" for their members to introduce Negroes into white neighborhoods.

Federal Housing Administration Policy

Nearly a year after the *Shelley* decision, in February, 1949, Charles Abrams wrote that the Federal Housing Administration was "the most serious government offender against racial equality." [75] Created in 1934 and placed within the Housing and Home Finance Agency by the reorganization of 1947, the F.H.A. neither makes loans nor builds houses. Its main function is providing insurance against loss on housing loans made by private lending institutions. In 1947, President Truman's Committee on Civil Rights had commended the Federal Housing Administration on its recent abandonment of "the policy by which it encourages the placing of racial restrictive covenants on projects supported by government guarantees." [76] Yet in 1949, Abrams charged that "discrimination is indulged in today as freely as ever on F.H.A.-insured loans." [77]

Acknowledgement of this practice had been made earlier by F.H.A. Commissioner Franklin D. Richards. Moreover, he said that the agency would insure properties subject to racial restrictive covenants in the future.[78] Obviously attuned to the interests and desires of real-estate and banking groups in the country, the F.H.A. made a practice of refusing to insure loans to Negroes in white areas.

The Abrams article on Federal Housing Administration support of racial discrimination in housing was not merely a statement of fact, but part of an effort to change this governmental policy. Letters of complaint were sent to President Truman by the American Jewish Congress [79] and by Walter White for the NAACP.[80] A number of civic groups then addressed a public appeal to the F.H.A. to refuse insurance for housing projects which excluded Negroes.[81] F.H.A. officials denied that the agency sanctioned racial discrimination,[82] but its critics were unconvinced.

On December 2, 1949, the lead story of the *New York Times*

appeared below this headline: TRUMAN PUTS BAN ON ALL HOUSING
AID WHERE BIAS EXISTS.[83] The spokesman for the administration
was Philip B. Perlman, the solicitor general. In New York City
he announced to a meeting of the State Committee on Discrimination in Housing a forthcoming revision in F.H.A. policy. The news story revealed that the new arrangement would
be less of an innovation than the banner headline suggested.
Actually, the new F.H.A. position would merely require insurance to be withheld if, after a date to be specified, a new racial
restriction were attached to the property in question. The policy
would not apply to covenants in existence, which meant it was not
likely to be significant in discouraging the perpetuation of segregated patterns in housing. Yet the announcement promptly received presidential blessings from Key West, and Philip Perlman
stressed that, in addition to Mr. Truman, he spoke for Attorney
General J. Howard McGrath, Home Finance Administrator Raymond M. Foley, and Commissioner Franklin D. Richards of the
Federal Housing Administration. It was made clear by the solicitor that the new policy was being fashioned to bring F.H.A.
mortgage operations into agreement with the Supreme Court's
action in the *Restrictive Covenant Cases* of 1948.

The prospective policy of refusing F.H.A. insurance for restricted
property seriously alarmed housing leaders in the South. Segregation was certain to continue which would mean the end of govern-
ment-insured private housing developments there. An official of
the Home Builders Association of New Orleans cracked, "That's
what I'd expect from Washington." [84] In Montgomery, Atlanta,
and Knoxville it was agreed that the new rule would not work
and should not be applied in the South.

Despite the dismay of white builders, colored people were not
assured of a complete Federal Housing Administration turn-
about. The National Negro Council urged President Truman to
clarify the meaning of the new policy.[85] This was done on December 12, 1949, by the F.H.A. itself through an official order signed
by Franklin D. Richards.[86] The new eligibility requirements for
insurance provided that the mortgage applicant establish that
no racial restriction "has been filed of record at any time subsequent to February 15, 1950." This confirmed the supposition that
covenants in force when the Supreme Court handed down its

decision in 1948, as well as those subsequently recorded until February 15, 1950, would be unaffected by the new F.H.A. order. Commissioner Richards said as much when he predicted little change in his agency's activities as a result of the order.[87] The order set the public record straight and cleared the administration's conscience. In its operation the rule tended to benefit Negroes but did not seriously interfere with the Caucasian objectives.[88]

Searching for New Protections

Hostility of Caucasians, the myth of "property values," and the interest of realtors and the F.H.A. in maintaining the status quo did not entirely prevent the movement of Negroes into white areas in many cities. Surveys in 1951 revealed that while segregated patterns were obvious, a sizable number of Negroes had moved beyond the 1948 racial boundaries in Chicago and Detroit.[89] The situation in New York, Denver, and Los Angeles was said to be even more favorable to Negroes. With respect to St. Louis a leader of the O'Fallon Park Protective Association has said recently that "the 1948 decision of the Supreme Court gave a decided impetus to the trend of Negroes moving into what, up to that time, had been white neighborhoods." [90]

Since informal pressures were too little to stem the color tide, overfearful Caucasians turned to physical violence, but found that it did not work either. In Birmingham, three houses sold to Negroes in a white section were dynamited,[91] and later burned.[92] In Cicero, Illinois, in the summer of 1951, a major race riot had its origins in the housing problem.[93] In Florida, later in the year, an NAACP official was murdered by bombs planted under his home.[94] In San Francisco, a Chinese, who was threatened if he moved into a white district, abided by a referendum vote against him.[95] While the implications of these incidents were not lost on Negroes, they did produce a reaction against the use of force and violence. The press defended the Negroes' right to life as well as liberty and property.[96] Public officials, like Governor Earl Warren of California,[97] sharply criticized lawlessness in race relations. Police protection for harrassed Negroes came into common use.

"A hostile attitude on the part of neighbors to unwanted newcomers will operate to a certain extent," said the *U.S. News*,[98] "but experience has shown that social pressure by itself will not keep a community's gates entirely closed to members of minority groups." The editors of this magazine and numerous other publicists, students, and attorneys after 1948 contributed ideas on methods of renewing legal enforcement of residential segregation. From Virginia, the president of the state bar association, John L. Walker, wrote to Gerald Seegers that practicing lawyers "will be interested in knowing whether or not there are any loopholes in the decisions [of 1948]. In other words, can any restrictive covenant plan be put into effect which will be upheld by the court?"[99] From St. Louis Seegers replied, "You probably realize that many lawyers around the country are thinking in terms of 'loopholes' in the Shelley-Kraemer decision. I am in correspondence with some of them and I suppose if anyone hits on a practicable plan I will hear of it. If and when I do I will disseminate it far and wide."[100]

After all, Chief Justice Vinson had said that the Fourteenth Amendment was not violated by the *making* of a covenant. A report from Tennessee based on interviews of "numerous real estate lawyers" reflected the universal attitude:[101]

> All the attorneys continued to insert the racial covenants when drafting a deed to property so covered stating "everyone does not know such covenants cannot be enforced by court action. The covenant is not invalid as between parties if voluntarily enforced. Furthermore it may have a moral or psychological effect upon a prospective purchaser encompassed by the restrictive covenant."

Before too many persons discovered that courts would not issue injunctions to enforce covenants, the mass search for new legal means of enforcement was well under way. Curiously enough the social views of many attorneys allegedly in favor of less racial discrimination did not prevent them from servicing the cause of the white property owners. The author of one study defined his position in this way:[102]

> The purpose of this paper is to investigate the effectiveness of legal devices, as a means of restricting a residential area to those of "pure Caucasian blood." The personal feelings of the writer are that such a result simply should not be permitted, regardless of

the means. Nevertheless, since prejudice cannot be adjudicated away, lawyers will still be called upon to draw instruments and set up plans to exclude as neighbors those of purportedly undesirable racial origins.

What methods for enforcing segregation by governmental action were suggested? Which ones were placed in operation?

One view was that alternate language in restrictive covenants, with no direct reference to Negroes, would be the best assurance of legal support for segregation. Court enforcement would be a possibility "if the agreement does not specifically mention the minority to be banned." [103] Before the 1948 decisions, in Chicago, the Oakwood-Kenwood Property Owners Association had employed community conservation agreements. The *Chicago Tribune* had recommended these devices.[104]

> Nothing in the decision prevents neighbors from agreeing on maintaining standards of occupancy, such as limiting the number of persons per room or requiring proper care of the premises.
>
> Such agreements are enforceable in the courts. They can preserve the neighborhood values perhaps more effectively than restrictive covenants have succeeded in doing. There are plenty of neighborhoods in Chicago where property values have declined without the presence of Negroes and plenty of other neighborhoods in which Negroes own homes without having brought about any deterioration of values.

Partisans of white property owners acknowledged that these agreements would be "indirectly achieving, to a high degree, the same ends sought by racial restrictions." [105] Simultaneously civil-rights organizations close to the Negro interest were welcoming the use of these agreements. For example, the executive secretary of the Chicago Council Against Racial and Religious Discrimination called the community conservation agreement a "democratic kind of restrictive covenant." [106] He added:

> This is not the complete solution to the problem of neighborhood disintegration. But it may prove a psychological substitute for the earlier covenants and a reasonably practical answer to the burning question asked by residents of many northern cities: Would you want to live next door to a Negro? Only the conservation agreements do not say "Negro."

The economic standards of the conservation agreement were not certain to preserve a community against inroads from well-to-do Negroes or Jews. As assurance that neither the rich nor the poor colored man would become a neighbor, it was suggested that exclusive property owners' clubs be formed.[107] Central control of the admission of new members would be maintained by a permit committee or board of directors. Or a real-estate firm selling property in a subdivision might retain the right to have first chance of buying it back if the new owner offered it for sale. Besides the option method, the *U.S. News* claimed that "approval of neighbors" was a plan in use.[108] Under it, "a majority of the five nearest neighbors must approve the new occupant before a residence can be sold or rented."

New Litigation: The Damages Cases

The possibility of collecting damages from individual white property owners who broke restrictive covenants by selling to Negroes was widely discussed after 1948.[109] The outlook for Caucasians was not too hopeful. First, damages could not be enforced through private action any more than an injunction could be obtained. "Once a breach occurs," it was pointed out, "the restriction can not effectively be enforced except by resort to the State courts, and this the [Supreme] Court has held can not be accomplished consistently with the Fourteenth Amendment." [110] Presuming an action was maintained, a second difficulty followed. What is the measure of damages? A friend of the white property owners answered gloomily in 1948: [111]

> I believe the court would refuse to enforce it on the fact that damages could not be proved nor measured and that the amount for which the breacher would be liable would be ridiculous. You see a suit by one owner would not preclude the other forty-eight from suing and if you brought a class action, how are you going to distribute the damages between the one living next door to the violation and the one further removed from it who logically would not be damaged as greatly.

Between 1949 and 1952 Caucasians in Missouri, Oklahoma, the District of Columbia, Maryland, Michigan, and California sought to collect damages from neighbors who sold property to

Negroes. An award of damages, said the courts of Missouri [112] and Oklahoma,[113] was constitutional. These decisions turned on a distinction between the application of covenants to Negro buyers as against white sellers who had signed the covenant. In each case it was agreed that the covenant could not be enforced by injunction to prevent the Negro purchasers from occupying the homes involved. This was on the authority of *Shelley v. Kraemer*. But in his opinion in that case, Chief Justice Vinson had sanctioned the rule that the Fourteenth Amendment erects no shield against private conduct no matter how discriminatory or wrongful. The Missouri and Oklahoma supreme courts therefore held that restrictive covenants were valid contracts between the white citizens who made them. These contracts could be enforced at law by awarding damages, for that remedy would not injure the right of Negroes to obtain property under equal conditions with whites.

These decisions, widely criticized in the law reviews, were matched by the refusal of courts in four other jurisdictions to enforce racial covenants by sustaining damages. The District Court for the District of Columbia interpreted *Hurd v. Hodge* as meaning that restrictions would not be enforced "by way of judicial action of any kind." [114] The Supreme Courts of Maryland [115] and Michigan [116] reached a like conclusion. In Michigan the trial court held that an action for damages following the breach of a racial restrictive covenant constituted an attempt to enforce it indirectly which, in practical effect, was repugnant to the Fourteenth Amendment. This view was followed by the Michigan Supreme Court, which declared: [117]

> Plaintiff's action for damages may not be regarded as involving individual conduct solely. The aid of the court is invoked on the theory that the agreement is valid as between the parties who signed it and their successors in title, and that the State acting through the courts will permit the recovery of damages for failure to observe it.

But the Court pointed out that if the recovery of damages were allowed in one case, others would follow, with the final result the same as if the covenant were enforced by the courts in equity. Finally, in California the state courts would not enforce a restrictive covenant through an award of damages either.[118]

An authoritative answer to the question raised by these damage actions was assured in the spring of 1953. At that time the Supreme Court of the United States granted certiorari in the California case, *Barrows v. Jackson*.[119] The six damage cases decided in lower courts after the 1948 covenant cases showed that there was great continuity in the participating interest groups. The white defendant in these cases had been represented by NAACP attorneys: Charles Houston in Washington, D.C., Willis Graves in Detroit, and Loren Miller in Los Angeles. *Amicus curiae* briefs were filed by civil-rights organizations. On the opposing side, improvement associations joined to make singular use of the *amici curiae* brief when the Supreme Court was asked to grant certiorari in the *Barrows* case. One brief came from the Affiliated Neighbors, Inc. and forty-eight other organizations in Los Angeles. Another was filed by Gerald Seegers for the Marcus Avenue Improvement Association of St. Louis. The United States Supreme Court was once again in the cross-fire of organized Negroes and white property owners.

X

THE SUPREME COURT AND

THE 1953 DAMAGES CASE

Summary of the Decision

The Supreme Court ruled, on June 15, 1953, the last day of its regular term, that a racial restrictive covenant may not be enforced at law by a suit for damages. Justice Sherman Minton spoke for the Court as it applied the rule of the 1948 cases one step further in *Barrows v. Jackson*.[1] An award of damages by a court would be state action as surely as a restraining injunction. This was the prevailing view of the majority of six justices, but Chief Justice Vinson vehemently dissented from this decision. He was alone, for Justices Reed and Jackson took no part in the consideration or decision of the case.

The restrictive covenant in this case had been entered into by property owners in the same Los Angeles neighborhood in October, 1944, and had been recorded the following May. By its terms each signer bound himself and his successors in interest that no part of his property "should ever at any time be used or occupied by any person or persons not wholly of the white or Caucasian race."[2] Each signer "also agreed and promised in writing that this restriction should be incorporated in all papers and transfers of lots or parcels of land" covered by the covenant. In September, 1950, one of the original signers, Mrs. Leola Jackson, broke the covenant in two respects. First, she sold her property without incorporating in the deed the restriction contained in the covenant. Second, the sale was to Negroes and she thereby permitted non-Caucasians to move in and occupy the premises.

For breaching the covenant in these two respects, Mrs. Jackson was sued for damages by three neighboring property owners. No legal action was taken against the Negro occupants for that would have been clearly violative of the doctrine of *Shelley v. Kraemer*. The action against Mrs. Jackson originated in the Superior Court of the State of California for the County of Los Angeles in February, 1951. The plaintiffs asked for damages of $11,600 plus reasonable attorney's fees and costs. Mr. and Mrs. Edgar W. Barrows claimed that their property had been "materially depreciated in value" and that it had become "less attractive as a residential area." They sought damages in the sum of $3,100. Richard Pikaar asked for $4,000 as he had purchased his lot "in the knowledge and belief that the premises . . . would at no time prior to the expiration of said Agreement in the year 2043, be used or occupied or permitted to be used or occupied as residence by any person or persons not wholly of the white or Caucasian race, except employees or servants of the occupants or owners of said premises." The other plaintiff, M. M. O'Gara applied for $4,500 in damages.

On March 26, 1951, Judge Daniel N. Stevens of the Los Angeles Superior Court declared that the suit for damages could not be maintained. His basic reason for concluding that the plaintiffs' complaint stated no cause of action that could be judicially recognized was rested on constitutional grounds. Judge Stevens said: [3]

> A reading of *Shelley v. Kraemer* . . . and *Hurd v. Hodge* . . . convinces me that the United States Supreme Court intended by its pronouncements therein to preclude State courts from giving judicial recognition to and enforcement of race restriction covenants contained in private agreements, whether such judicial enforcement be by way of injunction, declaratory relief, damages or any other type of action in which the remedy is predicated upon a judicial holding, express or implied, that such a covenant is valid.

This view was adopted by the District Court of Appeal for the State of California when it considered *Barrows v. Jackson*, on appeal, in a decision filed by Judge Vallée on August 6, 1952.[4] Pikaar, O'Gara, and the Barrows then petitioned the Supreme Court of California for a hearing but this was denied, over the wishes of three justices,[5] on October 4, 1952. Thereupon the United States Supreme Court granted certiorari on March 9, 1953 [6] and heard oral arguments on April 28 and 29.[7]

The first question faced by Justice Minton, in his opinion for the Supreme Court, was whether an award of damages by a court would constitute state action under the Fourteenth Amendment. He held that it does. This is how he regarded Mrs. Jackson's position: [8]

> To compel respondent to respond in damages would be for the State to punish her for her failure to perform her covenant to continue to discriminate against non-Caucasians in the use of her property. The result of that sanction by the State would be to encourage the use of restrictive covenants. To that extent, the State would act to put its sanction behind the covenants. If the State may thus punish respondent for her failure to carry out her covenant, she is coerced to continue to use her property in a discriminatory manner, which in essence is the purpose of the covenant. Thus, it becomes not respondent's voluntary choice but the State's choice that she observe her covenant or suffer damages. The action of a state court at law to sanction the validity of the restrictive covenant here involved would constitute state action as surely as it was state action to enforce such covenants in equity. . . .

Clearly if the covenant were to be enforced the state must participate, but would the state action in allowing damages deprive anyone of rights protected by the Constitution? Justice Minton did not think that Mrs. Jackson was being denied constitutional rights but he believed that the collection of damages from her would amount to a deprivation of equal protection of the laws of Negroes who were "unidentified but identifiable." [9]

> If a state court awards damages for breach of a restrictive covenant, a prospective seller of restricted land will either refuse to sell to non-Caucasians or else will require non-Caucasians to pay a higher price to meet the damages which the seller may incur. Solely because of their race, non-Caucasians will be unable to purchase, own, and enjoy property on the same terms as Caucasians.

Although non-Caucasians would be denied their constitutional rights, no individual representative of this injured group was before the Court in *Barrows v. Jackson*. This raised a most difficult question for the Supreme Court: May Mrs. Jackson, "whom petitioners seek to coerce by an action to pay damages for her failure to honor her restrictive covenant, rely on the invasion of the rights of others in her defense to this action?" [10]

Justice Minton recognized and reaffirmed the long-standing rule that "one may not claim standing in this Court to vindicate the constitutional rights of some third party." [11] Since the jurisdiction of the Supreme Court was restricted to "cases" and "controversies," the Court would not decide a dispute unless a real and direct injury might result to one of the parties. The justices had always used self-restraint in accepting cases so that "even though a party will suffer a direct substantial injury from application of a statute, he cannot challenge its constitutionality unless he can show that he is within the class whose constitutional rights are allegedly infringed." [12] This practice, said Justice Minton, "is a salutary rule."

There are exceptions to every rule, especially when the rule depends on self-enforcement. *Barrows v. Jackson* presented the Supreme Court with "a unique situation." The main reason for making an exception to the usual rule was that the basic rights of Negroes would otherwise be denied.[13]

> Under the peculiar circumstances of this case, we believe the reasons which underlie our rule denying standing to raise another's rights, which is only a rule of practice, are outweighed by the need to protect the fundamental rights which would be denied by permitting the damages action to be maintained.

A distinction was made between this case where *court* action was involved and the case in which *legislative* action was being reviewed. The United States Supreme Court would not permit the enforcement of segregation in housing through other means. Therefore it would be illogical and unwarranted for the Court to allow the same end to be accomplished indirectly through a suit for damages, "simply because the person against whom the injury is directed is not before the Court to speak for himself." Justice Minton regarded this case as one in which Negroes and Mrs. Jackson would both receive protection. "She will be permitted to protect herself and, by so doing, close the gap to the use of this covenant, so universally condemned by the courts." [14]

The exception made to the usual rule that one may not claim standing to vindicate the rights of some third party, was not being made for the first time in the *Barrows* case. Justice Minton recalled the 1925 decision of the Supreme Court in *Pierce v. Society of Sisters*.[15] There a state statute required all parents to send their children to public schools and the law was challenged by a parochial school. The parochial school's claim that its property rights were denied was supported by the assertion that the constitutional rights of parents and guardians would also be deprived by the statute. The Supreme Court permitted this even though the persons whose rights were invoked were identified only as "present and prospective patrons" of the schools. In *Barrows v. Jackson*, said Justice Minton, "it is not non-Caucasians as a group whose rights are asserted by respondent, but the rights of particular non-Caucasian would-be users of restricted land." [16]

In conclusion, Justice Minton disposed of constitutional claims made by the petitioners. They contended that for California courts to refuse to enforce the racial covenant was to impair the obligation of their contracts. There was a paradox in Justice Minton's answer, for while he was broadening the concept of state action in the scope of protection afforded Negroes by the Fourteenth Amendment, he followed the tradition of narrowly construing the contract clause of the Constitution. The provision is that: "No State shall . . . pass any . . . Law impairing the Obligation of Contracts." [17] His view was that this was directed only against impairment by legislation and not by judgments of courts. The petitioners also claimed that they were the ones being denied due process and equal protection of the laws by the failure to enforce the covenants. This was answered by reference to the *Shelley* case: "The Constitution confers upon no individual the right to demand action by the State which results in the denial of equal protection of the laws to other individuals." [18]

Chief Justice Vinson's Dissent

The author of the Court's opinion in the 1948 injunction cases would not accept the majority's position as expressed by Justice

Minton in 1953. Although not ordinarily given to sharp language, the chief justice opened his dissent on this note: [19]

> This case, we are told, is "unique." I agree with the characterization. The Court, by a unique species of arguments, has developed a unique exception to an otherwise easily understood doctrine. While I may hope that the majority's use of "unique" is but another way of saying that the decision today will be relegated to its precise facts tomorrow, I must voice my dissent.

Throughout his opinion, Vinson questioned the motives of the majority and the reasoning of Justice Minton. He reminded his colleagues that Supreme Court justices were obliged to rest their decisions "on the Constitution alone." He added, "we must set aside predilections on social policy and adhere to the settled rules which restrict the exercise of our power of judicial review." "A simple self-serving process of argument" described the Court's opinion in which the chief justice felt "personal predisposition" had been put "in a paramount position over well-established proscriptions on power." [20]

This bitter response in Chief Justice Vinson was provoked by the Court's application of the *Shelley* rule to a case in which the enforcement of a covenant did not cause any direct injury to an identified non-Caucasian. He first restated the rule of the *Shelley* case that it is not unlawful to make restrictive covenants. Added to this was a clarification that "it is not unlawful to enforce them unless the method by which they are enforced in some way contravenes the Federal Constitution or a federal statute." [21] Judicial enforcement of the covenants in the 1948 cases was struck down because it was directed against the Negro petitioners and deprived them of their property solely because of their race.

The chief justice believed that the *Barrows* case was different from the situation facing the Court in 1948. He observed that the majority had identified "no non-Caucasian who has been injured or could be injured" if damages were assessed against Mrs. Jackson.[22]

> Indeed, the non-Caucasian occupants of the property involved in this case will continue their occupancy undisturbed, regardless of the outcome of the suit. The state court was asked to do nothing

which would impair their rights or their enjoyment of the property.

This fact was decisive for Vinson for it meant that "the constitutional defect, present in the Shelley Case, is removed from this case." Because of this the Court "has no power to deal with the constitutional issue." To Chief Justice Vinson "the majority has failed to put first things first." [23]

Supreme Court practice, refraining from deciding a constitutional issue "until it has a party before it who has standing to raise the issue," said the chief justice, has a line of decisions supporting it "long enough to warrant the respect of even the most hardened skeptic of the strength of stare decisis as an effective limitation upon this Court's exercise of jurisdiction in constitutional cases." [24] The rule is sound and "no sophistry is required to apply it to this case." Under the standards of this rule, Mrs. Jackson must show that she, herself, "and not some unnamed person in an amorphous class, is the victim of the unconstitutional discrimination of which she complains." [25] The mere fact that Mrs. Jackson "decided to act as the self-appointed agent of these principals whom she cannot identify" permitted the majority to protect the rights of unidentified non-Caucasians. The chief justice also said that he did not think that broad constitutional limitations can spring from "such tenuous circumstances." Considering these facts, he continued, "there is no way in which a substantial case or controversy can be predicated upon the right which the majority is so anxious to pass upon." [26]

In conclusion, Vinson said: [27]

> Because I cannot see how respondent can avail herself of the Fourteenth Amendment rights of total strangers—the only rights which she has chosen to assert—and since I cannot see how the Court can find that those rights would be impaired in this particular case by requiring respondent to pay petitioners for the injury that she brought upon them, I am unwilling to join the Court in today's decision.

Mrs. Jackson and the NAACP

The Negroes who would be injured by the enforcement of the damages claim against Mrs. Jackson were "unidentified" but they were most emphatically "identifiable." The National Association for the Advancement of Colored People conducted Mrs. Jackson's case in order to protect the interest of Negroes. Loren Miller of Los Angeles defended Mrs. Jackson for the NAACP. Thurgood Marshall of the national office in New York and Franklin Williams, West Coast director for the NAACP, worked with him on the brief filed with the Supreme Court of the United States.[28] Loren Miller has recently commented that Mrs. Jackson's prime interest was in fending off damages and he does not know how she regarded the fact that she had established a precedent in the field of civil rights.[29]

After the victory in the 1948 injunction cases, the NAACP expected to be faced with the damages issue. In Los Angeles, Loren Miller had defended many Negroes in restrictive-covenant cases. His experience taught him to anticipate further legal difficulties. He had noted that there were many real-estate brokers and "a substantial number of property owners organizations" in Los Angeles "casting about for some way to enforce the covenants."[30]

When Mrs. Jackson broke her covenant, the suit against her was only one of at least a half dozen cases then filed in the Los Angeles Superior Court. Her own lawyers, Maurice Walbert and James Sims, were the attorneys of record in the state courts and appeared in the United States Supreme Court as "Of Counsel." Technically speaking, the appearance of the NAACP attorneys was that of counsel hired by the trial lawyers to present the matter on appeal, a not uncommon practice in appellate litigation. These developments have been described by Loren Miller in this way:[31]

> Mrs. Jackson's lawyers told us frankly that they had no funds to fight the case through the appellate courts. In turn, we took the matter to the local branch of the NAACP and through proper channels to the NAACP regional and national structures. We all agreed that the NAACP should assist in the case because we believed that our California courts would decide the issue favorably to us and that we would have the advantage of being respondents in the U.S. Supreme Court. Our calculations were correct in this regard. Because of the fact that the matter was a California case and because of my experience in the cases involving judicial enforcement of racial covenants the NAACP put the matter in my charge.

There can be no doubt that the NAACP acted in this case to defend the group interests of colored people. The Association's attorneys wanted to have control of any damages cases that got to the Supreme Court in order to "get a decision on the broadest possible grounds and to escape a technical decision." Loren Miller has said this about the nature of judicial processes and organized interests: [32]

> I am quite in agreement with you that Supreme Court cases involving larger issues are contests between opposing forces rather than law suits between individuals. They are cast as individual pieces of litigation because the Constitution guarantees the rights of individuals rather than those of groups. However, as a practical matter the individual is unable to pursue his rights to the ultimate and hence the job is done by groups of people who find themselves situated as the individual is situated and who secure their own rights by securing the rights of the similarly situated individual.

Amici Curiae *for the Negroes*

In the California District Court of Appeal some twenty organizations asked the judges to deny damages in the *Barrows* case.[33] These were led by the NAACP, Japanese-American Citizens League, and several Jewish groups. Labor support was in evidence as briefs were filed by the Los Angeles Central Labor Council and the C.I.O. Council as well as the Los Angeles International Ladies Garment Workers Union. The Southern California American Civil Liberties Union filed a separate brief. Finally, an assortment of groups, including the Santa Monica Y.W.C.A., the Eagle Rock Council for Civic Unity, and the Women's International Club, spoke as friends of the court in behalf of Mrs. Jackson.

When *Barrows v. Jackson* reached the Supreme Court of the United States, the national counterparts of these liberal, labor, racial, and religious groups relied upon the *amici curiae* briefs once again. Although the number of briefs dropped from the nineteen filed in the 1948 cases to four, the total of participating groups remained high. In the first brief, A. L. Wirin of Los Angeles expressed the interest of twelve organizations.[34] These included the NAACP, Japanese-American Citizens League, and other California organizations.

The Court was told that these groups were "committed to
the proposition that all men are created equal and that no state
action can be asked to enforce agreements based upon terms of
race or color." The brief also asked the Court not to permit the
deprivation of one of the basic rights of a property owner: the
right to dispose of property to a constitutionally qualified purchaser."

Two *amici curiae* briefs were filed with the Supreme Court by
Jewish groups. One was submitted by the National Community
Relations Advisory Council in behalf of twenty-nine member
organizations. Its policy position was as follows: [35]

> Discrimination in housing undermines the dignity that is the
> birthright of every man, woman and child. It squanders our human
> and social resources, fans tensions that destroy our national unity
> and presents powerful propaganda weapons to our enemies. It is
> unjust, uneconomic and indefensible. Its elimination is long over-
> due.

This brief observed that the Court's ruling in 1948 was "widely
hailed as one of the great landmarks of civil freedom and equality." The rule established then "meant actual release from galling
restrictions" to "thousands of minority group families" and "en-
abled them to buy homes in areas previously closed to them."
The National Community Relations Advisory Council brief went
on to say: [36]

> The present case represents an attempt to turn the clock back by
> restoring to the restrictive covenant some of the coercive effect
> that it was formerly given by the courts. The NCRAC and its
> constituent organizations are confident that this Court will reject
> this attempt to salvage a repudiated instrument of racial and
> religious discrimination.

An *amici curiae* brief on behalf of the American Jewish Committee and the Anti-Defamation League of B'nai B'rith was the
other one representing that religious group. A long historical
survey of the organizations introduced the brief. After a discussion of the evils of restrictive covenants based on race, color,
or creed, the brief concluded: [37]

> The organizations sponsoring this brief are peculiarly alert to
> the dangers to democracy arising from racial or religious residential

segregation. Jewish experience under European despotism gave rise to the word "ghetto." The threat of revival of that institution—implicit in the newest attempt to make racial restrictive covenants a deterrent to free use and occupancy of real property—demands our intercession in this case.

The fourth brief *amicus curiae* for the Negro position came from the American Veterans Committee. Phineas Indritz, counsel for the A.V.C., said that "this case is at attempt to undermine the rulings by this Court in 1948." [38] The veterans in the A.V.C. had "associated to promote the democratic principles for which we fought." [39]

> We believe that racial discrimination is inconsistent with our nation's basic principles, that it is harmful to our national welfare at home, that it adversely affects our relations with the peoples of the world, and that it is a potential catalyst for future military hostility against the United States.

Organized Property Owners and the Barrows Case

In the experience of the NAACP *Barrows v. Jackson* was different, as they believed that the case "was deliberately chosen by its protagonists as a test case." [40] For one thing, a large number of organizations of property owners in different sections of the country participated in the appellate courts as *amici curiae*. For another, the initiative at each stage was in the hands of the attorneys for Barrows, as plaintiffs in the Los Angeles Superior Court, as appellants in the California courts, and appellants again in the United States Supreme Court. Even when all seemed lost, further appeal was made to the Supreme Court for a rehearing. Thus, the NAACP was in the position of defense throughout.

Why was an all-out effort made to collect damages for the covenant violation by Mrs. Jackson? There were two reasons, one technical and one broad. First, one of the plaintiffs in the case happened to have been a successor in interest of a signer of the covenant. This was a fine point of interest to Caucasians for if they had won, both signers and their successors in interest would have been established as proper parties to secure damages. Had this point been made, then damage suits might then have been brought to make successors in interest of signers liable for damages when they sold to non-Caucasians.

The desire of the property-owning groups to establish this proposition belies their motivation to establish the damage suit as an enforcement device on a broad front. Since they had lost other cases in the Los Angeles Superior Court, it is evident that some deliberation occurred before appeal was taken in *Barrows v. Jackson.* Undoubtedly this was a test case filed to establish a right for a class of persons, not to protect the particular litigants. After all, since Mrs. Jackson's sale of property to Negroes was irrevocable, no levy of damages could enforce racial residential segregation in that neighborhood. In the United States Supreme Court the main brief by Loren Miller emphasized the point "that the end-purpose of a suit of this kind—chosen Petitioners said in briefs filed in the state courts, as a test case—is to create precedential substantive law that will have consequences far beyond the outcome of this case." [41]

In *Barrows v. Jackson* property-owners' organizations in many parts of the country relied on *amici curiae* briefs to register their views. In the District Court of Appeal of California a brief prepared by John W. Preston represented these fourteen Los Angeles organizations: Neighborly Endeavor, Inc., United Neighbors, Inc., United Homeowners, Inc., Vermont Square Neighbors, Inc., Harvard Neighbors Association, Neighborhood Protective Association, Steadfast Neighbors Committee, Angelus Mesa Neighbors Association, Loyal Neighbors Association, Citizens United, Inc., LaFayette Square Improvement Association, Hancock Park Neighbors, Inc., The Park Community Association, and the Associated Neighbors.

In the United States Supreme Court, organized white property owners in other cities joined those in Los Angeles to file one brief in support of the covenants.[42] The number of organizations in Los Angeles swelled to twenty. This brief was also signed by the Santa Fé Place Improvement Association of Kansas City, Missouri and the Southwood Improvement Association, Inc., of San Francisco. The organizations located in Highland Park, Michigan, were included. Twenty-four citizens' associations of Washington, D.C., were likewise listed in the brief filed by John Preston. The brief told the Supreme Court that the members of these forty-eight organizations "own several thousand homes which are protected by private contracts from monetary loss as real as loss by fire which inevitably results from the use and occupancy of a neighboring house by non-Caucasians. These valid contracts do not prevent the use and occupancy any more than fire insurance prevents fire but the loss is prevented in the same way." The decision of the California courts, it was pointed out, endangered their property rights.

Precisely the same reasons were given by Gerald L. Seegers and other St. Louis attorneys in filing an *amicus curiae* brief in behalf of sixteen organizations from that city.[43] These included two groups which had been active in the *Shelley-Kraemer* litigation, the Marcus Avenue Improvement Association, and the Council for Community Preservation.

A final indication of the petitioners' breadth of interest in racial segregation came after the Supreme Court's adverse decision in *Barrows v. Jackson* when a rehearing was sought. Although petitions for rehearing have averaged 180 per term in recent years,[44] the Supreme Court rarely grants such petitions as all cases decided have presumably received full and adequate consideration. In order to discourage unmeritorious petitions for rehearing, Court rules in 1947 had set the time for filing petitions at fifteen days after the decision.[45] In *Barrows v. Jackson* rehearing was denied by the Supreme Court so that no reply brief was necessary.[46] Nevertheless the petition for rehearing filed for the losing litigants by their counsel, J. Wallace McKnight, John Miles, and Charles L. Bagley of Los Angeles, is an unusual document that marks the depth of despair felt by the Caucasian position.[47]

Regretting that the case had been opened "to the rights of classes," the petition for rehearing spoke directly in defense of the rights of the class to which the petitioners belong. Racial restrictive covenants, said the petition, are not "just examples of some wilfulness of man and do not merely represent man's inhumanity to man." [48] Behind these covenants "are certain facts of life" which the petitioners "cannot escape facing." Following this, the petitioner for rehearing presents criminal statistics designed to establish a basis in reason for residential segregation. According to the *Uniform Crime Reports* issued by the Federal Bureau of Investigation for 1952, 64 per cent of the persons arrested for murder in 232 cities were of the Negro race. Other categories of crime show essentially the same division even though only 10 per cent of the population are Negro. "These are some of the facts of life that force peace-loving people to join racial restrictive covenants."

The petition went beyond this support for covenants to argue that "occupying houses in white neighborhoods is not all that Negroes want." With appendices made up of reprints of articles from Negro magazines, *Color, Sepia,* and *Ebony,* the petition concludes with this further reason for segregation in housing: [49]

> Every national Negro magazine known to petitioners on the newstands this month, June, contains one or more articles, either featuring or displaying intermarriage between Negroes and whites and in other ways illustrating the example being set for Negroes. There is no room in the philosophy being taught to Negroes for the white man's personal freedom of choice of associates. This attitude among Negroes who move into white neighborhoods adds to the other factors which, equally understandably, make them unwelcome neighbors.

With the old Caucasian bulwark of precedents swept away, the Los Angeles property owners had to fall back on the fear of intermarriage as the ultimate reason for segregation.

While litigation on the subject was largely foreclosed, precedent now favored the Negro position while the Caucasians were making sociological arguments.

XI

The Racial Covenant Cases in Perspective

The persistent note of interest-group activity struck throughout this study makes it essential in coming to fair and proper conclusions to review all elements that contributed to the Supreme Court's decisions in the *Restrictive Covenant Cases*. One way of telling why the Court ruled that neither a state or federal court may enforce a restrictive covenant barring the purchase or occupancy of real estate by Negroes is to accept the Court's own explanation. In 1948, Chief Justice Vinson wrote that the right to acquire, enjoy, own, and dispose of property is a civil right "intended to be protected from discriminatory state action by the Fourteenth Amendment." There was no question but that racial residential covenants restricted Negroes in the exercise of this right, but the crucial question for the Court was whether this resulted from individual action, or from state or federal governmental action. The restrictions had been drawn up by private citizens and their making was not illegal because of the well-established principle that the Fourteenth Amendment does not inhibit merely private conduct, however discriminatory. The chief justice pointed out that although the covenants were private they gained their force, as all contracts do, from the enforcement powers of courts. Without this judicial intervention the Negroes against whom the covenants were aimed could have disregarded the restrictions and occupied the properties in these cases without restraint. Enforcement by the courts, however, made available to individuals the full coercive power of government to deny colored people the enjoyment of property rights because of their race or color. Although the Fourteenth Amendment was inapplicable to the national government, it was ruled that the federal courts could not enforce racial restrictive covenants, because such action would be contrary to the right of all persons to have property guaranteed by the Civil Rights Act of 1866. Enforcement being otherwise inconsistent with the public policy of the United States, a federal court could not do that which is forbidden under the Fourteenth Amendment. In 1953 the Supreme Court, over the dissent of Chief Justice Vinson, ruled that the Fourteenth Amendment and their earlier actions forbade the enforcement of restrictive covenants by damage suit.

The words in these decisions are essentially legal or constitutional justifications for the result. They are of great importance in the interpretative development of the equal-protection clause of the Fourteenth Amendment. They form a significant application of public-policy considerations for the federal courts. These decisions in the *Restrictive Covenant Cases* marked a new sophistication in comprehending the power of the state, and particularly of courts as an arm of government, in enforcing rules of social conduct. In these ways the opinions of the Supreme Court play their part as the authority in constitutional law.

There can be no doubt that the personnel of the Court had an important bearing upon the outcome of the *Restrictive Covenant Cases*. It would, for instance, have been utterly inconceivable that Justice Frank Murphy could have voted in an opposite way. He had shown life-long sympathy for Negroes and was an arch foe of all discrimination based on race, color, or creed. Murphy had carried this attitude to the Supreme Court, where his voting record in defense of claims to civil rights was consistently above the other justices. In addition, Justices Black, Douglas, and Frankfurter had firm attachments to individual rights which were only different in degree from Murphy's. But the two new members of the Supreme Court, Chief Justice Vinson and Justice Burton, were less well known as advocates of civil rights for Negroes. More important than this was the fact that essentially the same Court refused to hear a racial restrictive-covenant case in 1945. There was nothing in the backgrounds of the justices' individual personalities or the Court's institutional history to account for this change of interest.

Another method of explaining the outcome of these cases is

to look to the times. The decisions were made in 1948 and 1953, not 1926, 1937, or 1945. In the years immediately following World War II there was tremendous interest in civil rights for Negroes in the United States. The Negroes themselves were able to exert influence toward this end, for they lived in the North in great numbers, and with the vote were becoming an extremely important bloc in the Democratic party. The threat of fascism with its racial theories, and the challenge of communism with its glowing promises of equality, helped to touch off a new reform movement toward practicing the preachings of American democracy. The administration of President Truman attempted to advance the social and economic position of Negroes and other minority groups in a variety of ways recommended by the report of the President's Committee on Civil Rights, including action to eliminate segregation in the armed forces. Although in Congress the power of the Southern delegation, especially in the Senate— the cloture rule being what it is—prevented any part of the program from coming into effect through federal legislation, the Supreme Court led the way in broadening the civil rights of Negroes. The decisions in the *Restrictive Covenant Cases* were in good company, for the Court had handed down a number of others of similar import. The situation in politics is a necessary ingredient in the story of major Supreme Court cases, but it is no magic explanation standing alone. The famous remark of Mr. Dooley that the Supreme Court follows the election returns is a limited explanation of judicial behavior.

It is not only in terms of the politics of the times that the decision in the *Restrictive Covenant Cases* may be looked at with illuminating results; equally important is the history of the social ideas which underlies the decisions. At the time of World War I, the belief of white people that they were biologically superior to the darker races was still very widely held. As a popular notion it was a natural accompaniment of racial segregation. Negroes were forced to live by themselves in the large northern cities, and in their squalid surroundings they were pointed to as inferior beings, incapable of anything better. The theory of biological inferiority comforted the vast majority, but uneasiness and conscience in a few produced studies during the 'twenties which questioned this assumption. Gradually there developed a new sociology, holding that environment, and not innate defects, was the cause of the Negroes' poor circumstances. This point of view gained the adherence of a large segment of public opinion, and was a belief necessary to the defense of civil rights by the Supreme Court. These last factors are peripheral to the *Restrictive Covenant Cases* themselves, for they are general in nature and difficult to detail satisfactorily. It is to the cases, though not particularly to the words of the opinions, that we must look for the essential story.

Who were the parties in the *Restrictive Covenant Cases?* The *United States Reports* tell that they were individuals: *Shelley v. Kraemer, McGhee v. Sipes, Hurd v. Hodge, Urciolo v. Hodge, Barrows v. Jackson.* However, research outside the law library shows that the individuals loaned their names to the larger causes of organized Negroes and white property owners. In the process of what appeared to be private litigation, then, a great struggle between two interest groups with contrary objectives was carried on.

It was through organized activity that white property owners protected their interest in living apart from Negroes. Neighborhood property associations functioned in Los Angeles, Chicago, New York, Detroit, Baltimore, St. Louis, Washington, and other cities. They drafted restrictions, had them officially recorded and guarded against violations. These associations usually worked closely with organized real-estate interests within each city to prevent sale of covenanted property to Negroes. Out of deference to these powers, local newspapers refused advertisements offering to sell real estate in white areas to Negroes. Individual owners were implored not to sell to colored people. When these informal means failed, the white property-owners' groups, called variously protective, improvement, or citizens' associations, brought legal action and gained injunctions from courts which forbade violators from owning or using particular property. Their success in gaining enforcement of these privately drawn covenants developed patterns of racial segregation in northern cities.

The power of white property owners was displayed by their persuasion of state courts throughout the country to use their equity powers to prevent violations of racial restrictive covenants. Each decision upholding a covenant was precedent for another court doing the same. By 1944 the American Law Institute reported that it was socially and economically desirable for courts to enforce these restrictions. This conclusion confirmed in convincing fashion the fact that the judiciary had accepted the values of the white property owners.

The political impotence of Negroes made possible the establishment of restrictive covenants as a workable means of keeping them out of white sections of cities, but by 1945 the number of precedents against them was an unreliable index to their strength. At that time their resources were marshaled by the National Association for the Advancement of Colored People in order to attack the validity of court enforcement of restrictive covenants. The Association's legal committee agreed to conduct the defense of any Negro sued for violating a covenant. With the postwar housing shortage forcing the issue, cases were soon under way in Los Angeles, Chicago, Columbus, Ohio, New York, Detroit, St. Louis, and Washington, D.C.

The actions brought by property-owners' associations were successful in all these cities, save for the loss of *Kraemer v. Shelley* on technical grounds in the trial court of St. Louis. This latter case was reversed by the Missouri Supreme Court, and appellate courts in the other jurisdictions affirmed enforcement of the other racial covenants. Precedent provided the justification for these holdings, but the nature of the Caucasian groups, as local organizations allied with powerful real-estate interests, may have had some effect on the judiciary at these levels. When the cases reached the Supreme Court of the United States, the provincialism of the white organizations was a debit where it had been an advantage before. Their lawyers were capable men. Their arguments had been sound enough to justify court enforcement of covenants for thirty years. But the Caucasians lacked national organization, strong allies, theoreticians, or an understanding of the new values of sociological jurisprudence. Their assets were not easy to capitalize in the Supreme Court of the United States.

The preparation of the Negro and white attorneys who conducted the cases for the Negro buyers was an enormous undertaking. The trials were conducted with finesse. The national scope of interest in ending covenants was indicated when in the Michigan Supreme Court, particularly, a number of organizations filed briefs to assist them. Although these beginnings were unsuccessful, they were continued along the same lines, and accelerated as the cases were taken up by the Supreme Court. Then the NAACP coördinated the presentation of the Negro position. Conferences to discuss the contents of main briefs and *amici curiae* briefs were held. Some volunteers worked on sociological data for use in argument. Others wrote law-review articles. The President's Committee on Civil Rights spoke out against court enforcement of racial restrictive covenants at a propitious moment and the Justice Department placed the weight of the United States government on the side of the Negroes by filing a brief *amicus curiae* with the Supreme Court. The Negro position had eighteen organizations as allies that prepared briefs and presented them as friends of the court. These organizations included the American Jewish Congress, American Civil Liberties Union, National Lawyers Guild, C.I.O., A.F. of L., American Veterans Committee, Congregational Christian Church, and American Association for the United Nations.

Analysis of the Negro victory in the *Restrictive Covenant Cases* forces the conclusion that this result was an outgrowth of the complex group activity which preceded it. Groups with antagonistic interests appeared before the Supreme Court, just as they do before Congress or other institutions that mold public policy. Because of organization the lawyers for the Negroes were better prepared to do battle through the courts. Without this continuity, money, and talent they would not have freed themselves from the limiting effects of racial residential covenants, notwithstanding the presence of favorable social theories, political circumstances, and Supreme Court justices.

Preface

[1] This restriction appears in a deed of the Crawford Realty Company in the office of the Register of Deeds for Cuyahoga County, Cleveland, Ohio. See vol. 5151, p. 15.

[2] The four injunction cases were *Shelley v. Kraemer, McGhee v. Sipes,* 334 U.S. 1 (1948); *Hurd v. Hodge, Urciolo v. Hodge,* 334 U.S. 24 (1948). The case involving the issue of damages was *Barrows v. Jackson,* 346 U.S. 249 (1953).

[3] First, two opinions were announced which dealt with school segregation in the states and in the District of Columbia. *Brown v. Board of Education,* 347 U.S. 483 (1954); *Bolling v. Sharpe,* 347 U.S. 497 (1954). The opinion as to the decrees was rendered a year later. *Brown v. Board of Education,* 349 U.S. 294 (1955).

[4] 271 U.S. 323 (1926).

[5] 163 U.S. 537 (1896).

Chapter I

Legal Precedents: Caucasian Bulwark

[1] *Parmalee v. Morris,* 218 Mich. 625, 628, 188 N.W. 330 (1922).

[2] For a criticism of this concept, see Arnold M. Rose, " 'You Can't Legislate Against Prejudice'—Or Can You?", *Common Ground,* IV (Spring, 1949), 61–67. Forceful arguments have been made that legal sanctions could enforce racial equality as easily as they have supported racial separation. See Morroe Berger, *Equality by Statute; Legal Controls Over Group Discrimination* (New York: Columbia University Press, 1952).

[3] Gunnar Myrdal, *An American Dilemma: The Negro Problem and American Democracy* (New York: Harper, 1944), Appendix 7: "Distribution of Negro Residences in Selected Cities," pp. 1125–1128.

[4] *Porter v. Johnson,* 232 Mo. App. 1150, 1160, 115 S.W. 2d 529 (1938).

[5] *Ridgway v. Cockburn,* 296 N.Y.S. 936, 943, 163 Misc. 511 (Sup. Ct. of Westchester Co. 1937).

[6] *Porter v. Johnson,* above, note 4.

[7] Copy in private legal files of James A. Crooks, Washington, D.C., taken originally from Liber 7424, folio 3, signed as Instrument 38445 on Dec. 18, 1939, Office of Recorder of Deeds, Washington, D.C.

[8] For a summary of racial classifications from the view of science, see Ashley Montagu, *Statement on Race* (New York: Henry Schuman, 1951). This provides "an extended discussion in plain language of the UNESCO statement by experts on race problems." For a discussion of the American legal view of race, see Charles Mangum, *The Legal Status of the Negro* (Chapel Hill: University of North Carolina Press, 1940).

[9] 18 Edw. I, Stat. 1 (1290). For a development of this rule, see Holdsworth, *History of English Law*, 9 vols., 3d ed. (Boston: Little, Brown, 1923), III, 73–87.

[10] Richard T. Ely and George S. Wehrwein, *Land Economics* (New York: Macmillan, 1940), p. 112; William F. Fratcher, "Restraints on Alienation of Legal Interests in Michigan Property: I," *Michigan Law Review*, L (March, 1952), 675, 701.

[11] American Law Institute, *Restatement of Property*, Sec. 406, comment a, p. 2394 (1944).

[12] According to the *Restatement*, there are six factors which when present tend to make restraints on alienation reasonable and valid. These are: (1) The one imposing the restraint has some interest in land which he is seeking to protect by the enforcement of the restraint; (2) the restraint is limited in duration; (3) the enforcement of the restraint accomplishes a worthwhile purpose; (4) the types of conveyances prohibited are ones not likely to be employed to any substantial degree by the one restrained; (5) the number of persons to whom alienation is prohibited is small; (6) the one upon whom the restraint is imposed is a charity. A.L.I., *Restatement of Property*, Sec. 406.

[13] 272 U.S. 365 (1926).

[14] For a full discussion of this rule, see Thomas Reed Powell, "The Supreme Court and State Police Power, 1922–1930, IV," *Virginia Law Review*, XVIII (Nov., 1931), 1, 18–33.

[15] 245 U.S. 60.

[16] *Harmon v. Tyler*, 273 U.S. 668, 47 S. Ct. 471, 71 L. Ed. 831 (1927); *City of Richmond v. Deans*, 281 U.S. 704, 50 S. Ct. 407, 74 L. Ed. 1128 (1930); *Clinard v. City of Winston-Salem*, 217 N.C. 119, 6 S.E. 2d 867 (1940).

[17] The avoidance of the race issue in *Buchanan v. Warley* was severely criticized. Note, "Race Segregation Ordinance Invalid," *Harvard Law Review*, XXXI (Jan., 1918), 475–479 stated: "It is apparent that the primary, the real interests involved in the ordinance are certain civil rights of the negro race guaranteed by the Fourteenth Amendment, and yet that the invalidity of the ordinance was determined professedly solely with reference to the property interest of a white man." *Ibid.*, 476. The outcome of the case was also attacked. S. S. Field, "The Constitutionality of Segregation Ordinances," *Virginia Law Review*, V (Oct., 1917), 5. Both the Buchanan rule and the theory behind it were questioned as late as 1941. Major Gardner, "Race Segregation in Cities," *Kentucky Law Journal* XXIX (Jan., 1941), 213–219.

[18] A.L.I., *Restatement of Property*, Sec. 406, comment 1, pp. 2411–12.

[19] *Ibid.*

[20] A.L.I., *Restatement of Property*, Introduction, I and II, p. ix; Benjamin N. Cardozo, *The Growth of the Law* (New Haven: Yale University Press, 1924), pp. 16–20.

[21] The Committee on Property of the American Law Institute was composed of the following: Richard R. Powell, Columbia University, reporter; A. James Casner, Harvard University; Julian S. Bush, New York University; Harry A. Bigelow, University of Chicago; Everett Fraser, University of Minnesota; J. Warren Madden, United States Court of Claims, Washington, D.C.; Oliver S. Rundell, University of Wisconsin; Lewis M. Simes, University of Michigan; Henry Upson Sims, Birmingham, Alabama; William Draper Lewis, American Law Institute, chairman, ex officio.

[22] A.L.I., *Restatement of Property*, Introduction, I and II, pp. vii–iii.

[23] 49 Fed. 181 (C.C.S.D. Cal. 1892).

[24] *Ibid.*, at 182.

[25] 109 U.S. 3 (1883).

[26] *People's Pleasure Park Co., Inc. v. Rohleder*, 109 Va. 439, 61 S.E. 794 (1908).

[27] *Queensborough Land Co. v. Cazeaux*, 136 La. 724, 67 So. 641 (1915).

[28] *Loc. cit.*

[29] *Los Angeles Investment Co. v. Gary*, 181 Cal. 680, 681, 186 Pac. 596 (1919).

[30] *Letteau v. Ellis,* 122 Cal. App. 585, 10 Pac. 2d 496 (1932).

[31] *Title Guarantee and Trust Co. v. Garrott,* 42 Cal. App. 152, 183 Pac. 470 (1919).

[32] *Hemsley v. Hough,* 195 Okla. 298, 157 Pac. 2d 182 (1945).

[33] *White v. White,* 108 W. Va. 128, 129, 150 S.E. 531 (1929).

[34] *Burke v. Kleiman,* 277 Ill. App. 519, 526 (1st Dist. App. Ct., Chicago 1934).

[35] *Wyatt v. Adair,* 215 Ala. 363, 366, 110 So. 801 (1926).

[36] H. J. Pasternak, "Real Property . . . Private Covenant Forbidding Sale or Lease to Negro," *Cornell Law Quarterly,* XII (April, 1927), 400.

[37] *Schulte v. Starks,* 238 Mich. 102, 104, 213 N.W. 102 (1927).

[38] *Kathan v. Stevenson,* 307 Mich. 485, 12 N.W. 2d 332 (1943).

[39] John Claggett Proctor, *Washington, Past and Present, A History,* 4 vols. (New York: Lewis Historical Publishing Co., (1930) IV, 709–710.

[40] *Torrey v. Wolfes,* 6 F. 2d 702, 703 (D.C. Cir. 1925).

[41] *Chandler v. Ziegler,* 88 Colo. 1, 5, 291 Pac. 822 (1930).

[42] *Title Guarantee and Trust Co. v. Garrott,* 42 Cal. App. 152, 183 Pac. 470 (1919).

[43] *Queensborough Land Co. v. Cazeaux,* 136 La. 724, 67 So. 641 (1915).

[44] *Vernon v. R. J. Reynolds Reality Co.,* 226 N.C. 58, 36 S.E. 2d 710 (1946).

[45] *Porter v. Pryor,* 164 S.W. 2d 353, 354 (Supp. Ct. of Mo., Div. 1, 1942, not officially reported).

[46] Herman H. Long and Charles S. Johnson, *People vs. Property; Race Restrictive Covenants in Housing* (Nashville, Tenn.: Fisk University Press, 1947) p. 41.

[47] "Washington's Citizens' Associations," *Washington Post,* March 2, 1952, p. 4B, col. 5, 6.

[48] Proctor, *Washington, Past and Present,* II, 907–908.

[49] *Ibid.*

[50] Long and Johnson, *People vs. Property,* p. 40.

[51] Harold U. Faulkner, *The Quest for Social Justice, 1898–1914* (A History of American Life, Vol. XI; New York: Macmillan Co., 1931), p. 9.

[52] *Buchanan v. Warley,* 245 U.S. 60 (1917).

[53] Long and Johnson, *People vs. Property.*

[54] *Ibid.,* p. 32.

[55] Gunnar Myrdal, *An American Dilemma,* p. 619.

[56] *Pickel v. McCawley,* 329 Mo. 166, 44 S.W. 2d 857 (1931).

[57] *Thornhill v. Herdt,* 130 S.W. 2d 175, 179 (St. Louis Ct. of App., Mo., 1939, not officially reported).

[58] *Ibid.*

[59] *Ibid.,* pp. 179–180.

[60] *Stone v. Jones,* 66 Cal. App. 2d 264, 270, 152 Pac. 2d 19 (1944).

[61] *Lyons v. Wallen,* 191 Okla. 567, 133 Pac. 2d 555 (1942), (70 per cent); *Hemsley v. Sage,* 194 Okla. 669, 154 Pac. 2d 577 (1944), (51 per cent); *Hemsley v. Hough,* 195 Okla. 298, 157 Pac. 2d 182 (1945), (90 per cent).

[62] *Oberwise v. Poulos,* 124 Cal. App. 247, 252, 12 Pac. 2d 156 (1932).

[63] *Foster v. Stewart,* 134 Cal. App. 482, 484, 25 Pac. 2d 497 (1933).

[64] *Dury v. Neely,* 69 N.Y.S. 2d 677 (Sup. Ct. of Queens Co., 1942).

[65] *Thornhill v. Herdt,* 130 S.W. 2d 175 (St. Louis Ct. of App., Mo., 1939, not officially reported). (75 per cent of total frontage owners.)

[66] *Queensborough Land Co. v. Cazeaux,* 136 La. 724, 67 So. 641 (1915); *Koehler v. Rowland,* 275 Mo. 573, 205 S.W. 217 (1918).

[67] *Porter v. Pryor,* 164 S.W. 2d 353 (Supp. Ct. of Mo., Div. 1, 1942, not officially reported); *Porter v. Johnson,* 232 Mo. App. 1150, 115 S.W. 2d 529 (Kansas City Ct. of App., Mo. 1938).

[68] *Vernon v. Reynolds Realty Co.,* 226 N.C. 58, 36, S.E. 2d 710 (1946); *White v. White,* 108 W. Va. 128, 147, 150 S.E. 531 (1929).

[69] *Foster v. Stewart,* 134 Cal. App. 482, 25 Pac. 2d 497 (1933).

[70] *Burkhardt v. Lofton,* 63 Cal. App. 2d 230, 234, 235, 146 Pac. 2d 720 (1944).

[71] *Ridgeway v. Cockburn,* 296 N.Y.S. 936, 163 Misc. 511 (1937); *Letteau v. Ellis,*

122 Cal. App. 585, 10 Pac. 2d 496 (1932); *Littlejohns v. Henderson,* 111 Cal. App. 115, 295 Pac. 95 (1931).

[72] *Lyons v. Wallen,* 191 Okla. 567, 133 Pac. 2d 555 (1942).

[73] *DuRoss v. Trainor,* 122 Cal. App. 732, 10 Pac. 2d 763 (1932).

[74] *Porter v. Pryor,* 164 S.W. 2d 353 (Sup. Ct. of Mo., Div. 1, 1942, not officially reported).

[75] *Porter v. Johnson,* 232 Mo. App. 1150, 115 S.W. 2d 529 (Kansas City Ct. of App., Mo. 1938).

[76] *Schulte v. Starks,* 238 Mich. 102, 213 N.W. 102 (1927).

[77] Henry Gilligan to LeRoy Brookmond, March 1, 1946, in the private legal files of James A. Crooks, Washington, D.C. The author saw numerous letters of this type while inspecting these files in 1952.

[78] *Clark v. Vaughan,* 131 Kan. 438, 292 Pac. 783 (1930), dissenting opinion by Jochems, J., 131 Kan. 438, 445.

[79] *Porter v. Pryor,* 164 S.W. 2d 353 (Sup. Ct. of Mo., Div. 1, 1942, not officially reported).

[80] *Koehler v. Rowland,* 275 Mo. 573, 205 S.W. 217, 9 A.L.R. 107 (1918).

[81] *Lee v. Hansberry,* 372 Ill. 369, 24 N.E. 2d 37 (1939), *reversed on other grounds, Hansberry v. Lee,* 311 U.S. 32 (1941).

[82] *Lyons v. Wallen,* 191 Okla. 567, 133 Pac. 2d 555 (1942).

[83] *Meade v. Dennistone,* 173 Md. 295, 196 Atl. 330 (1938).

[84] *Koehler v. Rowland,* 275 Mo. 573, 205 S.W. 217, 9 A.L.R. 107 (1918).

[85] *Corrigan (and Curtis) v. Buckley,* 299 Fed. 899 (D.C. Cir. 1924), *appeal dismissed,* 271 U.S. 323 (1926).

[86] *Grady v. Garland,* 89 Fed. 2d 817, 818 (D.C. Cir. 1937).

[87] *Ibid.,* p. 819.

[88] *Vernon v. Reynolds Realty Co.,* 226 N.C. 58, 61, 36 S.E. 2d 710 (1946).

[89] *Plessy v. Ferguson,* 163 U.S. 537, 539, 16 S. Ct. 1138, 41 L. Ed. 256 (1896).

[90] John P. Frank and R. F. Munro, "Original Understanding of 'Equal Protection of the Laws,' " *Columbia Law Review,* L (Feb., 1950), 131–169.

[91] Andrew G. McLaughlin, *A Constitutional History of the United States* (New York: Appleton-Century, 1935), p. 727.

[92] 14 Stat. 39 (1866).

[93] 18 Stat. L. 140 (1870).

[94] 18 Stat. L. 335 (1875).

[95] 14 Stat. 27 (1866).

[96] 18 Stat. L. 335 (1875).

[97] 109 U.S. 3, 3 S. Ct. 18, 27 L. Ed. 835 (1883). For an analysis of the *Civil Rights Cases,* see Milton R. Konvitz, *The Constitution and Civil Rights* (New York: Columbia University Press, 1947), pp. 8–28.

[98] 109 U.S. 3, 17.

[99] For a succinct discussion of the Negro problem in the context of American political development, see Ralph Gabriel, *The Course of American Democratic Thought* (New York: Ronald Press, 1940), pp. 132–140.

[100] 16 Wall, 36, 21 L. Ed. 394 (U.S. 1873).

[101] The Supreme Court invalidated state statutes on 212 occasions between 1889 and 1937 because they encroached on the rights of "persons." Of these but three referred to Negroes. Benjamin F. Wright, *The Growth of American Constitutional Law* (Boston: Houghton Mifflin, 1942), p. 148.

[102] 163 U.S. 537.

[103] Charles Wallace Collins, *The Fourteenth Amendment and the States* (Boston: Little, Brown, 1912), p. 78.

[104] Collins helped in developing theoretical support for Dixiecrat policies. Charles Wallace Collins, *Whither Solid South* (New Orleans: Pelican Press, 1947). For an analysis which stresses the importance of Collins, see Richard Hofstadter, "From Calhoun to the Dixiecrats," *Social Research* XVI (June, 1949), 135, 143–149.

[105] Collins, *The Fourteenth Amendment and the States*, p. 77.

[106] *Ibid.*

[107] *Ibid.*, pp. 79, 80.

[108] *Guinn v. United States*, 238 U.S. 347 (1915).

[109] 245 U.S. 60 (1917).

[110] 299 Fed. 899 (D.C. Cir. 1924), *appeal dismissed*, 271 U.S. 323 (1926).

[111] 299 Fed. 899, 902.

[112] 271 U.S. 323, 330.

[113] 109 U.S. 3.

[114] 14 Stat. 39 (1866).

[115] 271 U.S. 323, 331.

[116] *United Cooperative Realty Co. v. Hawkins*, 269, Ky. 563, 108 S.W. 2d 507 (1137).

[117] *Meade v. Dennistone*, 173 Md. 295, 301, 196 Atl. 330 (1938).

[118] *Lyons v. Wallen*, 191 Okla. 567, 133 Pac. 2d 555 (1942).

[119] *Doherty v. Rice*, 240 Wis. 389, 3 N.W. 2d 734 (1942).

[120] *Porter v. Pryor*, 164 S.W. 2d 353 (Sup. Ct. of Mo., Div. 1, 1942, not officially reported).

[121] *Ridgeway v. Cockburn*, 296 N.Y.S. 936, 163 Misc. 511 (Sup. Ct. of Westchester Co., 1937).

[122] See Robert E. Cushman, "Public Law in the State Courts in 1925–1926," *American Political Science Review*, XX (Aug., 1926), 583, 596.

[123] *Title Guarantee and Trust Co. v. Garrott*, 42 Cal. App. 152, 154, 183 Pac. 470 (1919).

[124] *Burkhardt v. Lofton*, 63 Cal. App. 2d 230, 146 Pac. 2d 720 (1944).

[125] *Ibid.*, pp. 238, 239.

[126] See pages 4–5, above.

[127] The states and the respective decisions follow: (1) Alabama; *Wyatt v. Adair*, 215 Ala. 363, 110 So. 801 (1926); (2) Colorado: *Chandler v. Ziegler*, 88 Colo. 1, 291 Pac. 822 (1930); *Stewart v. Cronan*, 105 Colo. 393, 98 Pac. 2d. 999 (1940); (3) Kansas: *Clark v. Vaughan*, 131 Kan. 438, 292 Pac. 783 (1930); (4) Louisiana: *Queensborough Land Co. v. Cazeaux*, 136 La. 724, 67 So. 641 (1915); (5) Missouri: *Koehler v. Rowland*, 275 Mo. 573, 205 S.W. 217 (1918); *Porter v. Pryor*, 164 S.W. 2d 353 (Mo., 1942, not officially reported); *Porter v. Johnson*, 232 Mo. App. 1150, 115 S.W. 2d 529 (Kansas City Ct. of App., Mo. 1938); *Thornhill v. Herdt*, 130 S.W. 2d 175 (Mo. App., 1939, not officially reported); (6) Oklahoma: *Lyons v. Wallen*, 191 Okla. 669, 133 Pac. 2d 555 (1942). The Court of Appeals of the District of Columbia has likewise enforced racial restrictive covenants over the objection that they constituted unlawful restraints on alienation. *Hundley v. Gorewitz*, 131 Fed. 2d 23, 24 (D.C. Cir. 1942).

[128] *Parmalee v. Morris*, 218 Mich. 625, 188 N.W. 330 (1922).

[129] *Koehler v. Rowland*, 275 Mo. 573, 205 S.W. 217 (1918).

[130] *Ibid.*

[131] *Queensborough Land Co. v. Cazeaux*, 136 La. 724, 727, 67 So. 641 (1915).

[132] *Lion's Head Lake v. Brzezinski*, 23 N.J. Misc. 290 (2d Dist. Ct. of Paterson, 1945).

[133] *Title Guarantee and Trust Co. v. Garrott*, 42 Cal. App. 152, 157, 183 Pac. 470 (1919).

[134] These are: (1) California: *Los Angeles Investment Co. v. Gary*, 181 Cal. 680, 186 Pac. 596 (1919); *Janss Investment Co. v. Walden*, 196 Cal. 753, 239 Pac. 34 (1925); *Stratton v. Cornelius*, 99 Cal. App. 8, 277 Pac. 893 (1929); (2) Michigan: *Porter v. Barrett*, 233 Mich. 373, 208 N.W. 532 (1925); (3) Ohio: *Williams v. The Commercial Land Co.*, 34 Ohio Law Rep. 559 (Ct. of App. for Franklin Co., 1931); (4) West Virginia: *White v. White*, 108 W. Va. 128, 150 S.E. 531 (1929).

[135] *Title Guarantee and Trust Co. v. Garrott*, 42 Cal. App. 152, 157, 183 Pac. 470 (1919).

[136] *Los Angeles Investment Co. v. Gary,* 181 Cal. 680, 186 Pac. 596 (1919). The code provision is section 711.

[137] *Porter v. Barrett,* 233 Mich. 373, 382, 206 N.W. 532 (1925).

[138] *Title Guarantee and Trust Co. v. Garrott,* 42 Cal. App. 152, 158, 183 Pac. 470 (1919).

[139] *White v. White,* 108 W. Va. 128, 150 S.E. 531 (1929).

[140] *Letteau v. Ellis,* 122 Cal. App. 585, 10 Pac. 2d 496 (1952); *Los Angeles Investment Co. v. Gary,* 181 Cal. 680, 186 Pac. 596 (1919); *Littlejohns v. Henderson,* 111 Cal. App. 115 (1931); *White v. White,* 108 W. Va. 128, 150 S.E. 531 (1929).

[141] *Meade v. Dennistone,* 173 Md. 295, 307, 196 Atl. 330 (1938).

[142] Arthur L. Corbin, *Anson's Principles of the Law of Contract,* 5th American ed. (New York: Oxford University Press, 1930), p. 303. See also Walter Gellhorn, "Contracts and Public Policy," *Columbia Law Review,* XXXV (May, 1935), 678; Holdsworth, *History of English Law,* VIII, 54–56.

[143] *Burkhardt v. Lofton,* 63 Cal. App. 2d 230, 239, 146 Pac. 2d 720 (1944).

[144] *Ibid.*

[145] *Queensborough Land Co. v. Cazeaux,* 136 La. 724, 727, 67 So. 641 (1915).

[146] *Parmalee v. Morris,* 218 Mich. 625, 188 N.W. 330 (1922).

[147] Walter Wheeler Cook, "Equity," *Encyclopedia of the Social Sciences* (1937) V, 582, 583.

[148] *Fairchild v. Raines,* 24 Cal. 2d 818, 826, 151 Pac. 2d 260 (1944).

[149] *Burkhardt v. Lofton,* 63 Cal. App. 2d 230, 240, 146 Pac. 2d 720 (1944).

[150] *Ibid.*

[151] *Ibid.*

[152] *Ridgeway v. Cockburn,* 296 N.Y.S. 936, 163 Misc. 511 (Sup. Ct. of Westchester Co., 1937).

[153] *Lion's Head Lake v. Brazezenski,* 23 N.J. Misc. 290 (2d Dist. Ct. of Patterson, 1945).

[154] *Ibid.,* p. 292.

[155] *Porter v. Johnson,* 232 Mo. App. 1150, 1152, 115 S.W. 2d 529 (Kansas City Ct. of App., 1938).

[156] *Ibid.*

[157] *Letteau v. Ellis,* 122 Cal. App. 585, 589, 10 Pac. 2d 496 (Sup. Ct. Los Angeles Co. 1932).

[158] *Fairchild v. Raines,* 24 Cal. 2d 818, 831–35, 151 Pac. 2d 260 (1944).

[159] *Ibid.,* pp. 832, 833.

[160] *Ibid.,* p. 834.

[161] *Hundley v. Gorewitz,* 132 Fed. 2d 24 (D.C. Cir. 1942).

[162] *Pickel v. McCawley,* 329 Mo. 166, 44 S.W. 2d 857 (1931).

[163] *Letteau v. Ellis,* 122 Cal. App. 585, 10 Pac. 2d 496 (1932).

[164] *Hundley v. Gorewitz,* 132 Fed. 2d 24 (D.C. Cir. 1942).

[165] *Ibid.,* p. 25.

[166] *Foster v. Stewart,* 134 Cal. App. 482, 25 Pac. 2d 497 (1933).

[167] 24 Cal. 2d 818, 151 Pac. 2d 260 (1944).

[168] 131 Kan. 438, 292 Pac. 783 (1930).

[169] Note, *Harvard Law Review,* XLIV (1931), 789–790.

[170] *Clark v. Vaughan,* 131 Kan. 438, 445–447, 292 Pac. 783 (1930).

[171] Note, *University of Chicago Law Review,* VII (June, 1940), 714.

[172] 89 Fed. 2d 817 (D.C. Cir. 1937).

[173] *Ibid.,* p. 820.

[174] *Ibid.,* p. 819.

[175] *Porter v. Johnson,* 232 Mo. App. 1150, 115 S.W. 2d 529 (1938).

[176] *Grady v. Garland,* 89 Fed. 2d 817 (D.C. Cir. 1937).

[177] *Vernon v. Reynolds Realty Co.,* 226 N.C. 58, 36 S.E. 2d 710 (1946).

[178] *Porter v. Johnson,* 232 Mo. App. 1150, 1152, 115 S.W. 2d 529 (Kansas City Ct. of App. 1938).

[179] 271 U.S. 323 (1926).

[180] The meeting was held Feb. 22, 1940. Minutes of the meeting taken by Emil Koob, secretary of the Marcus Avenue Improvement Association. Microfilm copy of the Association's papers are in the possession of the writer.

Chapter II

The Development of Negro Strength

[1] For a critical analysis of the educational theories of Booker T. Washington, see Merle Curti, *The Social Ideas of American Educators* (New York: Charles Scribner's Sons, 1935), pp. 288–309. Also, see Basil Mathews, *Booker T. Washington: Educator and Interracial Interpreter* (Cambridge: Harvard University Press, 1948); Samuel R. Spencer, Jr., *Booker T. Washington and the Negro's Place in American Life* (Boston: Little, Brown, 1955).

[2] Herbert Aptheker, ed., *A Documentary History of the Negro People in the United States* (New York: Citadel Press, 1951), p. 756.

[3] *Ibid.*

[4] E. Franklin Frazier, *The Negro in the United States* (New York: Macmillan, 1949), p. 546.

[5] Booker T. Washington, *Up From Slavery, An Autobiography* (New York: Doubleday, Page, 1905), p. 235.

[6] For accounts of the Niagara movement, see John Hope Franklin, *From Slavery to Freedom: A History of American Negroes* (New York: Knopf, 1950), pp. 437, 438; Frazier, *The Negro in the United States,* p. 545. For further background and a defense of NAACP methods, see Daniel Webster Wynn, *The NAACP Versus Negro Revolutionary Protest* (New York: Exposition Press, 1955). Also see E. Rudwick, "The Niagara Movement," XLII, *Journal of Negro History* (July, 1957), 177–200.

[7] Aptheker, *Documentary History of the Negro,* p. 907.

[8] *The Crisis,* XXXIV (June, 1926), 76.

[9] Editorial, "The 'Niagara Movement,'" *The Colored American Magazine,* XIII (October, 1907), 248.

[10] There is no adequate summary of the history and activities of the NAACP. The most useful books are autobiographical. See Mary White Ovington, *The Walls Came Tumbling Down* (New York: Harcourt, Brace, 1947); Walter White, *A Man Called White* (New York: Viking, 1948); and Walter White, *How Far the Promised Land* (New York: Viking, 1955). Some facts may be found in Robert L. Jack, *History of the National Association for the Advancement of Colored People* (Boston: Meador, 1943). A list of those who answered the *Call* to form the NAACP follows: Jane Addams, Chicago; Samuel Bowles, Springfield; Professor W. L. Bulkley, New York: Harriet Stanton Blatch, New York; Ida Wells Barnett, Chicago; E. H. Clement, Boston; Kate H. Claghorn, New York; Professor John Dewey, New York; Dr. W. E. B. DuBois, Atlanta; Mary E. Dreier, Brooklyn; Dr. John L. Elliott, New York; William Lloyd Garrison, Boston; Rev. Francis J. Grimke, Washington, D.C.; William Dean Howells, New York; Rabbi Emil G. Hirsch, Chicago; Rev. John Haynes Holmes, New York; Professor Thomas C. Hall, New York; Hamilton Holt, New York; Florence Kelley, New York; Rev. Frederick Lynch, New York; Helen Marot, New York; John E. Milholland, New York; Mary E. McDowell, Chicago; Professor J. G. Merrill, Connecticut; Dr. Henry Moskowitz, New York; Leonora O'Reilly, New York; Mary W. Ovington, New York; Rev. Dr. Charles H. Parkhurst, New York; Louis F. Post, Chicago; Rev. Dr. John P. Peters, New York; Dr. Jane Robbins, New York; Charles Edward Russell, New York; Joseph Smith, Boston; Anna Garlin Spencer,

New York; William M. Salter, Chicago; J. G. Phelps Stokes, New York; Judge
Wendell Stafford, Washington; Helen Stokes, Boston; Lincoln Steffens, Boston;
President C. F. Thwing, Cleveland; Professor W. I. Thomas, Chicago; Oswald Gar-
rison Villard, New York; Rabbi Stephen S. Wise, New York; Bishop Alexander Wal-
ters, New York; Dr. William H. Ward, New York; Horace White, New York;
William English Walling, New York; Lillian D. Wald, New York; Dr. J. Milton
Waldron, Washington, D.C.; Mrs. Rodman Wharton, Philadelphia; Susan P. Whar-
ton, Philadelphia; Mary E. Wooley (Mt. Holyoke College), South Hadley, Mass.;
Professor Charles Zueblin, Boston.

[11] Arthur M. Schlesinger, *New Viewpoints in American History* (New York: Macmillan, 1923), pp. 110–112.

[12] Storey to Ellen F. Mason, March 17, 1911, *in* M. A. DeWolfe Howe, *Portrait
of an Independent, Moorfield Storey, 1845–1929* (Boston: Houghton Mifflin, 1932),
p. 254.

[13] See James Weldon Johnson, *The Autobiography of an Ex-Coloured Man* (Boston: Sherman, French, 1912, republished with an introduction by Carl Van Vechten,
New York: Knopf, 1927); and *Negro Americans, What Now?* (New York: Viking,
1934).

[14] *Tenth Annual Report of the National Association for the Advancement of
Colored People* (New York, 1919), p. 7. These reports, whose titles vary slightly
year to year, are cited hereafter as NAACP, *Annual Report*.

[15] NAACP, *Annual Report*, 1919, p. 8.

[16] Note, "Private Attorneys-General: Group Action in the Fight for Civil Liberties,"
Yale Law Journal, LVIII (March, 1949), 574, 581.

[17] Johnson, *Negro Americans, What Now?*, p. 98.

[18] Roy Wilkins, "The Negro Wants Full Equality," in *What the Negro Wants*,
Rayford W. Logan, ed. (Chapel Hill: University of North Carolina Press, 1944),
pp. 113, 118.

[19] For a discussion of the crusade from the NAACP viewpoint, see White, *A Man
Called White*, pp. 102–119; Ovington, *The Walls Came Tumbling Down*, pp. 251–
257; NAACP, *Annual Report*, 1930, pp. 7–16.

[20] NAACP, *Annual Report*, 1930, p. 12.

[21] The speech may be found in *Hearings before Sub-Committee of the Senate Committee on the Judiciary* (Confirmation of Hon. John J. Parker to be an Associate
Justice of the Supreme Court of the United States), 71st Cong., 2d sess. (April 5,
1930), p. 74.

[22] *Guinn v. United States*, 238 U.S. 348 (1915).

[23] *Hearings on Confirmation of Judge Parker*, p. 74.

[24] *Ibid.*, p. 23. The decisions criticized by the A.F. of L. were *United Mine
Workers of America v. Red Jacket Consolidated Coal and Coke Co.*, 18 Fed. 2d 839
(4th Cir., 1927) and *Bittner v. West Virginia-Pittsburgh Coal Co.*, 15 Fed. 2d 652
(4th Cir., 1926).

[25] 72 *Cong. Rec.* 8357 (1930).

[26] 72 *Cong. Rec.* 7810, 7811 (1930).

[27] 72 *Cong. Rec.* 7793, 7794 (1930).

[28] 72 *Cong. Rec.* 8486 (1930).

[29] *Ibid.*

[30] 37 Fed. 2d 712 (C.A.A. 4th, 1929).

[31] 245 U.S. 60 (1917).

[32] 281 U.S. 704 (1930).

[33] 72 *Cong. Rec.* 8106 (1930).

[34] See Ovington, *The Walls Came Tumbling Down*, p. 253.

[35] 72 *Cong. Rec.* 8487 (1930).

[36] Two authorities on labor history do not consider the role of the A.F. of L. of
dominating importance in the Senate's rejection of Judge Parker. See Selig Perlman
and Philip Taft, *Labor Movements, 1918–1935* (*History of Labor in the United States,*

Vol. IV, New York: Macmillan, 1935), p. 691. However, a careful student of the Senate's power of confirmation does attribute the defeat of Judge Parker to the power of the A.F. of L. and NAACP combined. Joseph P. Harris, *The Advice and Consent of the Senate: A Study of the Confirmation of Appointments by the United States Senate* (Berkeley and Los Angeles: University of California Press, 1953), pp. 127–130.

[37] Herbert Hoover, *The Cabinet and the Presidency, 1920–1935* (*Memoirs*, Vol. II; New York: Macmillan, 1952), pp. 268–269.

[38] *Ibid.*, p. 269.

[39] White said of Judge Parker: "Since his rejection, his decisions on both Negro and labor cases which have come before him have been above reproach in their strict adherence not only to the law but to the spirit of the Constitution." White, *A Man Called White*, p. 114.

[40] *Congressional Quarterly Almanac* (1951), p. 719, *Congressional Quarterly Weekly*, May 23, 1952, pp. 487, 496.

[41] For a short account of this crusade see Franklin, *From Slavery to Freedom*, pp. 478–479. The methods used to make lynching a national issue are described in NAACP, *Annual Report*, 1919, pp. 13–33. For attacks on lynching by NAACP leaders, see Moorfield Storey, *The Negro Question*, an address delivered before the Wisconsin Bar Association, June 27, 1918 in the Wisconsin Historical Society Collection. Walter White, *Rope and Faggott, A Biography of Judge Lynch* (New York: Knopf, 1929). See also J. H. Chadbourn, *Lynching and the Law* (Chapel Hill: University of North Carolina Press, 1933).

[42] See Louis C. Kesselman, *The Social Politics of FEPC: A Study in Reform Pressure Movements* (Chapel Hill: University of North Carolina Press, 1948). NAACP efforts to improve employment practices have continued. See *The Crisis*, LVIII (April, 1951), 258; NAACP *Annual Report*, 1948, pp. 55, 56.

[43] NAACP, *Annual Report*, 1947, p. 5.

[44] NAACP, *Annual Report*, 1948, p. 50.

[45] NAACP, *Annual Report*, 1948, p. 50.

[46] NAACP, *Annual Report*, 1948, p. 44.

[47] NAACP alliance with trade unions has been condemned by its opponents. For example, see *Human Events*, XIV (Sept. 28, 1957), pp. 1, 2.

[48] Henry Lee Moon, *Balance of Power: The Negro Vote* (Garden City, N.Y.: Doubleday, 1948).

[49] *Ibid.*, p. 198.

[50] *Ibid.*

[51] See "Open Letter to President Wilson," *The Crisis*, VI (1913), 232–233.

[52] NAACP, *Annual Report*, 1942, pp. 6–13; 1947, pp. 45–47. For a full account of the success in ending segregation in the armed services see Lee Nichols, *Breakthrough on the Color Front* (New York: Random House, 1954).

[53] See Kesselman, *Social Politics of FEPC*, pp. 3–24.

[54] See NAACP, *Fighting a Vicious Film* (Boston: 1915).

[55] See White, *A Man Called White*, pp. 199–203.

[56] See Franklin, *From Slavery to Freedom*, p. 510.

[57] *Guinn v. United States*, 238 U.S. 357 (1915).

[58] *Buchanan v. Warley.*

[59] *Moore v. Dempsey*, 261 U.S. 86 (1923).

[60] White, *A Man Called White*, p. 53.

[61] See Charles Reznikoff, ed. *Louis Marshall, Champion of Liberty, Selected Papers and Addresses*, 2 vols. (Philadelphia: Jewish Publication Society, 1956).

[62] *Ibid.* In defense of minorities, Marshall appeared in the Supreme Court to challenge the California Alien Land Law, *Porterfield v. Weiss*, 263 U.S. 225 (1923); to protect a Jew convicted by a mob-controlled jury in Georgia, *Frank v. Mangum*, 237 U.S. 309 (1915) and to defend Catholic parochial schools in Oregon, *Pierce v. Society of The Sisters*, 268 U.S. 510 (1925).

[63] Max J. Kohler, "Louis Marshall," *Dictionary of American Biography*, XII, 326.

[64] 271 U.S. 323 (1926).

[65] *Nixon v. Herndon*, 273 U.S. 536 (1927). For excerpts of Marshall's brief and correspondence associated with the case see Reznikoff, *Louis Marshall*, pp. 425–459.

[66] The criticism refers especially to *Gong Lum v. Rice*, 275 U.S. 78 (1927). Herbert Hill and Jack Greenberg, *Citizen's Guide to De-Segregation, A Study of Social and Legal Change in American Life* (Boston: Beacon Press, 1955), p. 52.

[67] This observation is attributed to Mr. Justice Brandeis. Oliver Allen, "Chief Counsel for Equality," *Life*, XXXVIII (June 13, 1955), 141.

[68] The aid given to the NAACP by the American Fund for Public Service was called to my attention by Hill and Greenberg, *Citizen's Guide to De-Segregation*, pp. 56–59. However, my description of the role played by the fund is based on the original records at the New York Public Library pertinent parts of which were made available to me on microfilm. These will be cited as the AFPS Records.

[69] AFPS Records, Committee on Negro Work, Report of Oct. 18, 1929, p. 6, in series of *Correspondence with Members of Board of Directors*, II, 4.

[70] Roger N. Baldwin to L. Hollingsworth Wood, Oct. 21, 1929, in Series of *Correspondence with Members of Board of Directors*, II, 10.

[71] AFPS Records, *Applications Acted Favorably Upon—Gifts and Loans*, VIII, 27.

[72] *Ibid.*

[73] White, *A Man Called White*, p. 142.

[74] Margold and James Marshall, a son of Louis Marshall, argued the Negro cause in *Nixon v. Condon*, 286 U.S. 73 (1932).

[75] Walter White to Roger N. Baldwin, July 8, 1933, in AFPS records, *Applications Acted Favorably Upon—Gifts and Loans* VIII, 135.

[76] Hill and Greenberg, *Citizen's Guide to De-Segregation*, pp. 56–57.

[77] *New York Times*, June 26, 1950, p. 17.

[78] For a perceptive account of Thurgood Marshall's career, see Saunders Redding, *The Lonesome Road: The Story of the Negro's Past in America* (New York: Doubleday, 1958), pp. 315–329.

[79] 26 U.S.C.A. (Int. Rev. Code, 1939), sec. 23 (o) (2) as amended 26 U.S.C.A. (Int. Rev. Code, 1954) sec. 170 (c) (2). Names of new organizations qualifying under this section of the code are announced in the *Internal Revenue Bulletin*. For a full enumeration, see *Cumulative List*, Organizations Described in Section 170 (c) of the Internal Revenue Code of 1954. (United States Treasury Department, Internal Revenue Service, 1958).

[80] Robert L. Carter to author, July 20, 1956 and Feb. 20, 1958.

[81] In 1947 the National Legal Committee was composed of the following: *Atlanta*, A. T. Walden; *Birmingham*, Arthur D. Shores; *Charleston, W.Va.*, T. G. Nutter; *Chattanooga*, Maurice Weaver; *Chicago*, W. Robert Ming, Jr.; *Cincinnati*, Theodore M. Berry; *Cleveland*, William T. McKnight; *Dallas*, W. J. Durham; *Erie, Penn.*, William F. Illig; *Houston*, Arthur Mandell, Thomas L. Griffith, Jr.: *Los Angeles*, Loren Miller; *Louisville*, Charles W. Anderson; *Madison, Wis.*, Lloyd K. Garrison; *Nashville*, Z. Alexander Looby; *New York*, Donald Crichton, Morris Ernest, Osmond K. Frankel, Arthur Garfield Hays, Paul Kern, Karl N. Llewellyn, James Marshall, Shad Polier, Hope Stevens, Charles H. Studin, Andrew D. Weinberger; *Pittsburgh*, Homer S. Brown; *Richmond*, Spottswood Robinson, III; *San Francisco*, Bartley C. Crum; *Tulsa*, Amos T. Hall; *Washington, D.C.*, Charles H. Houston, William H. Hastie, Edward P. Lovett, Leon A. Ransom, Ruth Weyand; *Wilmington*, Louis L. Redding. NAACP, *Annual Report*, 1947, p. 95.

[82] Those who were members of the National Legal Committee in 1947 but no longer served in 1956 were: Weaver, McKnight, Mandell, Griffith, Anderson, Crichton, Hays, Kern, Stevens, Studin, Brown, Houston, Hastie, and Ransom. The new members in 1956 were from these cities: *Cambridge, Mass.*, Paul Freund, Benjamin Kaplan, and Albert Sacks; *Chicago*, Sidney A. Jones, Loring B. Moore; *Ithaca*,

N.Y., Milton Konvitz; *Kansas City, Mo.,* Carl Johnson; *New York,* Charles Black, Louis Pollack, Herman Zand; *Philadelphia,* William Coleman; *Richmond,* Oliver W. Hill; *St. Louis,* Sidney Redmond; *Washington, D.C.,* Arthur Goldberg, George M. Johnson, James M. Nabrit, Frank D. Reeves.

[83] This information was obtained through an interview with Dean George M. Johnson of Howard Law School, in Washington, D.C., March 27, 1956. See also Frazier, *The Negro in the United States* (New York: Macmillan, 1949), pp. 471–479.

[84] George M. Johnson to the author, April 25, 1956.

[85] George M. Johnson, "The Integration of the Negro Lawyer into the Legal Profession in the United States," a paper delivered to the Annual Conference of the Division of Social Sciences, Howard University, Washington, D.C., May 4, 1951.

[86] See the 8-page leaflet by Lucia T. Thomas, *History of the National Bar Association* (Chicago: 1950). For some years Negroes have been admitted to the American Bar Association although it was not until 1956 that the A.B.A. standing committee on membership could report that "the former long and troublesome membership application has been simplified and made attractive to members and one of the most troublesome questions thereon, the question of race, has been eliminated." *Reports of the American Bar Association,* LXXXI (1956), 193.

[87] Thomas, *History of the National Bar Association,* p. 1.

[88] The NAACP has been a bitter foe of the Communist party. For a typical criticism, see Herbert Hill, "The Communist Party—Enemy of Negro Equality," *The Crisis,* LVIII (June, July, 1951), 365.

[89] For full-length studies of the Communist party of the United States and Negroes, see Wilson Record, *The Negro and the Communist Party* (Chapel Hill: University of North Carolina Press, 1951); William A. Nolan, *Communism and the Negro* (Chicago: Henry Regnery, 1951). For a comment on the limitation of these books, see Vaughn D. Bornet, "Historical Scholarship, Communism, and the Negro," *Journal of Negro History,* XXXVII (July, 1952), 304–324. Also, see Fund for the Republic, *Bibliography on the Communist Problem* (New York: 1955), pp. 386–392.

[90] *Powell v. Alabama,* 287 U.S. 45 (1932). The second Scottsboro case, questioning the systematic exclusion of Negroes from the trial jury, was *Norris v. Alabama,* 294 U.S. 587 (1935). For the importance of these rules in constitutional development, see David Fellman, *Defendants' Rights* (New York: Rinehart, 1958).

[91] The contest between the NAACP and the Communist-dominated International Labor Defense is related in Quentin Reynolds, *Courtroom: The Story of Samuel S. Leibowitz* (New York: Garden City Books, 1951), pp. 248–314. See also Haywood Patterson and Earl Conrad, *Scottsboro Boy* (New York: Doubleday, 1950) and Allen K. Chalmers, *They Shall Be Free* (New York: Doubleday, 1951). For a defense of the NAACP on this count and others, see J. Edgar Hoover, *Masters of Deceit: The Story of Communism in America and How to Fight It* (New York: Henry Holt, 1958), pp. 247, 248, 252.

[92] Nolan, *Communism versus the Negro,* pp. 89, 90.

[93] *New York Times,* March 16, 1951, p. 1, col. 4.

[94] Note, "Bills Condemning Picketing of Courts Before Congress," *Journal of the American Judicature Society,* XXXIV (Aug. 1949), 53, 54.

[95] Joint Hearings before the Subcommittee of the Committee on the Judiciary on S. 1681 and H.R. 3766 *To Prohibit the Picketing of Courts,* 81st Cong., 1st sess. (June 15, 1949), p. 5.

[96] Public Law No. 831, sec. 31 (a), 81st Cong., 2d sess. (1950). The pertinent part reads: "Whosoever, with the intent of interfering with, obstructing, or impeding the administration of justice, or with intent of influencing any judge, juror, witness, or court officer, in the discharge of his duty, pickets or parades in or near a building housing a court of the United States . . . shall be fined not more than $5000 or imprisoned not more than one year, or both."

Chapter III

Evolution of NAACP Legal Strategy

[1] NAACP, *Annual Report*, 1915, p. 9.

[2] *Ibid.*, 1911, p. 7.

[3] *Ibid.*, 1911, p. 6.

[4] *Ibid.*, 1911, p. 7.

[5] *Ibid.*, 1914, p. 8.

[6] *Ibid.*, 1926, p. 9.

[7] *Ibid.*, 1931, p. 32.

[8] *Ibid.*, 1940, p. 30.

[9] *Ibid.*, 1940, p. 30.

[10] *Ibid.*, 1926, p. 9; 1927, p. 16; 1930, p. 21.

[11] The *Sweet* case is discussed in many histories of the Negro and of the NAACP. See also *New York Times*, 1925; July 12, II, p. 2, col. 4; Nov. 27, p. 11, col. 2; Nov. 28, p. 17, col. 8; Dec. 29, p. 16, col. 2.

[12] See Clarence Darrow, *The Story of My Life* (New York: Charles Scribner's Sons, 1932), pp. 301–311; Charles Yale Harrison, *Clarence Darrow* (New York: Jonathan Cape & Harrison Smith, 1931), pp. 329–351; Irving Stone, *Clarence Darrow for the Defense* (Garden City, N.Y.: Doubleday, Doran, 1941), pp. 469–486; Arthur Weinberg, ed., *Attorney for the Damned;* Foreword by Justice William O. Douglas (New York: Simon and Schuster, 1957), pp. 229–263.

[13] NAACP, *Annual Report*, 1926, pp. 7, 8. The victory was attributed to two factors: the money which was raised (as the NAACP said, justice in the courts costs money) and the skill of the lawyer, Clarence Darrow. "The Sweet Trial," *The Crisis* (July, 1926), p. 114. Another account credits Association lawyers with an assist. Arthur Garfield Hays, *Let Freedom Ring* (New York: Boni and Liveright, 1928), pp. 195–223.

[14] NAACP, *Annual Report*, 1926, p. 8.

[15] *Ibid.*, 1910, p. 10.

[16] *Ibid.*, 1914, pp. 7, 8.

[17] *Ibid.*, 1917, p. 8.

[18] *Ibid.*, 1917, p. 8.

[19] *Ibid.*, 1912, p. 6; 1913, p. 22; 1926, pp. 9, 10.

[20] 245 U.S. 60 (1917). See chap. i, pp. 4–5, above.

[21] NAACP, *Annual Report*, 1919, p. 48.

[22] AFPS Records, Committee on Negro Work, undated memorandum (approximately 1930), p. 14 in series of *Correspondence with Members of Board of Directors,* 1934–1938, II, 6.

[23] *Harmon v. Tyler*, 158 La. 439, 104 So. 200 (1927); *rehearing*, 160 La. 943, 107 So. 704 (1926).

[24] NAACP, *Annual Report*, 1926, p. 9.

[25] *Harmon v. Tyler*, 273 U.S. 668 (1927).

[26] AFPS Records, Committee on Negro Work, *op. cit.*, p. 14.

[27] 281 U.S. 704 (1930), *affirming without opinion* 37 Fed. 2d 712 (C.C.A. 4th 1929).

[28] 37 Fed. 2d 712, 713 (C.C.A. 4th 1929). Judge John J. Parker was a member of the three-man tribunal in this *per curiam* decision.

[29] AFPS Records, Committee on Negro Work, *op. cit.*, p. 15.

[30] *Ibid.*

[31] Louis Marshall to Moorfield Storey, Sept. 24, 1925. Charles Reznikoff (ed.), *Louis Marshall, Champion of Liberty*, Selected Papers and Addresses, 2 vols. (Philadelphia: Jewish Publication Society of America, 1957), I, 461.

[32] *Corrigan (and Curtis) v. Buckley,* 299 Fed. 899 (D.C. Cir. 1924), *appeal dismissed,* 271 U.S. 323 (1926).

[33] In 1926, Cobb was nominated by President Coolidge to be judge of the Municipal Court of the District of Columbia. Some senators opposed confirmation because of Cobb's membership on the Board of Directors of the NAACP and his position in the *Corrigan* case against the enforcement of racial covenants. Louis Marshall rose to Cobb's defense, the appointment was confirmed, and he served as judge for ten years. Marshall to Senator William E. Borah, April 19, 1926 in Reznikoff, *Louis Marshall,* I, 462–464.

[34] Louis Marshall to James Weldon Johnson, Sept. 25, 1924. Reznikoff, *Louis Marshall,* p. 459.

[35] Louis Marshall to Moorfield Storey, Sept. 24, 1925. Reznikoff, *Louis Marshall,* p. 461.

[36] Brief for appellants (summary), *Corrigan v. Buckley,* 271 U.S. 323, 324 (1926).

[37] The *Civil Rights Cases,* 109 U.S. 3 (1875) held that in enforcing the Fourteenth Amendment Congress could not penalize discrimination against Negroes by private persons. Marshall's comment is in a letter to Moorfield Storey, Sept. 24, 1925. Reznikoff, *Louis Marshall,* pp. 461–462.

[38] Louis Marshall to James Weldon Johnson, September 25, 1924. Reznikoff, *Louis Marshall,* p. 459.

[39] *Ibid.*

[40] Louis Marshall to Moorfield Storey, Dec. 12, 1924. Reznikoff, *Louis Marshall,* p. 460.

[41] Louis Marshall to James Weldon Johnson, Sept. 25, 1924. Reznikoff, *Louis Marshall,* p. 459.

[42] *Ibid.*

[43] Louis Marshall to Moorfield Storey, Dec. 12, 1924. Reznikoff, *Louis Marshall,* p. 460.

[44] *Ibid. Quia Emptores Terrarum* is discussed in chap. i, p. 2, above.

[45] AFPS Records, Committee on Negro Work, *op. cit.,* p. 14.

[46] The three cases identified as having been supported by the NAACP were *Corrigan v. Buckley,* 299 Fed. 899 (D.C. Cir. 1924), *appeal dismissed,* 271 U.S. 323 (1926); *Cornish v. O'Donoghue,* 30 F. 2d 98 (D.C. Cir. 1929), *certiorari denied,* 279 U.S. 871 (1929); *Russell v. Wallace,* 30 F. 2d 781 (D.C. Cir. 1929), *certiorari denied,* 279 U.S. 871 (1929).

[47] AFPS Records, Committee on Negro Work, report of Oct. 18, 1929, p. 3 in series of *Correspondence with Members of Board of Directors, 1934–1938,* II, 6.

[48] AFPS Records, Walter White memorandum to A. B. Spingarn and N. R. Margold, Oct. 29, 1931, p. 3 in series of *Applications Favorably Acted Upon—Gifts and Loans, 1934–1938,* VIII, 97.

[49] NAACP, *Annual Report,* 1948, p. 27.

[50] 311 U.S. 32 (1940), *reversing, Lee v. Hansberry,* 372 Ill. 369, 24 N.E. 2d 37 (1939).

[51] *Burke v. Kleiman,* 277 Ill. App. 517 (1931).

[52] Loring B. Moore, *Chicago Defender,* May 15, 1958, p. 1, col. 6.

[53] Florence Murray, ed., *The Negro Handbook, 1946–1947* (New York: Current Books, 1947), p. 33.

[54] *Mays v. Burgess,* 147 F. 2d 869, 152 F. 2d 123 (D.C. Cir. 1945), *certiorari denied,* 395 U.S. 858, *rehearing denied,* 325 U.S. 896 (1945). See *Georgetown Law Journal,* XXXIII (1945), 356; *Harvard Law Review,* LIX (1945), 293; *Illinois Law Review,* XL (1946), 432; *National Bar Journal,* III (1945), 364.

[55] Minutes of Meeting, "NAACP Lawyers and Consultants on Methods of Attacking Restrictive Covenants," Chicago, Illinois, July 9–10, 1945. Mimeographed minutes, 40 pp. All quotations in the author's account are drawn from these minutes. Those present were NAACP lawyers: Hon. William H. Hastie, Washington, D.C.; Theodore Berry, Cincinnati; Oscar Brown, Chicago; Sidney Brown, Chicago;

Francis Dent, Detroit; David Grant, St. Louis; Charles Houston, Washington, D.C.; Sidney Jones, Chicago; Maceo Littlejohn, St. Paul, Minn.; A. C. McNeal, Chicago; Jesse Mann, Chicago; Thurgood Marshall, New York; Loren Miller, Los Angeles; Irving Mollison, Chicago; Herman Moore, Chicago; Loring B. Moore, Chicago; Spottswood W. Robinson, Richmond, Va.; Eugene Shands, Chicago; Theodore Spaulding, Philadelphia; Hon. Charles E. Tovey, New York; George Vaughn, St. Louis; A. T. Walden, Atlanta; Andrew Weinberger, New York; Walter White, New York; Roy Wilkins, New York. Consultants in attendance were: Elmer Goertz, Chicago Council Against Racial and Religious Discrimination; William E. Hill, American Council on Race Relations; Homer Jack, Chicago Council Against Racial and Religious Discrimination and the American Civil Liberties Union; George B. Nesbitt, Racial Relations Advisor, Region III, F.P.H.A.; Harry Walker, Mayor's Committee on Race Relations, Chicago; Dr. Robert C. Weaver, American Council on Race Relations. NAACP Chicago Conference, p. 1.

[56] *Muller v. Oregon,* 208 U.S. 412 (1908). See Clement E. Vose, "The National Consumers' League and the Brandeis Brief," *Midwest Journal of Political Science* I (Nov., 1957), 267–290.

[57] Sheldon Glueck, "The Social Sciences and Scientific Method in the Administration of Justice," Annals, CLXVII (1933), 106, reprinted in Sidney P. Simpson and Julius Stone, *Law and Society* (St. Paul: West Publishing Co., 1949); II, 1406–1407. For discussions of newer approaches, see Tracy S. Kendler, "Contributions of the Psychologist to Constitutional Law," *American Psychologist,* V (October, 1950), 505; Jack Greenberg, "Social Scientists Take the Stand: A Review and Appraisal of Their Testimony in Litigation," *Michigan Law Review,* LIV, (May, 1956), 953–970; Arnold M. Rose, "The Social Scientist as an Expert Witness," *Minnesota Law Review,* XL (Feb., 1956), 205–218.

[58] Henry Steele Commager, *The American Mind: An Interpretation of American Thought and Character Since the 1880's* (New Haven: Yale University Press, 1950), p. 381.

[59] For a discussion of recent trends regarding judicial realism, see Alexander H. Pekelis in *Law and Social Action, Selected Essays,* Milton R. Konvitz, ed. (Ithaca and New York: Cornell University Press, 1950), pp. 1–41.

[60] For critical analyses of the political theory of race supremacy in the United States, see David Spitz, *Patterns of Anti-Democratic Thought* (New York: Macmillan, 1949), and Oscar Handlin, *Race and Nationality in American Life* (Boston: Little, Brown, 1957). For a contrary view, see Byram Campbell, *American Race Theorists, A Critique of Their Thoughts and Methods* (Boston: Chapman and Grimes, 1952).

[61] A historical treatment of Darwinian influence on theories of racial superiority in the United States, particularly in reference to justifications of imperialism, may be found in Richard Hofstadter, *Social Darwinism in American Thought, 1860–1915* (Philadelphia: University of Pennsylvania Press, 1945), pp. 146–173.

[62] E. B. Reuter, "Racial Theory," *American Journal of Sociology,* L. (May, 1945), 452.

[63] The Chicago Commission on Race Relations, *The Negro in Chicago; A Study of Race Relations and a Race Riot* (Chicago: University of Chicago Press, 1922), p. 445.

[64] *Ibid.,* p. 437.

[65] Alzada P. Comstock, "Chicago Housing Conditions, VI: The Problem of the Negro," *American Journal of Sociology,* XVIII (Sept., 1912), 241.

[66] The Chicago Commission on Race Relations, *The Negro in Chicago,* pp. 108–139; 152–230.

[67] *Ibid.,* p. 608.

[68] *Ibid.,* p. 610.

[69] *Ibid.,* p. 645.

[70] E. B. Reuter, "Racial Theory," *American Journal of Sociology*, L. (May, 1945), 456.

[71] See E. A. Shils, "The Present Situation in American Sociology," *Pilot Papers: Social Essays and Documents* II (1947), 10.

[72] Among the writings characteristic of the newer, sociological approach to Negroes relative to the housing problem are Louis Wirth, "Segregation," *Encyclopedia of the Social Sciences* (1937) VII, 643; Thomas J. Woofter, *The Negro Problem in Cities* (New York: Macmillan, 1928); St. Clair Drake and Horace R. Cayton, *Black Metropolis; A Study of Negro Life in a Northern City* (New York: Harcourt Brace, 1945); Charles S. Johnson, *Patterns of Negro Segregation* (New York: Harper, 1943); Gunnar Myrdal, *An American Dilemma; The Negro Problem and Modern Democracy* (New York: Harper, 1944); Richard Sterner, *The Negro's Share: A Study of Income, Consumption, Housing and Public Assistance* (New York: Harper, 1943).

[73] D. O. McGovney, "Racial Residential Segregation by State Court Enforcement of Restrictive Agreements, Covenants or Conditions in Deeds is Unconstitutional," *California Law Review*, XXXIII (March, 1945), 5.

[74] 271 U.S. 323 (1926).

[75] 109 U.S. 3 (1883).

[76] 245 U.S. 60 (1917).

[77] Roger J. Traynor, "Dudley Odell McGovney," *California Law Review*, XXXV (September, 1947), 327, 329. See bibliography of D. O. McGovney, *ibid.*, pp. 332–335.

[78] Loren Miller, "Race Restrictions on the Use or Sale of Real Property," *National Bar Journal*, II (June, 1944), 24.

[79] Harold M. Bowman, "The Constitution and Common Law Restraints on Alienation," *Boston University Law Review*, VIII (Jan., 1928), 1; A. A. Bruce, "Racial Zoning by Private Contract," *Virginia Law Register*, XIII (1928), 526; Bruce, "Racial Zoning by Private Contract in the Light of the Constitutions and the Rule against Restraints on Alienation," *Illinois Law Review*, XXI (March, 1927), 704; Arthur T. Martin, Segregating Residences of Negroes," *Michigan Law Review*, XXXII (April, 1934), 721; M. T. Van Hecke, "Zoning Ordinances and Restrictions in Deeds," 37 *Yale Law Journal*, XXXVII (Feb., 1928), 413.

[80] Harold I. Kahen, "Validity of Anti-Negro Restrictive Covenants: A Reconsideration of the Problem," *University of Chicago Law Review*, XII (Feb., 1945), 198, 207.

[81] The quotation is from the Foreword to *Yale Law Journal*, L (March, 1941), 737.

[82] The first case was *Minersville School District v. Gobitis*, 310 U.S. 586 (1940). That decision was overruled in *West Virginia State Board of Education v. Barnette*, 319 U.S. 624 (1943).

[83] *West Virginia State Board of Education v. Barnette*, 319 U.S. 624, 634, 635 (1943).

[84] *O'Malley v. Woodrough*, 307 U.S. 277, 281 (1938). This case overruled *Evans v. Gore*, 253 U.S. 245 (1920).

[85] The editorial appeared in the *Chicago Sun* on June 6, 1945.

[86] Details of these meetings have not been located. However, a pamphlet resulted from the conference. See Preston Bradley, *Racial Restrictive Covenants* (Chicago, 1946).

[87] NAACP *Annual Report*, 1948, p. 27.

[88] In Preston Bradley, *Racial Restrictive Covenants*, Loren Miller, "Restrictive Covenants vs. Democracy," pp. 5–23; Bernard J. Sheil, "Restrictive Covenants vs. Brotherhood," pp. 25–31.

Chapter IV

Covenants in the Capital

[1] Transcript of Record, *Hurd v. Hodge* [334 U.S. 24 (1943)], p. 77.

[2] *Corrigan v. Buckley,* 299 Fed. 899 (D.C. Cir., 1924), *appeal dismissed,* 271 U.S. 323 (1924); *Torrey v. Wolfes,* 6 Fed. 2d 702 (D.C. Cir., 1925); *Cornish v. O'Donoghue,* 30 Fed. 2d 983 (D.C. Cir., 1929), *certiorari denied,* 279 U.S. 871 (1930); *Russell v. Wallace,* 30 Fed. 2d 981 (1929), *certiorari denied,* 279 U.S. 871 (1930); *Edwards v. West Woodridge Theatre Co.,* 55 Fed. 2d 524 (D.C. Cir., 1931); *Grady v. Garland,* 89 Fed. 2d 817 (D.C. Cir., 1937), *certiorari denied,* 302 U.S. 694 (1937); *Hundley v. Gorewitz,* 132 Fed. 2d 23 (D.C. Cir., 1942), and other cases in the District Court not appearing in the case reports.

[3] *Hundley v. Gorewitz,* 132 Fed. 2d 23 (D.C. Cir., 1942). *Gospel Spreading Association v. Bennetts,* 147 Fed. 2d 878 (D.C. Cir., 1945).

[4] 147 Fed. 2d 869 (D.C. Cir., 1945), *certiorari denied,* 325 U.S. 868 (1945), *rehearing denied,* 325 U.S. 896 (1945).

[5] Testimony of Henry K. Murphy, executive secretary of the Commitee of Owners of the North Capitol Citizens Association, Transcript of Record, *Hurd v. Hodge,* pp. 70–75. This was corroborated by James A. Crooks, law associate of Henry Gilligan, in an interview, March 19, 1952. Crooks himself was active in citizen association work for twenty-five years. In the fall of 1945 he was nominated to be first vice president of the Washington Federation of Citizens Associations. *Washington Post,* October 7, 1945, p. 14, col. 2. Gilligan died October 6, 1950.

[6] 147 Fed. 2d 869 (D.C. Cir., 1945).

[7] Copies of this broadside are in the files of James A. Crooks, Washington, D.C. Inspected by the author in 1952.

[8] *Washington Post,* October 12, 1945, p. 18, col. 7. See Florence Murray, ed., *The Negro Handbook,* 1946–47 (New York: Current Books 1947), pp. 34–35.

[9] Crooks, office files.

[10] Testimony of Charles J. Rush, executive secretary and treasurer of the Washington Real Estate Board. Transcript of Record, *Hurd v. Hodge,* pp. 270–277. The Code of Ethics provided: "No property in a white section should ever be sold, rented, advertised, or offered to colored people. In a doubtful case advice from the Public Affairs Committee should be obtained."

[11] Testimony of Neville D. Miller, advertising manager of the *Washington Evening Star.* Transcript of Record, *Hurd v. Hodge,* pp. 258–259.

[12] Testimony of Charles J. Rush, Transcript of Record, *Hurd v. Hodge,* p. 271.

[13] *Ibid.,* pp. 78–79.

[14] Crooks, office files.

[15] Transcript of Record, *Hurd v. Hodge,* p. 7.

[16] Testimony of Raphael Urciolo, *ibid.,* p. 148. Testimony of Charles J. Rush, *ibid.,* p. 273.

[17] This was confirmed in an interview with Urciolo on December 19, 1951.

[18] Transcript of Record, *Hurd v. Hodge,* p. 147.

[19] Crooks, office files.

[20] *Ibid.*

[21] Transcript of Record, *Hurd v. Hodge,* p. 67. All quotations in this account of the trial are from the Transcript of Record unless otherwise identified.

[22] Transcript of Record, *Hurd v. Hodge,* pp. 7, 8.

[23] *Hurd v. Letts,* 152 Fed. 2d 121 (D.C. Cir., 1945).

[24] Testimony of Leonard S. Hayes, a Negro examiner, District of Columbia Rent Control Administration, Transcript of Record pp. 278–290.

[25] Testimony of Thomas W. Parks, *ibid.,* pp. 332–345.

[26] Testimony of Pauline Stewart, *ibid.,* p. 223; testimony of Herbert Savage, *ibid.,*

p. 227; testimony of James Hurd, *ibid.*, p. 241; testimony of Robert Howe, *ibid.*, p. 309.

²⁷ Testimony of Doris Wilkins, Board of Public Welfare, Washington, D.C., *ibid.*, pp. 353–357.

²⁸ Findings of Fact and Conclusions of Law, in Transcript of Record, *Hurd v. Hodge*, p. 379.

²⁹ *Grady v. Garland*, 89 Fed. 2d 817 (D.C. Cir., 1937).

³⁰ *Hundley v. Gorewitz*, 132 Fed. 2d 23 (D.C. Cir., 1942).

³¹ 147 Fed. 2d 869 (D.C. Cir., 1945).

³² *Hurd v. Hodges; Urciolo v. Hodge*, 162 Fed. 2d 233, 234 (D.C. Cir., 1947).

³³ *Ibid.* See American Law Institute, *Restatement of the Law of Property*, sec. 406, Comment 1 and 9, (1944). For a full discussion of the *Restraint*, see chap. i, pp. 4–5, above.

³⁴ *Hurd v. Hodge, Urciolo v. Hodge*, 162 Fed. 2d 233, 235–247 (D.C. Cir., 1947).

³⁵ *Ibid.*, p. 235. McGovney, "Racial Residential Segregation by State Court Enforcement of Restrictive Agreements, Covenants or Conditions in Deeds is Unconstitutional," *California Law Review*, XXXIII (March, 1945), 5.

³⁶ *Ibid.*, pp. 243, 245. Robert C. Weaver, "Race Restrictive Housing Covenants," *Journal of Land and Public Utility Economics*, XX (Aug., 1944), 183, 187.

³⁷ *Ibid.*, pp. 242, 244. Gunnar Myrdal, *An American Dilemma* (New York: Harper, 1944).

³⁸ *Ibid.*, p. 246. Remarks of the president in making the Wendell Willkie Awards for Journalism; press release, Feb. 28, 1947. General Eisenhower was also quoted as demanding the elimination of unfair practices against Negroes.

³⁹ United Nations Charter, Articles 55c, 56.

⁴⁰ 299 Fed. 899 (D.C. Cir., 1924). *Appeal dismissed*, 271 U.S. 323 (1926).

⁴¹ 14 Stat. 39 (1866). This provided, among other things, that Negroes have the same right "to inherit, purchase, lease, sell, hold, and convey real and personal property as is enjoyed by white citizens."

⁴² 147 Fed. 2d 259 (D.C. Cir., 1945), *certiorari denied*, 325 U.S. 868 (1945), *rehearing denied*, 325 U.S. 896 (1946).

⁴³ *Hurd v. Hodge; Urciolo v. Hodge*, 162 Fed. 2d 233, p. 237.

⁴⁴ *Ibid.*, p. 238.

⁴⁵ *Ibid.* The police-power cases cited as authority were *Nebbia v. New York*, 291 U.S. 502 (1934); *Euclid v. Ambler Reality Co.*, 272 U.S. 365 (1927).

⁴⁶ 245 U.S. 60 (1917).

⁴⁷ *Hurd v. Hodge; Urciolo v. Hodge*, 162 Fed. 2d 233, p. 239.

⁴⁸ 109 U.S. 3 (1883).

⁴⁹ *Hurd v. Hodge; Urciolo v. Hodge*, 162 Fed. 2d 233, p. 239.

⁵⁰ 245 U.S. 60 (1917).

⁵¹ *Hurd v. Hodge; Urciolo v. Hodge*, 162 Fed. 2d 233, p. 240.

⁵² See note 41 above, for the language of the Civil Rights Act of 1866.

⁵³ *Hurd v. Hodge; Urciolo v. Hodge*, 162 Fed. 2d 233, p. 241. All quotations in this section are from Judge Edgerton's opinion.

⁵⁴ Felix Frankfurter, "Judge Henry W. Edgerton," *Cornell Law Quarterly*, XLIII (Winter, 1958), 161, 162.

⁵⁵ Simon Rosensweig, "The Opinions of Judge Edgerton—A Study in the Judicial Process," *Cornell Law Quarterly*, XXXVII (Winter, 1952), 149.

⁵⁶ *Ibid.*, p. 166. Texts of his most important dissents are collected in Stanley D. Metzger, "Selected Opinions of Judge Henry W. Edgerton," *Cornell Law Quarterly*, XLIII (Winter, 1958), 163–195.

⁵⁷ Rosensweig, *op. cit.*, p. 149.

Chapter V

St. Louis, Missouri

[1] The account of the Marcus Avenue Improvement Association is based partly on interviews with Emil Koob, a leader of the association, and Gerald L. Seegers, its attorney, in St. Louis on Dec. 13 and 14, 1951. It also is derived from the records of the association, consisting mainly of minutes of meetings, from 1937 to 1948. These records were obtained from Emil Koob; a microfilm copy of them is in the author's possession.

[2] This figure, $10,000, was the estimate made by both Mr. Koob and Mr. Seegers.

[3] 335 Mo. 814, 198 S.W. 2d 679 (1947), *reversed*, 334 U.S. 1 (1948).

[4] M.A.I.A., *Minutes of Meeting*, Dec. 7, 1937.

[5] *Ibid.*, Feb. 24, 1938.

[6] *Ibid.*

[7] *Ibid.*, April 28, 1938.

[8] *Ibid.*, Aug. 22, 1944, p. 4.

[9] *Ibid.*, Feb. 24, 1938; Oct. 10, 1940; Dec. 9, 1940; Jan. 30, 1941; Aug. 22, 1944.

[10] *Ibid.*, March 10, 1938.

[11] *Ibid.*, March 3, 1941; June 18, 1941; Nov. 6, 1941; Feb. 5, 1952; June 3, 1942.

[12] *Ibid.*, April 28, 1941; June 3, 1942.

[13] *Ibid.*, May 25, 1943.

[14] *Ibid.*, Aug. 22, 1944.

[15] *Ibid.*, Oct. 10, 1940.

[16] *Ibid.*, May 15, 1942.

[17] *Ibid.*, Aug. 22, 1944, p. 3.

[18] *Ibid.*, Sept. 25, 1941, p. 2.

[19] M.A.I.A. *Records,* May 26, 1938; April 11, 1940; May 25, 1945; Jan. 11, 1948.

[20] M.A.I.A., *Minutes of Meeting*, Feb. 22, 1940.

[21] *Ibid.*, Sept. 25, 1941, p. 2.

[22] Printed in Scovel Richardson, "Some of the Defenses Available in Restrictive Covenant Suits Against Colored Americans in St. Louis," *National Bar Journal*, III (March, 1945), 50, 54.

[23] M.A.I.A., *Minutes of Directors Meeting*, Oct. 8, 1942.

[24] M.A.I.A., *Minutes of Meeting*, March 22, 1945.

[25] *Ibid.*, May 26, 1938.

[26] *Ibid.*, Oct. 8, 1942.

[27] M.A.I.A., *Minutes of Directors Meeting*, Oct. 13, 1942.

[28] M.A.I.A., *Minutes of Meeting*, Feb. 13, 1947.

[29] Transcript of Record, *Shelley v. Kraemer* [334 U.S. 1 (1948)] p. 88. Quotations not otherwise noted are drawn from the Transcript of Record.

[30] *National Bar Journal*, III (March, 1945), 50.

[31] *Ibid.*, p. 52.

[32] Interview, Emil Koob and Gerald Seegers, Dec. 13, 14, 1951.

[33] Transcript of Record, *Shelley v. Kraemer*, pp. 19, 20.

[34] *Ibid.*, p. 144. The Missouri precedents were *Thornhill v. Herdt*, 130 S.W. 2d 175 (Mo. App., 1939, not officially reported); *Porter v. Pryor*, 164 S.W. 2d 353 (No., 1942, not officially reported); *Koehler v. Rowland*, 275 Mo. 573, 205 S.W. 217 (1918).

[35] *Kraemer v. Shelley*, 355 Mo. 814, 821, 198 S.W. 2d 679 (1946).

[36] 147 Fed. 2d 869, 152 Fed. 2d 123 (1945), *certiorari denied*, 325 U.S. 868 (1945), *rehearing denied*, 325 U.S. 896 (1945).

[37] *Kraemer v. Shelley*, 355 Mo. 814, 823, 198 S.W. 2d 679 (1946).

[38] *Ibid.*, p. 824.

[39] *In the matter of Real Estate Brokers Association of St. Louis,* report of David A. McMullan, *amicus curiae,* to Circuit Court of St. Louis, Mo., undated. This report with other records of the Real Estate Brokers Association is in the possession of Mrs. Margaret Bush Wilson of St. Louis, henceforth cited as Brokers Association Records.

Chapter VI

Negro Lawyers and the Michigan Courts

[1] 218 Mich. 625, 188 N.W. 330, 38 A.L.R. 1181 (1922).

[2] The National Association of Real Estate Brokers, incorporated in March, 1948, is principally an organization of local Negro brokers' associations.—Graves to the author, Sept. 20, 1957. Also see *NAREB Report* (Chicago, Ill., 1957).

[3] 163 U.S. 537 (1896).

[4] See Charles S. Johnson, *Patterns of Negro Segregation* (New York: Harper, 1943), pp. 319–320.

[5] Bette Smith Jenkins, *The Racial Policies of the Detroit Housing Commission and Their Administration* (unpublished master's thesis, at Wayne University Library, Detroit, 1950), pp. 73–130.

[6] Alfred M. Lee and Norman D. Humphrey, *Race Riot* (New York: Dryden Press, 1943).

[7] Long and Johnson, *People vs. Property* (Nashville, Tenn.: Fisk University Press, 1947), pp. 78–79.

[8] Transcript of Record, *McGhee v. Sipes* [335 U.S. 1 (1948)], p. 13. Unless otherwise indicated the account of the trial is drawn from the Transcript of Record.

[9] Mich. Const., Art. II, sec. 16. "No person shall be compelled in a criminal case to be a witness against himself, nor be deprived of life, liberty, or property, without due process of law."

[10] This general classification is followed in *The UNESCO Statement by Experts on Race Problems.* Paragraph 7 reads: "Now what has the scientist to say about the groups of mankind which may be recognized at the present time? Human races can be and have been differently classified by different anthropologists, but at the present time most anthropologists agree in classifying the greater part of present-day mankind into three major divisions, as follows: The Mongoloid Division, the Negroid Division, the Caucasoid Division. The biological processes which the classifier has here embalmed, as it were, are dynamic, not static. These divisions were not the same in the past as they are at present, and there is every reason to believe that they will change in the future." Ashley Montague, *Statement on Race* (New York: Henry Schuman, 1951), p. 13. It is discussed in full at pp. 74–78.

[11] 218 Mich. 625, 188 N.W. 330, 38 A.L.R. 1181 (1922).

[12] 238 Mich. 102, 213 N.W. 102 (1927).

[13] 271 U.S. 323 (1926), *dismissing appeal from* 299 Fed. 899 (D.C. Cir. 1924).

[14] *Porter v. Barrett,* 233 Mich. 373, 206 N.W. 532 (1925).

[15] Brief for Appellants, *Sipes v. McGhee* [316 Mich. 614, 25 N.W. 2d 638 (1947)].

[16] D. O. McGovney, "Racial Residential Segregation by State Court Enforcement of Restrictive Agreements, Covenants or Conditions in Deeds Is Unconstitutional," *California Law Review* XXXIII (March, 1945), 5.

[17] Brief for Appellants, *Sipes v. McGhee.*

[18] 132 Fed. 2d 23 (D.C. Cir. 1942).

[19] Brief for appellants, *Sipes v. McGhee,* p. 25.

[20] *Ibid.,* pp. 26–29.

[21] *Ibid.,* p. 32.

[22] *Re Drummond Wren,* 4 D.L.R. 674 (1945).

²³ Unlike usual American practice, the counsel's affiliation with the organization, the Canadian Jewish Congress, is given in the official reports.

²⁴ *Brief for Appellants, Sipes v. McGhee,* p. 32.

²⁵ *Re Drummond Wren,* 4 D.L.R. 674 (1945).

²⁶ *Doss v. Bernal,* No. 41466, California Superior Court for Orange County, (Nov. 15, 1943 not officially reported). See Appendix B, brief for appellants, *Sipes v. McGhee,* pp. 63–64.

²⁷ Brief for appellants, *Sipes v. McGhee,* p. 44, note 59 above.

²⁸ See Appendix A, *ibid.,* pp. 49–62.

²⁹ Both these cases were decided against the Negroes after the decision in *Sipes v. McGhee. Northwest Civic Association v. Sheldon,* 31 Mich. 192, 27 N.W. 2d 36 (1947). *Mrsa v. Reynolds,* 31 Mich. 200, 27 N.W. 2d 40 (1947).

³⁰ Brief for National Association for the Advancement of Colored People as *amicus curiae, Sipes v. McGhee,* [316 Mich. 614, 25 N.W. 2d 638 (1947)].

³¹ Brief for National Bar Association as *amicus curiae, Sipes v. McGhee.* Counsel on this brief were Earl B. Dickerson, Loring B. Moore, Richard E. Westbrooks, and George N. Leighton, all of Chicago.

³² Brief for International Union, United Automobile, Aircraft and Agricultural Implement Workers of America (U.A.W.-C.I.O.) as *amicus curiae, Sipes v. McGhee.* The brief was signed by Maurice Sugar, general counsel and Morton A. Eden, associate counsel.

³³ Brief for Wolverine Bar Association as *amicus curiae, Sipes v. McGhee.*

³⁴ Brief for National Lawyers Guild, Detroit chapter, as *amicus curiae, Sipes v. McGhee.*

³⁵ The trade-union case was *Steele v. Louisville Railroad Company,* 323 U.S. 192 (1944). The case involving the Democratic party of Texas was *Smith v. Allright,* 321 U.S. 649 (1943).

³⁶ Brief for American Jewish Congress, Detroit section, as *amicus curiae, Sipes v McGhee.*

³⁷ Brief for appellees, *Sipes v. McGhee.*

³⁸ Answering brief for appellees, *Sipes v. McGhee,* p. 6.

³⁹ 147 Fed. 2d 869, 152 Fed. 2d 123 (1945), *certiorari denied,* 325 U.S. 868, *rehearing denied,* 325 U.S. 896 (1945).

⁴⁰ 162 A.L.R. 168 (1946).

⁴¹ Brief of twenty-five property-owners' associations as *amicus curiae, Sipes v. McGhee.* The names of these associations follow: Ardmore Association, Inc.; Broadmoor Improvement Association; Brookline No. 2 Association, Inc.; Brookline Outer Drive Association; College Woods-Southfield Court Civic Association; Embrook Civic Association; Evergreen Village Civic Association of Detroit; Grandmont Improvement Association; Grandmont No. 1 Improvement Association, Inc.; Grand River-Livernois Civic Association; Joy Road Community Association; Mayfair Park Improvement Association; Monnier Hgts. Improvement Association; North Redford Association; Northwest Redford Improvement Association; Parkdale Civic Association; Plymouth Tireman Improvement Association; Puritan Greenfield Improvement Association; Seven Mile Evergreen Association; Southfield Woods Civic Association; Tel-Craft Civic Association of Detroit; Tireman Joy Improvement Association; Linwood McGraw Civic Association, Inc.; Lothrup Duffield Blvd. Park Association; Tireman Park Property Owners' Association, Inc.

⁴² 218 Mich. 625, 188 N.W. 330, 38 A.L.R. (1922).

⁴³ Brief of twenty-five property-owners' associations, as *amicus curiae, Sipes v. McGhee,* pp. 5–10.

⁴⁴ 5 *Ruling Case Law,* pp. 599–600.

⁴⁵ *Sipes v. McGhee,* 316 Mich. 614, 25 N.W. 2d 638 (1947).

Chapter VII

Preparations for the U.S. Supreme Court

[1] Conference on Racial Restrictive Covenants, Howard University, Washington, D.C., Jan. 26, 1947. Mimeographed minutes, NAACP files, New York City.

[2] 147 Fed. 2d 869 (1945), *certiorari denied*, 325 U.S. 868 (1945).

[3] NAACP Howard University Conference, p. 1.

[4] *Ibid.* Those present were: Francis Dent, Willis M. Graves, George E. C. Hayes, Attorney Hall, Governor William H. Hastie, C. Alphonse Jones, Edward P. Lovett, Thurgood Marshall, Loring Moore, James Nabrit, Frank Reeves, Spottswood W. Robinson, III, Arthur D. Shores, Vertner Tandy, Andrew Weinberger, Robert L. Carter, Marian Wynn Perry, Franklin H. Williams.

[5] The case was *Tovey v. Levy*, No. 45-S-947, Superior Court of Cook County, Illinois. The decree enforcing the covenant was entered on Nov. 28, 1947. This decree was later reversed, 401 Ill. 393, 82 N.E. 2d 441 (1948).

[6] NAACP Howard University Conference, p. 2.

[7] *Perkins v. Trustees of Monroe Avenue Church of Christ*, 79 Ohio App. 457, 70 N.E. 2d 487 (1946).

[8] Two cases eventually reached the California Supreme Court: *Fairchild v. Raines*, 24 Cal. 2d 818, 151 P. 2d 260 (1944); *Cummings v. Hokr*, 31 Cal. 2d 844, 193 P. 2d 742 (1948). Eight other cases were consolidated with the last-named case.

[9] 24 Cal. 2d 818, 151 P. 2d 260 (1944).

[10] *Anderson v. Auseth*, L.A. No. 19, 759. The disposition of these cases by the California Supreme Court was never reported. Attorney General Kenney and Professor McGovney coöperated in filing *amicus curiae* briefs in later California cases. See *Cummings v. Hokr*, 31 Cal. 2d 844, 193 P. 2d 742 (1948); *Cassell v. Hickerson*, *Fairchild v. Raines*, 31 Cal. 2d 869, 193 P. 2d 743 (1948); *Davis v. Carter*, 31 Cal. 2d 870, 193 P. 2d 744 (1948).

[11] Brief of Attorney General of California as *amicus curiae*, p. iv, *Anderson v. Auseth*, L.A. No. 19, 759, appeal to California Supreme Court, Sept. 4, 1946.

[12] 69 N.Y.S. 2d 680 (1947).

[13] *Ibid.*, pp. 682, 683.

[14] *Hirabayashi v. United States*, 320 U.S. 81 (1943) quoted in *Kemp v. Rubin*, 69 N.Y.S. 2d 680, 683 (1947).

[15] 69 N.Y.S. 2d 680, 683 (1947).

[16] *Swain v. Maxwell*, 355 Mo. 448, 196 S.W. 2d 780 (1946); *Vernon v. Reynolds Reality Co.*, 226 N.C. 58, 36 S.E. 2d 710 (1946); *Northwest Civic Association v. Sheldon*, 317 Mich. 192, 27 N.W. 2d 36 (1947); *Mrsa v. Reynolds*, 217 Mich. 200, 27 N.W. 2d 40 (1947); *Schwartz v. Hubbard*, 198 Okla. 194, 177 P. 2d 617 (1947); Hawkins v. Wayne, 198 Okla. 400, 178 P. 2d 138 (1948).

[17] 43 Stat. 936 (1925), 48 U.S.C. secs. 645, 864 (1952).

[18] James Willard Hurst, *The Growth of American Law* (Boston: Little, Brown, 1950), p. 18. For a concise history of the principle that the Supreme Court's appellate functions are unique, see *ibid.*, pp. 117–121. For a collection of basic documents and references on the Supreme Court's certiorari policy, see Henry M. Hart, Jr. and Herbert Wechsler, *The Federal Courts and the Federal System* (Brooklyn: Foundation Press, 1953), pp. 1394–1422.

[19] Supreme Court Rule 38 (5).

[20] Fred M. Vinson, "The Work of the Federal Courts" (Address to the American Bar Association, Sept. 7, 1949), 69 S. Ct. v.

[21] Charles W. Bunn, *Jurisdiction and Practice of the Courts of the United States* (St. Paul, Minn.: West, 1949), p. 258.

[22] 299 Fed. 899 (D.C. Cir. 1924), *appeal dismissed*, 271 U.S. 323 (1926).

[23] *Cornish v. O'Donoghue*, 30 F. 2d 98 (D.C. Cir. 1929), *certiorari denied*, 279

U.S. 871 (1929); *Russell v. Wallace,* 30 F. 2d 781 (D.C. Cir. 1929); *certiorari denied,* 279 U.S. 871 (1929).

[24] *Grady v. Garland,* 89 F. 2d 817 (D.C. Cir. 1937), *certiorari denied,* 302 U.S. 694 (1937).

[25] 372 Ill. 369, 24 N.E. 2d 37 (1940), *reversed on other grounds,* 311 U.S. 32 (1940).

[26] 147 F. 2d 969 (D.C. Cir. 1945), *certiorari denied,* 325 U.S. 868 (1945), *rehearing denied,* 325 U.S. 896 (1945).

[27] See Joan Maisel Leiman, "The Rule of Four," *Columbia Law Review,* LVII (Nov., 1957), 975–992.

[28] NAACP Howard University Conference, p. 2.

[29] *Ibid.,* p. 3.

[30] *Shelley v. Kraemer,* 355 Mo. 814, 198 S.W. 2d 679 (1947), *certiorari granted,* 331 U.S. 803 (1947).

[31] *McGhee v. Sipes,* 316 Mich. 614, 25 N.W. 2d 638 (1947), *certiorari granted,* 331 U.S. 804 (1947).

[32] *Hurd v. Hodge, Urciolo v. Hodge,* 162 Fed. 2d 233 (D.C. Cir., 1947), *certiorari granted,* 332 U.S. 789 (1947).

[33] *Trustees of Monroe Church of Christ v. Perkins,* 147 Ohio St. 537, 72 N.E. 2d 79 (1947), Docket No. 153, U.S. Sup. Ct., 1947 Term. The chronology of a case is best followed in *United States Law Week.*

[34] *Amer v. Superior Court of California,* no. 429; *Yin Kim v. Superior Court of California,* no. 430. 1947 Term.

[35] Vinson, "The Work of the Federal Courts," 69 S. Ct. v (1949).

[36] NAACP *Annual Report,* 1948, p. 27.

[37] Indritz to Abrams July 23, 1947. Charles Abrams, public-housing authority, lawyer, and author, made his personal files available to the author in New York City in 1952. Abrams files.

[38] D. O. McGovney, "Racial Residential Segregation by State Court Enforcement of Restrictive Agreements, Covenants or Conditions in Deeds is Unconstitutional," *California Law Review,* XXXIII (March, 1945), 33.

[39] Form letter from Thurgood Marshall for the NAACP Legal Defense and Education Fund, Inc., New York, July 11, 1947. Abrams files. Also, see "Background Material for Newspapers," (Press Service of the NAACP; Sept. 6, 1947), 6 pp.

[40] Those present were: Charles H. Houston, Washington, D.C., Chairman; James T. Bush, St. Louis; Sidney P. Brown, Chicago; Irving Brand, Anti-Nazi League, New York; Robert L. Carter, New York; Francis M. Dent, Detroit; Frank Donner, C.I.O., Washington, D.C.; Phineas Indritz, Washington, D.C.; Harold Kahen, American Jewish Congress, New York; Edward Lovett, Washington, D.C.; Newman Levy, American Jewish Committee, New York; Loren Miller, Los Angeles; Loring B. Moore, Chicago; Robert Ming, Chicago; Constance B. Motley, New York; William K. Newman, Congregational Board, Home Missions, New York; James Nabrit, Washington, D.C.; Shad Polier, New York; Marion W. Perry, New York; Sol Roblin, Anti-Defamation League; S. Rosenwein, Lawyers Guild, New York; Spottswood W. Robinson, Richmond, Virginia; Stanley M. Riesner, American Jewish Congress, New York; Louis L. Redding, New York; S. Rosenzweig, Lawyers Guild, New York; Leon A. Ransom, Washington, D.C.; Jacob Schaman, American Jewish Committee, New York; Ina Sugihara, Protestant Council of Churches, New York; Lucia Thomas, National Bar Association; Raphael G. Urciolo, Washington, D.C.; George Vaughn, St. Louis; Franklin H. Williams, New York; Ruth Weyand, Washington, D.C.; Allen Wirin, Los Angeles; Walter White, New York; Richard Westbrooks, Chicago; Andrew Weinberger, New York; Willis M. Graves, Detroit; Prof. Robert L. Hale, Columbia University, New York; Dr. Frank Horne, Washington, D.C.; Will Maslow, American Jewish Congress; Byron Miller, Chicago; Annette Peyser, New York.

[41] Meeting of NAACP Lawyers and Consultants on Methods of Attacking Restrictive Covenants, Sept. 6, 1947, mimeographed minutes, NAACP files, p. 2.

[42] Charles Abrams, *Race Bias in Housing* (New York: 1947).

[43] Charles Abrams, "Homes for Aryans Only; The Restrictive Covenant Spreads Legal Racism in America," *Commentary*, V (May, 1947), 421.

[44] The comments, many of them questioning the correctness of court enforcement of racial restrictive covenants, were as follows: *Mays v. Burgess*, 147 F. 2d 869 (D.C. Cir. 1945), *certiorari denied*, 325 U.S. 868 (1945): *Georgetown Law Journal*, XXXIII (March, 1945), 356; *Harvard Law Review*, LIX (1945), 293; *Illinois Law Review*, XL (Jan.–Feb. 1946), 432; *National Bar Journal*, III (Dec., 1945), 364; *Rocky Mountain Law Review*, XVIII (Feb., 1946), 148. *Northwest Civic Association v. Sheldon*, 317 Mich. 416, 27 N.W. 2d 36 (1947): *Virginia Law Review*, XXXIII (Sept., 1947), 658; *Perkins v. Trustees of the Monroe Avenue Church of Christ*, 79 Ohio App. 457, 70 N.E. 2d 487 (1946), *appeal dismissed*, 147 Ohio St. 537, 72 N.E. 2d 97 (1947): *University of Cincinnati Law Review*, XVII (Jan., 1948), 77; *Kraemer v. Shelley*, 355 Mo. 814, 198 S.W. 2d 769 (1946): *Missouri Law Review*, XII (April, 1947), 221; *Sipes v. McGhee*, 316 Mich. 614, 25 N.W. 2d 638 (1947): *Minnesota Law Review*, XXXI (March, 1947), 385; *Detroit Law Review*, IX (Dec., 1947), 29; *Ohio State Law Journal*, IX (1948), 325. *Hurd v. Hodge, Urciolo v. Hodge*, 162 F. 2d 233 (D.C. Cir. 1947): *Cornell Law Quarterly*, XXXIII (Nov., 1947), 293; *Georgia Bar Journal*, X (Nov., 1947), 237; *University of Chicago Law Review*, XV (Autumn, 1947), 193; *Illinois Law Review*, XLII (Jan.–Feb., 1948), 812; *Notre Dame Lawyer*, XXIII (Jan., 1948), 256.

[45] Following is a list of articles which express opposition to court enforcement of racial restrictive covenants in the order of their appearance before the United States Supreme Court's opinion in the principal cases: Robert L. Hale, "Rights Under the Fourteenth and Fifteenth Amendment Against Injuries Inflicted by Private Individuals," *Lawyers Guild Review*, VI (1946), 627; S. A. Jones, Jr., "Legality of Race Restrictive Covenants," *National Bar Journal*, IV (March, 1946), 14; Charles Tefft, "*Marsh v. Alabama*—A Suggestion Concerning Racial Restrictive Covenants," *National Bar Journal*, IV (June, 1946), 133; Robert C. Weaver, "Housing in a Democracy," *Annals*, CCXLIV (March, 1946), 95; Note, "Anti-Discrimination Legislation and International Declarations as Evidence of Public Policy Against Racial Restrictive Covenants," *University of Chicago Law Review*, XIII (June, 1946), 477; Loren Miller, "The Power of Restrictive Covenants," *Survey Graphic*, XXXVI (Jan., 1947), 46; Note, "Restrictive Covenants Directed Against Purchase or Occupancy of Land by Negroes," *The American City* LXII (May, 1947), 103; Loren Miller, "Race Restrictions on Ownership or Occupancy of Land," *Lawyers Guild Review*, VII (May–June, 1947), 99; Clifford R. Moore, "Anti-Negro Restrictive Covenants and Judicial Enforcement Constitution State Action under the Fourteenth Amendment," *Temple Law Quarterly*, XXI (Oct., 1947), 139; John P. Dean, "None Other Than Caucasian," *Architectural Forum*, LXXXVI (October, 1947), 16; Loren Miller, "Covenants for Exclusion," *Survey Graphic*, XXXVI (Oct., 1947), 541; George Vaughn, "Resisting the Enforcement by Courts of Restrictive Covenants Based on Race," *National Bar Journal*, V (Dec., 1947), 381; Note, "Current Legal Attacks on Racial Restrictive Covenants," *University of Chicago Law Review*, XV (Autumn, 1947), 193; Irwin M. Taylor, "The Racial Restrictive Covenants in the Light of the Equal Protection Clause," *Brooklyn Law Review*, XIV (Dec., 1947), 80; I. N. Groner and D. M. Helfeld, "Race Discrimination in Housing," *Yale Law Journal*, LVII (Jan., 1948), 426. One book was also published, see Herman H. Long and Charles S. Johnson, *People vs. Property, Race Restrictive Covenants in Housing* (Nashville, Tenn.: Fisk University Press, 1947).

[46] See Robert C. Weaver, *Negro Labor, A National Problem* (New York: Harcourt, Brace, 1946); *The Negro Ghetto* (New York: Harcourt, Brace, 1948). Also see *Hemmed In* (Chicago: American Council on Race Relations, 1946); "Chicago: A City of Covenants," *The Crisis*, LXVII (March, 1946), and other articles by Weaver cited in note 45, above.

[47] Meeting of NAACP Lawyers and Consultants on Methods of Attacking Restrictive Covenants, Sept. 6, 1947, p. 4.

[48] Rule 27, Sec. 9, 306 U.S. 709 (1939).

[49] Both Gerald Seegers in St. Louis, and James Crooks have stated that they believe that all persons interested in the outcome of the cases were entitled to file briefs. However they were disquieted by the large number of *amici curiae* briefs on the opposition side presented to the Court.

[50] Marshall to Strong, Sept. 23, 1947. Abrams files.

[51] Statement of Perry Howard, Washington, D.C., on Dec. 21, 1951, personal interview.

[52] Frederick B. Sussman to Abrams, Nov. 7, 1947; Clifford Forster to Abrams, Dec. 2, 1947; Forster to Abrams, Dec. 9, 1947. Abrams files.

[53] Abrams to Levy, Nov. 13, 1947. Abrams files.

[54] 297 U.S. 288 (1936).

[55] Levy to Abrams, Nov. 14, 1947. Abrams files. The publicity motivation in the use of *amici curiae* briefs largely accounts for recent restrictions on the device by the Supreme Court. For a discussion of the excesses of organized groups, see Fowler W. Harper and Edwin D. Etherington, "Lobbyists before the Court," *University of Pennsylvania Law Review* CI (June, 1953), 1172–1177. The "Revised Rules of the Supreme Court," Rule 42.1, effective July 1, 1954, provide that an *amicus curiae* brief may be filed "only after order from the Court or when accompanied by written consent of all parties to the case." Justice Tom Clark, in conversation with the author, Cleveland, Ohio, Oct. 27, 1954, stated that he believed the *amicus* brief was too often used as a propaganda device. For further information on reasons for the limitation, see Frederick Wiener, "The Supreme Court's New Rules," *Harvard Law Review*, LXVIII (Nov., 1954), 20, at 80–81. On adoption of the revised rules, Justice Black made this objection: "I have never favored the almost insuperable obstacle our rules put in the way of briefs sought to be filed by persons other than the actual litigants. Most of the cases before this Court involve matters that affect far more than the immediate record parties. I think the public interest and judicial administration would be better served by relaxing rather than tightening the rule against *amicus curiae* briefs." *Supreme Court Journal* (Oct., 1953), 194. Justice Black's objection is appended to the Order Adopting Revised Rules of the Supreme Court, 346 U.S. 947 (1954).

[56] Marian Wynn Perry to Abrams, Nov. 21, 1947. Abrams files.

[57] Harry S. Truman, *Memoirs* (Garden City: Doubleday, 1956), II, 180.

[58] Walter White, *A Man Called White*, p. 203; *The Crisis*, LIII (Nov., 1946), 339–340; *New York Times*, Sept. 20, 1946, p. 1.

[59] President's Committee on Civil Rights, *To Secure These Rights* (Washington: Government Printing Office, 1947), pp. vii–ix.

[60] Truman, *Memoirs*, II, 181.

[61] *To Secure These Rights*, p. ix.

[62] *Ibid.*, pp. xi, 178.

[63] Joseph B. Robison to author, July 9, 1958.

[64] *To Secure These Rights*, pp. 169, 171.

[65] Philip B. Perlman to author, Feb. 6, 1953.

[66] NAACP Press Service Releases, Sept. 19, 1947, p. 3.

[67] *Ibid.*

[68] Miller to Clark, Sept. 3, 1947.

[69] Rev. Stat. sec. 1978, chap. 31, sec. 1, 14 Stat. 27 (8 U.S.C. 42).

[70] *Steele v. Louisville Railroad*, 323 U.S. 192 (1944).

[71] 5 U.S.C. 319.

[72] Supreme Court Rules, effective Feb. 27, 1939, sec. 27 (9), 306 U.S. 708–709 (1939).

[73] Clark to Miller, Sept. 11, 1947.

[74] Miller to Clark, Sept. 3, 1947, p. 2.

[75] For the text of President Truman's address to the NAACP conference, see *New York Times*, June 30, 1947, p. 3; *The Crisis*, LIV (July, 1947), p. 200.

[76] *The Crisis*, LIV (Aug., 1947), 283.

[77] Truman, *Memoirs*, I, 325–326.

[78] *New York Times*, Feb. 8, 1947, p. 7; March 1, p. 32; March 30, p. 44; April 16, p. 1; May 25, p. 46; Sept. 17, p. 23.

[79] Philip B. Perlman, "The Work of the Office of the Solicitor General of the United States," an address before the Maryland State Bar Association, Atlantic City, July 2, 1949, p. 4.

[80] See Current Biography (1952), pp. 465–467; American Bar Association Journal, XXXIII (Oct., 1947), 1008.

[81] Meeting of NAACP lawyers and consultants, Sept. 6, 1947, p. 4.

[82] *To Secure These Rights*, p. 169.

[83] Miller to Clark, Oct. 30, 1947.

[84] Perlman to Miller, Oct. 30, 1947.

[85] *The Crisis* (Sept., 1947), p. 275.

[86] John A. Huston, "Constitutional Law—State Court Enforcement of Race Restrictive Covenants as State Action Within Scope of Fourteenth Amendment," *Michigan Law Review*, XLV (April, 1947), 733.

[87] Robert L. Hale, "Force and the State: A Comparison of 'Political' and 'Economic' Compulsion," *Columbia Law Review*, XXXV (1935), 149.

[88] Huston (see note 86), p. 747.

Chapter VIII

The Supreme Court Makes a Decision

[1] For a list of former decisions overruled by the Supreme Court between the 1937 and 1947 terms, see C. Herman Pritchett, *The Roosevelt Court: A Study in Judicial Politics and Values, 1937–1947* (New York: Macmillan, 1948), pp. 300–301. Also, see Bernard Schwartz, *The Supreme Court: Constitutional Revolution in Retrospect* (New York: Ronald Press, 1957).

[2] *Smith v. Allwright*, 321 U.S. 649 (1944).

[3] *Elmore v. Rice*, 72 F. Supp. 516 (D. S. Car., 1947), affirmed, *Rice v. Elmore*, 165 F. 2d 387 (5th Cir., 1947), certiorari denied, 333 U.S. 875 (1948). For a trenchant analysis of the state-action concept in this line of cases, see Robert L. Hale, *Freedom Through Law* (New York: Columbia University Press, 1952), pp. 335–348.

[4] *Steele v. Louisville & Nashville Railway Co.*, 323 U.S. 192 (1944). See Elias Lieberman, *Unions Before the Bar* (New York: Harper, 1950), pp. 252–262.

[5] *Ibid.*, 198.

[6] *Marsh v. Alabama*, 326 U.S. 501 (1946).

[7] *Jewel Ridge Coal Corporation v. Local 6167, United Mine Workers of America*, rehearing denied, 325 U.S. 897 (1945). Justice Jackson's remarks, in a concurring opinion, were made in criticism of Mr. Justice Black for failing to disqualify himself in this case. For a discussion of the incident, see Alpheus Mason, *Harlan Fiske Stone, Pillar of the Law* (New York: Viking Press, 1956), pp. 642–646. On the general problem, see John P. Frank, "Disqualification of Judges," *Yale Law Journal*, LVI (March, 1947), 605–639.

[8] *New York Times*, Jan. 16, 1948, p. 30, col. 3; Jan. 17, 1948, p. 3, col. 1.

[9] *Memorandum from American Jewish Congress*, Feb. 2, 1948, p. 1.

[10] Statements to the author by Gerald Seegers and James Crooks.

[11] Either of two eventualities, lack of a quorum or a tie vote, would have meant affirmance of the lower-court decisions. Six justices are necessary to constitute a quorum. 28 U.S.C. sec. 1. When a quorum is lacking and "if a majority of the qualified justices shall be of opinion that the case cannot be heard and determined at the next ensuing term, the court shall enter its order affirming the judgment of the court from which the case was brought for review with the same effect as upon affirmance by an equally divided court." 28 U.S.C. sec. 2109.

[12] Summaries of Justice Murphy's career and judicial opinions are included in:

John P. Frank, "Justice Murphy: The Goals Attempted," *Yale Law Journal*, LIX (Dec., 1949), 1 ff.; Charles Fahy, "The Judicial Philosophy of Mr. Justice Murphy," *Yale Law Journal* LX (May, 1951), 812; Vincent M. Barnett, Jr., "Mr. Justice Murphy, Civil Liberties and the Holmes Tradition," *Cornell Law Quarterly*, XXXII (Nov., 1946), 177 ff.; Eugene Gressman, "Mr. Justice Murphy—A Preliminary Appraisal," *Columbia Law Review*, L (Jan., 1950), 29–47; John P. Roche, "The Utopian Pilgrimage of Mr. Justice Murphy," *Vanderbilt Law Review*, X (Feb., 1957), 369–394.

[13] See p. 57, above.

[14] For a discussion, see Robert K. Carr, *Federal Protection of Civil Rights* (Ithaca and New York: Cornell University Press, 1927).

[15] *Steele v. Louisville & Nashville Railway Co.*, 323 U.S. 192 (1944).

[16] Robert H. Jackson, *The Struggle for Judicial Supremacy* (New York: Knopf, 1941), p. 312.

[17] Letter to author from Leon Epstein, Nov. 12, 1953. See Leon Epstein, "Justice Douglas and Civil Liberties," *Wisconsin Law Review*, vol. 1951 (Jan., 1951), 125–157; Leon Epstein, "Economic Predilections of Justice Douglas," *Wisconsin Law Review*, vol. 1949 (May, 1949), 531–564; Marian D. Irish, "Mr. Justice Douglas and Judicial Restraint," *University of Florida Law Review*, VI (Winter, 1953), 537–553. For a popular portrait, see Richard L. Neuberger, "Mr. Justice Douglas," *Harpers Magazine*, CLXXXV (Aug., 1942), 312–321. The later extrajudicial writings of Justice Douglas revealed his disdain for racial discrimination. On the subject of restrictive covenants, see his *An Almanac of Liberty* (Garden City, N.Y.: Doubleday, 1954), pp. 132–133.

[18] John P. Frank, *Mr. Justice Black; The Man and His Opinions* (New York: Knopf, 1949), p. 139. Justice Douglas has said that "none will be rated higher than Justice Black for consistency in construing the laws and the Constitution so as to protect the civil rights of citizens and aliens, whatever the form of the repression may be." At the same time he believes Black's opinions include "plenty to disprove the charge that he is an 'activist' and a devotee of judicial power." William O. Douglas, "Mr. Justice Black: A Foreword," *Yale Law Journal*, LXV (Feb., 1956), 449–450. Also, see Eugene V. Rostow, "Mr. Justice Black: Some Introductory Observations," *ibid.*, 451–453; John P. Frank, "Mr. Justice Black: A Biographical Appreciation," *ibid.*, 454–463.

[19] Walter White, *A Man Called White* (New York: Viking Press, 1948), chap. 21: "Hugo Black and the NAACP," pp. 177–179.

[20] Charles F. Luce, book review of Charlotte Williams, *Hugo Black, A Study in Judicial Process* (Baltimore: Johns Hopkins Press, 1950), *University of Pennsylvania Law Review*, IC (May, 1951), 1043–1044.

[21] John P. Frank, *Mr. Justice Black; The Man and His Opinions* (New York: Knopf, 1949), pp. 138–139.

[22] *Chambers v. Florida*, 309 U.S. 227 (1940).

[23] See Samuel J. Konefsky, *The Constitutional World of Mr. Justice Frankfurter* (New York: Macmillan, 1949), pp. xi–xviii.

[24] See Felix Frankfurter, "The Hours of Labor and Legal Realism," *Harvard Law Review*, XXVIII (Feb., 1916), 353.

[25] Felix Frankfurter and Nathan Greene, *The Labor Injunction* (New York: Macmillan, 1930).

[26] Felix Frankfurter, *The Case of Sacco and Vanzetti: A Critical Analysis for Lawyers and Laymen* (Boston: Little, Brown, 1927). See G. Louis Joughlin and Edmund M. Morgan, *The Legacy of Sacco and Vanzetti* (New York: Harcourt, Brace, 1948), p. 319.

[27] White, *A Man Called White*, p. 157.

[28] For a thoughtful discussion of Justice Frankfurter's approach to the judicial functions in civil-liberties cases, see C. Herman Pritchett, *Civil Liberties and the Vinson Court* (Chicago: University of Chicago Press, 1954), pp. 201–226. The best overall analysis is Louis Jaffe "The Judicial Universe of Mr. Justice Frankfurter,"

Harvard Law Review, LXII (Jan., 1949), 357–442. Perhaps the staunchest defender of Frankfurter is Wallace Mendelson. See his "Mr. Justice Frankfurter and the Process of Judicial Review," *University of Pennsylvania Law Review*, CIII (Dec., 1954), 295–320; and "Mr. Justice Frankfurter—Law and Choice," *Vanderbilt Law Review*, X (Feb., 1957), 333–350.

[29] *Morgan v. Virginia*, 328 U.S. 373 (1946).

[30] Pritchett, *The Roosevelt Court*, p. 261.

[31] John P. Frank, "Fred Vinson and the Chief Justiceship," University of Chicago Law Review, XVI (Winter, 1954), 212–246. The most pertinent articles in a symposium on Vinson are Francis Allen, "Chief Justice Vinson and the Theory of Constitutional Government: A Tentative Analysis," *Northwestern Law Review*, XLIX (March–April, 1954), 3–25; and under composite authorship, "Chief Justice Vinson and His Law Clerks," *ibid.*, 26–35.

[32] Eugene Gressman, "The Coming Trials of Justice Warren," *New Republic*, CXXIX (Oct. 12, 1953), p. 9.

[33] Brief for Petitioners, *McGhee v. Sipes* [334 U.S. 1 (1948)].

[34] Brief for Petitioners, *Shelley v. Kraemer* [334 U.S. 1 (1948)]

[35] Brief for Respondents, *McGhee v. Sipes.*

[36] *Ibid.*, pp. 16–17.

[37] Brief for Respondents, *Shelley v. Kraemer.*

[38] Huston, "Constitutional Law—State Court Enforcement of Race Restrictive Covenants as State Action Within Scope of Fourteenth Amendment," *Michigan Law Review*, XXXXV (April, 1947), 733.

[39] Consolidated Brief for Petitioners, *Hurd v. Hodge, Urciolo v. Hodge* [334 U.S. 24 (1948)].

[40] *Ibid.*, p. 132.

[41] *Ibid.*, p. 7.

[42] *Ibid.*, p. 8.

[43] 312 U.S. 321 (1941).

[44] 310 U.S. 88 (1940).

[45] *Brief for Respondents, Hurd v. Hodge.*

[46] *Ibid.*, p. 8.

[47] Consolidated Reply Brief for Petitioners, *Hurd v. Hodge.*

[48] United States as *amicus curiae*, all cases. Citations are to Tom C. Clark and Philip B. Perlman, *Prejudice and Property: An Historic Brief Against Racial Covenants* (Washington, D.C.: Public Affairs Press, 1948).

[49] *Ibid.*, pp. 24–30.

[50] *Ibid.*, p. 30.

[51] *Ibid.*, pp. 31–34.

[52] *Ibid.*, pp. 34–35.

[53] Consolidated Reply Brief to the United States as *amicus curiae, McGhee v. Sipes, Hurd v. Hodge, Urciolo v. Hodge.*

[54] *Ibid.*, p. 2.

[55] *Ibid.*, pp. 13–14.

[56] Brief for Civil Liberties Department, Grand Lodge of Elks as *amicus curiae, Shelley v. Kraemer.*

[57] Brief for National Bar Association as *amicus curiae*, all cases.

[58] Brief for American Indian Citizens League of California as *amicus curiae*, all cases.

[59] Brief for Japanese American Citizen League as *amicus curiae, Hurd v. Hodge.*

[60] Brief for American Jewish Congress as *amicus curiae*, all cases.

[61] Brief for American Jewish Committee and others as *amicus curiae*, all cases.

[62] Brief of California as *amicus curiae, McGhee v. Sipes.*

[63] Brief for A.F. of L. as *amicus curiae*, all cases.

[64] Brief for C.I.O. as *amicus curiae*, all cases.

[65] Brief for Congregational Christian Church and others as *amicus curiae, Shelley v. Kraemer, McGhee v. Sipes.*

[66] Brief for Human Relations Commission of the Protestant Council of New York City as *amicus curiae, McGhee v. Sipes.*

[67] Brief for American Unitarian Association as *amicus curiae,* all cases.

[68] Brief for A.C.L.U. as *amicus curiae,* all cases.

[69] Brief for St. Louis Civil Liberties Committee as *amicus curiae, Shelley v. Kraemer.*

[70] Brief for American Association for the United Nations, as *amicus curiae,* all cases.

[71] Brief for A.V.C. as *amicus curiae,* all cases.

[72] Brief for Non-Sectarian Anti-Nazi League to Champion Human Rights, Inc. as *amicus curiae, McGhee v. Sipes.*

[73] Brief for National Lawyers Guild as *amicus curiae,* all cases.

[74] Brief for Arlington Heights Property Owners Association as *amicus curiae, Shelley v. Kraemer.* The other Los Angeles groups were Adams to Washington Association, Southwest Wilshire District Protective Association, Charles Victor Hall Tract Association, Community Protective Association and the Slauson-Figueroa-Manchester-Central Property Owners Protective Association.

[75] *Ibid.*

[76] Brief for Mount Royal Protective Association as *amicus curiae,* all cases.

[77] Brief for Federation of Citizens Association, Citizens Forum, of Columbia Heights, The Wheel of Progress, and the Columbia Improvement Association, Washington, D.C., as *amicus curiae, Hurd v. Hodge.*

[78] Brief for Mount Royal Association, *above,* p. 6.

[79] *Ibid.,* p. 8.

[80] Brief for the National Association of Real Estate Boards as *amicus curiae, Shelley v. Kraemer.*

[81] Oliver Allen, "Chief Counsel for Equality," *Life,* XXXVIII (June 13, 1955), 141, 144.

[82] *Ibid.* Many Negro leaders attended the practice session at Howard Law School. A Negro newspaper reported that a number came to Washington to attend the oral arguments before the Supreme Court. Among those present were Walter White, New York; David Grant and John A. Davis, attorneys, James T. Bush, real-estate broker, and J. E. Mitchell, editor of the *St. Louis Argus,* all of St. Louis; Joseph Clayton, Earl Dickerson, W. Ellis Stewart, Loring B. Moore, Cyrus J. Carter, J. S. Washington, Richard Westbrook and W. Robert Ming, attorneys, and Louis Martin, newspaperman, all of Chicago; Francis Dent, Willis M. Graves, Miss Clotel Macklin, Maceo Crutcher and Robert M. Simms of Detroit; James R. Golden, attorney, Battle Creek, Michigan; and Carter Wesley, editor, *Houston Informer,* Houston, Texas. *Washington (D.C.) Afro-American,* Jan. 20, 1948, p. 1.

[83] There is no verbatim record of the argument. Two partial accounts are available. *United States Law Week,* XVI (Jan. 20, 1948), 3219, and *Memorandum from the American Jewish Congress,* Feb. 2, 1948.

[84] *United States Law Week,* XVI (Jan. 20, 1948), 3219, 3224.

[85] A copy of this telegram is in the files of Gerald L. Seegers, St. Louis, Missouri.

[86] *Shelley v. Kraemer, McGhee v. Sipes,* 334 U.S. 1 (1948); *Hurd v. Hodge, Urciolo v. Hodge,* 334 U.S. 24 (1948).

[87] 334 U.S. 1, 4 (1948).

[88] 271 U.S. 323 (1926).

[89] 311 U.S. 32 (1940).

[90] *Shelley v. Kraemer,* 334 U.S. 1, 10 (1948).

[91] *Ibid.,* pp. 1, 13. The specific examples followed closely those given in Consolidated Brief for Petitioners, *Hurd v. Hodge,* p. 39.

[92] *Ibid.,* 18.

[93] *Hurd v. Hodge, Urciolo v. Hodge,* 334 U.S. 24 (1948).

[94] *Ibid.,* 30.

[95] *Ibid.,* 34.

[96] *Ibid.,* 36.

Chapter IX

Adjustment under the New Rule of Law

[1] *Detroit News,* May 4, 1948, p. 1, col. 2.

[2] *Times,* May 17, 1948, pp. 25–26.

[3] *Washington Post,* May 4, 1948, p. 3, col. 1.

[4] *Ibid.*

[5] *Ex parte Laws,* 31 Cal. 2d 870, 193 P. 2d 744 (1948).

[6] *Perkins v. Trustees of Monroe Avenue Church of Christ,* 79 Ohio App. 457, 70 N.E. 2d 487 (1946), *reversed,* 147 Ohio St. 537, 72 N.E. 2d 79 (1947), *certiorari granted and reversed,* 334 U.S. 815 (1948). For the early developments in this case, see pp. 152–153, above.

[7] *Amer v. Superior Court of California; Yim Kim v. Superior Court of California,* 334 U.S. 813 (1948). See *Washington Post,* May 11, 1948, p. 6, col. 5.

[8] 401 Ill., 393, 82 N.E. 2d 411 (1948). See p. 151, n. 5, above.

[9] 298 N.Y. 590, 81 N.E. 2d 325 (1948). See pp. 154–155, above.

[10] *Coleman v. Stewart,* 33 Cal. 2d 703, 204 P. 2d 7 (1949); *Morin v. Crane,* 32 Cal. 2d 895, 197 P. 2d 162 (1948); *Clayton v. Wilkins,* 32 Cal. 2d 895, 197 P. 2d 162 (1948); *Lippold v. Johnson,* 32 Cal. 2d 892, 197 P. 2d 161 (1948); *Cassell v. Hickerson,* 31 Cal. 2d 869, 193 P. 2d 743 (1948); *Davis v. Carter,* 31 Cal. 2d 845, 193 P. 2d 744 (1948); *Cummings v. Hokr,* 31 Cal. 2d 844, 193 P. 2d 742 (1948); *Claremont Improvement Club v. Buckingham,* 89 Cal. App. 2d 32, 200 P. 2d 47 (1948).

[11] *Rich v. Jones,* 142 N.J. Eq. 215, 59 A. 2d 839 (1948).

[12] *Goetz v. Smith,* 62 A. 2d 602 (Md., 1948), *certiorari denied,* 336 U.S. 967 (1949).

[13] *Malicke v. Milan,* 321 Mich. 102, 32 N.W. 2d 353 (1948).

[14] *Woytus v. Winkler,* 357 Mo. 1082, 212 S.W. 2d 353 (1948).

[15] *Barley v. Baughmann,* 200 Okla. 649, 199 P. 2d 210 (1948).

[16] *Pittsburgh Courier,* May 8, 1948, p. 1.

[17] Loren Miller, "A Right Secured," *The Nation* CLXVI (May 29, 1948), 599.

[18] *Washington Post,* May 6, 1948, p. 16, col. 2.

[19] Alfred L. Scanlan, "Racial Restrictions in Real Estate—Property Values Versus Human Values," *Notre Dame Lawyer,* XXIV (Winter, 1949), 157, 190.

[20] Note, "Restrictive Covenants," *New York University Law Quarterly Review,* XXIV (Jan., 1949), 227, 231.

[21] Note, "Restrictive Covenants and Equal Protection—The New Rule in Shelley's Case," *Southern California Law Review,* XXI (July, 1948), 358.

[22] John P. Frank, "The United States Supreme Court: 1947–48," *Univ. of Chicago Law Review,* XVI (Sept., 1948), 1, 22.

[23] Note, "State Action Reconsidered in the Light of Shelley v. Kraemer," *Columbia Law Review,* XLVIII (Dec., 1948), 1241.

[24] Editorial, "Answer to the Gentlemen," *New Republic,* CXVIII (May 17, 1948), 5–6.

[25] *Atlanta Constitution,* May 5, 1948, p. 8, col. 1; *Louisville Courier Journal,* May 4, 1948, p. 16, col. 5; *Chicago Tribune,* May 8, 1948, p. 10, col. 3.

[26] Homer Jack, "Racism and the Supreme Court," *Christian Century,* LXV (June 9, 1948), 571; editorial, "The Neighborhood and the Law," *Commonweal,* XLVIII (May 14, 1948), 93.

[27] Paul Sayre, "*Shelley v. Kraemer* and United Nations Law," *Iowa L. R.,* XXXIV (Nov., 1948), 1; Note, "Judicial Enforcement of Racial Restrictive Covenants," *Harvard Law Review,* LXI (Sept., 1948), 1450. Other comments, largely neutral and factual, were as follows: *Georgia Bar Journal,* XI (Aug., 1948), 88; *Louisiana Law Review,* IX (Nov., 1948), 394; *Mississippi Law Journal,* XX (Dec., 1948),

101; *Nebraska Law Review*, XXVIII (March, 1949), 461; *Oklahoma Law Review*, I (Nov., 1948), 290; *Tennessee Law Review*, XX (April, 1949), 679; *Wisconsin Law Review*, vol. 1949 (July, 1948), 508; *California Law Review*, XXXVII (Sept., 1949), 493; Yi-Seng Kiang, "Judicial Enforcement of Restrictive Covenants in the United States," *Washington Law Review*, XXIV (Feb., 1949), 1; William R. Ming, Jr., "Racial Restrictions and the Fourteenth Amendment: The Restrictive Covenant Cases," *University of Chicago Law Review*, XVI (Winter, 1949), 203.

[28] John H. Watson, Jr., "Restrictive Covenants as a Violation of Equal Protection Clause," *Illinois Bar Journal*, XXXVI (Oct., 1948), 88.

[29] James D. Barnett, "Race Restrictive Covenants Restricted," *Oregon Law Review*, XXVIII (Dec., 1948), 1.

[30] *Southern California Law Review*, XXI (July, 1948), 358.

[31] *Chicago Defender*, May 15, 1948, p. 14, cols. 1, 2.

[32] Walter White, *A Man Called White* (New York: Viking Press, 1948), p. 362.

[33] *Chicago Defender*, May 15, 1948, p. 14, cols. 1, 2.

[34] Walter White, "People, Politics and Places," *Chicago Defender*, May 15, 1948, p. 15, col. 2.

[35] *Ibid.*

[36] *Washington Post*, May 4, 1948, p. 3, col. 4.

[37] 86 Cong. Rec. 5256.

[38] *Ibid.*, p. 5257.

[39] *Washington Post*, May 4, 1948, p. 3, col. 1.

[40] *Detroit News*, May 4, 1948, p. 1, col. 2. This was true in Dec., 1952, when the author checked.

[41] Richard C. Baker, "Restrictive Covenants Reviewed," *South Carolina Law Quarterly*, III (June, 1951), 351, 364.

[42] James A. Crooks, "The Racial Covenant Cases," *Georgetown Law Journal*, XXXVII (May, 1949), 514.

[43] *Ibid.*

[44] Letter, Seegers to Irving Morris, June 2, 1948. Seegers file.

[45] John L. Walker, "Judicial Enforcement of Racial Restrictive Covenants—The Spurious Expansion of 'State Action,'" an address delivered to the Virginia State Bar Association at the Greenbrier, White Sulphur Springs, W. Va., Aug. 12, 1948. Copy in Seegers file.

[46] Note, "Restrictive Covenants," *George Washington Law Review*, XVII (April, 1949), 398.

[47] Joe S. Wilmetti, "Enforcement of Racial Restrictive Covenants," *Wyoming Law Journal*, III (Winter, 1948), 89.

[48] James A. Crooks, *op. cit.*, 514, 525.

[49] Richard C. Baker, "Restrictive Covenants Reviewed," *South Carolina Law Quarterly*, III (June, 1951), 351, 364.

[50] John L. Walker, *op. cit.*, pp. 12–13.

[51] Roger G. Mastrude, *If Your Next Neighbors Are Negroes* (Nashville, Tenn.: Department of Race Relations, American Missionary Association, rev. ed., 1951), p. 3.

[52] M.A.I.A. Meeting, Sept. 23, 1948, notes of Emil Koob. Koob papers.

[53] See p. 199, above.

[54] William Wilson, ed., "The Appraisal Docket," *The Appraisal Journal*, XVI (Jan., 1948), 79–85.

[55] William Wilson, ed., "The Appraisal Docket," *The Appraisal Journal*, XVI (July, 1948), 370–375.

[56] This section of the Code of Ethics of the National Association of Real Estate Boards was amended after the 1948 covenant cases. The new language is: "A realtor should not be instrumental in introducing into a neighborhood a character of property or use which will clearly be detrimental to property values in that neighborhood."

[57] Stanley L. McMichael and Robert F. Bingham, *City Growth and Values* (Cleveland: McMichael Publishing Co., 1923).

[58] Stanley L. McMichael, *Real Estate Subdivisions* (New York: Prentice Hall, Inc., 1949), p. 204.

[59] Arthur A. May, "Appraising the Home," *The Appraisal Journal*, XIX (Jan., 1951), 19, 20.

[60] *Ibid.*

[61] *Ibid.*

[62] Arthur A. May, *The Valuation of Residential Real Estate* (New York: Prentice Hall, Inc., 1942), p. 75.

[63] Charles Abrams, "The New 'Gresham's Law of Neighborhoods'—Fact or Fiction," *The Appraisal Journal*, XIX (July, 1951), 328.

[64] Luigi M. Laurenti, "Effects of Nonwhite Purchases on Market Prices of Residences," *The Appraisal Journal*, XX (July, 1952).

[65] *Ibid.*, p. 325.

[66] Mastrude, *op. cit.*, pp. 10–12.

[67] Harry Henderson, "Rugged American Collectivism: The Mass-Produced Suburbs, Part II," *Harper's Magazine*, CCVI (Dec., 1953), 80, 85, 86.

[68] Gerald L. Seegers to John L. Walker, June 24, 1948, Seegers papers.

[69] M.A.I.A. Meeting, Sept. 12, 1948.

[70] M.A.I.A. Records, Sept., 1948.

[71] *New York Times*, March 11, 1949, p. 5, col. 7; March 24, 1949, p. 22, col. 6.

[72] The [*Madison, Wis.*] *Capital Times*, Aug. 20, 1951, p. 1, cols. 3, 4.

[73] James D. Barnett, "Race-Restrictive Covenants Restricted," *Oregon Law Review*, XXVIII (Dec., 1948), 1, 6, note 30, quoting [*Portland*] *Oregonian*, May 4, 1948, sec. 1, p. 11, col. 6.

[74] *New York Times*, Dec. 11, 1948, p. 17, col. 8; Dec. 12, sec. iv, p. 8, col. 2.

[75] Charles Abrams, "The Segregation Threat in Housing," *Commentary*, IX (Feb., 1949), p. 123. For a fuller exposition by Abrams on this subject, see his *Forbidden Neighbors: A Study of Prejudice in Housing* (New York: Harper, 1955).

[76] Report of the President's Committee on Civil Rights, *To Secure These Rights* (Washington, D.C.: 1947).

[77] Abrams, "The Segregation Threat in Housing," p. 123.

[78] *Ibid.*, p. 124.

[79] *New York Times*, Dec. 22, 1948, p. 21, col. 1.

[80] *Ibid.*, Feb. 5, 1949, p. 8, col. 6.

[81] *Ibid.*, March 12, 1949, p. 19, col. 5.

[82] *Ibid.*, Jan. 30, 1949, p. 43, col. 4.

[83] *Ibid.*, Dec. 3, 1949, p. 1, col. 8.

[84] *Ibid.*, p. 2, col. 3.

[85] *Ibid.*, Dec. 5, 1949, p. 15, col. 3.

[86] 14 *Fed. Reg.* 7579–7582 (1949). *New York Times*, Dec. 16, 1949, p. 1, col. 2. The order has since been codified. 24 C.F.R. secs. 221.29, 221.37, 221.42 (1949 ed.).

[87] *New York Times*, Dec. 4, 1949, p. 84, col. 1.

[88] See B. T. McGraw and G. B. Nesbitt, "Aftermath of Shelley v. Kraemer on Residential Restrictions by Race," *Land Economics*, XXIX (Nov., 1953), 280–287; Jessie Parkhurst Guzman, ed., *The Negro Yearbook* (New York: William H. Wise, 1952), pp. 170–187. This section on housing was prepared by the Housing and Home Finance Agency.

[89] The surveys were conducted for the United Press and the New York State Committee on Discrimination in Housing, *New York Times*, Jan. 22, 1951, p. 19, col. 8; April 15, 1951, p. 60, col. 3.

[90] Letter to the author from Fred A. Niemoeller, Jr., Dec. 5, 1953.

[91] *New York Times*, March 26, 1949, p. 30, col. 4.

[92] *Ibid.*, May 7, 1951, p. 19, col. 1.

[93] This story appeared in the *New York Times* on 17 occasions during 1951. Also see Charles Abrams, "The Time Bomb That Exploded in Cicero," *Commentary*, XIV (Nov., 1951), 407–414.

[94] *New York Times*, Dec. 3, 1951.

[95] *Ibid.*, Feb. 17–24, 1952. Also, see Edward Howden, "Property and Prejudice: The Story of Sing Sheng," *New Republic*, CXXVI (April 21, 1952), 15–16.

[96] *New York Times*, Feb. 18, 1952, p. 18, col. 3.

[97] *Ibid.*, Feb. 19, 1952, p. 3, col. 6.

[98] *U.S. News*, XXIV (May 14, 1948), 23.

[99] Walker to Seegers, June 14, 1948, Seegers papers.

[100] Seegers to Walker, June 24, 1948, Seegers papers.

[101] Kenneth D. McCasland, "Practical Effects in Tennessee of the Non-Enforceability of Restrictive Racial Covenants," *Tennessee Law Review*, XX (June, 1949), 679, 681.

[102] Clare B. McDermott, Jr., "The Effects of the Rule in the Modern Shelley's Case," *University of Pittsburgh Law Review*, XIII (Summer, 1952), 647, 648–649.

[103] H. P. Livermore, "Circumvention of the Rule Against Enforcement of Racially Restrictive Covenants," *California Law Review*, XXXVII (Sept., 1949), 493.

[104] *Chicago Tribune*, May 8, 1948, p. 10, col. 3.

[105] *U.S. News*, XXIV (May 14, 1948), pp. 22, 23.

[106] Homer A. Jack, "Racism and the Supreme Court," *Christian Century*, LXV (June 9, 1948), pp. 571–73. Also see Mastrude, *If Your Next Neighbors Are Negroes*, p. 13.

[107] The suggestion appeared in the following places: *U.S. News*, XXIV (May 14, 1948), 22–23; H. P. Livermore, "Circumvention of the Rule Against Enforcement of Racially Restrictive Covenants," *California Law Review*, XXXVII (Sept., 1949), 493–498; Robert O. Hoelscher, "Use of Option To Purchase Land To Control Occupancy," *Missouri Law Review*, XV (Jan., 1950), 77–82; O. Max Gardner, Jr., "Judicial Enforcement of Racial Restrictive Covenants," *North Carolina Law Review*, XXVII (Feb., 1949), 224–228; Clare B. McDermott, "The Effects of the Rule in the Modern Shelley's Case," University of Pittsburgh Law Review, XIII (Summer, 1952), 647–665; Charles Howell, "Recent Developments in the Law of Racial Restrictions on Real Property," (St. Louis Univ. School of Law) *Intramural Law Review*, I (Spring, 1951), 222–240; Arthur N. Greenberg and Robert A. Franklin, "Discrimination in Ownership and Occupancy of Property Since Shelley v. Kraemer," (University of California at Los Angeles) *Intramural Law Review* (June, 1952), 14–22; John L. Walker, "Suggested Plans for Avoiding Effect of Shelley Decision," appendix to an address delivered to Virginia State Bar Association, Aug. 12, 1948.

[108] *U.S. News*, XXIV (May 14, 1948), 22–23.

[109] See articles listed in note 112, below. Also see 3 A.L.R. 2d 466, 473.

[110] Harry L. Gershon, "Restrictive Covenants and Equal Protection—The New Rule in Shelley's Case," *So. California Law Review*, XXI (July, 1948), 358, 365.

[111] Walker to Seegers, June 24, 1948. Seegers papers.

[112] *Weiss v. Leaon*, 359 Mo. 1054, 225 S.W. 2d 127 (1949). One critic had this to say about the Missouri Supreme Court's line of reasoning: "The Shelley case prohibits only judicial enforcement of the restictive covenant. Judicial enforcement is then converted into 'specific' enforcement, so that the holding of the Shelley case now reads, *specific* enforcement of a racially restrictive covenant is state action in violation of the Fourteenth Amendment. After this feat of alchemy, the rest was easy. Since only specific performance of the covenant was involved, the damages question was not raised or considered. Thus the Shelley case was no authority at all on the issue of damages." Clare B. McDermott, Jr., "The Effects of the Rule in the Modern Shelley's Case," *University of Pittsburgh Law Review*, XIII (Summer, 1952), 647, 651. Notes on this case appeared in the following law reviews: *Alabama Law Review*, II (Spring, 1950), 308–310; *Albany Law Review*, XIV (June, 1950), 217–220; *Boston University Law Review*, XXX (April, 1950), 273–274; *Georgia*

Bar Journal, XII (May, 1950), 498–500; Georgetown Law Journal, XXXVIII (May, 1950), 678–680; George Washington Law Review, XVIII (April, 1950), 417–422; Harvard Law Review, LXIII (April, 1950), 1062–1064; Missouri Law Review, XV (June, 1950), 313–315; New York University Law Review, XXV (April, 1950), 406–410; North Carolina Law Review, XXVIII (June, 1950), 442–445; (St. Louis University) Intramural Law Review, I (Spring, 1951), 222–240; Tennessee Law Review, XXI (June, 1950), 441–442; University of Pennsylvania Law Review, IIC (March, 1950), 588–590; Washington and Lee Law Review, VII (1950), 178–183; Washington University Law Review, Vol. 1950 (June, 1950), 437–442; Wisconsin Law Review, Vol. 1951 (Jan., 1951), 188–190.

[113] Correll v. Earley, 237 P. 2d 1017 (Okla. 1951). For comments, overwhelmingly critical, see Alabama Law Review, IV (Spring, 1952), 289–293; Buffalo Law Review, I (Spring, 1952), 304–307; Chicago-Kent Law Review, XXX (Sept., 1952), 350–355; DePaul Law Review, I (Spring-Summer, 1952), 293–296; Loyola Law Review, VI (1952), 154–155; Nebraska Law Review, XXXI (May, 1952), 304–307; North Dakota Law Review, XXIX (Jan., 1953), 81–84; Rocky Mountain Law Review, XXIV (April, 1952) 380–383; University of Pennsylvania Law Review, C (May, 1952), 1049–1054; Vanderbilt Law Review, V (April, 1952), 634–637; Virginia Law Review, XXXVIII (April, 1952), 389–390.

[114] Roberts v. Curtis, 93 F. Supp. 604 (D.C. 1950). This case provoked little comment. Alabama Law Review, III (Spring, 1951), 379–380; Baylor Law Review, III (Summer, 1951), 584–588; Georgia Bar Journal, XIII (Feb., 1951), 367–368; Syracuse Law Review, II (Spring, 1951), 367–368.

[115] Saunders v. Phillips, 191 Md. 707, 62 A. 2d 602 (1948), certiorari denied, 336 U.S. 967 (1949)

[116] Phillips v. Naff, 332 Mich. 289, 52 N.W. 2d 158 (1952). See Albany Law Review, XVII (Jan., 1953), 186–190; Georgia Bar Journal, XV (Aug., 1952), 71–75; Harvard Law Review, LXVI (Dec., 1952), 353–354; Michigan Law Review, LI (Dec., 1952), 288–290; University of Cincinnati Law Review, XXII (Jan., 1953), 97–99.

[117] Phillips v. Naff, 332 Mich. 289, 293.

[118] Barrows v. Jackson, 112 Cal. App. 2d 534, 247 P. 2d 99 (1952), certiorari granted, 345 U.S. 902 (1953).

[119] Ibid. Before being reviewed by the United States Supreme Court the Barrows case was noted in the following law reviews: Cornell Law Quarterly, XXXVIII (Winter, 1953), 236–240; Hastings Law Journal, IV (Fall, 1952), 57–59; (UCLA) Intramural Law Review, Vol. 1953 (March, 1953), 51–53; Minnesota Law Review, XXXVII (Dec., 1952), 65–66; Rocky Mountain Law Review, XXV (Dec., 1952), 112–114; Southern California Law Review, XXVI (Feb., 1953), 201–203; Temple Law Quarterly XXVI (Winter, 1953), 320–324.

Chapter X

The Supreme Court and the 1953 Damages Case

[1] 346 U.S. 249 (1953).
[2] Transcript of Record, Barrows v. Jackson.
[3] Ibid.
[4] Barrows v. Jackson, 112 Cal. App. 2d 534, 247 P. 2d 99 (1952).
[5] The three favoring the grant were Justices Sherik, Edmonds, and Schauer. Transcript of Record, Barrows v. Jackson.
[6] Barrows v. Jackson, certiorari granted, 345 U.S. 902 (1953).
[7] A full transcript of the oral argument was made by commercial stenographers In the Supreme Court of the United States, October Term, 1952: Barrows v. Jackson, No. 517 (Washington: Ward & Paul), 80 pp.

[8] *Barrows v. Jackson*, 346 U.S. 249, 254 (1953).
[9] *Ibid.*
[10] *Ibid.*, p. 255.
[11] *Ibid.*
[12] *Ibid.*, p. 256.
[13] *Ibid.*, p. 257.
[14] *Ibid.*, p. 259.
[15] 268 U.S. 510 (1925).
[16] *Barrows v. Jackson*, 346 U.S. 249, 260.
[17] U.S. Const., Art. 1, sec. 10.
[18] *Barrows v. Jackson*, 346 U.S. 249, 260.
[19] *Ibid.*, pp. 260, 261.
[20] *Ibid.*, p. 267.
[21] *Ibid.*, p. 261.
[22] *Ibid.*, p. 262.
[23] *Ibid.*, p. 263.
[24] *Ibid.*
[25] *Ibid.*, pp. 264, 265.
[26] *Ibid.*, p. 267.
[27] *Ibid.*, p. 269.
[28] Brief for respondent, *Barrows v. Jackson.*
[29] Loren Miller to the author, Nov. 10, 1953, p. 2.
[30] *Ibid.*, p. 1.
[31] *Ibid.*, p. 2.
[32] Loren Miller to the author, Nov. 25, 1953, p. 1.
[33] Brief for NAACP as *amicus curiae, Barrows v. Jackson* 112 Cal. App. 2d 534, 247 P. 2d 99 (1952).
[34] Brief for Japanese American Citizens League as *amicus curiae, Barrows v. Jackson.*
[35] Brief for National Community Relations Advisory Council as *amicus curiae.*
[36] *Ibid.*
[37] Brief for American Jewish Congress as *amicus curiae.*
[38] *Ibid.*
[39] *Ibid.*
[40] Loren Miller to the author, Sept. 13, 1957, p. 1.
[41] Brief for Respondent, *Barrows v. Jackson,* p. 28.
[42] Brief for Affiliated Neighbors as *amicus curiae.*
[43] Brief for Morens Avenue Improvement Association as *amicus curiae.*
[44] Frederick Bernays Wiener, "The Supreme Court's New Rules," *Harvard Law Review,* LXVIII (Nov., 1954), 83.
[45] *Ibid.*, p. 83.
[46] *Ibid.*, p. 84.
[47] Petition for Rehearing, *Barrows v. Jackson* [346 U.S. 249 (1953), *rehearing denied,* 346 U.S. 841 (1953)].
[48] *Ibid.*, p. 26.
[49] *Ibid.*, p. 31.

United Neighbors, Inc., 244
United States: decision to be *amicus curiae*, 168–174; *amicus curiae* brief of, 191–193; oral argument in behalf of, 200–201; role criticized, 193; role praised, 214. *See also* Department of Justice
University of Chicago, 67, 68, 162
Urciolo, Raphael, 83, 88, 89; on breaking covenants, 80, 81
Urciolo v. Hodge. See *Hurd v. Hodge*

Vallee, Judge, 234
Van Orsdel, Judge Josiah, 17, 18, 93
Vandenburg, Senator Arthur H., 36
Vanzetti (and Sacco), 182
Vaughn, George L.: 58, 64, 152, 164; comment on electing judges, 61–62; counsel in *Shelley v. Kraemer* trial, 112–119 *passim;* education and career, 121; obtains certiorari, 157; prepares brief for Supreme Court, 159, 160, 186; prepares *amicus curiae* brief, 165; oral argument, 199, 201
Vermont Square Neighbors, Inc., 244
Villard, Oswald Garrison, 31
Vinson, Chief Justice Fred M.: on Court of Appeals, 93–94; Supreme Court appointment and outlook, 177, 179, 183; explains certiorari policy, 156, 158; opinion in *Shelley* and *McGhee* cases, 205–208; opinion in *Hodge* cases, 208–210; dissenting opinion in *Barrows* case, 223, 237–239; position discussed, 213, 217, 228, 231, 247, 248
Violence: and formation of NAACP, 31; against Negroes over housing, 50; leads to *Sweet* case, 50–51; in Detroit, 124–125; condemned by Truman, 168; in housing disputes after 1948, 227
Virginia Supreme Court, 6

Walbert, Maurice, 240
Walker, John L., 228
Walling, William English, 32

Warren, Governor Earl, 227
Washington, Booker T., 30–31, 67
Washington, D.C., 2, 7, 12; litigation in, 57; federal question in test case, 62; *Hurd v. Hodge,* 74–99 *passim*
Washington Federation of Churches, 81
Washington Real Estate Board, 80
Wasson, Robert C., 187
Waters, Ethel, 57
Weaver, Robert C., 62, 95; contributes sociological material, 159, 162, 187; career, 162
Weinberger, Andrew D., 155, 186
West Virginia Supreme Court, 21
Westbrooks, Richard E., 138–139
Weyand, Ruth, 162, 186
White, Walter: NAACP secretary, 33; opposes confirmation of Parker, 35, 36; recommends Houston, 43; suggests method of attacking covenants, 55; at Chicago conference, 57; leads delegation to White House, 168; writes to Attorney-General, 170; friend of Black, 181; friend of Frankfurter, 182; on expense of litigation, 213; on need for continued action, 214; writes to Truman, 225
Wilkins, Roy, 33
Willer, Herman, 160, 186, 199, 201
Williams, Franklin, 240
Williams, Representative John Bell, 215
Wilson, Charles E., 168
Wilson, President Woodrow, 38
Wirth, Louis, 67, 162, 187
Wise, Rabbi Stephen S., 32
Wolverine Bar Association, 123–124, 140
Women's International Club, 241
Wren case (*In re Drummond Wren*), 134, 136

York, Ben F., 187

Zitver, Leon, 187
Zoning, 3. *See also* Residential segregation, Segregation ordinance